RESPECT YOURSELF

BY THE SAME AUTHOR

*Lost Delta Found: Rediscovering the Fisk University–Library of Congress
Coahoma County Study, 1941–1942*

Can't Be Satisfied: The Life and Times of Muddy Waters

The Elvis Treasures

The King on the Road: Elvis Live on Tour 1954 to 1977

It Came from Memphis

DOCUMENTARIES

Very Extremely Dangerous

Johnny Cash's America

Respect Yourself: The Stax Records Story

Stranded in Canton

The Road to Memphis

*Shakespeare Was a Big George Jones Fan: Cowboy Jack
Clement's Home Movies*

Muddy Waters Can't Be Satisfied

RESPECT YOURSELF
Stax Records and the Soul Explosion

ROBERT GORDON

BLOOMSBURY

NEW YORK · LONDON · NEW DELHI · SYDNEY

Published by Bloomsbury USA, New York

All papers used by Bloomsbury USA are natural, recyclable products made from wood grown in
well-managed forests. The manufacturing processes conform to the environmental regulations of
the country of origin.

LIBRARY OF CONGRESS CATALOGING-IN-PUBLICATION DATA

Gordon, Robert, 1961- author.
Respect yourself : Stax Records and the soul explosion / Robert Gordon. —First U.S. edition.
pages cm
Includes bibliographical references and index.
ISBN 978-1-59691-577-0 (alk. paper)
1. Stax Records—History. 2. Memphis (Tenn.)—History. I. Title.
ML3792.S78G67 2013
384—dc23
2013014533

First U.S. Edition 2013

1 3 5 7 9 10 8 6 4 2

Designed by Lawrence Kim

Typeset by Westchester Book Group
Printed and bound in the U.S.A. by Thomson-Shore Inc., Dexter, Michigan

For Deanie Parker, Mark Crosby, and Morgan Neville,
with gratitude

For Tara McAdams, with love

We're going to have to grapple with the problems
that men have been trying to grapple
with through history.
Rev. Martin Luther King
April 3, 1968, Memphis, Tennessee

What happened in this city is the result of oppression
and injustice, the inhumanity of man to man, and
we have come to you for leadership in ending the
situation. There are laws far greater than the laws of
Memphis and Tennessee, and these are the laws of God.
We fervently ask you not to hide any longer behind
legal technicalities and slogans, but to speak out at last
in favor of human dignity.
Rabbi James Wax to Memphis mayor Henry Loeb
April 5, 1968

CONTENTS

FOREWORD

by Booker T. Jones

I walked through the door on David Porter's heels, baritone sax in tow, not quite believing I had stepped into the studio. Before I knew it, I had my horn out and I was standing in the middle of a room of musicians. They played a short excerpt of the song, and asked if I could think of an intro. From out of the bell of my horn came the opening notes of "Cause I Love You," and the rest of the band picked up the opening bars. Rufus and Carla Thomas, who were even further back in the room behind a baffle with a small window, began to sing.

The tape was rolling, and my career as a session musician had begun—in lieu of a morning algebra class at nearby Booker T. Washington High School. That song, "Cause I Love You," put Stax on the map, and the place became my home away from home.

Years later, the song "Respect Yourself" galvanized a race of people that had tailspun across America in search of validation. A cry for healing, the song rivaled the "Negro National Anthem" for viability as an African-American theme and as a shove toward more self-esteem. The only place it could have been conceived was Stax Records.

"Respect Yourself" became an anthem on Chicago's South Side, and every other black ghetto in America, like a ship come to save drowning dark-skinned sailors from self-loathing. It is a proper title for this vessel as well. A work of gargantuan proportions, this tome is a labor of love, just as were the efforts of many of the characters that helped create Stax Records. It is lyrical writing about a lyrical subject from a son of Memphis.

I found the book compelling . . . unable to put it down. Many of the mysteries of the company's operations were clarified for me, its pages were that revealing. During those years, I often spent more time with Stax's constituents than I did with my own family. My mother's growing anger and distaste had always indicated there was something amiss in my alternate family. And, as you will discover, there were plenty of reasons to have situations obscured from a cloudy-headed young musical prodigy like me. When I reached the account of Otis Redding's plane crash, I realized I had arrived at the belly of the book. Emotion brimming, I wanted to call Robert. Not that I had anything in particular to say, I just wanted to hear his voice. But, it was 10:30 P.M. on the West Coast; it would be after midnight in Memphis. So I didn't call. But I thought he would understand what I was feeling—the sense of loss for the whole world, and for Stax and for Memphis.

Remembering that Sunday morning at the airport with the MGs, the scene at the bar—no one else really able to relate to what we were going through—and reading this account forty-six years later makes me think what a thin veil time can be, because the weight is just as heavy now . . . especially remembering the Bar-Kays or, as we used to call them, "the kids." But, the older, wiser Booker knows to be thankful for the time spent with them all, and to minimize regrets as much as possible by thinking of happy times, such as when I played harmonica with "the kids" on "Knucklehead"—or when I laughed with Otis in the hall of a Paris hotel late one night.

I know *Respect Yourself* will mean much to others who may read it, and I must say it has meant a great deal to me—for more reasons than I can list. So much of my life was given to the events in its pages, and I feel the author has been a careful, conscientious caretaker of the story. As a reader, I was transported back—given another view in many instances—of golden years I shared with a professional family, flourishing, toiling, suffering, and eventually graduating from the School of Stax Records in Memphis. It was a precious time for me that defined my life.

The Stax legend is fortunate to have been entrusted to my friend and fellow Memphian, Robert Gordon.

Enjoy,
Booker T. Jones

PREFACE: CITY STREETS

When I was a kid in 1970s Memphis, limousines were a rare sight. Used exclusively by the very wealthy, two would occasionally appear in traffic. From the backseat of our family station wagon, we'd scream for Mother to pull up closer. We'd know whose it was by the license plate. Elvis Presley's was not customized. Isaac Hayes's read MOSES, referring to his nickname, Black Moses. He was leading a people to the Promised Land.

I didn't appreciate it then, but Memphis is a place where people come to realize their dreams. In the vast rural area that surrounds us, where the light of opportunity glows dimly if at all, Memphis is the radiant destination. It is hope on the horizon. The disenfranchised, the hungry, the hopeful are drawn here, where a lone voice in the Delta multiplies, can gain mass and volume to become a political and economic force. Memphis is the crossroads, the grand intersection of information, commerce, and diverse citizenry. Dirt and gravel roads, train tracks, creeks and rivers—all paths lead to Memphis.

And the plantation prejudices still prevailed here. This is where the train out of the country discharges its passengers. Had there been another train depot beyond us, Memphis would have been like any of the racist, peckerwood towns around it. It became, instead, a racist, peckerwood big city. Publicly, as a civic enterprise, racism was embraced and enacted. From segregation to gerrymandering, from financial chicanery to murder, rape, and abuses physical and mental, African-Americans were beneath lower-class; one blues song reminded that if you shot a rabbit out of season, you'd wind up in jail, but "the season was always open on me / Nobody needed no bail." White farmhands shrugged at the brutality, saying, "Kill a mule, buy another. Kill a nigger, hire another." Memphis was one of those small towns, metastasized.

Contrary to its intentions, the oppression inspired great art, desperate art, lifesaving storytelling art. The blues that came from Memphis and Mississippi are a cry in the night for freedom, for justice, and at their foundation, for recognition. Dismiss me no more, I am a man. (The church and religious music fostered a similar narrative—I am a creature of God.) Despair and hope imbued the plea with immense beauty, extending beyond generations, beyond geography, beyond creed and race. The rule that intended to silence instead fostered a voice that outlives that of the tyrants. The blues, rock and roll, and soul music—all indigenous to Memphis and Mississippi—are expressions of the heart and soul in response to, in defiance of, the oppression. To be heard, the oppressed had to find entrance to the world of their oppressors. Ask Medgar Evers. Or the Memphis sanitation workers. Or Dr. King.

Stax Records was a little side project that became massive, an opening in the wall of subjugation, an accidental refuge that flourished, nourished by a sense of decency. Rays of hope, beams of trust, and the warmth of friendship cultured relationships that have become the legacy of the era and of the area. Stax songs are burned into our consciousness by their funky grooves and enduring appeal and are also resurrected time and again simply because of their good feeling. Stax is what we hear today on the radio, what we dance to at weddings, what brings a smile even when diluted as elevator music; it's an inspiration for hip-hop, a reliable source for sampling because the vibe of the music has meaning—of togetherness and of independence, of the conflict between the two and of their unification. The music made at Stax Records became the soundtrack for liberation, the song of triumph, the sound of the path toward freedom. In the country, you could dream big. But in Memphis, you could ride in a big limousine.

◆ ◆ ◆

ON HIS FIRST day of work, smack in the middle of the 1960s, Al Bell stepped into Jim Stewart's office. It was small for two people. There was

Al Bell, left, and Jim Stewart in 1967. (API Photographers Collection)

one desk and there were two chairs, one on either side of the desk. And there was one telephone.

Jim was white, Al was black. Jim owned Stax Records, Al was joining the staff to promote the records: get 'em played, get 'em sold.

It was 1965 in Memphis, Tennessee, the heart of the American South. Throughout this wide region, race mixing was nothing short of an assault on the social realm. Inside Stax Records, whites and blacks had worked side by side for half a decade. People who couldn't publicly dine together were making beautiful music that the public—black and white—loved to hear. Many times, however, they'd step outside the studio and white cops would stop to check on the whites' safety, to hassle the blacks.

On Al's first day, Jim Stewart gestured him to his seat at the desk. Stax had scored several hits, but money was tight. Stax could make the hits, but they needed Al's promotional whizbang to get more out of their success. His job would involve contacting disc jockeys across the country.

Jim showed Al the stationery drawer. Stamps were inexpensive. There wasn't much of a long-distance budget, but calls would be necessary.

One telephone and one desk. While Al situated himself, Jim made a call. When he hung up, Al watched as Jim slid that phone across the desk, toward him.

Al Bell made his call. When done, like his boss, he slid the phone back across the desk. It was such a quotidian act, yet revolutionary in 1965. Marchers in support of African-American voting rights were being beaten by police in Montgomery, Alabama. Malcolm X had recently been assassinated. Chaney, Goodman, and Schwerner—three Freedom Riders—had the previous year been delivered to the Ku Klux Klan for murder by Mississippi police. In Memphis, thirty-three African-American men had been recently fired from the sanitation department for fomenting strike talk, seeking better wages and union recognition. Downtown, while sit-ins broke barriers at banks and businesses, the City of Memphis defied integration orders by closing its public swimming pools—for two consecutive hot summers—rather than having blacks and whites share the same water.

The expanse of the desk was either a great divide or a cultural bridge. Jim may have looked at Al or not. His heart was beating fast, or it wasn't. Al's was. But no handkerchief came out of Jim's pocket to wipe clean the phone, no sanitizing spray. Jim had another call to make. He picked up the phone and he placed the call, sharing the earpiece, sharing the mouthpiece, sharing responsibility for the company.

"I was amazed to sit in the same room with this white guy who had been a country fiddle player," says Al. "We had separate water fountains in Memphis and throughout the South. And if we wanted to go to a restaurant, we had to go to the back door—but to sit in that office with this white man, sharing the same telephone, sharing the same thoughts, and being treated like an equal human being—was really a phenomenon during that period of time. The spirit that came from Jim and his sister Estelle Axton allowed all of us, black and white, to come off the streets, where you had segregation and the negative attitude, and come into the doors of Stax, where you had freedom, you had harmony, you had people working together. It grew into what became really an oasis for all of us."

◆ ◆ ◆

RACISM HAS LONG been the grit that produces musical pearls in Memphis. When Stax Records settled into its South Memphis home, it had only to open its doors and the warm, welcoming air attracted those who'd received

Beale Street, late March 1968, after Dr. King's march supporting the striking sanitation workers turned violent. (University of Memphis Libraries/ Special Collections)

society's cold shoulder. It quickly—accidentally—unleashed a torrent of talent. People who wanted to be heard, to contribute, gravitated to Stax's embrace. Stax would release eight hundred singles and three hundred albums between 1960 and 1975, becoming a national business entity on a scale that no other Memphis label ever did. Stax had 167 top-100 pop songs, nearly 250 top-100 R&B songs. Stax established the careers of Otis Redding, Isaac Hayes, the Staple Singers, Sam and Dave, Booker T. & the MG's, and Wilson Pickett. Isaac Hayes became the first black American to win the Academy Award for Best Original Song ("Theme from *Shaft*"). Stax created the Wattstax concert in 1972, dubbed "the Black Wood-stock," which spun off into a movie and two best-selling double albums. Many of the company's achievements are notable for their cross-cultural appeal. Previously, even twenty years prior, the go-to civic response to such expressions of African-American pride would have been lynching. Through the 1960s and into the '70s, when every step toward equality seemed to bring two back steps of repression and retraction, a small group of people in Memphis quietly reveled in racial harmony.

The story of Stax is more than a record-label history. It is an American story, part Horatio Alger, part Alexis De Tocqueville—where the shoe-shine boy becomes a star, the country hayseed an international magnate. It's the story of individuals against society, of small business competing with large, of the disenfranchised seeking their own tile in the American mosaic. In Stax and its miraculous and foolhardy struggle for success, both the better and worse angels of our nature are interlocked, engaged in a righteous battle that, even now, remains undecided.

In its time, Stax was the rare place where everyone had a chance. The sound of the street could walk in the door. Regardless of age, background, and race, inside Stax you could get someone's ear. In the city where segregation reigned, where the civic laws screamed "No!" Stax Records sang, jubilantly and simply, "Yes."

PART 1
INTEGRATION

1. CUTTING HEADS AND HAIR
1957–1959

Jim Stewart sat in his barber's chair. Jim's hair was short, his face boyish and scrubbed clean. He wore thick-rimmed glasses and a necktie, his jacket on the barber's coat hook. It was 1957 and Jim was twenty-seven years old, working in a bank and taking business classes at night on the GI Bill, with an eye toward becoming a lawyer. He played fiddle in a country swing band on weekends.

Within ten years, this man would be responsible for some of the most soulful, swinging, and hip music ever made. Black people—of which he presently knew approximately none—would be his closest associates. The Beatles, to be unleashed in just a few years, would reach the height of their popularity, and in the thick of Beatlemania, the Beatles would phone Jim Stewart and ask if they could record at his studio. In ten years, Jim would have a hep goatee and his hair would be much longer than it was before he sat down for this trim. But in this barber's chair, 1957, there was no indication any of that would, or could, happen.

Jim had always inclined toward music. In his rural west Tennessee home, not only did he play country fiddle, but also his sisters, father, and uncle were a gospel quartet. The church music was staid but powerful—big broad notes that moved up and down like ballast on heavy

Jim Stewart in Middleton, Tennessee. "I used to tease him that he played the fiddle," says his sister Estelle. "Then he went to college and played the violin." (Stax Museum of American Soul Music)

machinery; it wasn't rafter-shaking, but with enough voices this style of "shape note" singing could, like Samson, tear this building down.

Where Jim had been raised, about seventy miles east of Memphis in rural Middleton, Tennessee, his sister Estelle, twelve years his senior, had been his schoolteacher in the one-room schoolhouse. She soon moved to Memphis, the middle sister followed, and then Jim arrived after finishing high school in 1948. He worked a couple years as a stock clerk, finished his military service in February 1953 (his fiddle got him into Special Services), and went to college. With his degree in business, he took a job in the bond department at Memphis's First National Bank. He'd finish the desk job, attend law school at night, and still find time to play fiddle in the Canyon Cowboys—"My love in music was Bob Wills, Leon McAuliffe, Spade Cooley—Texas western swing," Jim says. "If I could only fiddle like Johnny Gimble . . ."

Snip snip. Snip. Back in the 1957 barbershop, Mr. Marshall E. Ellis worked the scissors. Jim had become particularly interested in Ellis's recent experience with a record label. A fiddle player himself, Ellis had invested in a portable tape recorder, and he'd made records for a few bands around town. His deal was pretty simple: It would cost the artist nothing, and if the record became successful, they'd get better gigs that attracted more people. If the distributors paid Erwin Records—Erwin was the barber's middle name—then he'd pay the artist. The trick, Jim's barber explained, was to make sure that the song was an original and that the artist signed over the publishing. Because—and surely the *snipping* stopped here—the money in the music business was in owning the publishing rights. For every record sold, a penny or two always went to the publisher. The publishing company filed some brief paperwork, and then if anyone else ever covered the song, the publisher got a check in the mailbox. And out of the dozen or so records that Ellis had been involved in, one had led to good money when country music star Hank Locklin released his own version. *Ka-ching*—the publisher had to be paid. The artist might get screwed by the label, the label might get screwed by the distributor, the musicians may never see a dime, but the publisher who registered his song in Washington, DC, was paid. Ellis hadn't made hit records, but they'd sold farther than he could throw them, and twice a year he opened his front door and money walked in.

Jim fancied this scenario. "I recognized my limitations," says Jim. "I knew that I could not make it as a musician, so producing was the next best thing. It was an outlet for me to express myself musically. I knew nothing about copyright, publishing, BMI—absolutely no knowledge how to get a record pressed, how to get a label started."

A little more than a year before this haircut, in November 1955, a former mortuary employee and radio technician across town named Sam Phillips had made a fortune selling the contract of his star player, Elvis Presley, to RCA Records. Now Phillips had a bundle of money and a stableful of other artists who were selling nationally. Ellis pointed out that if you looked on the records themselves, you'd see that Phillips also controlled the publishing rights for the original songs, so you could be sure that he was making more money than you knew about.

A barber. A mortuary technician. In South Memphis, an appliance salesman and some guys associated with Phillips's Sun Records had broken away and formed Hi Records in an old movie theater. How hard could it be?

Stewart, trained in pen to paper, estimated the costs involved in cutting a record would be more than he could handle himself, so he pooled

$1,000 by partnering with a country singer, bassist, and disc jockey named Fred Byler; with a rhythm guitarist named Neil Herbert; and with a blind female songwriting piano player named Nadine Eastin, for whom Jim named the publishing company, East. They called the record label Satellite, since Russia's October 1957 Sputnik launch was the hottest topic in years. Jim composed the song "Blue Roses" (it would be his only recorded composition), Fred sang it, and they hired Jim's barber to bring his recording deck to Jim's wife's uncle's garage, where they'd hung a few drapes so they could call it a recording studio. The recording deck was monaural, meaning the singer and all the instruments had to be recorded at once onto one track, and if anyone messed up, everyone would have to redo the whole thing. Technically, the project was a success, in that a song was recorded. The slow, controlled rhythm indicates promise from Jim as a producer. But the melody and production are so sappy that by song's end your teeth hurt. Jim remembers the record being so bad that he couldn't get a single station to play it.

"Right after they made the first record is when I entered," says Estelle Stewart Axton, Jim's sister. In addition to her family quartet singing, she'd played organ at church in Middleton. But Estelle really loved to dance, and she had taken quickly to the rock and roll beat. Entrepreneurial, she also had a sideline selling records to her coworkers at a another Memphis bank, Union Planters National Bank, where she'd been a clerk since 1950. "There were a lot of people that didn't want to

The Converted Garage That Started Stax Records

Guitarist Steve Cropper says, "At least it was a start, a place to be."
(University of Memphis Libraries/Special Collections)

take time to go to the record shop," she explains, "so they'd give me a list and I'd go to Poplar Tunes and buy whatever they wanted. I'd pay sixty-five cents for the singles and I'd sell them for a dollar." Jim knew Estelle loved music. "He brought the record over and asked me what I thought about it. I played it on a little tiny record player that somebody had given the kids. I said, 'It's all right, but the production seems a little thin.' He said the only way to make it better is to have better equipment to record it on. That's when he asked me if I'd be interested in investing any money. I guess he thought I had money because I was working and my husband was working." Having a love for music is one thing, and having capital to gamble is another altogether. Estelle's husband, Everett, a unit tender at the Kimberly-Clark factory in Memphis (he oversaw a group of women that made Kleenex), was against investing, afraid they'd wind up living in a tent. Nonetheless, she agreed to consider her brother's proposition.

About a month after the first session, Jim and his barber returned to the garage, accompanied by Satellite's next artist and the guitarist who'd found him. The artist, singer Don Willis, had his own composition, and he gave Jim's consortium the publishing rights. Willis was more modern than Stewart and Ellis, and the guitarist who'd brought him had recently come from California and working at Gold Star Studios, where modern recording techniques were being crafted. Willis cut a mean little rockabilly number, "Boppin' High School Baby." It couldn't be more different from "Blue Roses." The guitarist's production drenched the song in echo and flaunts the searing guitar work. It's the kind of record that might have sold well if people could have found it. But Jim Stewart and friends were still figuring out the record business, and one essential component yet lacking was distribution. It's one thing to make a record, and it's easy enough to take the master tape to a pressing plant and have five hundred copies pressed. But then what?

Record distribution was, and remains, a tricky business. Lots of money changes hands, and by the late 1950s the accounting was convoluted. "Sam Phillips and his peers," Jim explains, "they didn't know what returns were. You sent out a record to the distributor, he bought it. No free goods, no returns. If you sold ten records you got paid for ten records. When I got into the record business, freebies had come into the picture. It was three hundred on a thousand. It had progressed, or regressed, to that." That means that for every one thousand records that a distributor ordered, he expected to also get an additional three hundred free, reducing the label's profit by a third before getting out of the gate, and significantly

increasing the distributor's profit potential. Many distributors were owners of jukebox services, so they could stock their machines with freebies.
Or the distributor could simply sell the freebies outright. If he could find
nothing else to do with them, he could give them to disc jockeys and
encourage airplay. It didn't bring immediate profits, but radio play, with
its promise of wide and democratic reception, was the best way to increase sales. "Three hundred on a thousand" was the way you got records
played.

Jim had one record that sounded terrible and one that rocked, and neither got very far out of the box. But the work had given him a charge. "I
really got hooked on it after the first record," Jim says. "I got the fever,
decided I wanted to be in the record business."

The nascent company then got hit hard, twice. Jim's wife's uncle
wanted his garage back, and Jim's barber moved. They'd lost both their
studio and their recording equipment. But grace once again gleamed from
the silver shears: The new barber, Mr. Mitchell, had a place of his own that
Jim could use. It was a storage building in Brunswick, Tennessee, about
twenty miles east of Memphis. "This barber had a young daughter, about
fourteen or fifteen," Estelle explains. "He wanted so much to get her recorded that he had an old store building that he said we could use if we
wanted to clean off the old shelves and get stuff out of it. We went out
there, fixed it up, nailed up our tiles for the acoustics." The free building
came with a price, Estelle continues: "There was a railroad track right
next to it and it seemed like any time we tried to do a professional session,
these trains would come by and jar the building." Nor did Brunswick
greet these tinkerers with open arms; Jim had to stand before the town
council and testify to his own integrity, and promise that drug addicts,
thieves, and other lowlifes attracted to the music business would not infil-
trate the crossroads and poison the minds of Brunswick's fine children.

Estelle, meanwhile, wouldn't let the idea drop at home. "They were
using a little portable machine to record, so they needed a console," she
says. "We couldn't talk anybody into believing you could make money in
the recording industry, even though Sam Phillips had already proved you
could. People thought there wasn't another Sam." Estelle had no ready
cash; her husband was making eighteen dollars a week. But their house
note was only twenty-one dollars a month, and they were seventeen years
into paying it down. "My husband, he couldn't see nothing in the music
business. I had to talk an awful lot to get him to mortgage our house to
get twenty-five hundred dollars to buy a console recording machine. So I
got into the business by mortgaging our house, and the new note was

Estelle Axton mortgaged her house so the company
could buy an Ampex 350, the recorder that established
the Stax studio. (Courtesy of René Wu)

about five times higher than the original." They purchased a new Ampex 350 mono tape recorder.

The turmoil was more than Fred Byler could handle. He took a job at a radio station in Little Rock, Arkansas, and parted ways with the company. Partner Neil Herbert raised an eyebrow, could see nothing in the work they'd done that indicated anything was going right, and, so, thank you but no, he'd not part with any more of his hard-earned dollars. Ms. Eastin, too, found other keys to tinkle, leaving Jim and Estelle as sole partners, with Estelle's house riding on the company's success.

◆◆◆

BRUNSWICK WAS A significant trek from Memphis in 1958, and the siblings found that inviting bands to drop by was not so productive. And they were surprised by how heavy the trains were, and the way the recording equipment could pick up their rumblings even before their ears could detect them. But enthusiasm abounded, if success did not, and in the year at

Brunswick they managed to release one record of note. It's a surprising re-cord, considering the label's history to date, a portentous one considering the future about to unfold. The band was an African-American vocal group, the Veltones, who performed regularly in West Memphis, Arkan-sas. West Memphis is across the Mississippi River from Memphis and was a refuge from the law for Memphians, a playground of vice where bands played louder, longer, and more salaciously; where craps games were an assumed component of a nightclub's business; where drive-in movie the-aters showed nudist-colony films; where bartenders would serve alcohol to anyone tall enough to set their silver on the bar.

None of these activities appealed to Jim or Estelle. Nor, particularly, did black music. So how a group from a place they didn't frequent, play-ing music they were not familiar with, landed in their converted grocery store in a part of the woods where the races did not mingle is unclear. (Neither Jim nor Estelle recalls the provenance.) But they had two asso-ciates, one of whom likely was the link between the Veltones and the Stewart siblings: Estelle's son Packy Axton, and the guitarist who'd become Jim's engineer, Chips Moman.

Charles "Packy" Axton came from parents who were not much alike. Estelle's husband, Everett Axton, believed in putting in his hours for the company, and in getting his check for the work. He liked to drink beer from a quart bottle at Berretta's BBQ, and if he wanted to have more than one, he'd earned the money and he didn't want to be told no. ("My father was just not a man who took responsibility," says his daughter, Packy's sister, Doris.) He was a product of his time: Segregation was nor-mal and, thus, right. He'd fallen in love with Estelle, an adventuresome, independent-minded woman, and that indicated untapped depths in his personality. Estelle never drank to speak of, and had grown up leery of alcohol's devilish ancestry. In her part of the rural country, there were very few African-Americans, but she and her brother had been taught that all people were created equal in the eyes of God. She was not an activist or rabble-rouser, and though segregation seemed inherently mistaken to her, she was not one to join a movement.

Packy Axton embraced parts of each of his parents. His mother would never understand her son's commitment to drunkenness. His father would never understand why he wasted his life fooling around with "niggers" and their music. Packy's acceptance of others not like him pleased her, and irritated his father. In the mid-1950s, when African-American culture was reaching into the mainstream through its artists—musical, literary, and others—and through its politics, Packy supported the new thinking.

He wasn't political, unless one counted the simple act of respecting blacks a political act. He was a hard-drinking boy who liked a good time. He was hep, and he was in Elvis's hometown; music was everywhere, and Packy went everywhere to find it, including West Memphis. He may have brought the Veltones to Brunswick.

Or maybe it was Lincoln Wayne Moman—a poker player whom everybody called "Chips." He'd hitchhiked to Memphis from LaGrange, Georgia, around 1950, when he was fourteen. There was money to be made with his aunt's son, who was a housepainter. Some neighborhood kids had guitars; Chips couldn't afford one, but he'd learned his way around the six strings before leaving home. He was picking someone else's instrument at a drugstore one day after work, paint still on his pants, when Sun Records' rising star Warren Smith ("Rock 'n' Roll Ruby," "Ubangi Stomp") heard him. "He asked me if I wanted a job," says Chips, "and I said, 'Doing what?' That's how it started."

"Doing what?" It's just that attitude—mixed suspicion and aggression, with a taste for adventure—that made Moman one of the twentieth century's great record producers; he'd write some of soul, pop, and country's greatest songs, and he revived Elvis Presley's latter-1960s career by drawing out the singer's talent, which had been long dormant. Moman became legendary, but in the late 1950s he was just eager. So he traveled the two-lane highways with Warren Smith and then he moved to California with Johnny and Dorsey Burnette, two Memphis Golden Glove boxers who were just busting out nationally as a musical act. Moman's reputation spread around Los Angeles, and he found his way in and out of many studios. He hit the road as part of Gene Vincent's brooding rockabilly band until a car wreck sent him back to Memphis to recuperate. It was 1958, and Jim Stewart's barber was still M.E. Ellis. When Chips showed up with the boppin' Don Willis, the barber figured Chips, who had seen lots of "real" recording studios in California, might be able to help Jim Stewart, who was trying to create one. "Jim had one tape machine and four microphones," Chips recalls. The mikes all ran into a four-channel mixer, where the sound levels were balanced, and out from there to the mono recorder. Chips began to wrangle more contemporary talent to Jim's studio. He hung out in West Memphis, where the beer was cheaper. Perhaps he brought the Veltones to Brunswick.

One way or another, the Veltones, five black men, made their way beyond the outskirts of Memphis to the former grocery store. The song they recorded, "Fool in Love," was written by Moman and his drummer, Jerry Arnold. It's a good record, featuring the group's doo-wop style vocals and a vibrato-heavy guitar sound. It's a unique and appealing combination, a song that brings a smile to your face.

Though Jim was a country musician, black music was not totally foreign to him. His favorite bandleader, Bob Wills, led a country swing band called the Texas Playboys. Wills's style, while decidedly white, was heavily influenced by blues and boogie. Many of his songs were built around the same lyrics and riffs as blues standards, and he was influenced by African-American meter, tempos, and rhythms. Country swing didn't have R&B horns, but the pedal steel guitar played variations of their parts, the string arrangements were similar, and the vocalists emulated the casual and easy delivery of the blues singers. Jim's swing outfit, the Canyon Cowboys, had followed Wills's model of adapting jazz and blues to a country setting. Stewart may not have been familiar with what influenced his sound, but through playing, he'd gained a feel for those styles.

With an R&B record on his hands, Jim had to promote it. That led him to WDIA, a Memphis radio station staffed by all-black on-air talent. A decade earlier, WDIA opened as a white station and Jim's Canyon Cowboys held a live lunchtime slot during the station's first year. But Memphis didn't need another station like the five others, and before going under, WDIA tried an African-American announcer. After weathering the initial bomb threats, "the Mother Station of Negroes" rocketed to the second-highest rated station in Memphis. In 1958, WDIA was well established. Jim brought free copies of "Fool in Love" to hand out, and while at WDIA, he met Rufus Thomas, who hosted a popular afternoon show. Already in his early forties, Rufus had been performing since the age of five, when he'd portrayed a frog in a show on Memphis's Beale Street, the center of African-American culture in the South. Half a decade before Jim Stewart met him, Rufus recorded "Bear Cat" for Sam Phillips's Sun Records, a musical response to Big Mama Thornton's "Hound Dog," and the song had put both Rufus and Sun on the national map. There were a few other black-oriented stations in the area for Jim to visit—WLOK opened to emulate WDIA in 1956; West Memphis had a black station; there was one in Helena, Arkansas; and in Little Rock, KOKY had begun, where a DJ named Al Bell was becoming a local sensation.

"I see Jim right now in that little section between the door and the control room," says Al Bell, recalling his first meeting with Jim Stewart, long before they knew how the Fates would entwine their lives. "I saw a little small guy, short, but a smile on his face, and I immediately related to him. He was bringing me an African-American record, and I was excited when I heard it. I think it was a chemistry starting at that early stage between Jim and myself."

The Veltones' record brought a smile to Jim Stewart's face after he released it in 1959 and nationally distributed Mercury Records, home to Frankie Laine and Patti Page, offered a few hundred dollars for national distribution rights. It did not take off, but there was some money in this game after all.

2. A NEW PLANET
1960

MEMPHIS IS A city that hums and thrums. Its song is constant, a part of the soil, river, and air, and because it is everywhere, it can be hard to detect. Most white Memphians have been oblivious to the city's song, largely because African-American culture is essential to it, and most white people—certainly well into the 1960s—were trained to disregard that culture. Memphis is the capital of the mid-South, a vast rural agricultural area that spreads for hundreds of miles, encompassing a world divided between the landed and the landless, the rich and the poor. Cotton was king, and cotton determined who had bread and who had butter, who lived in the big house and who worked for the big house, who dressed in silk and who wore flour sacks. All roads led to Memphis, for there the cotton was paid for and shipped to the world beyond. With the cotton came the field hands, and with the field hands, the city's tune grew ever more intense.

This paradigm had been set since the early 1900s, as the Mississippi Delta became more cultivated. By the 1920s, Beale Street had become the Harlem of the South. Beale is on the south side of Memphis, which is the Delta side—no need to have *them* getting all the way to the *center* of town—and it runs about five blocks extending from the river. Beale was the backbone of a thriving black neighborhood. Beale Street was like New

Orleans's Storyville, and like what West Memphis later became—the laws were less enforced, the good times more pronounced.

One Memphian who heard the city's song, and who helped others tune their ears to it, including Elvis Presley, Packy Axton, and many future Stax stars, was a disc jockey named Dewey Phillips. A white man totally unsuited for broadcasting—his tone was not mellifluous, his diction not precise, his patter not soothing—he pestered his way onto an evening show at a Memphis station that was doing so poorly in the ratings that it was willing to take a chance on him. The notion at WHBQ was that, because WDIA went off the air at sundown, maybe they could capture some of that listening audience by playing black music at night. But none of their dulcet-toned DJs knew anything about African-American music. Dewey started in 1949 with fifteen minutes, soon had three hours, and by the late 1950s, in addition to his nighttime show, he was on for the kids after school, simulcasting on TV and radio. The success of someone so patently unsuitable for the job is a testament to the South's long embrace of the eccentric.

Dewey exploded the constricted 1950s notions of radio programming. He did not play songs from a dedicated genre throughout his show. He programmed by essence, hearing the similarities between Bill Monroe, Hank Ballard, the Spaniels, Louis Jordan, and Bob Wills. He'd follow a Sister Rosetta Tharpe rocking guitar gospel song with a Tommy Dorsey big beat, and if you thought the twain should never meet, his program either confirmed your notions of the world's imminent demise or it knocked down the walls of the box you had never realized you were living in. Elvis's career at Sun was a tribute to Dewey—a bluegrass song played as a blues? A blues song given a country swing? Like "That's All Right" and "Blue Moon of Kentucky," his first Sun release, Elvis regularly condensed Dewey's three-hour program onto two sides of a 78-RPM disc.

"We used to listen to the Grand Ole Opry," says Donald "Duck" Dunn, who would became the bassist in Stax's house band, "but when I heard Dewey play Little Richard, Bill Doggett, and Bo Diddley, it just changed my life."

"I used to listen to Dewey Phillips with the kids," says Estelle Axton. "I wouldn't even know how to go to the office and have a conversation if I didn't listen to Dewey the night before." Her home was in a modest working-class neighborhood established in the early 1940s, part of the city's constant march east, absorbing farmland. (Jim always preferred a more rural feel, favoring the area north of town, which is where his two studios had so far been located.) Though neighborhoods were still segregated by race, listening to Dewey Phillips wasn't considered radical or communist. "The neighborhood kids used to come to our house," says Estelle's daughter Doris. "This was before she got into the record company—and we'd play canasta. Mother was part of the group. She'd set up two tables in our tiny house—just me and the guys and Mother, no other girls. Dewey Phillips was a big thing for us to listen to."

Between Dewey Phillips, WDIA radio, and the sound made on the streets of downtown Memphis when black and white shoulders rubbed together, when rich and poor, rural and urban converged on the sidewalks, someone like Packy Axton couldn't help but dive headfirst into the world that the segregationists believed held no worth. And there were increasingly more people like Packy. Many, in fact, went to his high school, and the board of education had, however inadvertently, established a place for them to meet.

"The smoking room at Messick High School was a dungeon," says Don Nix, who would soon play saxophone in the Mar-Keys, one of Memphis's early white R&B bands. "The school had designated a smoking area for boys—girls couldn't go in there—and that's where we all smoked. Duck Dunn, Steve Cropper, Charlie Freeman, Packy Axton, and Terry Johnson—the first Mar-Keys guys." Many of these kids would become core players at Stax, and all would help establish the label. They lived in the neighborhood around Messick High, and they hung out together after school, sometimes taking the number 57 Park Avenue bus downtown to look in the shop windows, especially where musical instruments were displayed.

"This music was everywhere!" says Terry Johnson, who would play drums in the Mar-Keys. "We would sneak over to the Plantation Inn in West Memphis and get the band to buy liquor for us, and they would let us in Curry's Tropicana in North Memphis, or we'd spend all night down on Beale by the old Club Handy and listen to Evelyn Young play saxophone, sitting on the curb with beer that some black guy had gone around the corner and bought for us. That was how it got started."

"Sometimes they'd let us in and sometimes they wouldn't," Steve Cropper remembers. Soon Steve's guitar would become a signature of the Stax sound, but in high school he was still absorbing diverse influences. "They knew we were underage, but on Beale Street they'd let us stand in the stairwell and you could look past the ticket booth and see a mirror in the back of the Flamingo Room, and you could see the reflection of the band in that mirror. The first time I saw [future bandmate] Booker [T. Jones] was in the Flamingo Room playing bass, an old red Gibson."

The Mar-Keys inside the Stax recording studio on McLemore.
L–R: Charles "Packy" Axton, Donald "Duck" Dunn, Wayne
Jackson, Terry Johnson, Don Nix, Steve Cropper, Jerry Lee
"Smoochy" Smith.

These young fans became a refraction of that reflection. After seeing an upperclassman in high school perform "Bo Diddley" at the talent show, Steve had begun saving up for a guitar. "Everybody in those days had a Sears and Roebuck catalog—we called it 'the Wish Book,' and my mom could attest to this: I mowed yards and I set bowling pins and did every little odd job I could do to save enough money to buy me an eighteen-dollar Sears Roebuck Silvertone guitar. When the truck pulled up, they said, 'That'll be a twenty-five-cent delivery charge.' My mother always says, 'I'm the one that loaned you that twenty-five cents to get that guitar.'"

The guitar needed tuning, the bridge was loose, and Steve couldn't make much sense of the instrument. But there was a kid at school named Charlie Freeman who was a guitar whiz. "He had been taking guitar lessons, and I asked him to help me," Steve continues. "We went back in his bedroom and fixed it up and he started showing me a few things." Steve and Charlie, tenth graders, began hanging out after school and soon friends were joining them, to listen. Charlie Freeman had an ear beyond his years and was fluent in jazz, R&B, and blues; he could dispense listening suggestions as well as technique. The duo wound up auditioning for a DJ who, impressed, offered them a spot on his weekly sock hop—if they could find a bass and drum. "Boy, we were asking everybody in school," says Steve. "We found this kid, Terry Johnson, who played drums in his father's country band. So he had a little bit of experience, even though he was only in the ninth grade." Cropper's friend Donald Dunn—he was already "Duck" back then, a redhead with a perennial grin—tried moving from the ukulele to the guitar, but couldn't figure out what to do with the extra couple strings. He showed up one day with a bass guitar and found he had a natural feel for the bottom—he loved to dance, and the bass and drums dictated the rhythms. Steve found a Fender Princeton amplifier, and the electricity gave them the jolt to be heard over crowds. They got a gig at the Starlight Club, playing for three bucks a night and all the fried fish they could eat.

"Before I was with them," says Don, "I'd go see them at Neil's, across a bridge and down in a bog, somewhere outside town near the Millington Naval Base. It was the kind of place where people left their teeth at home so they wouldn't break their dental work in a fight. They played Jimmy Reed, Bill Doggett's 'Hold It,' James Brown. I heard Charlie [Freeman] saying, 'Should we do the floor show?' The floor show was Charlie, Steve, and Duck getting up on the bar and doing steps and moves together, then jumping onto the floor." They called themselves the Royal Spades, explaining that they loved poker and a royal spade flush was the game's highest hand. The name's racist overtone smacks of teens believing they're getting away with something, and reveals society's blunted sensibility; the name would soon change.

One day at high school, Steve, the band's lanky and serious leader, was approached by someone he'd seen in the smoking room. "This guy come up to me that I didn't have any classes with, so I didn't really know who he was. He says, 'Hey, man, I hear you guys have a good band.' He said, 'I'd like to be in your band.' And I said, 'Well, we're not looking for anybody. What do you do?' And he said, 'I play saxophone.' And I said, 'Oh, that's real good, but we're two guitars, bass, and drums, and we're not really looking for any horns.' I said, 'How long you been playing?' He said, 'Oh, I've been taking lessons for three months.' And I'm thinking, Yeah, okay, great. Somewhere in the conversation he mentioned something about his mother or his uncle having a recording studio and I went, 'Oh really?' And it ended with me saying, 'Can you be at rehearsal this coming Saturday?'" Their musical interests were entwined, and soon Packy brought Steve to the studio. "He took me out to a garage where Jim Stewart had some equipment. That was the extent of the studio, but at least it was a start, a place to be."

More than a place to be, it became a place to be themselves. These kids came from dry, hardworking worlds—Don's father drove a truck for a small cleaners, Duck's father drove a cab, and Steve's was a railroad detective. The "studio" became their practice space, where they could live their Beale Street dreams. The boys helped move from the garage to Brunswick, and they helped Jim and Estelle clean the new place. Jim had to learn his way around this new equipment, so it was helpful to have the boys rocking and honking while he figured out how to make it all work. "Jim said we'd never make it," Steve remembers. "Jim liked all kinds of music, and he was a country fiddler. I think he was looking to the pop market. But, to be loyal to his sister, he allowed Packy to bring his band out on Saturdays." The players also met Chips Moman there, who regaled them with road stories—recording studios in California, touring with Gene Vincent after his hit, "Be-Bop-A-Lula," and fists flying and knives drawn on average Saturday nights outside Memphis.

"I'd put all those guys in my car on Saturday, with all those instruments, and we'd go out to Brunswick," says Estelle, sounding more like a den mother than a record producer. "They'd jam and practice, jive, carry on. Jim knew the engineering—it doesn't take much engineering for a one-track machine. The machine only had a few knobs, even I learned to run it. And that's what we'd do on Saturday. They thought Packy was great because his mother owned half that company."

Once Packy joined, an expanded horn section was natural. Don Nix was slow to master the guitar, but the fast talker and class clown had plenty of breath for the baritone sax and he'd recently seen how essential an instrument it was. Don's uncle worked downtown in a seat-cover factory and spoke of a black trumpet player named Willie Mitchell who manned the assembly line with him. Mitchell led one of Memphis's most swinging bands, and had a regular gig across the river. Don's uncle didn't take him there, but Don went on his own and was bowled over by the intensity of the horn section. "Now if you can imagine, white kids had never heard R&B music before. It was like going to another planet, a real good planet. It was just unbelievably good vibes—Where has this been?" Then Dewey and Elvis primed the pump, and Memphis's young hep cats wallowed in the gusher.

"We wanted to sound like Willie Mitchell's band," Don continues. Don was a natural on the stage, where his class-clown antics won him applause instead of detention. "So we needed a trumpet player and we met Wayne Jackson. Wayne was a go-getter, a people person. He could play all the old standards. Somebody wanted to hear 'Stardust,' and we don't know how to play it, but Wayne knew how so we could fake it. He was the only one from outside the Messick smoking-room guys."

Wayne was from West Memphis, which is where Willie Mitchell held his regular gig. "Willie was my mentor," says Wayne, who remembers sneaking out to see—or rather to hear—him. "At the back of the bandstand was a big fan that sucked out the smoke and hats and ladies' wigs. And I would stand outside and listen to the band. So Willie Mitchell always sounded like: *wwwwwuuhhhwuuuhhhhhwuhhhh*. Then, when the Mar-Keys got together, we copied Ben E. King and Chuck Jackson and the local black bands of the day. They all had horns. It's a hangover from the big bands, but all they could afford was one or two." Wayne played trumpet; Don and Packy were on saxophones. Soon the band's pay went up to ten bucks a night and all the beer they could drink.

"I was a pretty good student but after I found music . . . no more. I just knew I was gonna play music," says Duck Dunn. "I looked in the mirror every night and tried to do Elvis or whatever Frankie Lymon was doing. We used to sneak over to the Plantation Inn in West Memphis and I just said to myself, Man, I can do this." He began taking lessons in South Memphis, close to where Stax would soon move; his teacher was Larry Brown, the Plantation Inn bassist. "I had a feel that Larry taught me, and Bill Doggett's records taught me, and Little Richard—I just wanted to kick ass. I didn't know a whole lot of notes but I just wanted to make people smile. I was in love with Hank Ballard and the Midnighters, the Five Royales, James Brown, Ray Charles—great R&B artists."

While the band honed their chops, the adults figured out the business. One obvious issue facing them was cash flow, and the lack thereof. The rent in Brunswick was free—and they'd soon be ready to record the landlord's daughter—but as they accumulated microphones, up to seven from four, and bought tape, no money was coming in to replace that which was going out. Estelle and Jim's wife, Evelyn, took care of that. They cleaned the abandoned ice cream stand extending from the former grocery; it had a walk-up window. "We were looking for small dollars, not thousands of dollars," Estelle explains (ever practical). "All I went through to run that ice cream place!"

During the summer, Estelle sent her kids to the ice cream stand before she got off work at the bank. "Packy and I would get in his old '49 Ford, and it was our job to go out there and open up the ice cream place," says Doris. She and Packy didn't get along. "He always called me the goody-goody." Indeed, young Packy had already committed himself to a life of drink. "People said, 'What do you want to do when you grow up?'" Don remembers. "Packy always said he wanted to be an alcoholic. He loved to drink."

Packy was an established problem between Jim and his sister. There

The Brunswick studio building. The dairy bar was to the left, the train tracks to the right. (Courtesy of René Wu)

were two issues, one a principle, one personal. In principle, Jim was uncomfortable with any hints of nepotism. "None of my family worked at the company," he says. "I wanted to run a company that was totally objective and gave people a chance. If it's a small company and you've got a half dozen nieces and nephews and brothers and sisters, people would know they never have a chance of making it." Personally, Packy aggravated Jim's last nerve. His happy-go-lucky attitude, his irreverence, his carousing—these were antithetical to how Jim did business. (These same tensions also existed between Jim and Estelle's husband, Everett.) When Jim solicited his sister's backing, he knew Packy would be part of the package, but his eyes were on the new equipment, not the old conflicts.

Meanwhile, tending to the business at hand—recording—they were constantly reminded of the location's shortcomings. "We didn't do a lot of renovations work at the Brunswick studio," Jim explains. "We felt like it was temporary. It was too far out, too inconvenient for everybody. But it was better than the garage that we had worked in previously."

If the third time were to charm, it would need to be nearer the talent, sound better than an abandoned grocery store, and allow for a secondary cash flow. "We made the decision to move to a location where we could have a record shop and a studio combined," Jim says, "the record shop being the primary means of survival for the studio."

While searching Memphis for a suitable location, they were influenced by the recent success of Hi Records. In 1958, this offshoot of a record distributorship established itself in a movie theater and quickly released more than a dozen records. At the end of 1959, Hi scored a national hit with "Smokie (Part 2)" by the Bill Black Combo, a band led by Elvis's ex-bassist. "At that time, movie theaters were out of business," says Estelle.

Television was sinking the industry. "In Memphis, a lot of theaters were vacant." After considering several other venues, Jim, Estelle, and Chips Moman decided on the Capitol Theater in South Memphis, at the corner of College and McLemore (pronounced "*Mack*-le-more"). Built in 1931, the Capitol had, after twenty-seven years of movies, briefly become a Pentecostal Holiness Church, then a square-dance venue on weekends. It was in a commercial area with a lot of foot traffic on the wide sidewalk, and in the lobby Estelle could establish a record stand. The rent was one hundred dollars per month, which the siblings felt they could manage. Jim recalls no consideration given to the studio's geography, but Moman remembers being intent upon pursuing rhythm and blues and looking specifically for a space in an African-American neighborhood.

The neighborhood had no particular name. Residents called it either the south side, which encompassed a broader area, or College and McLemore, because that corner had been the center of the commercial district since the 1920s. Until the early 1950s, the area was mostly but not entirely white, with working-class families living in single-story bungalows; the two-story dwellings were usually duplexes. Some families expanded their homes, often to take in boarders. There were lumberyards and a rail yard nearby, and the McLemore streetcar ran straight downtown, connecting many husbands to jobs in the Ford Motor plant. Throughout the 1950s, whites were moving east and the neighborhood became increasingly African-American.

In addition to a recent government housing project called LeMoyne Gardens, built in 1940 for the African-American community, there were pockets of black housing elsewhere. The area just west of the Capitol Theater, beyond Neptune Street, had long been black, and was home to Booker T. Washington High School. "Those were the homes of the middle-class black in Memphis. Doctors, lawyers, schoolteachers, as well as some professors at LeMoyne College, which was located nearby," says Logan Westbrooks, who was raised there and later would work with Stax. "But this is segregated Memphis, and that was a white theater. As a black youngster, that theater would not be a concern of mine, not under any circumstances. I would not even be standing out there looking at the marquee, and I certainly wouldn't be attending." Other commerce at College and McLemore—"the corner"—had always been integrated. The theater was the anchor building in a complex that included a barbershop and other small businesses. On Sundays, at nearby Bellevue Park, there were regular football games, whites versus blacks; in a town of long memory, no one could recall racial altercations there. The area also had some musical history, though it was probably unknown to the Satellite staff; the famed Blackwood Brothers, one of white gospel music's brightest lights, came from a church a couple blocks east of the Capitol, and songwriter Rev. W.H. Brewster, who composed "Move On Up a Little Higher" and "Surely God Is Able," the first million-selling black gospel songs, preached for decades from a church several blocks away.

Satellite was not lost in space, even if they were a little directionless. The handful of white-oriented records they'd made had all stiffed; the one with the black group had drawn some attention. On McLemore, they'd be nearer to both groups instead of far from everything. Early in 1960, Satellite Records packed up their gear, the country mouse moving to the city. The Brunswick landlord's daughter never did get recorded.

3. A CAPITOL IDEA
1960

Booker T. Jones stood outside the second-floor nightclub and listened to the music. The Club Handy was perhaps the most storied of all the Beale Street joints, the one from which B.B. King was launched, the one where Bobby "Blue" Bland cut his teeth. This club never closed, attracting all the musicians after their own gigs to jam, to "cut heads"—play unfettered and for themselves, without the restraints of pleasing an audience. Booker, who would soon become a pillar for the foundation of Stax Records, was only in high school, but he already knew the insides of many clubs—mostly from the bandstand's perspective, a high schooler substituting for the regular player who'd taken a night's society gig or gone on the road with some of the marquee talent that regularly passed through Memphis.

"These bandleaders had to come to my house," Booker explains about his teenage years, "persuade my mom and dad that they were okay and to let me go with them. Most of the time I was playing baritone sax or piano, but I did have that Silvertone guitar and a little amp. We'd be in these cow pasture joints playing up-tempo blues, and when it gets a little too late and a little too loud and the sheriff is in there and everybody's dancing and it's hot and it's grinding and the guitar gets turned up and it starts to crunch—I could make that guitar do that. And I'd make five or

A young Booker T. Jones.

six bucks a night with people like [local bandleaders] Robert Tally and Johnny London and Tuff Green."

Booker took the nightclub gigs as they came, and the lessons that came with them. Dexterous on several instruments, Booker often subbed on bass with Willie Mitchell's popular band, and with one led by Al Jackson Sr. Al's son, Al Jackson Jr., soon to be Booker's bandmate and a driving force at Stax, became a strong—maybe strong-armed—influence. "I never worked with anyone who thought keeping time was so important," says Booker of Al Jr. "Al, if I would rush or slow down, he would yell and curse at me—onstage, in front of people. He would hit you over the head with the drumstick if one eighth note or a sixteenth note was off. I mean, he was up and cussing. Al Jackson's place onstage was behind me and the important thing for me was to keep on time so I didn't get hit, so he didn't throw anything or yell at me. That's pretty good incentive for a fourteen-year-old playing with a borrowed bass."

Booker had been inside Curry's Club Tropicana, the Flamingo Room across Beale Street (where his future bandmates Steve Cropper and Duck Dunn saw his reflection in the mirror from the stairwell), the Plantation Inn in West Memphis. He'd played for white rednecks in Millington and for African-American society in South Memphis. But the Club Handy remained a mystery. Where the other clubs hired larger groups like Willie Mitchell's band, Al Jackson Sr.'s band, the Newborn Family band, Tuff Green's Rocketeers, Gene "Bowlegs" Miller's Orchestra, or Ben Branch, Club Handy had a secret weapon: Blind Oscar. Oscar Armstrong played the Hammond organ, and he made the instrument into an orchestra. He had only a drummer and sometimes another instrument behind him, but that was all he needed. "Club Handy would chase us away," Booker laughs. "'You boys go on, get away from here.' They didn't need us kids to substitute. Oscar could fill that room with music and make it pulsate with the Hammond organ."

Booker, when he first heard the organ, couldn't identify it. "I heard the Hammond sound coming out of a Pentecostal church and coming out of Club Handy on Beale Street. Blind Oscar was playing bass on it, and I heard it from Jack McDuff records. But I wasn't sure what the instrument actually was." Pentecostal churches, also called sanctified churches or holy rollers, often featured a full band that would help the pastor whip the congregation to a spiritual frenzy. Booker had been warned not to go inside those churches, and he was chased away from Club Handy, so he experienced the intense power of the Hammond organ without being sure exactly what was creating it.

(He finally saw a Hammond organ when he asked his piano teacher what was always kept covered across the room. "I thought it was a china cabinet," he remembers. His teacher demonstrated the instrument but admonished him not to become entranced by it as he could not afford the lessons he'd need. Soon, Booker was throwing a paper route after school to pay for those lessons, folding the newspapers outside Phineas Newborn's house, so he could hear the great jazz pianist practice.)

By the late 1950s, going from a Memphis club to the national stage was an established career path. Several decades earlier, a band teacher at Manassas High School in North Memphis named Jimmie Lunceford had taken his students to New York, where he quickly earned the house gig at Harlem's Cotton Club, from which both Duke Ellington and Cab Calloway had recently broken out. Lunceford's Orchestra was famed through the 1930s. B.B. King had leapfrogged from a Beale Street talent show to headlining the Club Handy to becoming a national star by 1951. Rufus Thomas had put Sun Records on the map in 1953, and Sun soon launched Junior Parker (Bobby Bland was his valet), Rosco Gordon, Howlin' Wolf, and then Elvis Presley, Johnny Cash, Jerry Lee Lewis, and Carl Perkins. Bobby "Blue" Bland became his own star. Johnny Ace and Johnny Burnette too. In the jazz world, Phineas Newborn went from local clubs to prestigious New York recording artist in 1956.

While the pay for a musician in southern cities was not as high as for a doctor or lawyer, the job had as much respect. "If the Dixie Hummingbirds came through town, or Pops Staples and the Staple Singers, or Sam

Cooke and the Soul Stirrers came through, they were ambassadors of hope," says Rev. Jesse Jackson, a future Stax artist who was raised in the rural South. "These were bona fide stars. They belonged to us." Musicians were pollinators, traveling with the wind of applause beneath their wings, serving not the practical matters of an MD or jurist but rather the essential spiritual side, serving the soul. "So much of our survival capacity came through music and imagination," Rev. Jackson continues. "People living in the worst of conditions, picking cotton or tobacco, or waiting tables, against all odds—music creates for us a great sense of imagination."

◆ ◆ ◆

STANDING IN FRONT of the Capitol Theater, Jim Stewart was approached by a neighborhood boy, African-American, less than ten years old. A white man in the neighborhood was not unusual—if by 1960 the area was weighted more toward blacks, it was still plenty mixed. But no one had poked around the shuttered theater in a long time, and the lad—William C. Brown—had been dreaming of that stage inside nearly all his life. "Jim Stewart was standing outside looking at the building and I was a little kid.

The neighborhood movie theater where Stax would make its home. (Stax Museum of American Soul Music)

So I asked him, 'What are you getting ready to do?' He said, 'It's going to be a recording studio.' And I said, 'I sing.' Just like that. He started laughing. So when he opened the door, I ran under his arm, right into Stax." He would soon work for Estelle in the record store, then sing for Stax with the Mad Lads and learn there to engineer recordings.

Brown set the model for getting in the door—walk right in, sit right down, baby let your mind roll on—though it wasn't quite Stax yet. The company was still called Satellite. Nor was it yet a recording studio. "I had already mortgaged my house, and then to get the operating capital, I had to refinance it," says Estelle. "I'm one of these that likes to take a chance." Money in hand, they began transforming the building. "The theater was too big," Estelle continues. "So we put a partition in. Up on the stage where the screen usually was, that made a good control room, set above the theater floor." They built a wall with a large window so Jim could see the performers. The slanted floor helped deaden the sound, keeping it controllable.

The kids in Packy's band, when not in high school classes, helped with the renovation. It would be their rehearsal space when sessions weren't going on. "It was a very big room," says Steve Cropper, estimating the studio as two thirds of the theater's original size; the Capitol had been a neighborhood theater, not a movie palace, but it seated several hundred. "We had to take the seats out and a lot of the bolts wouldn't come out of the concrete. Packy Axton and I would spend hours with a hammer trying to break these things off so we could lay down carpet."

"We did the acoustic stuff ourselves," says Estelle. "We were always do–it–yourself. We put down carpets, we zigzagged acoustic tile down the walls. I had made some drapes for the studio in Brunswick, and we hung those all the way from the ceiling. That stayed there a long time because it was too hard to get down."

"Jim Stewart and I built these sound panels out of pegboard and burlap," says Steve. "And we put windows in them, so we could see each other—separate the sounds but have eye contact."

Inside the control room was the original Altec Voice of the Theater speaker, eight feet tall and five feet wide. It had filled the building with the sound of James Cagney's bullets and Lash LaRue's snapping whip, and since the studio only needed to hear it in the control room, they could keep the volume low and get very clear playback. The original echo chamber was the men's bathroom, tiled from the theater days.

The theater was one entrance in a strip of several adjoining businesses. Immediately to the east, sharing a wall, was the Capitol Barber Shop.

Beyond that, a shoeshine stand, then a beauty shop, and on the corner a small grocery store and produce stand, complete with a soda fountain serving kids cherry Cokes after school. West from the theater was a TV and small-appliance-repair service, and then a beer joint that had a variety of names (and commonly known, later, as Slim Jenkins' Joint, though it was never incorporated as that). As the Stax musicians matured, their foot traffic shifted to the west, from the soda fountain to where people took their blues home in a brown paper bag.

That commercial strip was a complete universe in which the kids could orbit. "One end was a food store, and the other way was May's Grill," says future Mar-Key Don Nix. "May was an alcoholic lady, white, and she lived in the place. She'd just pass out at night, wake up in the morning, and take off again. Carl Cunningham, who became the Bar-Kays' drummer at Stax, was the shoeshine boy at the barbershop. Everybody hung out together and got along. And that was the neighborhood. We'd rehearse all day sometimes, go down to May's Grill and eat lunch. We'd go to the food store and get sliced baloney and crackers. It was like a job almost, though you didn't get any money for it. But we were learning something."

The theater's entrance was midblock. The ticket booth was still out front, and just inside was the lobby, with the concession stand forming a triangular area that guided you through the curtain and into the theater. Estelle Axton saw the concessions space and saw opportunity—a home for her record shop. "I had been selling records all along," she says. "Now I'm trying to build some stock. This was a largely black neighborhood so I had to get into the rhythm and blues records, and I'm still buying the other kind too because I'm still working at the bank." No one gave real consideration to the advantages that would develop—no one conceived *what* would develop: The store would be a way to gauge what shoppers were buying, would provide immediate customer response to new and developing songs, and would yield a working library so writers and musicians could keep current. The initial purpose was plain and simple: cash flow to help pay the rent.

◆ ◆ ◆

THE STUDIO'S FIRST real boost came from the postman. He heard about the new place in the neighborhood and spread the news. That he was retired and that the studio wasn't on his old route—well, this is a story filled with such improbabilities. The postman's name was Robert Tally, and he was also a keyboard player and bandleader.

Rufus Thomas, left, at the textile mill, watching the vats, making up songs.

"A fella by the name of Robert Tally came by my house and told us that there's a new recording studio over there at the corner of McLemore and College," says Rufus Thomas, whose work at Stax would soon make him known as the Funkiest Man Alive but whose superlative then might have been Busiest, as he was working several jobs to make ends meet (despite his local and national fame as an entertainer). He worked full-time at a textile mill, with half an hour to get from there to his afternoon shift on radio. But even on the job, music was on his mind. "I'm watching the cloths fill up in these big old vats," he says, "and I'm bobbing my head up and down as I watch them, trying to make up songs." In addition to his work at Sun Records, he'd recorded for Meteor and was active in several other studios around town. "Tally said, 'I think you oughta go over there.'"

Musicians had been crossing proscribed thresholds in the city for years. B.B. King had gotten his radio show on WDIA by walking through the front door on a rainy day and asking for an audition. Howlin' Wolf walked into Sun, having heard that the white man Sam Phillips would give you a fair shake. The door Elvis walked through was metaphorical, but his success grew from his knowledge of music on the other side.

Tally had heard about the studio from a mortician in the neighborhood with whom he wrote songs. They'd gone there and cut some demos, been hospitably treated. "They had this Ampex 350 recorder," says Tally, impressed by the gear purchased with funds from Estelle's mortgage. "So I told Rufus Thomas, 'Hey, man, let's go over there and do some demos on McLemore.' And that's how we got hooked up."

Uninvited, Rufus and his seventeen-year-old daughter Carla drove the mile and a half from their home. "We came right off the street," says Rufus, "went right in." In the lobby, they'd have been greeted by Estelle's Satellite Record Shop: boxes of records spread across the candy counter, and by Estelle herself. She was a radio hound, and would have known Rufus by voice if not by sight; when Jim came forward from the back, he recognized Rufus from his rounds promoting the Veltones. Rufus, however, reveals that he remained suspicious. "At that time, really, I thought nothing about white folks," he says, as frank as he is funky. "Nothing at all. When I was young, I had some rough experiences—wrong experiences, bad experiences—with white folk. I'm thinking that all white folks are the same. But I know I had to work, and the white folks had the jobs so I did what I had to do. It took me some time to get these things outta my system, and my system was pretty tight."

Rufus's simple act of entering on his own terms was actually no simple act at all. As James Baldwin wrote: "[W]hen the black man, whose destiny and identity has always been controlled by others, decides and states that he will reject the identity imposed on him, and control his own destiny, he is talking revolution."

A revolt of that very nature was fomenting in public on the streets of Memphis. The fear of arrest, and the certain brutality in jail, had quelled activism for generations. But after serving the country in World War II and the Korean War, the black community had a new sense of entitlement. At the start of February 1960 in Greensboro, North Carolina, a sit-in of four students at a white lunch counter grew to three hundred protestors in less than a week; shortly thereafter, Memphis students began a series of similar direct actions, forcibly integrating lunch counters, public libraries, and the art museum. Ministers joined, urging African-Americans to make their economic contributions felt by boycotting downtown businesses on Mondays and Thursdays. Even the most devalued were rumbling. The sanitation department employees worked the worst job in the worst conditions for the worst pay. Many of the department's full-time employees were eligible for welfare, and many had been there for decades because they knew that, lacking education, lacking training and skills, hauling garbage was as far as they'd go in Memphis jobs. (The head of the Department of Public Works in the latter 1950s, Henry Loeb, had taken to hiring black men with arrest records, knowing they'd have fewer options and thus would be easily victimized.) So the headline on February

6, 1960, stating SANITATION MEN WANT MORE PAY became a call to action; if the garbagemen were standing up for themselves, then many of the city's African-Americans who'd been afraid to publicly demonstrate had to take stock.

When organizers in 1960 began to unionize the sanitation workers, the city's new mayor, that same Henry Loeb, responded that he would dissolve the department and hire private contractors before he'd recognize a union—despite the city's recognition of unions for white-skinned white-collar workers, including those in the sanitation department. Six weeks later, the black public's anger had increased: NEGROES AT FEVER PITCH. An interracial citizens' council was formed, and desegregation of public facilities began in earnest, though slowly. The progress at the sanitation department was negligible.

Rufus meeting Jim on McLemore was taking place five years after the nearby Emmett Till murder; three years after the Little Rock Nine defied the city and upheld the nation's law, integrating their Central High School. It was four years before the federal government passed the Civil Rights Act forbidding hotels, restaurants, gas stations, theaters, and the like to segregate or discriminate "on the ground of race, color, religion, or national origin." It was five years before the Voting Rights Act, which was passed to buttress the Fifteenth Amendment, created ninety-five years earlier.

The entertainment culture, music particularly, moved at a faster pace than social changes. The year prior to Rosa Parks and the Montgomery bus boycott, in Memphis a white kid had embraced the disenfranchised culture of blacks, recording songs in their musical style—white and black musical styles were decidedly distinct then—and Elvis Presley's popularity had soared. Adjacent to a 1960 newspaper article about the expanding protests on Main Street is an advertisement for one of the city's most prominent record stores, Pop Tunes, with the simple statement RECORDS FOR EVERYONE.

Social issues were not on Jim's mind when he leased the Capitol, but music was. While Stax was getting into rhythm and blues, rhythm and blues was working its way into Jim. The only music by African-Americans that he'd ever heard had been on warm 1940s evenings as a teenager in Middleton, when he and a date would sit outside the black church near town and listen to the congregation sing. Both soul music and rhythm and blues would grow from church music, reworking the exuberant spirit and exulting lyrics into secular songs. For Jim, Elvis had not done the trick in the middle 1950s, and if his passion for Bob Wills had unwittingly introduced him to blues styles and roots, his conversion to black music had not come until 1959. In the wake of his lone studio success with the Veltones, Jim had shifted his radio dial. "You're going to listen to the station that plays your records," he says. "I listened to WDIA and WLOK and I became exposed to black music. When I heard a record called 'What'd I Say' by Ray Charles"—the sense of wonder remains in Jim's voice decades after the fact—"I was baptized in soul music and I never looked back. When I heard that record it was like a lightning bolt hit me, something I never, never felt before. And that's what I wanted to do, that's where I wanted to go." Jim was responding not only to the record's exciting energy, but also to the deep sense of character that the artist imbued in the music. Like Bob Wills, Ray's music was embossed with his personality. And that's why Jim will always discover new talent—he's not listening for what sounds hot, he's listening for the individual. In 1960, Jim heard Ray's new live record, *In Person*. "That really blew me away. Like the addict, that was the second fix and I was gone, hooked, never looked back from there." His musical landscape was about to synchronize with his studio's physical geography.

Rufus reacquainted himself with Jim Stewart and introduced his daughter Carla. Jim showed them the studio that was still taking shape. With Chips Moman, he'd been honing the system, recording Royal Spades rehearsals. They'd gotten to where they could produce radio commercials, and, as Tally had already discovered, they were amenable to being a demo facility for the local professional talent. In addition to the R&B players, they still worked with some of the rockabilly cats, fishing around for something that sounded right. Jim knew about Rufus's Sun hit, so when Rufus inquired about recording, it was music to Jim's ears. "When you have a recording studio, you always have disc jockeys that come in," says Estelle. "You want to take a chance on them because maybe they'll play some of your other records."

Not long after—the very next day, by some accounts—Rufus was at Satellite with Carla, his piano-playing son Marvell (then eighteen years old), and Bob Tally's band, featuring seventeen-year-old drummer Howard Grimes (who would later achieve fame on Al Green's records as a member of the Hi Records rhythm section). "I had a little four-piece group and we took Rufus Thomas into the studio," says Tally. "We had this tune we worked on, 'Deep Down Inside,' and we got it down so they would record it. And then they had to have another song for the flip side."

"Daddy had to stay right in the studio and write the other side," Carla remembers. "Jim said, 'Let's cut—let's keep going so we can get both sides.' That's Jim: 'While we're on a roll, let's go.'"

"Rufus," says Estelle, "he always had a song."

This song would announce the new studio's presence, and would introduce a young Booker T. Jones to his future career. "On this song Rufus was coming up with," says Tally, "I had the rhythm to play a certain way. Do you remember a record called 'Ooh Poo Pah Doo'? The feel of that rhythm is what I had them do." Once the drums and bass found the groove, the others could fall in. Marvell was on the piano, so Tally played trumpet; he realized it would sound great with a baritone sax. The vocalist for Tally's band, David Porter (soon to be one of Stax's main songwriters), knew a baritone sax player. David was an eager and ambitious young man skipping a day of twelfth grade because he wasn't going to miss the chance to be in a recording studio.

"I was in eleventh-grade algebra class and David Porter comes with a hall pass and tells the teacher the band director wants to see me," remembers Booker T. Jones. "David had been singing around the high school and in male vocal groups. We were friends. David had the keys to the bandmaster's car—Mr. Martin would let David borrow it. It was a '57 Plymouth, had a lot of pickup. The music-room key was on the same chain, and the baritone sax was in the same room as the bass I always borrowed. David said, 'Go get your horn, we're going over to the studio on McLemore.' I had heard the music coming from behind the curtain while I listened to hundreds of records in the store. I would hang around for hours, and I knew there was something going on back there, but I had never put my foot through the door. So down we went to get the baritone sax out of the instrument room and into the borrowed car and over to Satellite Records and through the door, and there I was."

"I knew he could play guitar and trombone and all of this," says Tally, "so we gave him the baritone sax."

Booker made the most of his opportunity. "Steve [Cropper] played guitar on that Rufus Thomas session," says Booker. "I knew him because he was the clerk at the Satellite Record Shop. We didn't have a lot of interaction [on the session] because I was behind a baffle [sound divider] with a little window. But he was the guy. Before I left, I made sure that Steve and Chips Moman knew that I could play piano." Moman was recording the session. (Though Carla remembers Jim being there, he may not have arrived until the first song was nearly done; if Booker was being pulled out of class, Jim was likely still at the bank. Moman remembers playing the track for Jim that evening.)

The new studio had its first record, the playful " 'Cause I Love You," a back-and-forth between Rufus and Carla, with great dynamic breaks for the piano and baritone sax. Rufus, always a little bit of a clown, is endearing as the man who wants his woman back; Carla sounds very adult (she'd been singing onstage with WDIA's high school singing group, the Teen Town Singers), and the rhythm evokes the exchange between New Orleans and Memphis.

"We didn't sit down and say, 'We're going with black music,'" says Jim. "'R&B' was a foreign word to me. It happened quickly, but not in a manner that was conscious and direct." The gears of the unimagined machine began to turn when calls came in to the record shop asking for this new song, "'Cause I Love You." The calls indicated that people were hearing the song and that the store was becoming established in the neighborhood; they weren't associating the song with the studio in the back, they were just hunting down something they wanted to own. "Locally, we sold four or five thousand records in a couple weeks' time. We'd never sold that many records on anything." Rufus's job at WDIA gave the record a solid tie-in there. "It was so loose back then," Jim continues. "There was no program director. It was about the friendship with the individual jocks. They played what they wanted to play—as long and as many times as they wanted to play it. It was not uncommon to hear a record played five times consecutively. It was easy to get exposure, especially with black radio. So between DIA and LOK, we broke the record locally. Then Rufus had contacts through the Sonderling Broadcasting chain—he sent the record to San Francisco, it started getting action."

Jim rode the wave as best he could, expanding his promotion outside the city limits. He found stations east of Memphis in Tennessee, others in nearby Mississippi and Alabama. "Some stations we'd just find the call letters and send the records out," he says. He and Rufus hit the highway, delivering some in person, hoping the extra attention would be repaid. "So," says Jim, "we had a local hit."

◆ ◆ ◆

SMALL INDEPENDENT LABELS were an essential part of the record industry ecosystem. Able to mine talent in their neighborhoods, cities, and regions, these businesses may have had national aspirations, but they functioned on a local level. Recording a song that sounded like a hit was much easier than distributing enough of those records to make it sell like a hit. And more than one label went broke from a hit, going into debt to keep up with demand, then finding out that distributors who'd ordered all those records wouldn't pay. The way up and out for the indie was through allying with an established national label. RCA and Columbia, for example, were machines that could readily sell millions of records—the new seven-inch 45s, twelve-inch LPs, and ten-inch 78s—not only in America but also across the globe. An indie would send the master tape of the song to the national label, and the national would incur the costs of manufacturing and distributing; in return, they'd take the lion's share of the revenue, paying a royalty—10 to 15 percent—to the indie. Smaller labels—Chess in Chicago, Jewel in Shreveport, Dot near Nashville—beat the bushes to find local talent. In many instances, they were farm teams: Memphis's Sun Records couldn't keep up with Elvis's popularity and sold his contract to RCA; Johnny Cash made his name on Sun, but made his money at Columbia.

At Atlantic Records in New York City, Ahmet Ertegun and his brother Nesuhi, sons of America's first ambassador from Turkey, began building a label that specialized in rhythm and blues. The more established labels didn't believe the African-American market had enough disposable cash to warrant cultivating; Ahmet, along with his brother and partners Herb Abramson and Jerry Wexler, recognized that their burgeoning popularity was taking it into the white market (first through publishing—the original songs being covered by whites, then by the black artists breaking through). Paramount Records had begun because its parent company manufactured phonographs and it needed product to play; Warner Bros. Records began as an outlet for its movie stars and soundtracks. Atlantic began because it loved the music. As its success mounted—with Ruth Brown, Ray Charles, Big Joe Turner—Atlantic could afford to buy up smaller labels, or sign distribution contracts with them. Smaller and poorer than the major labels, its distribution network cobbled together like a patchwork, Atlantic became an indie that functioned on a national scale.

In Memphis, Atlantic's distributor was an entrepreneur named Robert "Buster" Williams. He'd fallen into the music business through the vending machine industry. First he sold peanuts at local football games in Enterprise, Mississippi; that led to snack machines, which took him to jukeboxes, and in short order he had a record-pressing plant, Plastic Products in Memphis, which sold records to his distributorship, Music Sales, which sold records to his jukebox company, Williams Distributing. He would make a profit three times on the same record (twice before it left the warehouse), and soon Buster was a ready friend for younger record entrepreneurs like Jim Stewart, extending easy credit on the condition that if any money came in, he'd be paid first—which was easy to enforce since Buster's distribution company was collecting the proceeds that would go to Jim.

Sales of Jim's " 'Cause I Love You" were brisk enough for the Music Sales staff to notice, and when an Atlantic Records promotions man came through, they brought it to his attention. In short order, Jim's phone rang and on the other end was Jerry Wexler from Atlantic Records. Wexler's name may have meant little to Jim, but Atlantic's name meant a lot—they were the company that released the Ray Charles lightning bolts! When Wexler identified himself as producer of Ray's "What'd I Say," Jim realized the call's significance. "I didn't know what label distribution was, or a production deal," Jim says. "The royalty rate Wexler offered was so small that it's unreal, but it was a start. And that was big time for me." Atlantic paid Satellite $5,000; the exact nature of that five grand was not etched into the lines of the handshake, and its vagueness would later cause significant problems. One thing Atlantic definitely got for its money was the opportunity to pick up any future records with Rufus and Carla. They released that first one on the Atlantic subsidiary label Atco. The record's success, the interaction with Wexler—Jim was bitten. "From there," says Jim, "it just sort of mushroomed."

It all sounds very matter of course, but it can take years for this series of events to fall into place. There were record labels working out of garages and living rooms all across America, and many great songs never found their way up for air, so receiving a call from Wexler was a very big deal, and hearing him say you'd done something that he wanted a piece of was a significant indication that you were doing something right.

Not that that made Jim's work any easier. Jim was working his day job at the bank, nights and weekends at the studio, and also gigging in clubs. (Steve says Jim used to sit up nights and calculate royalties down to the penny.) Word about his facility was getting out—the room was large and the sound was good—so musicians would book time there to cut demos, the small-change payment reverberating through the empty coffers. Someone might find an account and they'd cut a furniture commercial or radio spot of some kind for cheap. Chips, who was overseeing the studio while Jim was at work, ran deep in the music community and could pull together a jam session, and had an ear for pulling songs from rough ideas. "Usually it was just someone that would walk in," Moman remembers. "That's how David Porter came in. And William Bell. After school was out, Booker would come in wearing an ROTC uniform—him and David Porter. We'd just start recording. When Jim would get off in the evenings, I'd play him what I did that day."

When no one else was there, the Royal Spades were ready to make noise. "Hanging out there was like going to Disneyland every day," says Don Nix, who often came in earlier than the other kids because he'd either skipped school or been kicked out. "What a education that was. If you didn't do anything else, you stood in the record shop and listened to records. And every day was something new. Jim didn't know anything about recording equipment, and I'm not sure that Chips knew that much—just enough to get a one-track machine and some microphones up and running, kind of hit-and-miss. There was a lot of recordings at Stax that never saw the light of day. They weren't all hits, and some of them weren't even records. But there was always somebody cutting something. You're at the right place at the right time and the right stuff happened."

When Estelle opened her record counter, Steve Cropper quit his job at a grocery store to work for her. Steve was always more serious than the other guys in the Royal Spades; he was a natural leader, he had a tendency toward the staid and reserved, but like his bandmates, he liked his music loose and fun. He was attending college and may not have been anticipating a career in records, but he knew that working at Satellite kept him closer to the studio than the grocery did. "We didn't get paid very much for playing music in those days," Steve says, "and I had to eat. I talked to Miz Axton about working in the record shop, and my main reason for that was to be close to the studio—that's what I wanted to do."

Jim, too, had found what he wanted to do, even if the monetary rewards were not yet evident. "Music can bring people together, emotionally as well as socially," he reflects. "You begin to see inside of each other's minds and understand where we came from. We were looking for good talent, it didn't matter how old, how black, how white. We were looking for good writers, good musicians, creative people. Once we opened the studios on McLemore, I don't think we cut any more pop or white records for a long time. It was as if we cut off that part of our lives that had existed previously, and never looked back." That change may have been market-driven—Jim's white records had flopped, his black ones had sold. But there were plenty of white people who couldn't have worked with African-Americans, no matter the success. Jim was feeling the power of the music in his soul. "As it grew, it didn't matter whether I was getting encouragement. It was striking an emotional fire within me and that was all I was going by. I had no way of knowing whether it was going to be successful or not, I just knew it moved me."

4. THE SATELLITE'S ORBIT
1960–1962

THE SATELLITE RECORD Shop drew in life's blood and pumped it to the enterprise. Estelle hung speakers outside the entrance to attract passersby—the trolley stopped near the store's entrance, and those extra-wide sidewalks on this active commercial street could foster a real neighborhood bustle. "College and McLemore was kind of like the Times Square of Memphis," says Don Nix. "At night, there was lots of lights from the grocery store and all the shops. Everybody hung out and was friends. [Future Mad Lads] William C. Brown and John Gary Williams, they'd be out on the street corner singing doo-wop just like in the movies."

The record store lured the kids. "We would dance out on the sidewalks," says William Bell, who'd soon sign with the company as a vocalist. "I'm sure it was good for business because the kids dancing would attract potential buyers. Satellite Record Shop was like the entertainment center for the neighborhood."

"They gave me a job working around the place when it first opened," says William C. Brown, the kid who'd run under Jim's arm when he'd opened the door. "One thing about it—you could go in Stax as a floor sweeper and end up a producer or writer or a star."

One of those customers who'd work his way back to the studio was Booker T. Jones. "We never had a record store in our neighborhood before," he says. "It was something of an oasis for me. Before that I had to drive twenty minutes out to Sears to look at records, and all the records there were country. At Satellite, you could listen to your record at the counter. That's the first place I heard Ray Charles, the first place I heard John Coltrane. Going there was an enlightening experience. I listened to hundreds of records, for hours, and I never had any money to buy anything."

Listeners suited Estelle just as much as buyers. She'd quiz the kids about what they liked, and why, and then share that information with the budding writers and musicians. "She positioned herself with that record shop to be the research and development division for Stax Records," says Deanie Parker, who began working for Mrs. Axton in 1960. "Estelle had more common sense than twenty people put together." All the kids warmed to her, and when she wasn't referred to as "Miz Axton," they called her Lady A.

Estelle studied the radio, and she would do her own buying at the distributorship because she knew what she wanted. "I had very faithful customers," she says. "I had a card system. When they'd buy ten records, I'd give them a free one of their choice. And the minute they'd give me their name, I'd pull the card, see what they like, and I'd play whatever I had bought at the distributorship. My brother always said that anybody who'd come in with twenty dollars, I'd get nineteen of it—leave them enough money to get home on." And her store wasn't only for moving product; it was also for developing it. "I could also test the records they made in the back. If I had one that several customers said, 'Give me one of those too,' I could tell them in the back, 'Go ahead and press that one, it'll sell.' That's why we were successful with nearly everything we put out for a few years—we tested them at home before we let them go."

The studio was also developing relationships with the disc jockeys, especially at Memphis's two black radio stations. Jim could take them a test copy of a record, and they'd add it to their rotation. Audience response could be judged by requests at the record shop. "We'd either get calls for it or we didn't," says Jim. "They'd come in, wouldn't know the name, just a line. I used to spend Friday nights, Saturdays, and Saturday nights in the record shop if we weren't cutting. They'd get their checks, the winos were in—it was a great experience for me and one of the happiest times in my life, working behind the counter and really dealing with the consumer, finding out his preferences in music. I would spend as much time as I could in there."

The trade was in 45s—seven-inch pieces of vinyl lacquer with one song on each side spinning at forty-five rotations per minute. And usually, it was just the one song that mattered, the A-side. A few artists released albums, but mostly these were after-the-fact collections of singles; making statements in a series of songs—the Beatles' *Sgt. Pepper*, Marvin Gaye's *What's Going On*—was a concept years from commonplace. The business was built around the hit. And there was no better place to read the winds than at record stores. Estelle's, with its turntable at the front, its young, hip, and vocal crowd tuning in, drew DJs and traveling stars, promotions men and label representatives, because she was an outspoken and articulate critic, and they liked to hear her assessment. "Rufus Thomas, Dick 'Cane' Cole, Al Bell, and a lot of the disc jockeys hung out," Don says. "We all knew who they were. They were stars to us. And if Solomon Burke or other stars came through town, the next morning they'd come through Stax."

Another character who'd hang out at the record store was Estelle's husband, Everett. He'd arrive in the evenings after his factory job with a quart of Stag beer in a brown paper bag, replenishing his supply from the neighborhood store. He smoked Picayune cigarettes, a strong, caporal tobacco (the American version of the French Gauloises) with the motto "Pride of New Orleans." He wore black brogue irons (a metal-tipped work shoe), white socks, and his work clothes. He was mostly quiet—grumbling occasionally about the lateness of the hour. "I'm not certain that Everett was ever very comfortable being around an organization that was predominantly African-American," says Deanie Parker. "I certainly never felt the warmth from Everett that I experienced from Estelle." Everett had his house riding on Stax's success. His discomfort participating in race mixing was sometimes palpable, but he mostly kept it to himself. An investment is an investment.

And his wife was her own person, proceeding according to her own ways. "Estelle was the nucleus," says Marvell Thomas, Rufus's son. "She is what made Stax Records be Stax Records. Her attitudes about people and her love for people was the reason why the racial harmony existed in that place. Everybody loved her. Black, white, green, purple, we all liked Estelle."

◆ ◆ ◆

As THE DUST began to settle—"'Cause I Love You" racked up a powerful thirty or forty thousand copies in sales—Jim Stewart saw what was before his eyes: Carla Thomas. She was young, radiant, and possessed a real talent. When there was a performance by WDIA's Teen Town Singers, eyes always stopped on Carla.

Carla Thomas with Al Jackson Jr. (Stax Museum of American Soul Music)

"Carla was somebody we was always *oohing* and *ahhing*," Wayne Jackson says. "It was like a fraternity house in that studio. We'd show up and nothing would get done for an hour or two while we talked about everybody that wasn't there. We always said Marvell had a better ass than Carla, and then we'd fall out laughing."

"Everybody was infatuated with Carla," says Duck Dunn. "Her voice, and she was a beautiful girl—how could you not love Carla Thomas?"

Carla would pass time on the piano, and Jim began to really see her, to hear her. With the passion and innocence of a teenager imagining love, Carla would pour her whole heart—and have fun pouring her whole heart—into her favorite self-penned folly. "I knew 'Gee Whiz' was a great song when I first heard Carla do it," says Jim. "A hit record. You just get this feeling." Seventeen at the time, Carla had written the song two years before in her tenth-grade notebook. "I wrote short stories and songs and I just was enjoying myself," she remembers. "I was in the glee club and all the little clubs. I don't know how I wrote it. I was through within thirty minutes. It just kind of flowed, like angels came down and gave it to me."

Jim's concern was keeping the lights on at the studio, but with "'Cause I Love You" working its way into the public eye, and with the Atlantic money in the bank, he recognized an opportunity. They could raise their stake, sinking their income into another record. "I was at the bank, so all I could work was nights and on weekends," Jim says. Juggling a variety of responsibilities—including the arrival of his third child—Jim relied on Chips Moman, who was always ready to take the reins. "I was thinking, Now that I've got a hit record," Jim says, "I need to make the next one better quality." Jim didn't yet believe in his facility—the Ampex tape machine, seven microphones, and a four-channel mixer—and he sent Chips to record Carla at the Hi Records studio in the former Royal movie theater, the next neighborhood over. But when Jim heard the result of the session, he was dissatisfied: "It was too fast. I didn't hear the magic. So I cut it again in our studio." It was folly upon folly: three or four years into a business that was at best a crapshoot, he'd had one lucky roll, and now, with a finished song in the can—paid for, including studio rental, string players, and everything—he was going to pay again for the same session. Only this time, he'd be in charge.

The technology in late 1960 in Memphis still demanded that all the musicians and instruments be recorded together, live to tape. If one person messed up, all would have to start over. The background singers shared Carla's mike; she'd step back to allow them room, they'd then make room for her. Jim hired string players again, and hired Robert Tally to write out arrangements. Jim was, for the second time on the same song, laying out pay for about ten musicians, a very serious investment for a company that was, to date, a losing proposition. (The standard payment was fifteen dollars per musician per session, and if the song got released, it got filed with the union and they received full pay—about sixty-five dollars.) The day of Carla's redo, the investment seemed to go from bad to worse: the string players arrived, but Tally's arrangements didn't. Leaving the studio with everyone there and the clock running, Jim drove three miles to Tally's house, 1425 Eloise Road. His furious knocking woke Tally—he'd played a gig the previous night, it ran late, he was still asleep . . . and he'd forgotten to write the charts.

Jim hightailed it back. "What a hassle that session was," he says. "An all-day affair." A union session was supposed to run three hours; if it went over, it was considered another session, with additional pay. But the

Memphis union and the Memphis players were more lax than in the big cities. That day, they made up a simple arrangement they could play without fully written parts. "String players never make up parts as they go along," says Marvell, "like horn players do all the time. But they did that day." With Jim producing, the song landed in the right spot. "Gee Whiz" captures Carla's innocence and her earnestness. It's a silly little song, as Jim has described it, but the piece is really about Carla's delivery, which all the supporting instruments bring out. The strings and backing vocals give it a maturity and presence that would usher it from the youth market to broader appeal. Jim pressed copies, then watched somewhat agog as it took off, first in Memphis, then in St. Louis, then beyond.

"I got a call from an old pal of mine, Hymie Weiss," says Atlantic's Jerry Wexler, referring to a music business insider behind an array of hits ("one of the lovable roughnecks in the record business," as Wexler describes Weiss). "[Hymie] was in Memphis and he said, 'Hey, schmuck, you got a hit record down here. It's Carla Thomas, 'Gee Whiz.' He said, 'If it wasn't you I'd pick it up for myself. You better come down and get it.'"

Jerry Wexler telephoned Jim, putting on the *harrumph*: Atlantic had signed Carla, he said, so why was Jim sneaking out records on her? Jim's first argument with his mentor ensued. Not three moons prior, Jim Stewart had been thrilled when Atlantic picked up his record and made a distribution arrangement. With their help, "'Cause I Love You" had sold tens of thousands of copies, reaching people at greater distances than the fledgling company could ever have reached. So now, the same opportunity presenting itself, Jim Stewart had the opposite reaction; he bristled at Atlantic's intrusion. Why? His legal angle was that Carla was a different act from Rufus and Carla, and Atlantic had optioned the duo. But the gut of his reaction was emotional. The first time Wexler had asked, the second time he'd come in bullying, and Jim's back ridged when he was being told what to do. Being told what to do is one step from being told what *not* to do, and Jim Stewart did not want to be told he had no right to release his own records how and when he wanted. He was an *independent*.

The disagreement led to a negotiation. Jim's brief taste of success had made him aware of several issues, one being that "I was not making the money. So I had been contemplating going into independent distribution." If he cut out Atlantic, he'd make more money per record. Wexler told him, "You'd be making a big mistake. You don't know how bad collections are. You need a sales force." Jim understood that a hit had killed many a burgeoning record label: Distributors were known not to pay for what they ordered, and labels found themselves in debt—they'd paid for the recording, the shipping, the manufacturing, and received back nothing. Allying with Atlantic would allow Jim to focus on making records, with the burden of distributing them, and collecting the money, left to others. Jim decided he could forsake distribution, but he wanted his own label, as opposed to delivering master tapes that would be released on Atlantic. A "production deal" was arranged, with Stax delivering the masters for Atlantic to manufacture and distribute on the Stax label, and to pay Stax a portion of the profits, approximately fifteen cents per single sold. "So we made the contract, five years," Jim says. The contract was a handshake, so the terms were general, not specific. Specificity on the front end would have solved a lot of problems, but as Jim recollects, "In those days, no one hired an attorney to do these things. It was a one-on-one deal, and my deal was with Jerry Wexler."

In three months, "Gee Whiz" went to number five in the nation, breaking into the pop top ten. Working with Atlantic clearly had its benefits.

And its obligations. Carla had begun college in Nashville, but Atlantic wanted to promote her in New York as part of an R&B revue show. To secure her appearance, Wexler boarded a plane for Memphis. Satellite's two hits were different enough, interesting enough, and successful enough—who were these people and what was this place? He found the theater-cum-studio a marvel: If the hits hadn't proven it, there'd be no reason to think this facility could produce them. He wanted to take Jim Stewart to dinner—smoothing any ruffled feathers from their recent renegotiation, and also to meet the It-girl, Carla Thomas. (Atlantic had established itself through vocalist Ruth Brown, so Jerry had a particular interest in meeting the new female vocalist.)

There was, however, no place in Memphis or its surrounding environs that a mixed table could dine. Jerry and Jim: white. Carla, Rufus, and Lorene Thomas, Carla's mother: black. Not in public in Memphis in 1960, or for several more years.

So they decided to meet in Jerry's hotel room, where they'd order room service. "We're going to his hotel room to talk—money that is," says Rufus Thomas. "I'm sharp, I got on my good clothes, and I'm cleaner than nineteen yards of chitlins, and you clean them up good enough to eat 'em."

At the front door of the Claridge Hotel, the party was reminded how far they were from the embrace of Jim's studio. "Instead of going in the front," says Wexler, "we had to go in the back way. Blacks couldn't use the front door."

"I told them, 'Hell no, I ain't riding no service elevator,'" Rufus remembers. "'Don't have to ride it, won't. See, I can go back right back in the street where I was and forget you people. I am *not* riding that elevator!' But my wife said, 'Well, maybe let's do this this one time, and you never have to do it again.' So I did, went up on that service elevator."

The contingent—blacks and whites, dressed for dining—traipsed around the building and through the slop alley to the back door. Wexler never forgot Rufus's resigned comment: "And Rufus says, 'Here it is again, walking through the garbage cans.'"

Jim Stewart recoils today as he recalls the event, citing the freight elevator as possibly the most embarrassing event of his life. He and Carla had become very close, grateful for the gifts each had shared with the other. They'd known only respectful, pleasant terms. Here, the real world intruded; the alley, the freight elevator—the humiliation.

Privately ensconced, the group began rebuilding their bridges. Dinner arrived, wheeled in on carts by members of the hotel staff. "We had dinner in there and we talked," Rufus remembers. "They talked real good about what Satellite and Atlantic was gonna do, how they were gonna market the records, about New York and Tennessee, the North and the South coming together for one common cause, and that was records." Amends were made, new promises put forth, and the company left in good cheer.

But the waiters had noticed—and reported—the transgression of blacks and whites in consort. An invisible empire of cogs began turning and promptly the Memphis police knocked on Wexler's door. "'Open up! You got a woman in there,'" Wexler remembers them saying. "They were all long gone. I said, 'Bring up the manager, I'm not opening up.' I had an idea of them putting me in the trunk of a car and dumping me in Arkansas." The errand for the manager allowed Wexler to scrawl a desperate note to his company in New York and put it in a stamped envelope. When the manager arrived, Wexler flung the door open and dashed to the hallway mail chute, praying for the letter's New York arrival before the oxygen was depleted in whatever horrible chamber he was soon to be held.

The management and the police saw the room was empty. "Someone saw these black people, including Carla, who was beautiful, and they figured there was unwarranted miscegenation happening on their premises." Wexler wasn't done. "I called the lieutenant in charge and said thanks for welcoming me to Memphis with this. I said, 'This is Stone Age, and that's what you are and your cops are, Stone Age.'"

But Wexler left with what he wanted, and Carla performed in New York. "It was one of the highlights of my life," says Carla. "The Brooklyn Paramount Theater. All I had was those two little songs. [She'd cowritten the B-side with Moman.] But people whose records I'd bought—Little Anthony, Jackie Wilson, Chuck Jackson—now I'm on the show with them."

5. A BANKER AND A GAMBLER
1961–1962

SOME DAYS THE studio felt like a bad talent show, people hoping to be the next Carla Thomas—but their tenth-grade songs sounded like tenth grade, their performances juvenile. A neighborhood doo-wop group cut a pretty good piece with Chips Moman that Jim felt was worth releasing. The group renamed themselves for the producer; Atlantic did not pick up the Chips' "You Make Me Feel So Good," but it was a worthwhile exercise for Satellite. Everything was; it was all so new.

Chips kept the studio active. He had a good ear, and plenty of time to audition those who felt they belonged in the studio making records, not in the front buying them. One player who made his way to the back was Floyd Newman, a saxophonist who had recently returned from college in Detroit. His family lived near the corner of College and McLemore. Last he'd seen, white people were watching movies at that address; four years later, black people were dancing outside the front door. "It was a record shop, and I went in there to buy some records," he remembers. "Some of the musicians saw me and they hired me." Floyd hung out with his old friend and fellow saxophonist Gilbert Caple, and they came up with a riff. "Gilbert and I, we were just messing around," Floyd continues. "Goofing off. And I happened to put in that response, 'Ooh, last night.' It had the feel, and the feel is what sells songs." Chips heard a song beneath the fun, and he put Gilbert and Floyd with Packy and his rowdy friends; Gilbert and Floyd were black, a bit older, and they could really play. So could some of Packy's friends, but not all of them. Chips brought in his honky-tonk friend Jerry Lee "Smoochy" Smith, who had a piano riff that seemed like it would meld with Gilbert and Floyd's idea, and it did.

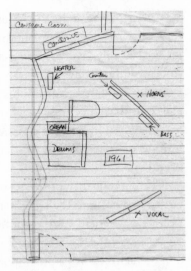

The studio setup in the early 1960s. (Drawing by Steve Cropper/Courtesy of René Wu)

"We were just kids having a good time," says Wayne. "Poor old Jim, it was life and death to him." Chips could corral and focus their energies. "Jim was a nervous fellow," Wayne continues, "took nerve pills. A country redneck fiddler in a black neighborhood—a banker really. And working on borrowed money. But Miz Axton was selling 45-RPM records to black kids and she knew they wanted to dance. She told us, 'I want you to make a record these kids can dance to. And I want it to be an instrumental.' So that's how we came up with 'Last Night.'" Wayne's use of "we" is casual, but exactly who the "we" was would soon become a heated conflict.

With the rehearsals taking shape, Chips called a recording session. Steve Cropper was on the session, and Duck Dunn was supposed to be, but his father had recently lost his job and, to earn money, he was working with a friend giving helicopter rides on weekends. "My dad was going through financial stuff," says Duck. "He needed help." Duck was giving other kids a thrill and missing his own. On bass was Lewie Steinberg, another older black player who, at twenty-seven, was active in the night-club scene; he played with Al Jackson Sr.'s band (alongside Al Jr.), and with Willie Mitchell's band (where Al Jr. also played, and Booker often subbed). "I was at home minding my own business and Gilbert Caple come by my house," Steinberg says. Caple, one of the new song's writers, invited him to the studio. "I said, 'What studio and for what?'" Steinberg hadn't been to Satellite yet; in fact, he'd just come from a tour through Louisiana, and his playing was saturated with a New Orleans feel that he lent to the song's bottom.

Somewhere between the country soul of Chips and Smoochy and the funky hearts of Floyd, Gilbert, and Lewie, the song "Last Night" emerged.

It is, perhaps, the archetypal Memphis song of that era, the "What'd I Say" for locals. The horns tease out their opening notes, so playful; the rhythm—it's surprisingly layered, like a comic team's banter, and much too kinetic to hear without physically responding. The drummer (Curtis Green) was from the Plantation Inn and his playing suggests how raucous and fun that club must have been. As gleeful a song as ever recorded, the instrumental is punctuated by Floyd's occasional vocal refrain—"Oooh, last night!"—hinting of salaciousness, of secrets being told between friends. It is fun, funkified.

The sonic quality of the record is also great—it leaps out of the speakers, etched hot into the tape, with the needle in the red but not distorting. "Chips was actually at the controls," says Jim of the production. "Insisted on it. Two little four-channel mixers tied together, and a little Ampex mono machine." It's a poker player's recording, not a banker's.

Before its release, the tape sat on the shelf for weeks. Jim pursued his recordings with Carla, and Chips kept the studio humming. Time passed, the tape languished, an exercise in recording, another testing of the equipment. And that might have been the end of the story but for one important fan: Estelle. She heard the record's blend of rhythm and blues and country, and knew, too, that instrumental songs were popular (it was thought by many that Hi Records stood for "hit instrumentals"). "I was selling those blues numbers," she says, "and I could put two and two together." She had Jim make a test pressing for the store's turntable. "I had become close to WLOK and WDIA, talking to the disc jockeys," says Estelle, referring to the two black music radio stations. When she played it for one of WLOK's lead jocks, he took the copy to the station, swearing it was a hit. "From the very first day he put it on," Estelle says, "people began stopping at the shop looking for that instrumental. They'd say, 'I don't know what it is, but it goes, "Ooh, last night."'"

While the requests continued, Jim's attention was on Carla. He heard pop potential and took her to Nashville. "I thought I'd get a better string sound," he says. "I was misleading myself, actually. I didn't know what I had in that studio." Soon he'd recognize the difference between the foothill sound of Nashville's country and the thick funk of Memphis's swamp, vowing never to cut an R&B record in Nashville again.

"Jim was so involved with Carla and the other vocalists," Estelle says, "he wasn't pushing this instrumental bit. But because my son was in there, I was pushing that instrumental. They'd played it on the radio and they were coming into the shop to buy it but I didn't have a product. It was getting very irritating." Estelle believed it could sell nationally, and she played it for Jerry Wexler. "Mr. Wexler said, 'It's all right, it needs this, that, and the other.' He used to say, 'Just because it's selling in Memphis doesn't mean it's a national hit.' I said, 'Mr. Wexler, I know enough about the record business in Memphis, Tennessee, that if it sells here, by God it'll sell anywhere in the world.' This was the hardest market. I knew we had a product that would sell, and I knew we needed the money, and here we are wasting that time."

Weary of telling customers that the record wasn't available, pining for the easy income, Estelle made a decision. "One night I was in the record shop, didn't close till nine, my husband standing there anxious to go home. I said, 'Nope, I'm not leaving here tonight till we settle something. We're either going to put that record out or we're going to pull that dub [copy] off the air.' Jim and Chips came up about nine o'clock. Started out, I asked them in a nice way about the record. They began to hem and haw. Then I started crying, trying to get their sympathy. That didn't work. I started cussing and my brother had never heard me cuss before. I blew his mind. He said, 'All right, in the morning have Packy get the tape and take it to the plant for mastering.' When I believe in anything, I'm going to keep on until I get it done."

The next day, Estelle had no trouble rousing the usually indolent Packy. "Packy went back to get the tape, starts to play it, and would you believe that about sixteen bars off the front end of that tape had been erased? We found out that they had taken that tape to Nashville when they cut Carla's album, and someone had erased that up there. I said, 'As many times as y'all have done that tape back there, there's got to be another one with the same tempo.'" She adds, "To this day, I know exactly where the splice is in that record." Before releasing it, Estelle insisted the band change its name; all-white kids playing black music and calling themselves the Royal Spades just wasn't going to play. She suggested the Marquis. Words with a *q*, however, intimidated some of the band members, and this word—meaning noblemen—seemed unrelated in any way to the boisterous group. Estelle considered the movie marquee that hung over the front of the building, and the keys of the piano, and she overcame the challenge of the difficult letter by suggesting the Mar-Keys. Ah, phonetics. The boys could drink to that.

"Nobody ever thought it was a record," muses Don Nix. "And it wouldn't have been a record had it not been for Miss Axton." "Last Night" caught on quickly, going from a popular unreleased song on local radio to a regional and national hit, easing its way to number two on the R&B chart, number-three pop.

"The first time I heard that song on the radio," says Wayne Jackson, "I was driving to a gig and just as we got to the bridge on Lamar, it came on the radio. I damn near wrecked the Plymouth. It's a onetime thing, like sex—there's only one first time when you hear yourself on the radio, something that you don't expect to have happen. It just lit me up, and I've been lit up ever since."

"Jim realized that Estelle had her finger on the pulse of what was going on," says Steve, and Don Nix adds, "They started listening to her after that. And she started having a little bit more say."

"When we put that record out," says Estelle, "it exploded like nothing had exploded before. I sold two thousand one by one over my counter. They certified a million, it was a national hit, and I've never been as proud of a record in my life."

◆ ◆ ◆

WHILE MUCH GOOD came from the success of "Last Night," it also marked a certain loss of innocence, the recording *business* emerging from the recording sessions. First was the issue of authorship and its rewards; then, who would reap the glory on the road. The authorship question was tied to the publishing royalties, a long-term issue; the glory was short-term; both were financial. The money from a hit goes to the songwriters (collected by their publishing companies) and, if the artist has a good contract, they share in some of the royalties on uses of their master recording. Many artists never see a dime after they get the union pay for the session, and that's the case with the Mar-Keys; those who played that day got paid, and most never saw another cent from record sales. But the songwriters continue to be paid—for every record sold, for every use licensed, for every new version recorded—and after being certified for a million, it has continued to sell, and to this day is licensed for movies, TV shows, commercials, games, and has been covered by other artists. Each of those usages is money for the songwriters. Saxman Floyd Newman is adamant that the authors of "Last Night" were solely him and Gilbert Caple. "We were just messing around and that's the way a lot of hits come up," says Floyd. "Two people wrote 'Last Night.' Gilbert and I."

When the record came out, there were three names on it in addition to Gilbert's and Floyd's. The piano part is essential to the song, and it came from Smoochy Smith; his name is on it. Moman, as the song's producer, brought the piano riff to the horn riff, fashioning one song from many pieces; that's part of the producer's job, but his name's on it as a writer. The final name is Packy Axton. Packy didn't solo, didn't really contribute anything essential; his name is there because his mother could put it there, because she saw others carving their piece from the publishing, knew that other label owners who couldn't hum a tune had affixed their names to songs—and so she put her son's name on it. ("I couldn't even spell *publishing* then," says Wayne, "much less have asked to be included in it.")

Gilbert and Floyd weren't around when the credits were being divvied on their song, and they might not have gotten anything but for the virtue of an unexpected someone: the cranky Everett Axton. He spoke up for the artists. "He called us outside," Floyd explains, "said, 'I want you to know that you gonna get your money, and nobody gonna beat you outta your money.'" He was mostly right: "Instead of Gilbert and I getting fifty percent each, we get twenty percent," says Floyd. "A lot of money's been made off that song, and I'm glad Everett Axton spoke up, 'cause we were gonna wind up with nothin'."

Bright lights beckoned, or dim lights did, and smoky rooms smelling of stale beer. The band went on the road to promote the new song. Or a version of the band. That is, not the band that recorded it, but the band that smoked in the Messick High School dungeon, that played for sailors at Neil's, that helped Jim test the wiring in Brunswick, tore out the seats in the Capitol. It was approaching the summer of 1961, and most of the boys revved their engines and spun their wheels waiting for their drummer Terry Johnson to finish twelfth grade and be dismissed for summer break. Then they'd hit the road. The label sent Carla out with the boys, and Miss Axton to chaperone, in a late-model Chevrolet Greenbrier that she signed for, and on which the boys paid the note.

"We were very young and life was magical, especially because we were playing music," says Wayne. "No one ever said, 'You're gonna take that trumpet and make a living with it.' My band director, all the people in Arkansas—nobody. They said, 'How you gonna plow with that thing, boy?' We never expected to get off the dirt farm, and it was magic when it happened."

The communal ideal of the Mar-Keys with Carla and Miz Axton soon collapsed; traveling with eight teenage boys was not an environment for ladies of any age or type—well, except for one type. After the first run of dates, the Mar-Keys slowed the van and the women jumped out near home. With no chaperone and no Carla, it was, Steve laughs, "like letting a bunch of monkeys out of the cage."

But this was no picnic at the zoo. The band that went on the road—the white guys—didn't include the two black guys who'd cowritten the hit. "'Last Night' became a hit record and Jim didn't send me and Gilbert," says Floyd. "He sent all the white group out on the road, a bunch of kids. And I never thought that was fair, not at all, because Gilbert and I was a part of that group, but we were black. They had been out there for quite a while before we found out." There is truth in what Floyd charges, though there was also a benefit in sitting out this tour: He was finishing college, training to be a band teacher, and as exciting as the variety of stages would have been, he'd have been one furious and frustrated college guy as he watched the Mar-Keys squander, in an alcoholic frenzy, most every opportunity presented them.

"You had eight guys between the ages of eighteen and twenty who just wanted to get out on the road to play and party their butts off," says drummer Terry Johnson. "And that's exactly what we did and that's probably why the band was a one-hit wonder. It's hard to be a two-hit wonder when you leave the Dick Clark show and he's waving at you on film and everybody's shooting him the bird. It's hard to be more than a one-hit wonder when you've got a tour of Texas booked and the whole band takes off to Mexico and then calls back and says, 'We've lost our bus because we sold it.' We wanted to have fun, chase women, drink beer. We did it the storybook way and to hell with the consequences. 'Let's have this memory burning in our brains when we're sitting in the old folks' home, incontinent.'"

They played it for all it was worth, working the road and pushing the record up the charts. "We played on top of the popcorn stand at the Sunset Drive-In in West Memphis," says Wayne, and his smile is so big that it almost reaches back in time. The roof was slanted backward; Packy set his bottle down, and as it started sliding back, he chased it, tumbling off the roof onto the gravel below. The bottle didn't break, nor did Packy, but he refused to return to a place so inhospitable to bottles. "We played the New Moon Club in Newport, Arkansas, where they had chicken wire around the bandstand," Wayne continues. "We didn't know whether it was to keep the musicians from getting in the crowd or the crowd from throwing bottles at us. If they had told us to play in the sewer, we would have crawled down in there and played. We were making money, for God's sake! I was eighteen when all that happened. I had been working at the Big Star grocery store in West Memphis making eighteen dollars a week and tips. And I had a paper route too. I made as much in a night onstage as I made in a week at the grocery store."

They'd show up at black clubs and the owners would be very skeptical that the eight pimply white kids pouring out of the Greenbrier were the ones who could play the record they'd been looking forward to hearing.

But when they took the stage, the band earned the audience's respect. A club didn't need the precision of a studio band, and these guys were full of passion, hot as fire, and they had the feel. Playing black music for black audiences is where these kids had dreamed of being since they'd heard bands like the Five Royales, Hank Ballard, and Bo Diddley. They'd been motivated by the liberation they heard in the music, the looseness released in a society that was otherwise so constricted. Their motivation was the good times, and if there was any social result, that was accidental. "People who had never known each other, who had never eaten a barbecue together, who had never done the things that typically people do," says Terry Johnson, "all of a sudden were doing those things."

Fun as it was, eight guys in a Chevy van was a petri dish for tensions, their personality differences incubating. Before too long, a noble fight was brewing among the Mar-Keys for leadership of the band. "I used to wear white socks, march around in ROTC," says Duck. "And so did Don Nix. But, you know, we were just rebellious. Steve was a little different. Steve was pretty strict and disciplined and I commend him for that."

On the one hand, the guys could rib Steve and he could take it. "None of us liked to pack that Greenbrier," says Don. "But Steve was really good at it. So we'd make a little effort and then say, 'Gosh Steve, how do you make all this fit?' And he'd push his way up there and we'd all stand around smoking cigarettes every night while Cropper packed the van."

On the other hand, Steve could not tolerate the complete lack of discipline that defined Packy. "One night we all got in a bar fight and it was because of Packy," Duck remembers. "While we was on a break some guy made some insinuations about Packy, and Packy slashed the guy's tires and this guy pulled out a twenty-two rifle—looked then like a twelve-gauge shotgun—and a fight broke out. Some lady got hit, the owner's wife—it was just a complete misunderstanding. A drunken brawl is what it was."

Most galling of all (to Steve), Packy considered himself leader of the band—when Steve had the band long before Packy joined and was obviously the responsible one. Packy cared nothing for responsibility, but he made it known that they'd be nowhere but for his mama, so it was his band. "These guys went crazy on the road," Steve says. "It was just pure unadulterated madness. So we'd come down through Myrtle Beach and were in Bossier City, Louisiana, playing the Show Bar." This was a strip joint where the band played behind and above the bar, and a schoolteacher on summer vacation would shimmy herself down to her nipples while the band coaxed the audience toward frenzy. "We had a three-week engagement," Steve continues, "and somewhere in the second week we went to the bathroom on a break and I looked at Packy and I said, 'Packy, you got it. I'm gonna turn it over to you.' I said, 'I can't take this anymore, I'm going back to college.' I caught a bus, headed back to Memphis, and got reenrolled in Memphis State. And I asked Miz Axton for my old job back in the record store, which she gave me." Steve went home to Packy's mama.

The success of "Last Night" wrought another change: In September 1961, Satellite changed its name. When the record reached California, another label there named Satellite learned of the Memphis operation, and they sent a wire ordering Memphis to cease, but offering to sell the name for a thousand bucks. "I said, 'Screw that, I hate that name anyway,'" Jim remembers. "And the next pressing of 'Last Night' we changed to Stax. My wife came up with the name, from Stewart-Axton." Combining the first two letters of Jim's and Estelle's last names, "Stax" cleverly conveyed a proprietary sense while evoking the stacks and stacks of records they hoped to make and sell. The label's emblem was a stack of records in motion.

The Mar-Keys roared on down the road. Since they hadn't played on their big hit, the studio didn't need them around for their next release, or their next several. Fumbling around some no-name town, they entered a record store and saw they had a new single on the market. "The second one sure as hell couldn't have been us because we were gone the whole time!" says Terry. "But Floyd Newman and those guys, they put a nice one together."

When neither "The Morning After" nor "About Noon" got the same response as "Last Night," the theme was retired. The band, however, forged on, running on gas, running on fumes, then finally running empty. "The Mar-Keys died in St. Paul, Minnesota, on a cold fall morning when eight guys looked at each other and said, 'It's over,'" says Terry. "And then it looked like rats leaving a sinking ship."

◆ ◆ ◆

"Last Night" had, essentially, walked in off the street. "We were surrounded by talent after we moved onto McLemore," says Estelle. "The neighborhood had become a black area. In our little hometown [Middleton], I doubt there was half a dozen black people in the whole area. When I taught school, we didn't have integration then, and not much at the bank. At the studio, we just looked at people as talent, not the color of their skin."

A dozen singles were released in the six months after "Last Night," and another one that walked in the front door also hit the charts. Stewart and Moman had regular players they could call on, and sessions were mix and match depending on availability. When the Mar-Keys were home for a break, some of them were called to help William Bell record an unusual tune, "You Don't Miss Your Water (Till Your Well Runs Dry)." It was a country music ballad that had been baptized in a black church feel. (Later it would be covered by soul great Otis Redding and country-rock pioneers the Byrds.) William was one of the kids who'd been dancing on the sidewalk when Estelle hung speakers by the front door. He'd been singing with the Phineas Newborn Sr. Orchestra, one of Memphis's premier club bands and a training ground for many future stars. In 1960, the orchestra lucked into a six-week club date in New York City, and when it was extended to three months, Bell, homesick, became aware of what he'd taken for granted in Memphis. Using the metaphor of a foolhardy lover, the twenty-one-year-old wrote about his pining. The following year, he was making plans for a medical career—like his father wanted—when he encountered Moman, who'd been impressed by Bell in the clubs; Moman invited him to audition at Stax. "I had been to Stax to sing backing vocals on 'Gee Whiz,'" William says. "And I knew Estelle because she had the record shop. And I knew Chips Moman. So I was comfortable in that atmosphere." Under Moman's direction, Bell imbued the song with longing, and it has remained evergreen, a song through which you can hear life whispering urgently: Appreciate the fleeting moment, it is a gift.

Before the music business took hold of him, William Bell intended to be a doctor.

The song came out in November 1961 with Atlantic's muscle pushing it; everything Stax released now had a shot. It got just enough attention to be lingering in January after the rush of Christmas records. Its sound was new and nostalgic, cloaked with a melancholy appropriate for winter. "Starting in January, it just skyrocketed," says William. "The first city that it hit in was Baton Rouge and then New Orleans and Pensacola." Atlantic had the reach to build city upon city, and it did. "I think Jim thought it was a little bit too churchy," he continues, "and he wanted the up-tempo stuff that he had been selling."

It hit *Billboard*'s Hot 100 in late April. Jim had released it because Moman and Estelle pushed him; with the sales building, Jim came around.

◆ ◆ ◆

SUCCESS, AS IT does, brought bubbling tensions to the surface. Expenses had gone up with the new location, and they'd been operating on a tight budget. Estelle counted on Packy for help before he went on the road. "I was depending on my son to open up while I was at the bank. He'd finished high school, didn't want to go to college." Giving Packy the responsibility of the keys, Estelle knew, meant accepting a responsibility herself: "Usually I'd have to call him from the bank to get him up to go open the doors."

Two things about that situation grated on Jim. "Nepotism always bothered me," he says. "But Packy, there was no question—Packy was not an organizational man. You can't put people in positions if they can't do the job. Packy would show up one week and the next week he's gone. He was not reliable, and he didn't want that responsibility either. But my sister always tried to give him the responsibility. She wanted him to be head of the studio. That would lead, in my opinion, to total destruction."

"Mother was fighting for something that was never to be," says Doris, Packy's sister. "But that's what parents do. He was so talented, but he didn't have that management sensibility."

Jim's business couldn't survive on shenanigans. "She brought her family into the thing, and that clouded her perspective," he says. "She thought I was just a cold bastard. But it was nothing personal. I was looking out for Stax Records. If it's good for Stax, it's good for her, it's good for me, it's good for everybody that works there." And what was good for Jim was to give Chips more responsibility. "When we moved to McLemore, Moman and I were very close," he says. "Chips was my right-hand man. I was still working at the bank, Chips would open the studio, take care of whatever we needed." But there was a problem. "My sister didn't get along with him at all."

By late 1961, her record shop had become successful enough, and demanding enough, for Estelle to quit her job at the bank. "At one point, the doctor put me in bed for three days, nothing but nerves," says Estelle. She'd been juggling two careers and home life. "I had two kids in school, was leaving home about six thirty in the morning to get to work on the bus. Leave there at four thirty, get to College and McLemore at about five, stay till nine o'clock. When I came home from that, I had to get clothes together for the kids to go to school, do what I had to do in the way of housework—and it got the best of me. There wasn't a minute for anything extra. Doctor said to me, 'You're going to have to get rid of one thing or another,' so that's when I left the bank."

When her Stax hours increased, so did the tension with Moman. Chips and Estelle were from different worlds. Estelle had a vision, and a practical sense for actualizing that vision. She'd proven her mettle at the bank, and she was set on proving it again in the music business. Chips also had a vision, but his approach to achieving it was unlike anything Estelle could comprehend; his nickname, after all, came from his poker playing. ("Chips would rather go to a two-dollar card game," says Duck, "than produce a million-selling record.") Estelle remembers Chips living beyond his means: "Chips loved to drive fancy cars. He'd have them financed, then he'd run to keep from paying notes. You could always tell when they was after him." Further, Estelle didn't like Chips's friends. He was someone who liked a drink, and in this beatnik era, she suspected his friends might be into other, more criminal recreations: "I'd be kind of upset at the characters that were coming in and out of there in the daytime. Jim and I talked about the drug scene, which was just opening up. If the law caught 'em, it'd be the end of our place. And we didn't want to have the name that we were harboring drug addicts."

When Jim would arrive after work, he'd find himself in the middle. "I would get the flack when I walked in the door," says Jim. He speaks of Chips with respect and admiration, though they too were very different: Chips was a gambler, Jim was a conservative banker. Chips played electric guitar with an ear for rock and roll, Jim played the country fiddle. Chips was headstrong—working under Jim for Jim's company.

By early 1962, the fighting came to a head. Chips had recorded an instrumental, "Burnt Biscuits," an exchange between a popping organ and a harmonica, that he thought was every bit as good as "Last Night" and better than the other Mar-Keys singles that had followed. He named the band after the car he was driving, the Triumphs, and just like he'd hoped, it was gaining traction in Memphis and a couple other cities as well. The single inaugurated Stax's first subsidiary label, christened Volt Records. (A subsidiary allowed a successful label to spread out; in the wake of the 1950s payola scandal, radio stations were careful not to show favoritism and avoided playing too many songs by one label, no matter how good those songs might be. Subsidiaries allowed for a pretense of fairness: Chess Records formed Checker; Atlantic had Atco. Stax established Volt.)

Chips believed "Burnt Biscuits" had been a hit, but the payment he got from Jim didn't reflect that. Chips told Estelle that Jim was beating him out of his money. "I knew better because I had seen the sales on it," says Estelle, "so he and I got into it. Chips told Jim that I was trying to run the business, and Jim jumped on me. I told Jim, 'I defended you. Chips accused you of stealing his money on "Burnt Biscuits."' That didn't sit too well with Jim."

Moman had proved himself a strong engineer and producer, and as reassuring as that was, it was also something of a threat. Jim wanted to be a producer too, not an executive. "I could see Chips taking over," Estelle says, "and I didn't want that taken out of Jim's hands." Jim knew he couldn't handle the studio while working at the bank, and despite the successes (mostly recorded under Chips's hand), the company was far from strong enough to support him and his family. Jim needed help. And there seemed to be a new solution: Since returning from the Mar-Keys road band, Steve Cropper was proving himself reliable, resourceful, and friendly. Steve was a quick study, absorbing technique from both Jim and Chips. He was the support that Jim needed, both less threatening and more dependable. So when Chips got hot about the money from "Burnt Biscuits," Jim felt safe in letting Chips go.

"I was supposed to get a third of the Satellite label," is how Chips recalls the setup. He'd turned the label from schmaltz to popular music, and he'd been the force behind several of their biggest hits. "We had two or three records goin' at the same time. It started getting to be a madhouse. And I wrote one side of Carla Thomas's 'Gee Whiz,' and I wrote one side of 'Last Night.' And so I asked Jim about my money, and he said, 'Well, the only thing I can tell you, Chips, is I'm fucking you out of it.'"

Wayne Jackson was sitting in the lobby when what he describes as "the explosion" occurred. "Jim and Chips came into that hallway in a snit. They were at each other. Jim just put his hands on his hips and said, 'Well if I screwed you, you'll have to prove it.' And Chips said, 'Well, okay then,' and he slammed out the doors, got in his TR3, and purred on off down the street."

"I hated to see him go," says Jim, "but I was in the middle. I ran the company with an iron hand, and I had to. I had to."

A new calm followed. Jim no longer had to play referee between Chips and Estelle. Steve moved into Chips's place in the studio. Packy was finally doing something he was good at—leading the besotted Mar-Keys, with plenty of miles between him and Jim. And Chips acquitted himself quite well, though he had to pull himself up from the mire. He got a lawyer who got him a $3,000 settlement. "I was a broke kid," says Chips. "A thousand of it went to a lawyer. [Leaving Stax] is a bad memory. It affected me all the way through." It did, however, let him know he wanted to be in charge. After a year in Nashville, Chips opened his own studio across Memphis, American, and became a huge hitmaker through the 1960s and '70s, responsible for some of Elvis Presley's best-known and respected work, as well as hits with Neil Diamond, Wilson Pickett, Dusty Springfield, and Waylon Jennings—among many others. Working for himself, everything he touched turned to gold.

Steve picked up the daytime responsibilities, as much as college allowed, until something had to give, and it wasn't going to be music. "I wound up marking tapes and sweeping the floor, cleaning the piano and doing whatever I could do," he says. "I didn't mind calling the musicians or going to their house and waking them up. And I turned in the contracts, edited tapes, and did all of the little odd jobs that nobody else wanted."

"With Steve," says Estelle, "Jim didn't have nearly the headaches that he had before." Nor did he have the experienced assistant he'd had before, the hitmaker. Jim had cut "Gee Whiz," and now he'd have to prove that that wasn't a fluke.

6. "GREEN ONIONS"
1962

BOOKER T. JONES, with the successful Carla Thomas session under his belt, was making his presence more known at Stax. He was no longer another neighborhood kid bugging Steve Cropper and the other clerks to play him records; he was a player in the pool of musicians who helped Stax create sessions. He'd moved from sax to keyboards. "We were always having to call somebody to come in and play piano," says Steve. Marvell Thomas was attending college; Joe Hall, popular at Hi Records, was great except for his drinking problem; Smoochy Smith was on the road. When Jim said he wanted a reliable keyboard player, Steve turned to Floyd Newman, the baritone sax player; he suggested Booker. Floyd knew the kid was as good on one instrument as another, and moving him from horn helped Floyd protect his own gig. The youngster took up the keyboard duties, usually playing the piano but exploring the possibilities of the studio's Hammond M3 organ.

A friendship was developing between Booker and Steve, and it expressed itself not only in their playing; they began to hang out together, telling an interviewer in the 1970s:

"I'd pick Booker up at school," says Steve.

"Baritone sax in the backseat," Booker affirms.

"You had marching band," says Steve. "I'd wait out there on you."

Nineteen-year-old Steve had a car, seventeen-year-old Booker didn't, and giving Booker a ride one day to his girlfriend's, a song came on the radio and the seed for Stax's next hit was planted. "There was one bar in there where they did this one little thing," Booker remembers. He turned to Steve. Cropper nodded. He'd heard it. "The song never did come back on the radio again," Booker continues. (Neither he nor Cropper was ever aware of the song's name.) But next time they were in the studio, they "took those few notes," says Booker, "and started messing around." It wasn't so much a song they came up with as a pattern, a series of riffs that hung together. Then they parked it on the back shelf of their minds.

Usually, sessions seemed to materialize without forethought. A musician from the neighborhood wandered back to show Steve a cool riff; Steve picked up the guitar. An aspiring songwriter appeared, ready to demo the next great tune . . . there was always something to do, and often something to play for Jim in the evenings. Records were released: Jim's DJ friend Nick Charles, from one of the pop stations, recorded a couple insipid pop songs, the direction Jim pursued before hearing Ray Charles. Another artist, Macy Skipper, told jokes with a raunchy groove behind him; while his "Goofin' Off" is a lot of fun, it didn't aid much in keeping the operation solvent.

In the summer of 1962, a vocalist named Billy Lee Riley was scheduled for a session. Success always circled Riley but never quite landed upon him. In the 1950s, he cut some notable records with Sam Phillips during Sun's heyday, but circumstances never conspired to make him a star. With fellow Sun alumnus Roland Janes, he formed Rita Records in 1960. Their little Memphis label had a huge success in 1961 with Harold Dorman's "Mountain of Love," which almost broke the top twenty nationwide, and nearly broke their company (they assumed a debt to keep up with demand, then had to endure a long wait for distributors to pay). In a few years, Riley would be one of the coolest guys in Los Angeles, leading the house band at the Sunset Strip's Whisky a Go Go. On the day he was due at Stax, however, he was picking up small change as the vocalist for a radio jingle.

Or he was due in to lead a session, either at the studio's behest or of his own initiation. The facts are unclear. Al Jackson Jr., Booker T. Jones, and Lewie Steinberg remember Riley as a "country and western" guy. He didn't fit musically because he didn't fit personally either. He was coming off the boppin' fifties, a hyped-up feel, and the groove at Stax was much cooler, a later-at-night feel, hep on its way to hip. Steve remembers Riley not showing up; Estelle recalls him there, but with a problem. "He got drunk," she says. "Showed up but was so drunk he couldn't do the commercial."

"We worked a few hours with Billy Lee," says Jim, "and nothing was happening. We took a break and got ready to start again, and we were looking for Billy. We couldn't find him. He just took off."

Booker remembers Jim not identifying with what Riley was doing. "Jim was sitting up there in the control room," Booker says, "making all kinds of funny faces. And finally the cat left, walked out on the street and didn't come back."

This is where the different versions fold back into one: The band was left in the studio without a vocalist. "We're standing around looking at each other," says Booker. "We didn't want to waste time—Sunday afternoon." Sunday—when Jim wasn't at the bank.

The four guys on the floor all knew each other musically, but this was the first time they'd played together as a quartet. It may have been Al Jackson's first day inside Stax. He was considered the best drummer in town, and getting him on a session was an accomplishment. "Al wasn't anxious to get in there at all," says Booker, who'd played alongside him in Willie Mitchell's and Bowlegs Miller's groups; Booker brought Al to Stax. "Al had his hands full with those two bands. And his dad had a band. Al was hard to get." Howard Grimes had been the first-call drummer, playing on Carla's earlier hits; Al Jackson was Howard's mentor. Lewie Steinberg played with Al in the clubs, and he'd been in and out of the studio a few times since he'd played on "Last Night." He had a funky feel, walking and rolling his bottom notes. But the four were not an obvious band. Al and Lewie were each approaching thirty; Cropper, the only white guy, was twenty; Booker was a teen. But they'd all been listening to the same music for several years, so finding a groove together was no problem. Booker shared a slow blues jam he'd been doing at dances. The others fell in. "I had been playing that in the clubs," he says, "and people liked it and would slow-dance to it."

Jim, in the control room, recorded one of their takes. "Jim said, 'Hey guys, come in here and listen to this,'" Steve remembers. "And we go, 'You recorded that?'"

"I was up in the record shop," says Estelle of that Sunday. "That was the only time I had to work on my books, to keep up with the inventory and all that. [Commerce closed for church in Memphis—and in much of the USA—then.] Jim came running up front, said, 'Come back here, I want you to hear something. It's a hit!'" Estelle agreed with Jim's assessment; it captured that late-night slow-dance feel when hands began to wander, and she suggested "Behave Yourself" as a title. Then, disbelief mingling with enthusiasm, the band heard Jim, who'd been leery of releasing both "Last Night" and "You Don't Miss Your Water," present the new problem: They needed a song for the other side of the single. "We just kind of looked dumbfounded," Steve remembers, "and wondered if he was really serious." They'd come in to record a jingle, now talk was of a single.

Talk turned to that recent afternoon and what they'd heard in the car. "I started playing that riff," says Booker. "I had played it a few times on piano but this was the first time on the organ. It sounded different through the little organ speaker. It had more urgency, more attitude." The band quickly fell into an arrangement of the song. Steve was playing a Fender Esquire guitar, favored among country musicians (it's the distinctive sound on Johnny Cash's hits); he was playing it through a Harvard amp. Booker's organ was filtered through the African-American church. The song's charge came from an honesty that underlaid it, the meeting of styles anticipating a racial reality on the streets that many people preferred to deny. Al Jackson suggested the song's dynamic build. Jim suggested Steve move his punctuating chords from the song's middle to the front.

"Booker goes down to the organ and starts playing," says Steve, "and Al Jackson and Lewie fell in on it. And I think two cuts later, we had what we know today to be 'Green Onions.'" The instrumental had its own sound, while suggesting several references: It was sinister, with a staccato emphasis on the beat like the popular TV detective show theme song "Peter Gunn." ("We were fascinated by 'Peter Gunn,'" Lewie remembers. The Henry Mancini song had recently won a Grammy.) "Green Onions" also evokes the deceptive simplicity of a John Lee Hooker song, and the beat-heavy "Think" by the Five Royales, a popular R&B band who were a big influence on the Mar-Keys. The guitar and bass often double, playing the same notes, guided by Booker's left hand; it gives the band a fat sound, uncomplicated.

"They come up with this fantastic groove," says Jim, "a funky, unbelievable groove. Everybody came into the control room and was jumping up and down." Lewie listened to the playback and said the music was so stinky it should be called "Onions." Someone else suggested "Funky Onions"—"We wanted to be funky and stinky," says Lewie. "Miz Axton changed it to 'Green Onions.' So, that was that."

Now that there was a record, the group needed a name. Chips Moman had named his band after his car—the Triumphs. The competing British sports car was the MG—named for Morris Garages (the dealer who customized the British Morris sports cars). There was no denying the rhythm

Booker T. and the MG's, 1962. L–R: Booker T. Jones, Steve Cropper, Al Jackson Jr., Lewie Steinberg. (Promotional photo by API Photographers/ Earlie Biles Collection)

inherent in combining "MG's" with "Booker T.," and there was a certain mystery in the initials—Memphis Group, Mixed Group. Whatever it meant, Booker T. & the MG's worked.

Promptly, Jim had Steve take the tape to Scotty Moore at Sam Phillips's Sun Records, where they had a lathe, and Scotty cut an acetate of the single—a cheap but playable version of the record. Within hours, not more than a day, that acetate and a popular local DJ, Reuben "Mad Lad" Washington, found each other; either he came into Estelle's shop and heard it playing or Steve brought it to him at WLOK—but the DJ put it on the air. "Behave Yourself" was the featured side, but Washington liked the flip. "Before that record was over," Steve remembers, "the phones were ringing off the wall. 'Who is that?' 'What band is that?' 'Where's that from?'" Calls came in to Estelle at the record shop, and she phoned Jim at work, and he authorized pressing the records. Al Jackson recalls Jim first offering it to Atlantic. "They said, 'Where's the rest of it? This needs horns,'" says Al. "Jim said, 'Naw, I'm going on this record.'" Jim, after all, had wanted his own label so he could release songs the way he liked.

Disc jockeys loved the record, but they were not featuring "Behave Yourself," playing the B-side instead. "'Green Onions' broke overnight," says Jim. "We couldn't even get the records out fast enough." In Memphis it got airtime on WLOK, where Al Bell and Dick "Cane" Cole added it to their shows. WDIA, the leading black station in town, took to it. Steve drove to stations in Arkansas, Mississippi, Tennessee, and Alabama, promoting the record. "The neat thing about it," Steve says, "was that they were glad to see anybody. Nobody ever called on a lot of these outlying stations. They thought, These guys drove all the way from Memphis, sure, we'll play your record." Worries about the gap left by Moman, who'd been instrumental in the earliest hits, were eased; Jim's confidence in his own abilities was renewed.

As radio play, fans, and sales grew like spring weeds, "Green Onions" got Wexler's attention in New York. He suggested reissuing it with "Green Onions" on the A-side, and moving it from the new subsidiary label, Volt, to Stax; he thought Stax's association with the earlier hits would help draw DJs. He was right. Pushed by Atlantic, the song went to number-one R&B and number three on the pop charts.

Stax was releasing a variety of material, but after "Green Onions," a core sound coalesced. The preceding three singles indicated a lack of direction: "The Pop-Eye Stroll" by the Mar-Keys is a light, humorous instrumental, followed by Nick Charles's "The Three Dogwoods," a sappy Christian allegory, and then the Canes' "Why Should I Suffer with the Blues," a nightclub ballad salacious enough to make Mr. Charles's dogwood wither. "I think 'Green Onions' was the beginning of the Memphis funk sound," says Booker. "This attitude of making it as funky as it can be, as simple as it can be, and let's do it together—let's understand each other. I think 'Green Onions' was the beginning of that part of the Memphis sound."

More than creating a hit single, the musicians that day created a unit. A studio doesn't need a house band, but when one can offer a versatile backing group, the studio can attract a lot of vocalists. A ready group saves time in assembling a session, and if the players are in sync, the time becomes more productive. A house band can become a studio's lifeblood. "Before Al Jackson, we did not have a unit," says Jim. "We had Steve, and different guys that we used on a regular basis." They'd connected with each other, they'd connected with Jim—they'd established a level of communication that transcended race and age. "That's what made Stax," says Lewie. "We integrated Stax and didn't think no more about it than the man on the moon. We couldn't go and play on the same *bandstand* together in Memphis! But we'd get together inside the studio and do everything we want to."

Outside this oasis, the city had some catching up to do: At nearly the same time that "Green Onions" was recorded, thirteen black first graders had integrated four white schools, prompting some white parents to remove their kids. "We'll move out into the county," one mother told the newspaper, "and if they [African-Americans] go to school there, we'll move back to Mississippi." Change comes slowly to Memphis. The sanitation workers had begun believing it wouldn't come at all. With the city making no real progress, over nine hundred men signed Teamsters Union cards—the Teamsters represented sanitation workers in Tennessee's other major cities—and hundreds had shown up at a mass rally asking for tubs that didn't leak maggots onto their heads, showers to get clean after work, a bathroom they could use at their headquarters instead of the sewer, and other common decencies. This was the largest ever public statement by the garbagemen and their power was approach-

1961. Sanitation workers asked for buckets that didn't leak maggots on their heads, among other requests for respect. (University of Memphis Libraries/Special Collections)

ing critical mass when Mayor Loeb called the Teamster leaders to a meeting. What was said was said in secret, but following that, the Teamsters—apparently having been threatened—abandoned the sanitation workers. They cut off contact with O.Z. Evers, the men's representative, who stated, "I think the union has sold the men down the river." He quit the project in hopeless disgust, but a younger man, T.O. Jones (no relation to Booker T.), took up the lead. T.O. Jones, after serving in the navy, had worked the shipyards in Oakland, California, and there had experienced the benefits of union work, the power of one voice amplified by many. Jones returned home to Memphis in 1958 and began hauling garbage the following year. He took over the organizing efforts and found solidarity at the Retail Clerk's Union, where he was given office space and telephones to pursue his cause. The sanitation workers were asking for respect and they were determined to get it.

"If you think about it," Booker mused about creating a mixed-race band, "you'd be stupid to start something like that in 1962 in Memphis." Starting it had not been a conscious decision, but continuing it was. "In those days in Memphis, there were some terribly inhuman acts that happened. The emotion was very extreme in the South and in this country—it was out of control. If we'd thought about it, there'd be no way the band could work." Memphis was their common home, but within its borders they lived in separate cities. Life for blacks there was very different from life for whites.

Race was not the only issue in the studio. Another was money. Al Jackson was glad to have the song work out, but he was making a living in the clubs and had no interest in giving that up for a series of fifteen-dollar demo sessions, of which only a few might pan out to the union's full sixty-five-dollar scale. Thanks, but no thanks. Jim, however, had seen how strong Al's contributions were—not just his playing but also his ear for arranging. Jim decided the gamble was worth it; Steve was on staff, Lewie was amenable to the present situation, Booker was still a kid but anxious to play any sessions that didn't conflict with high school or ROTC, so if Jim put Al on some minor salary, he'd save time pulling sessions together and get better results from a group that knew each other's styles. So Booker T. & the MG's became the house band at Stax.

As "Green Onions" spread, the MG's began to travel; mixing races on the bandstand was not forbidden everywhere. "We got to go to all the big cities," says Steve. "St. Louis, Kansas City, Detroit, Chicago, Washington, DC, New York, Atlanta, and we'd get to see what these people were dancing to." Each city had its own sound; radio stations were programmed locally, and understanding who liked what was essential information in figuring out how to break records. (Philadelphia liked doo-wop; Atlanta had a gritty edge; Houston and Dallas needed a twang.) "Al Jackson was the guy that would pick up on the rhythm of what people were doing," Steve continues, "and first thing Monday morning, we'd be working on the grooves that we saw happening. So we were demographically staying on top of things."

Traveling as a racially mixed group was not without its challenges. They were sometimes refused hotel accommodations, gas station bathrooms, and restaurant service. At a truck stop in Alabama, when the four were told to go outside to the rear window to place their order, they left instead; Duck lingered (this occurred after he joined the group), and went back in alone. He ordered forty hamburgers, staying at the counter to see them go on the grill, to see the buns laid out and dressed, and even the bags come out to hold the order. But when the counter help looked up to deliver the food and settle the bill, Duck had vanished, the MG's on their way to a place where they could all dine together.

The gigs were mostly confined to weekends, because the band was in the studio during the week. With their coming together, Stax had a foundation. "Al Jackson had come into the picture," says Jim, "and we concentrated on some real serious production work, on tightening. We had a few hits prior to '62, but that was the year we started the Stax sound."

◆ ◆ ◆

WHILE STAX WAS establishing itself as a new source for contemporary R&B hits with pop potential, there was another company in Detroit well down that path. Berry Gordy had established Motown in 1959, and he'd turned early success into a hit factory. Coming from his job applying chrome and upholstery at a Lincoln-Mercury assembly plant, Gordy applied the assembly-line technique to music—a real contrast to the organic group think at Stax. He built a departmentalized company that could handle all aspects of the record business: songwriting, production, mastering, distribution; Motown even had a staff choreographer, and their deportment specialist trained its artists in manners and etiquette. (No souse, hoop cheese, and grape bellywashers for them.)

"We were a factory," says Motown staff musician Jack Ashford, known as "the tambourine man." "We had an assembly-line-type procedure. The A&R department would okay the song, then the producer would put it up for review. Once he had his players, the musicians would cut the track. Then, if the music was found good enough, it would go out to the lyricists. At Motown we [the musicians] very seldom saw the vocalist. They recorded later, and several artists would record [using the same backing track], and whoever sang it best is the one that ended up being released."

Motown's songs were manufactured for pop success. They were bright and inviting, emphasizing the backbeat with a tambourine. The call-and-response of gospel was adopted, eschewing the grittiness of the form, creating an opening for audience participation. Motown's music was full of appeal, easily digestible. It worked under the slogan "The Sound of Young America," defining itself not by race but by age. Though its artists were black, its music was not necessarily categorized so. The company was calculating, shrewd, and austere. Its first hit, written by Gordy, was "Money (That's What I Want)," and that's what they were getting. The Motown party was fun to attend, but the swinging good times stopped at the dance floor, replaced in the studio by dictatorial edicts, autocracy, and repression.

"Otis Redding was an incredible artist," continues Ashford. "And I liked Rufus Thomas; he knew how to do what he was doing. But I wasn't too much aware of the other artists. Carla was a nice singer. But the Stax sound was more earthy than ours. The Motown rhythm section were all jazz musicians, so instead of playing a B-flat chord, we'd have a B flat with a flat five on it, and get a different sound. But not to the point where it confused the public. Our sound was more pop."

"Motown was a big deal for us," says Jesse Jackson, noting the roads that it paved. "We could never own our own talent. And here comes Berry Gordy, producing and writing and distributing and owning his own company." Like the car manufacturers that surrounded him, Gordy conceived a reliable product, shiny and universally appealing, on which to build a national—nay, international—empire. Stax had no such vision. It was careening from session to session, stumbling onto hits, unaware of the larger effect it was creating. In Detroit, they built cars; in Memphis, the big factory with the good jobs made tires. The scope of vision was different.

The sign at Motown read, HITSVILLE USA. The marquee at Stax answered, SOULSVILLE USA. "That whole Memphis-soul feeling—outside of the southern nightclubs, nobody had ever heard that laid-back, barely-make-it-to-the-next-measure bluesy soul feel," says Mar-Key Terry Johnson. "It was different from Motown with the strings and the background voices and trying to pop up black music so white people would buy it. What came out of Stax was really not a very commercial music. It's amazing the commercial success it had."

Motown songs made you want to sing along. Stax music—you were the singer. "Motown had appeal to the urban areas of the North and they had a lot of pop crossover," says future Stax star Isaac Hayes. "Stax was down-to-earth, raw, very *honest* music that represented the common man—the common black man. It was real-life experiences on a very ethnic level. Stax was just a music of the people."

"It wasn't a preconceived kind of goal or concept that I had that Stax would be a black-music-oriented record company" says Jim. "As I got more and more into the music, I began to understand and have a feeling for it. I got into it by chance, but it was becoming a labor of love."

7. WALK RIGHT IN
1962–1963

THE LITTLE STUDIO hummed along. Estelle would open the record shop and Steve the studio. Customers entering the old theater doors could be coming in to buy a song or to make one. Buying one was easy, and making one not much more complicated. Steve would audition the talent and, if it seemed like something was there, he'd have the room ready when the band would fall by. "People were always coming by the record shop and saying, 'Could you hear me sing?'" says Steve, "'Could you hear me play? Would you listen to my song?' And usually during the week there were sessions going on." By the time Booker showed up after school, Lewie and Al were there. They might have a radio ad to knock out, a job sent by a local ad agency; a producer or musician might rent the studio, sometimes bringing his own staff, sometimes hiring the band and engineer. If Steve had heard something good, there'd be fresh tape on the machine and a nervous kid—or adult—from the neighborhood, pacing about. If no one had a seed from which a song might grow, they'd gather around the turntable in Estelle's shop, let her play them the most exciting singles she'd recently found, and then parse the trends and melodies, finding something to build on. There was forward motion, but no overarching direction.

In August of '62, they got stroked a little. A record promotions man named Joe Galkin, based in Atlanta and a fan of Estelle's shop and Jim's studio, booked a session for an up-and-coming act. Talent coming all the way from Georgia! Galkin was familiar with the studio because Memphis was part of his territory. Promo men worked as hired guns for national labels, making sure that in specific regions (like the South) their records reached the front lines of the disc jockeys and retailers. Joe watched Stax grow, and was impressed by the players. "Joe was promoting records for Atlantic," says Estelle. "That's how he came in the picture. We'd talk about records since I had the shop. He recognized the product we were putting out was very successful." Joe had watched a regional guitarist, Johnny Jenkins from Macon, build a following with his local instrumental release "Love Twist," and when it kept on selling, he brought it to Atlantic, which gave it national distribution. Sales were strong enough to warrant a follow-up, and Galkin hoped to marry the success of the "Green Onions" sound with Jenkins's flashy guitar.

On Sunday, August 12, 1962, the group now calling themselves the MG's was out front beneath Estelle's record-store speaker. The temperature was pushing ninety but not breaking it—a relatively mild summer day, though hot and thick enough to remind Memphians of their city's proximity to a swamp. Air conditioners were still not common, and the studio had no windows, so waiting out front was not just hospitable, it was also a relief. "We're all out there," says Steve, "and here comes this car, Georgia plates on it. We go, 'Well, that's gotta be them.'" "Them" was two people, a star and a driver. Johnny Jenkins was tall and slender, fashionably cool and laid-back. The driver, an African-American, set to work. "This big, tall guy gets out of the driver's seat," Steve continues, "goes around to the trunk, and he starts pulling out amplifiers and microphones and guitars, like he was setting up for a gig." Steve told the driver that, this being a recording studio, they had their own equipment inside and, in fact, it was already set up.

"I remember them pulling up," says Booker. "I remember the driver being the guy that carried the stuff—the food and the clothes—for Johnny's demo session."

Johnny's demo session—how quickly the excitement faded. Jenkins was a showman, a guitarist who danced, did acrobatics, put the guitar behind his head and played solos. His live show was all fire, and when people left, they wanted a reminder of the fun, which they could get by purchasing "Love Twist." But creating a new record that would draw people to the show—that proved harder. His showmanship and the MG's groove couldn't find a place to synchronize, the session never hit its lick, and it was

Johnny Jenkins, left-handed guitarist, 1963, dancing the "Love Twist."

ending in disappointment. The players had gigs, disbursing to play "Stardust," "Roll with Me Annie," and "Apple Blossom Time" to good citizens sipping highballs and swishing across the dance floor. Hits or misses in the studio notwithstanding, these guys put food on their tables by playing in clubs.

"During the session, Al Jackson says to me, 'The big tall guy that was driving Johnny, he's been bugging me to death, wanting me to hear him sing,'" Steve remembers. "Al said, 'Would you take some time and get this guy off of my back and listen to him?' And I said, 'After the session I'll try to do it,' and then I just forgot about it."

"He had really sat over there all day long," says Al, "and he kept talking about, 'I can sing.'"

The guy had made no impression on Jim during the course of the day (the session was scheduled around Jim's bank duties). But Joe Galkin, who was sitting in the control room with Jim, had heard him sing as part of Jenkins's club act, and he was hoping to leave the session with a twofer—two records for the price of one. Now that Johnny hadn't jelled, he was in danger of leaving the session with nothing. "Joe and I had a great relationship," Jim continues. "He'd scream at me and I'd scream at him. We were great friends." The vocalist was badgering the band, and Galkin was working Jim. Almost too late—some of the guys were packing up for their night gigs—Galkin played his trump card. He'd give Jim half of the publishing royalties in return for half of Stax's royalties on sales of what they cut. The publishing was worth more: It would begin paying with the first sale, and would pay on others' versions should they be recorded, while the master royalties wouldn't pay until the expenses had been recouped, and applied only to this version. "Everybody was tired and a couple of the musicians had already left," Jim continues. "It was like, 'Well, we gotta do this. The guy's been sitting here waiting all day, let's see what he sounds like.'"

Steve called the guy down to the piano. He asked Steve to play some "church chords." "'Church chords,'" says Steve, "meaning triplets. And we started playing and he started singing 'These Arms of Mine' and I know my hair lifted about three inches and I couldn't believe this guy's voice." Steve ran outside to wrangle the departing musicians. "Lewie Steinberg was putting his bass in the trunk of his Cadillac," says Steve, "and I said, 'Lewie, get your bass out, man. I need you real quick.' Al Jackson was there and Johnny Jenkins wound up playing guitar since he was already plugged up. So we cut 'These Arms of Mine.'"

"When you're in a moment like that, you're not thinking that it's gonna sell a lot of records," says Booker T. Jones. "It's all heart, and time gets frozen. I'd never been with anybody that had that much desire to express emotion. 'These Arms of Mine,' it's the longing. And it translates to the listener and the player and anyone who hears it. When that happens, millions of people listen. There's no choice."

"He was a very humble person," says Estelle. "I don't think he had any inkling we'd even pay attention to what he did. But we were always analyzing people for their uniqueness, and he was definitely different from anyone else we had. He had that different sound. But we didn't think he'd bust it all wide open."

The driver's name was Otis Redding.

◆ ◆ ◆

NOBODY AT STAX knew at the time that Otis had already recorded two singles, one in California, the other in Georgia, nor that he was a featured attraction in Johnny Jenkins's band. Or that he earned $1.25 an hour as a water-well driller, and was fired from his job as a hospital orderly for singing in the hallway. That day, to those people, he was Jenkins's valet. (Another fact not then known about Otis was that he was under contract to an enterprising producer and former used-car salesman in his hometown. That did not stymie Galkin. He snowed the snowman, tough-talking him that Otis wasn't twenty-one when he signed—despite the fact that, when recording at Stax, he was still a month shy of his twenty-first birthday.)

By Thursday the sixteenth, Stax had Otis under contract, assigning him to the Volt subsidiary label. While some were excited by the new signing, Jim felt more a sense of obligation than exuberance; as far as he was concerned, the deal was really about Joe Galkin, not Otis Redding. "The black radio stations were getting out of that black country sound," he says. "We put it out to appease and please Joe." When the single came out, three months had passed and it was bundled with two other releases, one by Carla Thomas ("I'll Bring It Home to You," an answer record to Sam Cooke's recently released "Bring It on Home to Me") and another by the Mar-Keys (their version of Cannonball Adderley's "Sack O' Woe"). These releases had the contemporary sound and feel, not Otis's. His A-side was "Hey Hey Baby," which sounded like a Little Richard imitation; "These Arms," spare and "country" sounding, was buried on the back.

The world seemed to agree with Jim Stewart—Little Richard was the best Little Richard, and Otis's record was going nowhere. A couple more months passed, and then the influential Nashville DJ John R., no doubt influenced by Galkin, flipped over the record. John R. broadcast on WLAC, one of the first stations to adopt "clear-channel" technology, meaning that at night its fifty thousand watts reached twenty-eight states. The station's influence increased as radios proliferated, especially with the introduction of the transistor radio in late 1954. John R. broadcast when kids were going to bed, their radios tucked up under their covers. On his show *After Hours*, he serenaded them—America's future songwriters—with hepcat talk and very un-lullaby-like rhythm and blues. John R. called to tell Jim he was promoting the wrong side and that the ballad was a smash. As pleased as Jim was to hear it, he was looking at months of little response. Figuring that something was worth more than nothing, Jim passed to John R. his portion of the publishing monies he'd gotten from Galkin. (The Federal Communications Commission would soon curtail such practices.) The gift had potential value; if John R. made it a hit, he'd get half a 1963 penny for every record that was sold. This, Jim had learned, was how records got played.

John R. set about playing the record every night of his show.

◆◆◆

AT STAX, IT was a period of comings and goings. Two weeks after Otis came through and weeks before "These Arms of Mine" was released, Booker T. Jones—namesake for Stax's biggest act, rising star of the house band, and recent high school graduate—left Memphis altogether to attend Indiana University, four hundred miles away. He'd been saving since folding newspapers outside Phineas Newborn's house. With $900, he had enough for out-of-state tuition, and off he went. "I never thought, What am I doing going to college?" he says. "Lots of other people did. But it meant everything to my family for me to have a degree. My father was a high school teacher. He had a degree. His father had graduated from Mississippi Industrial College in the late 1800s and was able to purchase seventy acres of land in Marshall County, Mississippi, on which he built a school and became a teacher."

As Booker settled into his freshman year, "Green Onions" was climbing to number three on the pop charts, overtaking Elvis Presley's "She's Not You." But Booker didn't give it a second thought. "Indiana changed my life. The standards they have—I don't think I had any respect for regimen before I went there. And I was finally learning about all this music I was hearing in my head and playing—what it meant and how it translated and how to translate it to other people. How to write strings, how to write horns, what were the origins of this scale, how to conduct an orchestra—I found these things out at Indiana. I always heard music in my mind but I didn't have the ability to translate so much of that music to the outside world."

Though Indiana had an applied music degree, Booker pursued a broader education, studying business, art, and history. "Music gives you a way to organize not only notes, but all sorts of ideas. You think of twelve notes in the scale, and twelve colors in the spectrum, twelve months in the year, and twelve bars in blues. That's Western music, but what about Eastern music? What if you have sixteen bars, or thirteen? Thirteen is the magic number if you use it in conjunction with eight and five. And that's the golden ratio." He smiles. "There are so many possibilities to link music with mathematics and beauty, with nature and art." He soon received a $5,000 check from Stax for "Green Onions," paying his upcoming tuition, and making a down payment on a Ford Galaxie 500 convertible. "I was styling. I went back to Memphis as often as I could and played sessions."

No one fully appreciated the space that this quiet musician filled until he was gone. "Booker wanted to continue with his education," says Steve. "How can you deny a guy that?" The studio knew they'd need a piano player, and saxophonist Floyd Newman, once again, was the linchpin: He brought Steve to his gig, at a South Memphis nightclub, to check out his keyboardist. "I heard a couple sets," Steve says, "and I talked to the guy, asked if he'd be willing to do some sessions at Stax. And he says, 'Oh, man, that would be great.' So I told Jim, 'I think I found us a piano player.'"

The young man's name was Isaac Lee Hayes. He was working days at a meatpacking plant ("Hogs and cows being slaughtered," Hayes says, "I couldn't hardly sleep, but it was a living"), and he'd already been rejected by Stax twice, first auditioning with a blues band, then with a rock group. "Nobody would hire Isaac," says Floyd. "Isaac used to hang around the studio and he would hear things that were beyond his knowledge. He was just a natural, but he wasn't a very advanced player. When I hired Isaac, he could only play piano with one hand." He'd since learned a thing or two, and Jim called Floyd to see if he'd endorse the idea. "I said yes," Floyd remembers, "because you could drop a fork or spoon or plate on the floor, and Isaac would tell you what note it was. He was hearing everything."

Isaac's budding talent found fertile ground at Stax. He'd had no formal training on the keyboards—"I feel so limited, so restricted," he says even years after he'd become a superstar. "It's in my head, but I can't get it to my hands." But he was innately musical, with a strong sense of a song's arrangement: He knew when to play, and when not to play. That endeared him to the musicians in the studio.

His first session was for one of Otis Redding's early returns to Stax, after "These Arms" had hit but before Otis was anything like a star. "I was nervous," says Isaac. "I was scared to death—they were gonna find me out, that I'm not good as Booker T. Jones. Well, Otis was a dynamic person. He was easy to work with. It was like a party whenever Otis came to town.

Isaac Hayes, songwriter. (Stax Museum of American Soul Music)

We'd gather around the piano, work up the tune—the horn players, Al Jackson, Steve Cropper, David Porter did a lot of the backup singing—and I sat at the piano. After a few takes I just fell in line and it was like a big family."

◆ ◆ ◆

THE FAMILY WAS growing. The woman who would develop and run the company's publicity department, Deanie Parker, came through the door with her high school singing group that won first prize in a local contest: a chance to audition for Jim Stewart. "Mr. Stewart indicated that he was impressed," says the petite chanteuse who'd moved to Memphis from Ohio a couple years earlier, "and then he asked a question that I had never heard before: 'Do you have any original music?'" Deanie returned to her bedroom, dominated by an upright piano, and wrote lyrics, a melody, and taught the group. "And Jim was even more impressed. And then he said, 'What are you gonna put on the B-side?'" She laughs, "'B-side? What is a B-side?'" Her song "My Imaginary Guy" came out in February 1963 (with her "Until You Return" on the flip), as Otis's "These Arms" was finding its audience. A playful song, it reaches back to the fifties for a mambo beat, with rich backing vocals; it also calls to mind Carla's "Gee Whiz," with its dreamy, youthful melody. It makes you reach for your ink pen and school notebook to doodle.

Deanie hit the road with her musical ensemble—and the road hit right back. "These artists were leaving their homes to go on the road," she explains, "where they did not have hotels where they could rest, did not have restaurants where they could eat. At any given time, a sheriff might appear out of a cotton field and stop you just for the sport of stopping you, tell you that you were speeding when you know that you were driving under the speed limit. As an African-American, you knew that any excuse and no excuse was good enough to be stopped, and humiliated, or treated as a second-class citizen. I didn't have the soulfulness of Aretha Franklin, I could never belt out a song like Gladys Knight, and I certainly didn't have Tina Turner's legs. So, I thought I needed to find something else to do."

Deanie pursued her college education and found a part-time job. "Estelle Axton hired me to be a salesperson at the Satellite Record Shop. And she asked me for recommendations for other salespeople, so my popularity soared." Others, too, were taken by her spunk and charm. "Jim Stewart made me the first publicist for Stax Records, even though I had no experience. We contracted the services of Al Abrams, who had done marketing, PR, and publicity for Motown. He really, by mail and by phone, taught me how to structure a press release, how to pursue the media, how to prepare the artist for the interview—fundamental things." In 1964, Deanie Parker would become the company's first salaried African-American office employee.

◆ ◆ ◆

IN THE FALL of 1963, Stax released a record that would rival the success of "Green Onions." Since giving the company its first hit, Rufus Thomas was proving himself an endless source of song and fun. He followed "The Dog" from earlier in the year with a sequel that was promptly covered by the Rolling Stones on their debut album and has been often imitated, but never equaled.

There was a certain happenstance to the recording of the song, extending from Jerry Wexler's New York restiveness. He'd been expecting a new song from Carla Thomas for several weeks, and every time he'd phone Jim, Jim reported that the equipment was broken. Wexler turned to Tom Dowd, trained as a nuclear physicist and working as Atlantic Records'

Rufus Thomas in Estelle's Satellite Record Shop, early 1960s. (Photograph by Don Nix/Courtesy of the Oklahoma Museum of Popular Culture, Steve Todoroff Collection)

chief engineer. "Jerry was thinking they were up to something down there so he called me in, said, 'Dowd, you're going to Memphis tonight.' He said, 'There's no equipment in life that's gonna be broken for two weeks, so find out what are they doing.' Okay, fine. Jim Stewart picked me up at the airport on a Friday evening, took me right to the studio, and I saw there was a brake band broken, a few normal malfunctions on a machine. Jim said, 'We can't find the parts.' So I called my engineer in New York, said, 'You bust into Harvey Radio first thing in the morning, get me a pair of brake bands for a 350, get me a couple 65K resistors, get me two capacitors, an on-off switch, and then go straight to the airport, give a stewardess on the first plane to Memphis twenty-five dollars to carry them, and I'll meet her.'

"Next morning I asked Jim to take me to the airport to pick up the parts. I think he was a little taken aback. But we returned to the studio, I plugged in a soldering iron, *boom boom boom*, had the machine running in about thirty-five or forty minutes, said, 'Okay, we're ready to record.'" Dowd couldn't get a flight out until late Sunday afternoon, and arrangements were made to play golf on Sunday morning with some of the guys. Dowd was about to confirm yet again that Memphis is the town where nothing ever happens, but the impossible always does. "We played ten or eleven holes and all of a sudden Steve says, 'Well, we'd better be heading back to the studio, we just about have time to get coffee and doughnuts.' And I was surprised because it was Sunday. Well, on Sunday when people come out of church, they fall by the studio. Al Jackson shows up and Isaac [Hayes] and David [Porter] and the horns mosey in. We're talking and they were asking me questions and playing me things. Then Rufus Thomas comes walking in the door and says, 'Hi everybody!' He says, 'Everything workin'?' And they said, 'Yeah, it's working now.' And Rufus says, 'I got a song!' So Rufus runs this song by them once or twice, and I'm up in the control room to engineer and I'm laughing. Steve looks up and says, 'You ready to record?' And I say, 'You got it, let's go!' *Boom,* right? Rufus never broke stride. He sang it for the band twice, says, 'See y'all later!' and he walked back out the door, going home to have Sunday dinner. It was very casual." The Stax folk listened to the playback and were in awe of Dowd's work. Through experience and science, he knew how to capture the most life and make it stick to the tape. Jim said it was the best-sounding record yet to come off their console. Dowd continues, "It was pleasant people enjoying each other's company and having good conversation. And I had under my arm when I went back to New York, I had 'Walking the Dog.'"

For Dowd, Stax had been a walk through the looking glass. In New York, sessions were by the union book, with the clock ticking off three hours and the pressure always on. Sessions proceeded in proscribed ways: Music was put on charts by the arranger, which the musicians played according to the instructions of the producer. Certain people worked in the control room, others on the studio floor, and they communicated on microphones through the glass, with neither invading the other's space. Not in Memphis. It was a revelation to see the free passage between the control room and the studio floor. Everyone was welcome everywhere. It was a fluid environment, even with the song arrangements. No musician's parts were written, nothing was worked out in advance. For "Walking the Dog," Rufus hummed his ideas to the players, they improvised. He dictated the rhythm by getting close to the player's ear and clacking his teeth. It worked. The song is extra funky, a tight, bouncing stroll down a young and sunny

Packy Axton, left, and Don Nix. (Photograph by Don Nix/Courtesy of the Oklahoma Museum of Popular Culture, Steve Todoroff Collection)

street. Steve's guitar leads the parade, loose like a rubber band. Every bend he ever played, he made his own. Packy's saxophone grins its way through a verse. ("Packy was not the greatest saxophone player in the world," says Duck, "but he had the heart of the greatest saxophone player in the world.") Musical charts would have been less useful than racing charts. "Head charts," they called this—making it up and using the good parts.

In New York, Wexler was more amazed by the process than the song—and he *loved* the song; soon he'd visit Memphis to produce there himself. "Memphis was a real departure," he told author Peter Guralnick, "because Memphis was a return to head arrangements, to the set rhythm section, away from the arranger. It was a reversion to the symbiosis between the producer and the rhythm section. It was really something new."

It was also really something old. The studio maintained a mono machine and a mono sensibility well past the advent of stereo, when two tracks of playback enhanced the sound's dimension. Not a company to lead the technological charge, Stax captured what the others couldn't—spirit. Jim had no reason to argue with what was working. But Tom Dowd did. "When I came down here, 1962, I was appalled. These people were still recording on a machine like I abandoned in 1952. And when I said, 'We should replace this machine with a new two-track machine,' it was an appalling suggestion. They thought their sound was gonna be destroyed if they went into this."

Dowd was motivated by more than technology. Albums manufactured in stereo sold for a higher price, garnering more profits. It would be the summer of 1965 before he connected a stereo machine to the front of the mono machine, allowing Stax to work, as was their custom, in mono, but simultaneously producing a stereo tape. "I said, 'You just listen on the one speaker in mono and whenever you send me a tape, send it to me off of this stereo machine. You make it sound good in mono, I'll worry about the stereo.'" Stax got comfortable with stereo, and in 1966, Dowd would install a four-track recorder. More tracks expanded the possibilities for overdubbing and mixing. For the players, more tracks meant that when one person messed up, not everyone had to redo their parts. More peak performances could be kept.

◆ ◆ ◆

STAX WAS BECOMING a company of national renown, but in its South Memphis neighborhood, it was the rising home team for which everyone root-root-rooted. For those African-Americans who had recently ascended to the middle-class neighborhood, Stax was a validation. Neighbors could insert themselves into the success: *My* record clerk was a recording star, a songwriter, a tastemaker.

The democracy—the opportunities—of the studio was already legend. Rufus and Carla walked in the front door, danced onto the national charts. High school kids were leading bands—with songs on the national charts. The dang driver from Georgia who walked in carrying amps recorded his own song there—and was rising again and again on the national charts. Still, it was an unreliable way to run a business.

As the legend spread, more unknowns would enter, expecting to get heard. But with the studio growing, more sessions were going on, leaving less time to cater to the individual potential legends. Since the musicians worked late on weekend nights, the studio was quiet earlier in the day. "We just told people to come back on Saturday morning, and starting about nine until noon or so, I got to hear a lot of stuff," Steve says. "I don't recall any superstars coming out of that, but it kept things flowing." These Saturday-morning auditions became a weekly conduit between the neighborhood and the studio. Sometimes it was a duo, a man playing solemnly at the piano, harmonizing with the woman standing stiffly beside him. Sometimes a lone white guy, strumming country guitar and crooning; or four guys from the street corner harmonizing like pros, in amateurs' outfits that paid homage to the day's natty dressers. Most had never seen the inside of a studio before.

"If you had talent—if you thought you had talent—you could go there," says Rufus, his racial wariness eased in this sanctuary. "Nobody else was doing that around here. No studios—no nothing—ever gave any of the black artists that kind of a chance."

Elsewhere in Memphis, blacks stepped to the curb when whites walked by. The city closed its public swimming pools rather than integrate them. And in June 1963, over one hundred sanitation workers came to a meeting called by organizer T.O. Jones, an effort to solidify the group's complaints. The city, however, sent informants, and less than two weeks later, thirty-three men who'd attended the meeting—including T.O. Jones—were fired. Jones spent months fighting to get those jobs back, and was mostly successful, though he chose not to return to the daily humiliation and instead devoted himself entirely to forming a union. He soon had reason to be optimistic: The intransigent Mayor Loeb resigned in October after a death in his family, and an African-American community banded together to elect a moderate, Judge William Ingram, who had distinguished himself on the bench as a voice for the common man, publicly rebuking the police force for unlawful tactics. The community also supported a new Public

T.O. Jones organized the sanitation workers and fought for union representation. (University of Memphis Libraries/Special Collections)

Works commissioner, Pete Sisson, though he turned on them shortly after being sworn in, stating in early January 1964, "I do not expect, nor will I tolerate, agitation within my department. I receive applications daily from too many prospective employees who are ready and willing to go to work immediately to allow discord within the ranks of this department." When Mayor Ingram did not come to the sanitation men's rescue, the new optimism quickly dimmed.

At Stax, everyone had a chance. One neighborhood group in their early teens became reliable assistants to the studio regulars (*valet* was the fancy term used), and as they learned to play, they would soon form their own group, the Bar-Kays. "I used to get my hair cut up there next to Stax when I was a kid," says James Alexander, who was born in the clinic (925 E. McLemore) across the street from Stax. "Carl Cunningham was the first one who started getting into Stax because he shined Al Jackson's shoes at the barbershop and he aspired to be a drummer. Al used to let him sneak in and get on the drums. I wanted to get in there too. Al, Isaac and David, Booker T.—they took us under their wing. When there were no sessions, we'd start beating on the instruments and when they saw we wasn't gonna leave, we became part of the family. Otis Redding, soon Sam and Dave, and all these people, they always needed stuff done—clothes to the cleaners, cars need washing, shoes need shining. We were like little puppies running around in the studio."

"The Bar-Kays used to come in there and just sit and listen to us the whole time we'd be recording," says bassist Lewie Steinberg. "They sat, listened, and learned from us."

"We were playing the songs that you hear on the R&B radio stations," continues future Bar-Kay James Alexander. "We would play Brook Benton. We learned to play the Stax stuff that was getting popular, 'The Dog' by Rufus Thomas, things like that. Monkey see, monkey do—wasn't no such thing at that point as trying to play originals. We would just learn the songs off the radio and play them."

They'd gather around the record player in Estelle's shop to deepen their understanding of the songs. Despite all the studio-centric work that went on in the store, records did get sold. Business got so good that Estelle expanded into her own place, taking the front of the bay next door when the barbershop folded.

The Bar-Kays came into their own at Booker T. Washington High School, a few years after Booker T. Jones, William Bell, and William Brown graduated from there. Booker T. was the African-American public school on the south side of town (a mile from Stax), and it had a large auditorium. It often hosted major events, one of the largest being a talent show that since the 1940s had been known as the Ballet. It was the premier showcase for up-and-coming talent, rivaling the Palace Theater's Amateur Night, which in earlier years had sprung Rufus Thomas, B.B. King, Bobby Bland, and many others. "The thing during those days was to get your talent good enough to be on the Ballet," says James. "We played that night and I'll never forget it. We got suits from Lansky Brothers on Beale Street, maroon shiny suits, pink shirts, black patent-leather shoes, and we had—you had to have—black silk socks. We had a pretty hot horn section and we always liked to move around onstage. We played 'Philly Dog' by the Mar-Keys, and that really brought the house down."

These kids paid tribute to the rising national stars who had graced the same stage not long back. The 45s by the recent graduates from Booker T. Washington were in every record collection alongside James Brown, Brook Benton, and Etta James.

◆ ◆ ◆

ONE OF STAX'S biggest fans left town in 1963. Local disc jockey Al Bell was offered a job in the Washington, DC, radio market, where his swinging sophistication quickly became popular on drive time, mornings *and* evenings. "Al Bell would come by the record shop," remembers Steve Cropper, "and he'd invite us to the station. We got to be friends. I was allowed to bring him and other DJs brand-new product and demos, and if they liked it, they actually put it right out on the air. Didn't need anyone's permission, just played it. And the day that Al Bell went to Washington, DC,

I lost a buddy. He was such a part of us—he'd hang out at the record shop, helped write songs with us, played our records—and when he left, we lost a big part of the whole thing that Stax was into."

Bell made the most of his outsider status, bringing the sounds of southern soul to this North–South border, introducing Otis, the MG's, Carla, and all the talent from Stax, Fame, Hi, and the myriad of southern labels to a new audience. He would soon use Otis's 1964 recording "I Want to Thank You," the flip side of his "Security" single, as his sign-off song. When the sound found favor in DC, DJs elsewhere on the East Coast could justify playing the music.

No one at the time could know, but Al's foray on the East Coast would prove propitious in just a few years' time.

8. THE GOLDEN GLOW
1963–1965

WHAT VERY WELL could have been a fluke—the driver who steered into a hit—was proving to be no accident at all. As if testing disc jockey John R.'s resolve, "These Arms" finally hit the R&B charts on March 23, 1963, half a year after its release, landing at a solid number twenty—if only for a single week. John R. wasn't done, however, and neither were other disc jockeys around the country. Two more months passed, and on May 25, "These Arms" hit the pop charts, staying there for three weeks. The gentleness of the song, its emotional depth, its simple yet gripping musicality, were indicative of Otis's latent talent, which Stax began to extract. "Otis did not catch fire overnight," Jim says. "Each record was a step above the last one in his interpretations of the music, and his arrangements, and his whole persona onstage. It was a process that took time."

"He put a spark under Stax," says Steve Cropper. "No question about it. And with all due respect to all the great artists that came through those doors, Otis Redding was the one artist that everybody looked forward to recording with."

"Otis Redding seemed to be a person with a mission," muses Booker T. Jones, "and we picked up that mission and it became all of ours. His intent was so strong and so powerful when we were recording that it translated to more than the music." More than being heard, Otis wanted

Estelle Axton and Jim Stewart, late 1963 or early 1964. Rufus
Thomas has a hit, Otis's release is hanging in. In two years, Jim will
quit his day job at the bank.

to be felt. He wanted his recorded performance, his impersonal piece of
vinyl, to physically affect the detached listener. He wasn't able to do that
right away; it took time to master the intricacies of recording, of conveying his ideas to the musicians around him, of getting the sounds in his
head to stick to the magnetic tape.

In the wake of the first single, Otis formed a touring band with players from Macon, and he promoted "These Arms" as best he could. Well

OTIS REDDING

over half a year passed before he
returned to Stax. Working with
the MG's, he recorded "That's
What My Heart Needs," a ballad
in the mold of "These Arms" that
expanded the sound with horns,
and indicates a blossoming ease
between Otis and Steve's musi-
cianship; it broke the top thirty on
the R&B charts. Redding's powers
of persuasion were also evident
away from the microphone, convincing Jim Stewart to record singles by three members of his road
band, which buoyed their draw at
shows.

When Redding returned a third time, his musical ideas had significantly crystallized. He recorded a treatment of "Ruler of My Heart," a song by Irma Thomas and Allen Toussaint. Otis's "Pain in My Heart" is a full-on realization of the textures in his voice, a beautiful interaction with the band. The MG's, who backed him in the studio but did not tour with him, lay down a deceptively simple backing track, allowing Steve's guitar to play sinuous fills that accent the embellishments in Otis's singing. The love affair between Otis and the horn section is in its springtime. "I really think Otis was a genius," says Wayne Jackson, trumpeter. "Genius means being touched by God. In your mind and your heart, you're able to focus that power. That's a genius." The three horn players would each take a note to form a chord, and they played whole notes. Otis, however, would get right in the player's face—horns, guitar, drums—and imitate the sound or rhythm in his head by using his whole body to convey the impact he desired. You'd feel what he was saying before you heard it, but you'd hear it soon enough. Fans sent "Pain in My Heart" to number sixty-one on the pop charts. (The industry magazine *Billboard*, ruler of the charts, was not maintaining an R&B chart during this period, not because it was discounting R&B, but because the African-American sound had so influenced the pop sound that *Billboard* no longer recognized a distinction. Black music—once segregated at best, and often simply dismissed—was being fully embraced by America. However, the R&B chart returned the following year; in its absence, the chart's influence on sales became very clear to the labels and artists, and they welcomed its return.)

In the spring of 1964, with the recording of "Security," Otis was a new man in the studio. The horns sound like him singing, the guitar sounds like his hands waving about between lyrics. He's learned to commandeer the ineffable and give it his own accents. "He made everybody smile and he made everybody a better musician," says Duck. "After that, when Otis came in to cut, no one was late. He wore a halo."

This sense of Otis in a golden glow, a firmament of goodness, is universal at Stax. In his hometown of Macon, there are those who claim authorship of some of his biggest hits—notably "These Arms" and "Respect"—and there, Otis is judged differently. (Not giving proper credit is a form of theft, substantial theft when the song becomes a hit; it's possible others wrote those songs and Otis stole them outright, but his personal imprint is so individual that whatever elements others supplied, he surely supplemented and finished, making him at least coauthor. A Macon bandmate of Otis's, Benny Davis, is one of several people who claim authorship of "These Arms," and he says, "I always thought he'd do the right thing about it,

Mid-1965, Stax signs Otis Redding and Rufus and Carla Thomas to new contracts. The future looks bright. Jim quits the bank. "My suits were a little more continental than bankers appreciated," he says. (Promotional photo by API Photographers/ API Collection)

you know? But he never did.") At Stax, Otis was beloved. "Otis was the nicest person I ever met," says Steve. "He didn't have any vices, and he didn't have any faults—which sounds like you're making it up. Everybody loved him. Kids gravitated toward him. Women worshipped the guy. His fans were unbelievable. He was tall, good-looking, and he sang his gazoo off, so why not? He was always on time, always together, loved everybody, made everybody feel great. He was like a country preacher, always wanting to help people out and always paying people compliments."

Otis's drive to find his own voice—his brute power, his insistence on precise backing, his consistent drive and demand to be pushed—reverberated throughout Stax, influencing a change in the MG's, a retuning of their own voice. Though Lewie Steinberg and Al Jackson were the same age, they played from different generations. Steinberg had a classic "walking bass" sound, loping up and down the scale, common especially in big bands and jazz-based combos; it's a fun sound, makes you feel like you're taking a walk on a pretty day, bobbing your head and humming a little tune. But by the mid-1960s, with the growth of rock and roll, the bass was becoming more of a power tool, an automatic weapon, a car that rumbled instead of a pedestrian that ambled, and Duck Dunn, who'd been playing on sessions at Stax since the earliest days of the Mar-Keys—and who was a prizewinning dancer—knew how to wield the same instrument (a Fender Precision bass) in the fashion of the new era. "Times changed," says Duck. "Lewie could play the hell out of that walking bass, but then music went in the syncopation thing, like with Otis's 'Security.' Maybe I was a little bit faster, but rhythm and blues went from walking to syncopation."

Duck played on "Security," and the change in the MG's lineup was public with their early 1965 single featuring one side with Steinberg and the other with Dunn (and neither with Booker T. Jones who in his final year at Indiana University was replaced by Isaac Hayes). The Steinberg side is the hard-driving but somewhat carnivalesque sounding "Outrage"

Duck joins the MG's in 1965. L–R: Donald "Duck" Dunn, Booker T. Jones, Steve Cropper, Al Jackson Jr. (Promotional photo by API Photographers/Earlie Biles Collection)

(named, perhaps, to acknowledge Steinberg's hurt), while the Dunn side, "Boot-Leg," is as hard-rocking and exciting as anything the MG's had released to date. A walking bass couldn't run to keep up with it.

There was one other issue. "The group talked to me about problems they were having with Lewie and his drinking," says Jim. "It's no secret. But I didn't say, 'Get him out.' The decision came from the group that they were going to have to do something." Al demanded a command of the beat, and demon alcohol wasn't improving anyone's timing. Clean living was still the order of the day in 1964; beatniks may have introduced marijuana on the coasts by now, but in the insular Bible Belt, booze was considered wild and even the Mar-Keys knew to separate the fun from the studio work.

Steinberg has his own theories, and his own magnanimity: "Every time Stax would get a hit record, I would be the one that would put the bass to it. And every time it comes out, somebody else is reaping the benefits. I'm in there recording as one of the Mar-Keys. The next thing you know, Duck Dunn is the Mar-Key. I recorded with Booker T. & the MG's—next thing you know, Duck Dunn is in Booker T. & the MG's. There's a reason for that: Duck and Steve were childhood friends, all through life, which is very beautiful. I admire that two people are able to stick together like that."

Indeed, whatever other issues there were, Cropper, the boss's right-hand man, wanted the company of his friend since fourth grade. Ability was not an issue—Duck could play, and in a style that helped modernize the sound. And the replacement presented a beautiful racial symmetry onstage, a message no one looking at the band could ignore.

For Steinberg—thirty-one years old in 1964—although the big time was about to pass him by, he'd made his mark. He'd contributed to several MG's classics, including "Green Onions," "Chinese Checkers," and "Soul Dressing" (and shared in the songwriting royalties). With his band mates, he was inducted into the Rock and Roll Hall of Fame in 1992, and awarded a Lifetime Achievement Grammy Award in 2007. In 1964, he remained a favored bassist in the era's better bands and combos—Willie Mitchell, Al Jackson Sr., and Bowlegs Miller sought him. And he had his day job, where he was able to do all the blending he wanted, and all that he couldn't achieve at Stax. "I was working with United Paint Company, what they call a mixologist. Any color you might want, I can make it. Ain't no such thing I can't make that color."

Duck's ascension was the realization of a dream that began with the Royal Spades. "Here's a bunch of white guys trying to do a bunch of black guys' music," he says. "And eventually it led to Steve and I playing with Booker and Al. I didn't care about the money. I just wanted to be accepted by these great musicians." He'd been listening to Al Jackson in clubs since he'd been tall enough to sneak in, and he continued to seek him out. "I was working at King Records during the day and playing a hillbilly club called Hernando's Hideaway and I'd stop by and see Al before going home. He was my mentor. Watching him, he taught me how to play, when to play and when not to play—and it's mostly when not to play." Now he was playing alongside him, and in the beginning every session felt like a test. "I was young then, but I knew I had to kick ass. You got Al Jackson over there looking at you, saying, 'Here it is, Dunn, get it.' You had to get it or your ass is out of there."

The Mar-Keys had been drunken teens playing fun music; the MG's were a serious band. "Al Jackson was the pulse," says Steve. "His playing said, 'Here's a groove, sing to this. Play to this.' He was *demanding* that way in the studio, and he was that way onstage. A lot of good drummers want to follow the singer, or they're watching the guitarist, or trying to lock with someone. At Stax, we all followed Al Jackson. More than any other musician on those records, he was probably the biggest influence in how they sounded."

Steve's own style developed in relation to what Al played. "I treated the guitar more as a percussion instrument," he says. "I treated the guitar very much like I would a set of drums, picking up from the little things that you do on the high hat, on the cymbals, and little stabs and rim shots. I would weave in and out of Al and play where he didn't and lay out when he did. It was a great combination and we always kept that rhythm going."

"Al played a cross between jazz and blues," says Booker. "Al's idol was Sonny Payne, who was Count Basie's drummer. Sonny Payne was untouchable. Al's background was playing blues in Memphis clubs, and at Stax that got combined with rock and rockabilly. Al played that music with his jazz background, so that type of drumming was completely unique—the simplicity that he brought to it combined with the jazz chops."

"The first thing that Al used to do when he would come to a session was reach in his back pocket, pull out this big fat billfold, and plop it on the snare," says Steve. "That way the snare didn't ring too much. And there's not a lot of cymbals because we didn't mike the cymbals."

Otis Redding was a perfect vehicle for Al Jackson's talent. Otis was guided by his gut, and Al could anchor him, could determine the rhythm, the groove, and the feel that would hold the song and allow Otis to get his ideas across. Their increasing synchronicity and the resulting hits were making Redding ever more confident, and a trio of songs he released in late 1964 and the spring of 1965 were three small steps for the artist, one giant leap for the record label.

"That's How Strong My Love Is" was written by Roosevelt Jamison, an entrepreneurial music lover with a day job in the lab of a Memphis blood bank. Jamison had begun managing the careers of O.V. Wright and James Carr, two deep-soul singers who came up in the church and were ill-prepared for the temptations of the pop world; Wright would enjoy many R&B hits before withering under a heroin addiction, and James Carr's notable career was blunted by mental health issues. But in the early 1960s, the future looked bright, and Jamison wrote the song, recorded it with Wright, and brought it to Stax to see if they were interested. Steve Cropper thought Wright's version was too churchy, but he liked the song and recorded Jamison singing it. At a session, Steve played "That's How Strong My Love Is" for Otis.

The song is startlingly simple, the music a bed for a plea for understanding from one lover to another: simple yet precise in its emphases—the drums set up the horns, the drums drive the guitar and its fills, the drums anchor the recurring piano chords. This wide but spare foundation allows Otis to stretch out his vocals, to moan low, to rasp and roll and plumb the depths of the imploration. He takes us inside his hurt.

"I loved Otis doing ballads," says Jim. "To me that's where he stood out, and that's where you got the real Otis and the real warmth, and everything about him." The song became a top-twenty R&B hit, and broke the Hot 100 pop list; within a year's time, the Rolling Stones would cover it on their first album. Stax was flowering on national—international—soil.

Redding's musicality reached new heights with "Mr. Pitiful," the flip side to "That's How Strong," which went even higher on both charts. A.C. "Mooha" Williams, a disc jockey on WDIA, Memphis's premier African-American radio station, would play a Redding ballad and, referring to the sorrow infused in the song, dubbed him "Mr. Pitiful." On Otis's next visit to Memphis, Steve suggested an upbeat tune based on the downbeat name, and between the airport and the studio—fifteen minutes—they had most of the song. "They call me Mr. Pitiful," Redding sings, "that's how I got my fame." Al Jackson drives the song but the horns bring the funk, adding their swooping riffs and jive punctuation. They shine midsong when they solo and set up the bridge; Wayne remembers Otis leaning into the section to sing them the part. The notes are so fast, the part so unique, that they were both exhilarated and taken aback. "When he had the rhythm section cooking along, then he'd come back to the horns," Wayne says. "We were behind a partition. He'd get right in your face with his fist and sing the part, *da, da-da, da-da, da-da.* And he'd have you breaking out in a sweat and dancing. He was like a big football coach, a huge man, and he had all this energy aimed at you and *di-di-li-di-li-de-da, di-di-di-di-di-di-dee-da* while we were scrambling to find those notes and play with the rhythm pattern that he was singing."

"Otis would always have us play in funny keys," says saxman Floyd Newman. "He had us in sharp keys, like A and B and F sharp, and nobody ever played in those keys. It's difficult to play in a sharp key, but it's more of a brilliant sound. And it made us think. There were funny little lines that he would hum to us that would fit perfectly—Otis would know every riff he wanted you to play." The song hit number ten on the R&B charts.

Redding's confidence was infectious, and before he cut "I've Been Loving You Too Long (to Stop Now)" in the first quarter of 1965, Jim Stewart finally found the label reliable enough to do what every dedicated musician would love to do: He quit his day job. His company had been creating chart singles for five years. They'd had hits with established artists, discovered new talent, been so overrun with opportunity that they'd opened on Saturday mornings to give everyone a chance to be heard. But Jim was interested in calculated safety. At the bank, his day was spent analyzing risk. "Stax might not make it, better hold on to my job," Jim remembers thinking. "But my job began costing me money. And I really didn't fit in with that banking atmosphere either. My hair started growing longer. My suits were a little more continental than bankers appreciated. The company was growing rapidly and it needed my services twenty-four hours a day. It was a business decision."

One thing about this new work he was fully committing to—it was fun. He had no training for running a record label, had never worked at someone else's and wasn't schooled in the business. Every day was different. And Otis was coming through the studio several times a year, each session a long stride toward artistic success and financial reward. Always ready to write a song, Otis arrived in early spring 1965 with a collaboration that had begun in a nondescript hotel room with Jerry Butler, former lead singer of the Impressions; hanging out after a show together, Butler shared an idea he'd begun but couldn't finish. It was the first couple lines of "I've Been Loving You Too Long." For three years Butler had been trying to figure out where to take it, and he'd taken it nowhere. Otis called him not long after—he'd not only figured out where to take it, he'd taken it there, recording and releasing the song (and sharing the writer's credit with Butler). "I never would have approached it the way he approached it," Butler said. "It was just beautiful." Otis wrenched all the dynamics from the song, building it slowly, the horns teasing the excitement of the lover who wants to go on, then suddenly cutting off to the spare sounds—the lover who wants to quit the relationship. The recurring rise and fall of the melody, the building and disassembling of the instruments, his moans of pity and woe—it's an artistic triumph not only for Redding but for all of Stax, an indication of how far they'd pushed themselves. "That song, to me, was the beginning of him being that superstar that you always dream of working with in your lifetime," says Jim. "Just the words, to hear him say, 'I've been loving you too long to stop now'—what more do you have to say? It makes you want to cry. He was such a sincere person. He was so intense. This man—I've never known anybody like him."

"Otis became that power-packed, raw, gutsy, emotional, serious performer," says DJ Al Bell. "You felt him. You heard the tear in his voice, and that captivated me, and when I went on the radio, it was Otis Redding and me. We were having an affair on the air."

It was that "tear" in Otis's voice, the crying and the ache that it evoked, that made him a transcendent vocalist. His songs were about love, but the sense of longing he conveyed was deeper than the love between a man and woman; Otis touched the heart of desire. He sang about love but summoned the poignancy of his times, of people used and being used and wanting an embrace instead of a fist. Black, white—no matter the listener's race, only the listener's empathy. Those seeking comfort found it in Otis Redding's songs.

9. SOUL MEN
1963–1966

STAX'S ONGOING SUCCESS was a boon to all associated with the label, but perhaps most to Atlantic. Creating the songs was much harder than feeding them through the distribution machine, and Stax's creativity was on fire. So in the summer of 1964, when Atlantic's Jerry Wexler and Ahmet Ertegun found themselves propelled to wild dancing by two singers in a Miami nightclub, they immediately thought of pairing the duo with Stax.

The two men—Sam Moore and Dave Prater, the rafter-shaking singers who would become famous as Sam and Dave—did not know each other when they began performing together. The success of their first duet, as impromptu and unplanned as a high-wire fall, revealed that each had an innate understanding of how the other would move, physically and vocally.

Sam Moore had scuffled his way into hosting a talent show at a nightclub, the King of Hearts, in his hometown of Miami. Dave Prater was a bread baker. Sam remembers that when Dave signed up for that week's show, he was wearing his baker's whites; wherever he walked, he left behind white flour shoe prints. At the auditions, Dave sang a Jackie Wilson song, "Doggin' Around," but realized he didn't know the verses. Sam, whose job depended on selecting acts that would produce a good show, agreed to stay close during the performance and feed him the lines. But that night, Sam's foot caught the microphone cable, and as the mike began to fall, Dave went down to catch it and Sam went down to catch Dave. Choreographers couldn't have written it better: They came up together, singing and with the mike in hand. In that little mix-up, an act was born that would last the better part of twenty-two years and would remain forever a part of the public consciousness.

Both were high-energy performers, and their force mushroomed when they were together. Unlike many partner acts—the Righteous Brothers, the Simms Twins, the Everlys—Sam and Dave weren't known for subtle harmonies, one voice buttressing the other. They were double dynamite, each at full tilt, exploding together with exponential force. Roulette Records had been unable to capture the live magic in the studio, and Jerry Wexler flew to Miami with partner Ahmet Ertegun to see them at the King of Hearts.

"I'd always heard about Jerry Wexler, Tom Dowd, and Ahmet," says Sam of Atlantic's triumvirate. "I had always wanted to be on Atlantic, to get produced by those ears."

"It's a hundred and ten degrees inside this club," says Wexler. "Ahmet and I are boogalooing our asses off in there, and we signed Sam and Dave." Sam moved to New York, and when Wexler summoned him, Sam was ecstatic. Like Jackie Wilson and Sam Cooke, this soul crooner imagined crossover potential. Then, from behind his desk at Sixty-first and Broadway, Wexler conveyed the news: You're being shipped to Memphis.

Memphis? That's country music, thought Sam. His eyes were on the city that never sleeps, recording like Ruth Brown, Big Joe Turner, and Ray Charles—the Atlantic Records dream team! Memphis? The southern poll tax, enacted after the Civil War to prevent blacks from voting, had only recently been constitutionally abolished. Southern blacks had marched on Washington in massive numbers calling for jobs and freedom the previous year, around the same time that four smiling Sunday-school girls had been slaughtered in a Birmingham church bombing. He'd just arrived in New York and he was being shipped off to the land where Chaney, Goodman, and Schwerner, three Freedom Riders, had been delivered to the Ku Klux Klan for murder by local police. The assassination of Medgar Evers was recent. James Meredith had recently become the first African-American graduate of the University of Mississippi, but it had taken five hundred US Marshals to get him there. Sam remembers his muted reaction: "God have mercy."

The social conflicts may have obscured Sam's knowledge of the music coming from Memphis, but Wexler was tuned in. "I didn't have enough production chops available to do Sam and Dave right," Wexler acknowledges. "So I said to Jim Stewart, 'How about you go ahead? The contract is with us, but we will treat this exactly as a Stax record in terms of royalty and so on.'" Wexler was proposing a "loan" to Stax, an unusual arrangement with a few important caveats—most notably that Stax agree to split publishing royalties on any songs written by Stax staff for Sam and Dave, and that Atlantic retain ownership of the duo's contract. "The deal was that they made the Sam and Dave masters at Stax, they did the mixes, send them up to us, and from there on we took it," explains Wexler. While the lawyers were drafting that contract, someone at Atlantic—either Wexler or the lawyers—realized that the distribution arrangement between Atlantic and Stax that had been in place since Rufus and Carla's 1960 hit had grown into a significant arrangement worth a lot of money, and it had never been formalized. So the contract discussions ensued, encompassing now not only a unique arrangement with Sam and Dave, but also the basics of the relationship between the two companies. For Jim Stewart, their arrangement was less about the company and more the man he dealt with—Wexler—so he requested a "key-man clause," making Stax's connection to Atlantic dependent upon Wexler's presence there. The distribution deal took longer to work out than the Sam and Dave arrangement, but because it was only affirming a deal long in place, no one hesitated to continue business as usual.

Once in the hinterlands of Memphis, Sam and Dave stood outside the theater with Jim Stewart, getting acquainted. Sam remembers he was acclimating to the idea of being in an old theater within a languishing retail district, taking it all in, when a colorful neighborhood character in a pink shirt, chartreuse pants, white belt, white shoes, pink socks, and bald head stopped his afternoon stroll in front of Jim Stewart. Jim introduced Sam and Dave to the songwriter and piano player Isaac Hayes. Along came another guy in a small hat and a large alpaca sweater, looking like the insurance salesman he was—David Porter, another writer for the studio.

"Then I find out that during the daytime Jim works at the bank and at night he plays country music," Moore continues. "Oh my God, the tears started streaming down my face. I looked at Dave and I said, 'How could Atlantic do this to us? How could they?'"

Oh, but for a crystal ball: Then Sam Moore could believe what Jerry Wexler was doing for him. Mr. Chartreuse and Mr. Alpaca were going to custom-fit the voice of Sam and Dave, writing the hits and coaching the singers so closely that, for a period of time, the four individuals were a single voice. The hits that were to come, the reputation for their stage act, the enduring legacy—all were unseen but in place.

◆◆◆

THE PAIRING OF Hayes and Porter as a creative team further tightened the weave at Stax. Isaac had replaced Booker T. Jones during the school year, and when Jones was home, Isaac supplemented the band; he and Booker could trade off piano and organ. He'd also begun to write arrangements and help produce sessions, learning his art on the job. "I saw how Otis was working with the horns and doing the head arranging—nothing is written down. And during those days, there was no multitrack tapes—we had one track, and Jim Stewart was known as King of the One Track. If somebody screwed up, everybody had to start all over again."

David Porter was a regular at Stax long before he was hired there as the first staff writer. Since the late fifties when he was in high school, he'd been singing in clubs as Little David. When the record store opened in the concession stand, David was quickly inside, eager to be associated in any way with anything musical in his neighborhood. He met Estelle Axton, then Jim Stewart and Chips Moman; when he found out they had a recording studio in the back, he auditioned, essentially, near where the popcorn machine had been. Porter's eagerness and intensity were charming, and if the owners didn't think he yet had the chops as a vocalist, he certainly won their favor when, hearing they needed a baritone sax for the first Rufus and Carla session, he introduced them to Booker T. Jones.

Estelle Axton thought David Porter had talent. She appreciated his drive and encouraged him. Fatherless, he'd been raised in government housing not far from Stax, singing at Rose Hill Baptist Church in a quartet with future Earth, Wind & Fire vocalist Maurice White. He wanted to write and sing, so when stars like Jerry Butler came through Memphis, he'd insist they let him carry their bags; in return, he'd seek advice. (Butler advised him: "You can have a hit record, but you better learn how to diversify.") Still a teen, Porter borrowed $500 from a local preacher to start Genie Records, and released himself singing "Ain't That a Lot of Love," a fine song written by Deanie Parker and future Stax employee Homer Banks. (The song made little impression at the time, though by the mid-1960s, after a few copies had made their way to England, the heavy staccato opening and soaring melody morphed into the Spencer Davis Group hit "Gimme Some Lovin'.")

Soon after the studio opened, with an eye toward keeping himself nearby, David took a job sacking groceries at the Big D Supermarket across the street. The scene at Stax—it was less a scene than another world—was especially appealing to Porter. At his grocery store job, his supervisor made a habit of kicking black employees from behind as they walked past, an everyday humiliation that the others accepted. Porter was younger, and of a generation not afraid to demand respect. The athletic high school graduate grabbed the kicking foot, pressed his supervisor against the wall, and stated his opinion of the man's practice, with a prediction about what would happen next time he tried it. The produce manager no longer kicked the produce man in the ass. The distance between that grocery store and the Stax family could be measured in inches, though the chasm would take years for the public to traverse.

When not on the market's clock, Porter returned to Stax's embrace. He brought lyrics that spilled over several pages, and Estelle played him Motown songs to help him decipher the structure of verses, chorus, and bridge. ("David would have a good idea," she says. "But he'd expand upon it so much that he'd have two or three songs in one. I had to teach him how to cut out the junk.") She played him writing teams like Bacharach-David and Holland-Dozier-Holland, helped him hear the writer in the production, hear the personal stamp.

In 1962, Porter recorded—as Little David—for the local label Golden Eagle and then for Savoy, and also as Kenny Cain for Hi Records; if the records had little impact, Porter's enthusiasm and ambition were undiminished. Nor was he slowed by becoming a teen father, marrying the woman and adding "insurance salesman" to his responsibilities so he could provide a home.

David picked up gigs as a vocalist with Booker T. & the MG's. When they'd go out on weekends—weekdays they stayed in the studio—they'd flesh out their set with soulful covers of contemporary hits, sung by Porter. Estelle pressed Jim to audition David as a vocalist. Jim didn't share her faith, but the value of her taste had long been proven, so he dutifully listened. Stax released Porter's first single as a vocalist in January of 1965. He was twenty-four years old and the father of two, working at the grocery, selling insurance, and traveling with the MG's. That's busty, it's no wonder that his song title was "Can't See You When I Want To."

"David and I went to rival high schools and we sang in rival groups," says Isaac Hayes, reflecting upon their partnership's genesis. "I had known David, but not that well." Hayes's stock at Stax had been on the rise. His talent for arranging the instruments was increasingly respected. "I always had ideas but I was the last resort. If they'd get stumped on a session, then

David Porter (left) and Isaac Hayes, songwriters. (Promotional photo by API Photographers/Deanie Parker Collection)

they'd say, 'What you got, Ike?' I'd offer them my little ideas and they started to work, and before you knew it I was arranging a lot."

David had no shortage of song ideas, but he needed a musical partner to fully realize them. He and Steve Cropper collaborated on what became the first single for Sam and Dave, but Porter had yet to find the yin to his yang.

"David approached me with the intention of selling me an insurance policy," remembers Isaac, who was finding himself cowriting with the MG's, individually and as a group. ("Banana Juice" by the Mar-Keys is evidence of the fun Isaac was having.) "During our conversation, we discovered that we had similar interests. He said, 'Ike, I'm a lyric man, and you're a music man, let's do like Holland-Dozier and Bacharach and David!'" Porter was working with Raymond Moore, a high school friend who wrote poetry, and they brought in Hayes to help finish the song "How Do You Quit (Someone You Love)," which Carla Thomas recorded. Hayes and Porter felt like something might click, and they persisted. "After fifteen or twenty duds we began to find our niche," Isaac says. "We experimented a lot. That's why we had so much success for Sam and Dave, because I would try new types of melodies and new horn riffs and different sounds."

Sam and Dave did not initially find Stax a welcoming environment. "I don't think Jim ever laughed," says Sam Moore. "It was always business: Get in there and do your job. We'd take a break and when it's time to go back, he would come through and say, 'Gentlemen, are we ready?' That was it. I felt no warmth from him towards Sam and Dave."

But Hayes and Porter were feeding them fire. "Sam and Dave didn't have a style," Sam reflects. "Isaac Hayes gave us a style." Isaac Hayes was someone who could sit at the piano and put a song together, pointing to each person and playing their part, then standing in the middle of the room to coach everyone together. He was producing and didn't know it, and he produced Sam and Dave right onto the hit charts. "When we first started, there was just a verse, chorus, and then try and harmonize it out. Isaac Hayes, bless his heart, he gave me and Dave the style, all the call-and-response, the horns became the background singers, the rhythm keeping the beat—it's Isaac Hayes."

For Sam and Dave, it began to come together a few months later with "I Take What I Want," written by Hayes and Porter, along with a sixteen-year-old guitarist named Mabon "Teenie" Hodges. Hodges was a rising star in Willie Mitchell's band, and when he protested that he knew nothing about writing songs, Teenie remembers them saying, "All you've got to do is play like you play onstage. Just do it your own way. You do it all the time." The experience unlocked a door inside him, and he'd go on to write several huge hits for Al Green, Bonnie Raitt, and others.

"David had this old Ford, and you could tell where we'd been because we'd leave a trail of seat-cushion foam," Isaac laughs. "It'd fall out the bottom of his car. And we rode in that car for—it seemed like forever. We'd walk down the street, they'd see us with attaché cases, and they'd tease us. 'Hey hitmakers, how many hits y'all write today?' But we just kept trudging on, relentlessly, and finally we struck it. And then everybody wanted to be a songwriter."

"I Take What I Want" didn't sell well enough to land on the charts, but it gave Hayes and Porter the material they needed to begin honing Sam and Dave into the breakout act they were about to become.

◆ ◆ ◆

IN MEMPHIS, STAX existed largely in a vacuum. Outside the black community, it was largely unknown, because most whites simply never acknowledged the black community, ghettoized mostly to the north and south of downtown. Similarly, the sanitation workers were invisible men, keeping the city clean, seen but rarely acknowledged. T.O. Jones, however, was relentless in seeking the formal acknowledgment of the city for the sanitation workers, despite being shut out seemingly everywhere he turned. The recognition he sought was for fair treatment on the job, respect as human beings, and for the same opportunities that whites were offered—all of which could come through workers united in a union. Jones made contact

with AFSCME—the American Federation of State, County and Municipal Employees—and at a November 1964 meeting attended by sanitation
workers, supported by leaders from the black community and churches
(no longer afraid of offending the mayor they'd helped elect), a charter
was adopted for the Local 1733—the "33" in honor of the men fired the
previous year. Jones was elected president. Pete Sisson, the commissioner
they'd supported, responded by firing the five, though, from the department who'd been elected as the new union's officers. The city was clearly
stating it would recognize no union for these black men.

A couple months later—long enough to suggest the adoption of the
union was not compelling him—Sisson began getting his thirteen hundred "unclassified" workers onto the Social Security rolls. These were the
employees on the trucks who were subject to whimsical firing and labor
abuse, and Social Security had been one of their requests. Sisson also stan-
dardized the department's pay scale, and on some trucks he added heat.
The workers remained "unclassified," and when in the swelter of August 1966 Commissioner Sisson received word that a strike might be imminent, he sent letters to seven hundred former workers announcing
available jobs should the sanitation employees strike; he would fire en
masse those on strike and hire those ready to take the abuse.

The unionized men—about five hundred of them—met on Saturday
night, August 21, 1966. Jones informed them that the city was not going to
recognize Local 1733 as their bargaining agent, it was not going to proffer
a written contract to the men, and it would not agree to better working
conditions. The men voted to strike, but the following day, after a special
session of the City Commission, a chancellor issued an injunction ordering
the municipal workers not to strike, saying the action would "cause an
emergency condition . . . greatly affecting the health, safety and general
welfare of the people of the City of Memphis." Though some men showed
up to picket in the wee hours of Monday morning, a defeated T.O. Jones
told them the city had outmaneuvered them. Public Works again, after a
time, made further concessions; it introduced three-wheeled carts to replace the leaky tubs men carried on their heads, it gave the men rain gear,
open trucks were replaced with mechanical packers, and the men received
a ten-cent-an-hour raise.

◆ ◆ ◆

AROUND THIS TIME, though nothing changed at Stax, everything changed.
Without really becoming aware of it, Stax had become an entity to be
reckoned with. It was a supplier of hits to Atlantic—*relied upon* for hits.

Atlantic still produced its own material in New York, but the hot stuff on the label came from Memphis, from Stax. Sam and Dave were on the rise, Otis Redding was raging, and the MG's and Carla and Rufus were each regularly landing on the pop charts. Further, Stax was expanding its sound with new vocal groups: The Mad Lads hit number-eleven R&B with "Don't Have to Shop Around," and the Astors hit number twelve with the catchy, post-doo-wop Cropper-Hayes collaboration "Candy." Even as there were grumblings that Atlantic wasn't doing enough to promote Stax's material, Atlantic expanded its reliance on Stax, sending to Memphis an artist they knew was capable of hits but who'd been unable to find his groove.

Wilson Pickett was a popular singer in New York City nightclubs, but to the rest of the world he was basically a has-been if he was known at all. He'd been singing with a Detroit vocal group named the Falcons, who'd enjoyed a minor hit with "I Found a Love." The Falcons had three lead vocalists—Pickett, Eddie Floyd, and Bonnie "Mack" Rice. They harmonized beautifully, and they passed around the lead microphone. But Pickett wasn't prone to share; the spotlight throws a large circle, and he believed he could fill it. Instead of breaking out, though, he was going broke.

Jerry Wexler at Atlantic saw the stealthlike beauty of Pickett onstage, could hear in his growl the latent soul power, and quickly agreed to make a solo star of the man who looked like he just walked out of *Esquire* magazine. "Before Black Panthers were a political issue I used to call him the Black Panther," Wexler says. "It was like he was made out of steel and baling wire, so handsome, and I just loved his voice. When James Brown used to scream, it was a scream. When Pickett screamed, it was a musical note—a great advantage."

But so far Pickett was all gas, no fuse. "I was very critical about material," Pickett says. "Wexler used to bring me a whole suitcase full of records he wanted me to do. Me and him almost had a falling-out because he was bringing too many Rascals records, Rolling Stones, Beatles—these kind of things. I was trying to create an original career of Wilson Pickett." Pickett had been spending time on the road, playing the radio while the car crawled between distant chitlin-circuit towns, and one voice with the sound he wanted kept coming over those stations. "I was touring through the South and I kept hearing on the radio this guy, Otis Redding"—and Pickett breaks into singing "Pain in My Heart"—"and the horns and everything. So I said, 'Jerry, this is the direction I want to go.'"

Wexler produced a single with Pickett in New York that made little impact, and the Panther was pacing. "We could never get together on material—ever," says Wexler. "So his manager, a little mobbed-up Italian guy that was very nice to me, finally said, 'Listen, do it or else.'"

"Jerry said, 'Okay, baby, I'll hook you up with it,'" Pickett recounts. "So he hooked me up with the Stax family down in Memphis. And then it was no turning back."

"I said, 'Okay, Jerry, send him down,'" Jim says. "I was really trying to help them out." So Stax paused in its own work to help Pickett, who wasn't even on the label. (Jim arranged for the studio to have points in the profits of their collaborations.)

Jim told Steve about the upcoming project, asking him to prepare some material for consideration. "I said, 'Who is Wilson Pickett?'" remembers Steve. He tried to buy Pickett's albums, but there were none. He did find a single or two in the Satellite Record Shop, and there was an album from the Apollo with a variety of Atlantic acts—including Rufus Thomas and Pickett. "Wilson had one track at the end of the album," Steve says, "and it was maybe four minutes long but for two minutes all he said was, 'Hey baby, I'm going to get you the midnight hour. I can't wait until the midnight hour,' and so that's all I had to go on."

In May 1965, Wexler flew to Memphis ahead of Pickett. He had business to do, a client to ready, a handshake that needed warming: His lawyers had drafted the distribution agreement. And in addition to those business needs, there was a personal need. Wexler wanted to share the recording experience Tom Dowd had talked about: freedom from the three-hour session clock, the excitement of head charts and making up the arrangements on the spot, conviviality and a sense of teamwork for the greater good. Just seeing it done would be touching the hem of the garment.

On the eleventh, Wexler and Jim (sporting a goatee, now that he was free of the bank) delivered Pickett from the airport to a hotel where Steve was waiting, and the two musicians sipped from a bottle of bourbon and listened first to a handful of singles that Pickett brought—recent releases that he liked. "Cropper got a good idea of which way he wanted to take these things," says Pickett. Steve adds, "He had this tune that he'd been working on and he played a couple verses for me, and I said, 'That's out of sight, so let's build it around that one.' And that's what happened."

"We left," says Wexler, "and the next morning they came in with the song 'In the Midnight Hour.'" Booker T. was off at school, Isaac Hayes had his day job in a slaughterhouse, so piano that day was Joe Hall. He'd played at the Plantation Inn, and was the original piano player at Hi Records, helping to establish the Bill Black Combo.

"Steve Cropper and that group of fellows were so together, they knew what each was going to do—break here, or cut there, or leap there," says Pickett. "There were no music charts. Race didn't matter. We were wailing away on 'In the Midnight Hour,' trying to find the right groove to put that sucker in. Jerry Wexler was in the control room, and was unhappy about something."

He was unhappy about the song not having found its groove, though considering that twenty-four hours before there'd been no such song on earth, one could say it was coalescing speedily. But Wexler was not hearing the *oomph* that he needed, that he could feel nascent in the song. Dowd's story about participation was fresh in his mind. After giving various suggestions over the intercom, he realized that the issue was with the bass and the rhythm, and that the best way to explain how he was hearing it was to dance to it. "I get this idea about a beat from [the song] 'The Cool Jerk,' delaying at two and four. So I go out in the studio and I start dancing—like a fool. I'm sure they couldn't hide their mirth, you know, this old man doing the Cool Jerk."

The embers were smoking, but the song wouldn't flame. "I had a different guitar part worked out that was the major lick," says Steve. "And Jerry said, 'Can you just do a backbeat thing?' And he's, like, pulling his arms down, and doing this dance that he'd seen somewhere. He made it go, 'I'm gonna wait till the midnight hour,' *boom*, 'that's when . . .' It was great, and it certainly simplified my part."

"In the Midnight Hour" entered the R&B chart on May 26, 1965, at number thirty-five. Over the next six weeks it climbed to number one and spent nearly three months on the chart; it spent about the same time on the Hot 100, reaching number twenty-one. "My experience in Memphis was the first time I'd encountered southern recording," Wexler continues. "Instead of working from written arrangements, they built the record organically—not deductively. I'd see the MG's come to work in the morning, hang up their coats, gather up their axes, and start playing music. Maybe it was some chord changes, maybe it was a lick, maybe it was a song, but they started playing, they started building it. I said, My God, this is fantastic."

Not only was Wexler's joy in the creative process revived: He also took care of business. On May 17, 1965, the handshake between Jim and Jerry was formalized as a contract between Stax and Atlantic. The numbers were standard, such as "standard" exists in the record business: Stax would receive fifteen cents for each single sold, and 10 percent of the retail list price on albums, and Stax would be responsible for paying the artists. Jim, not wanting to be stuck in a deal with a bunch of strangers he didn't trust, had asked for a key-man clause, and there it was, written amid the thirteen pages of agreement. That seemed like a lot of words for expressing what had worked with none for five years already, but Jim figured Atlantic was a large company and lawyers had to earn their money too. If Atlantic were making any changes, surely they'd have discussed it, like he would have with them. Jim was a southern man, forthright, decent. His word was his bond. "I didn't bother to go down and read the whole distribution agreement," Jim says. "I did not read the fine print in the contract. I more or less went on a gentlemen's agreement." When the Atlantic contract was placed before him, when he confirmed that his key-man request had been satisfied, he signed. He signed like Jerry knew he would, like anyone who knew Jim knew he would.

10. A ROCKET IN WING TIPS
1965–1966

THE SUMMER OF 1965 was hot even without feeling the temperature. President Johnson had escalated the war in Vietnam and would commit half a million troops before year's end, opening a ground war. In April, 28,500 soldiers were there, and the next month, the number more than doubled to 68,500. William C. Brown, the neighborhood kid who'd run into the building when Jim first explored it, and his Mad Lads bandmate John Gary Williams both shipped out to the war overseas. "Miz Axton would pack them a box every month," says Don Nix, "candies and things, and anybody who was around could throw stuff in. She'd ship it. When William came home, he said those things kept him alive over there." Songwriter Homer Banks had returned the year before and landed a job in the record shop. Booker would have gone as a second lieutenant without his college deferment. "I was the battle group commander for Booker T. Washington High School," he says. "I could dismantle an M1 blindfolded by the time I cut 'Green Onions.' I knew that gun inside and out."

William Bell returned from his two years of service and memorialized the time in his single "Marching off to War," the B-side of "Share What You Got." Set to a martial beat, this story of a soldier being shipped out and saying good-bye to his sweetheart captures the mid-1960s zeitgeist, the young man's quandary: duty versus freedom, R-O-T-C versus L-O-V-E.

Five years since Rufus and Carla put Stax on the map, the label and studio were coming into their own. The company released about thirty-five singles in 1964, double what it had done two years earlier, and it would maintain that output in '65. Jim Stewart was no longer distracted by his day job at the bank, Otis Redding's "I've Been Loving You Too Long" was working its way to number two. Most important, the cogs had locked into place: the MG's and Isaac supplied the music; Lady A, from behind the store's sales counter, oversaw a creative songwriting team (David Porter, Deanie Parker, Steve Cropper, and, well, just about everyone there); and Jim Stewart supervised it all. The machine was well-oiled, in fine shape, and breaking with ease into high gear.

Estelle, from the counter of the record shop, handled much of the promotional duties. DJs were fun to talk to—jive artists with effervescent personalities and strong opinions on the music. DJs were always on the make, angling to earn a little extra scratch—free copies they could sell, touring artists they could book for their local sock hop, anything to make a dime. (Distributors, on the other hand, were not as fun to talk to; they often owed money and were slow paying. Jim handled those calls, which usually ended with shouting. Jim had quit the bank and here he was, still chasing the unpaid accounts.)

Estelle kept up with the hits, and she could give with the DJs as good as she got. She'd become tight with the top R&B jock in Los Angeles, the Magnificent Montague. His catchphrase "Burn, baby, burn," had become part of the LA street lexicon. On the phone, they hatched a plan to bring a Stax Revue to Los Angeles. DJs made side money promoting performances, and Montague was deep into the Stax sound; he'd be a good promoter. The West Coast was where Stax needed help. As the plan developed, the trip grew to two weeks and included radio appearances and TV shows. A broadcast on KGFJ, Montague's station, was arranged— that would get the general word out. Carla Thomas and the Astors were booked on Dick Clark's TV show, *Where the Action Is;* Carla's "Stop! Look What You're Doin'" was breaking the top forty, and the Astors were hot with "Candy." The MG's were booked on *Hollywood A Go Go* playing one of their most aggressive songs, the guitar-heavy R&B top-ten hit "Boot-Leg." It features the bar-walking sax of Packy Axton, who shares cowriting credit with Isaac Hayes, Al Jackson, and Duck Dunn. Ostracized at the studio due to his alcohol abuse, Packy was woven into this trip; his mom was organizing and chaperoning it. ("It was a very strange thing to watch him drink himself to death," says Don Nix, from the Mar-Keys. "You went to school with this guy since the fifth grade and to watch him turn into an old man in just a few years, it was tough. He knew it was gonna kill him.") Rufus Thomas, William Bell, and Wilson Pickett were part of the entourage, and their other television appearances included *Shindig* and *The Lloyd Thaxton Show*. It was a media frenzy, generating coverage in *Billboard* (an August 7, 1965, headline reads, STAX AND VOLT ARTISTS ON TV) and guaranteeing packed houses for the two nights of the gig Montague was promoting. He booked them into the 5-4 Ballroom, one of the hottest venues in Watts, a large African-American neighborhood in LA akin, somewhat, to Harlem in New York. (The 5-4 has been described as the Apollo of Watts.) Playing there, they'd reach the heart of their audience, a solid foundation on which the label could build.

The group's live sound was aggressive, playing faster and harder without losing the feel—sharp-edged. Montague was all over the mike, hyping the audience with his trademark chant, the audience fueling the artists' flames with their enthusiasm. "Boot-Leg" may be the show's highlight, the MG's crunching the music like a hard rock band. It was summer and hot, and many in the state were angry over a proposition that overturned recent fair housing laws, giving landlords and sellers the right to openly discriminate; the proposition was so reactionary that all federal housing funds to California were terminated. No one could have known during the trip's planning that long-standing racial tension in this community would explode coincidental with the Stax appearances. "They were holding lighters and matches and saying, 'Burn, baby, burn,'" says Steve. "And we thought they just loved us to death but, naw, they were talking about something else."

While in California, Estelle took advantage of the distance between herself and her brother. Packy may have become a drunk, but he was still her son. So with Montague's connection to recording studios and the greatest house band in the world among her entourage, and in a land where being female and an older sister didn't restrict her like back home, she booked studio time and paid out of her pocket. Packy and the MG's cut an album's worth of instrumentals, including "Hole in the Wall," a relaxed, jazzy tune in the mode of the recently released "The In Crowd"—perfectly catchy. Montague dropped in audience sounds and released the single on his own label, calling the band "The Packers." "Hole in the Wall" took off, and word—or sound—got back to Memphis as it spread across the nation. The song hit number five on the R&B chart, nearly cracked the top forty on the pop chart, and the album hit number seven.

"Estelle could make a recommendation, or try to persuade Jim to do something, or be very adamant about something that she felt strongly about," says Deanie Parker, "and Jim would just—he would be a typical little brother. 'Oh, Estelle, you don't know, how can you know what you're talking about?' And she had that pose: She liked to smoke Parliament cigarettes, and she would fold one arm underneath her elbow, hold that cigarette, and she would say without looking at him, 'Yes-I-do-know-what-I'm-talking-about. This is a hit. And all we need to do is add some horn lines to this, Jim, and put it out.'"

The Stax hit on another label really heightened the pressure between the siblings. It can't have helped that Packy—who Jim saw as an irresponsible derelict—was at the center of it. "I hit the ceiling," says Jim. "It was like giving away a hit record." (Not that he'd have allowed Packy in to cut it at Stax.) Montague's publishing company claimed every track, and the writing credits all included Montague, with the present MG's sharing in "Hole," and Packy sharing in only one track, which was not coincidentally the single's B-side. Estelle's response to Jim's "how could you" was likely simple: Since you wouldn't listen to me, I did it myself.

"My sister has a lot of ideas," Jim says. "She's got a great ear for certain kinds of records, especially a left-field record. But after that fiasco with Montague, I really shut her down. I had to. I was very adamant about my artists playing on other records." Jim wanted Packy banned from Stax, but with his mother as co-owner, he was never completely out of the picture.

By the time most of the artists were flying home on August 11, the tense energy felt at the gigs was just being released—a highway patrol car had stopped a couple of black men in Watts, a crowd gathered, unrest fomented, and rocks were hurled. Several Stax artists saw smoke from the city as their plane departed. The next day, protests grew in Watts, and shortly, four thousand California National Guard troops were called out. Rioters numbered nearly thirty-five thousand. Over six days, thirty-four people were killed, hundreds injured, and tens of millions of dollars in damages occurred. "The story I got," says Steve, "was that one of the first buildings to burn was the liquor store next to the 5-4 Ballroom." Only days earlier, President Johnson had signed the Voting Rights Act, with Martin Luther King and Rosa Parks among his special guests.

◆ ◆ ◆

As a promotional trip, Los Angeles had been a huge success, and it confirmed that many and varied promotional possibilities awaited if Stax had someone devoted to creating them. Estelle, Steve Cropper, and Jim had all come to this realization independently, though Estelle's trip brought the need to the fore. "Jim Stewart recognized that if he were to continue doing what he loved doing most—and that was discovering and developing new talent, and recording hit after hit in Studio A," says Deanie, who worked to get reviews and newspaper articles about the artists, "then he needed someone else to make certain that that product was being promoted on the radio. After all, the money came from the sale of records." Only one person was really considered for the job, because the Stax folk knew who it should be: Al Bell, the former Memphis disc jockey who had moved to Washington, DC, and been responsible for breaking many Stax artists on the East Coast.

Al Bell was the Otis Redding of business. A head taller than almost everyone, he shot like a rocket in wing tip shoes. "Walk with me as we talk," he'd say, on the move and getting things done, two at a time, minimally. His manner was authoritative, his demeanor approachable. He favored suits, always a necktie, a color-coordinated handkerchief, and he presented like a bank vice president, a career yet beyond reach for African-Americans. "Sales?" he might say. "Have you seen our sales thermometer this month? Nearly double last month's sales and that's the fourth month running." Then he'd stop and look in your eye, hold your arm above your elbow, say something like, "But better than the income, the money is flowing back to the community. The way out of this social mess is economic empowerment, getting the money into the hands of the people." Al Bell—his full name was Alvertis Isbell—inspired people, opening their eyes to possibilities accessible and dreams attainable.

The ken of Al's vision was a testament to the depth of his soul. He'd been raised in rural, racist Brinkley, Arkansas, and that which was intended to keep him down had planted the very seed from which his vision grew. "I grew up in a neighborhood that was obviously segregated. You had your blacks together and whites together, and then you had your various socioeconomic groups. Not too far from us was the working white community. There was a white man who had a fruit stand and small grocery about a half a block from where we lived, and he raised pedigree bulldogs. And that's a place I was able to go and make a little money cleaning up after those filthy bulldogs. And this man inspired me, 'cause I heard him say one day, he said, 'Niggers can't do nothing but sing and dance.' Well, it offended me. But it kept me thinking. And one day, for some odd reason, I realized: Singing and dancing, you make a lot of money. So that's not a problem, that's an opportunity."

In the latter 1950s, Alvertis prepared for the ministry at an Alabama

Bible college, and for the business world at Arkansas's Philander Smith College, where he hosted a radio program on the newly established KOKY, Little Rock, Arkansas's first radio station programmed for an African-American audience. He established a small record label and began promoting concerts and dances, both gospel acts and sock hops, forging relationships with the Staple Singers among others. "Being in the record business was fun in college," he says. "The DJ at the dance—everyone wanted to talk to you. You brought the band in, they carried your name to the world beyond, so after the Staple Singers liked you, you might get a call from Dorothy Woods's manager, or Albertina Walker." DJing, Al had a powerful sense of what moved

AL BELL

A **KOKY** *personality*
1440

Your six-feet-four bundle of joy, 212 pounds of Miss Bell's baby boy.

people. During his morning show, the white kids from Central High and the black kids from Dunbar High would congregate in the studio and dance together. While the National Guard was called in to Little Rock in 1957 to desegregate Central High, Al Bell had created one safe interracial haven a few blocks away.

He'd announce, "This is your six-feet-four bundle of joy, two hundred and twelve pounds of Miss Bell's baby boy. Soft as medicated cotton and rich as double-X cream. The women's pet, the men's threat, and the playboy's pride and joy, the baby boy, A-a-a-a-l"—he'd pause to ring a *jingaling*—"Bell."

In 1959, Al left Arkansas and radio to join Dr. Martin Luther King's civil rights movement in Georgia, attending leadership workshops sponsored by the SCLC—the Southern Christian Leadership Conference. "I realized during that period that I desired, like Dr. King, to have peace among us as ethnic groups," Al says, "but I thought we needed to be in pursuit of economic empowerment and building an economic base for us as a people. I believed that our natural resource was music and that we could use it like the Irish used the whiskey, and the South Africans used diamonds. And if we built that economic base, then we could elect representatives in local, state, and national government to put forth laws that would assure that we had equal rights, and we would not be perceived as a liability but as an asset because of the contribution that we would be making to capitalism in this country."

Bell diverged from Dr. King in specifics: "At that time I carried a switchblade knife and was fairly prolific in the utilization of that instrument. On one occasion we had a march in Savannah, Georgia. The whites would holler, 'You nigger!' 'Black SOB!' and all this stuff. The words didn't bother me. But there was a white gentleman, he spit and the spit hit me and I lost my cool. Before I knew it, I was out of my pocket with my switchblade knife, broke rank, and was going through the crowd after this guy. Hosea Williams and Ralph Abernathy came and got me. Doc [Dr. King] talked to me first about my knife. I said, 'Well, Doc, I'm a Bible student myself and Jesus had Peter with him and Peter carried a sword.' He laughed, because he couldn't argue that point. Doc said to me, 'But what I'm doing must come first. The people have to see us on television. They have to recognize that we even exist on the earth as a people and secondly, these dogs have to bite us, some of us have to be killed, we have to be beaten by these police and all of that so that the rest of the world could see how we have been treated.'"

Al left Georgia but not the movement, and in short order he was on radio in Memphis. The Satellite Record Shop and Stax studio provided him with material for his program, and when he moved to DC, a significantly larger, more active, African-American market, he took the sounds of Memphis with him and maintained his contacts at Stax. "Jim would send me dubs [preview copies of songs] and call me," Al says. "He knew I had my fingers on the pulse of that market."

In DC, Bell had formed Safice Records with two new friends—singer and songwriter Eddie Floyd and promotional man Chester Simmons. (The name Safice is a jumble of the three men's first and last initials.) The label cut a good song on Eddie Floyd, which Atlantic picked up for distribution, establishing a relationship between Al and Jerry Wexler. Al knew that Carla Thomas was at Howard University in Washington, DC, and early in 1965 he pitched her a couple songs he and Eddie Floyd had written, "Stop! Look What You're Doin'," and "Comfort Me." Carla was fond of Al from his Memphis days and liked the songs; under Al's direction, she cut demos at the radio station after it shut down at 5:30. He sent the demos to Memphis, and they came back with an invitation for him and Eddie Floyd to attend the Stax sessions. Soon, Bell and Floyd were in and out of town, writing songs with Steve Cropper and others, attending sessions. These occasional visits back to the fold energized the idea of inviting Al into the organization. The only problem was the perennial one: money, and the lack thereof.

Jim didn't like the idea of adding more staff, and he argued that

Atlantic was doing fine promoting its product to DJs. "We needed promotion," Estelle says. "We were making some hit records, and we needed help getting them played all over the country. Al was a good communicator, and he could convince these disc jockeys and program directors to play the records. That all goes along together—you can have a hit, but if you can't get it heard, you can't sell it."

"Business-wise, we were getting a little lost in the shuffle," says Steve. "If a promotion guy walks into a radio station and he's got six Atlantic records and one Stax record, what's gonna happen?"

Weighing his options, Jim liked the idea of lightening his business responsibilities, assuring him more creative time in the studio. He'd known Al since pitching him the Veltones record during Al's college radio days. "My sister kept screaming we needed somebody to promote our product," Jim says. "Al and I were friends when he was in Memphis, and when he went to Washington, I kept in touch. In my meager way, I had to promote the records." Al had the skills and connections, and though Jim claims not to have weighed skin color in his decision—"I never thought of it in terms of needing to hire a black man"—hiring Al would enhance the administration's credibility among the employees. They were already walking the walk, but assigning this authority to an African-American would mollify any potential political undercurrents. "Al was into what we were doing," says Jim, "and he was very aggressive. Whatever he believes in, he's going to try to make it happen."

Jim found he could readily agree to the need for a promotions man, but he was adamantly against paying for it. The record business had begun to treat him well. He was driving a Cadillac at the time, but he was a cautious, frugal businessman. "I told Wexler we were bringing in a promotion man," Jim says, "and I felt they should pay half of Al's salary. He would be promoting product they were making money on, too." Wexler agreed to match Stax's $100-per-week offer to Al Bell. This was how you got records played.

"We weren't a professional company before Al," says Booker T. Jones. "We didn't have big business going on. We had big music going on, but not big business. Al Bell was a businessman and a preacher. He wore a suit and tie, but he had a beard and he was announcing Blackness–which wasn't done very much then. So we rallied around him. With Al, someone came in who could talk, who could sell, who knew how to dress, how to bring people together. It galvanized the whole operation. This was 1965 and there were black activists. You could see the cloud building; society was going to change."

Shortly after Al Bell joined Stax. L–R: Shirley Wexler, Jerry Wexler, Betty Cropper, Steve Cropper, Al Bell. (Stax Museum of American Soul Music)

"Jim called me," says Al, "and said, 'I've been talking with my sister and we want to convince you to take over as national promotion director of Stax.' So I said, 'Well, what can you pay me?' He said, 'I can give you a hundred dollars a week, and I talked to Jerry Wexler and he'll also give you one hundred dollars a week.' I said, 'Two hundred bucks?' My involvement in radio, in concert promotions—I was booking in the Howard Theater and Wilmer's Park in Brandywine, Maryland—and my record hops, I was making high five figures in 1965. And he's saying two hundred bucks?" Al laughs at the memory of the conversation.

The salary was not going to draw Al back home, but the potential would. "I had a great love for Stax music, and having seen the reaction of the people in Washington, DC, to that music, and the experiences that I was having with the people at Stax, I had a greater appreciation and belief in what could happen with their music." *That* spoke louder than the paycheck. "At some point," says Jim about the negotiations, "Al said, 'I've got to have more than just a salary.' And we agreed to promising him a percentage of the company."

◆◆◆

THINGS HAPPENED FAST upon Al Bell's arrival in the early autumn of 1965. He fostered an environment with an emphasis on growth. "I took a poster board and drew a thermometer and filled it at the bottom with red ink. As sales increased, and revenue increased, I would increase the mercury. And at the very top of the thermometer, I had it explode out into what I called Heaven. And that was after we had achieved our goal."

"Al said when we filled that bubble at the top," relates Steve, "he's gonna give everybody a bonus. Man, we couldn't wait to come in there on Monday morning and see where that mark was gonna be."

"So every week I'd calibrate the red in the thermometer," Al continues, "and the producers and the writers and any visitors, they'd see that thermometer just increasing, increasing, increasing. And as it increased, the morale increased, and eventually it exploded into Heaven."

The price for all the increased sales was mostly paid by Booker T. & the MG's. Jim worked them hard, but with a passion. "More important than the record," says Jim, "was the making of the record. The fun became work after the tape stopped rolling."

"You could sense Jim's dissatisfaction," says Booker about Jim as a producer. "He would have a tendency to be quiet and look away. But you could tell when he was happy. When he liked a song he'd snap his fingers and dance around." Duck concurs: "He didn't like too many augmented changes, he liked natural. He sat in the control room, would have his head leaning on his hand, and I'd think, What the hell is wrong? We'd be on the floor thinking we were playing our butts off, and he's sitting up there acting like he's bored. I thought, Are you really getting what we're doing out here? But Jim had a great musical ear." "Jim could hear well," Floyd Newman says. "Violin players, they hear concert notes right off. He would say, 'That doesn't sound right, let's change it to this.' There was no browbeating, no domineering. It was very casual, very loose."

Sharing Jim's office, Al received a full course in the Stax world. "What was precious about working in that one office with Jim and spending so many hours with him was his determination to record and release authentic music. I was amazed to hear his passion for Little Walter and Jimmy Reed and Lightnin' Hopkins and B.B. King and all of these blues giants. And it was fascinating to see him go into the studio and with that same passion work those MG's to the point of near exhaustion. Jim would sit behind the board and have the MG's playing and he would not stop or give them a decent look until they had gotten a groove. His favorite criticism was, 'That's too busy.' And it forced them into playing less so you got more. But he worked them, and it got too bad until the guys came to me on one occasion and said, 'Can you do something to convince Jim to get out of the studio a little bit more so we can get a break?' But it was that drive that was in Jim Stewart that really caused Stax to become what it became."

Al also learned from Estelle. "We could always go to Miz Axton and get those words of wisdom," Al says. "I shared with her the problems that I was having with disc jockeys resisting our music. She said, 'Al, have you read a book called *The Power of Positive Thinking*? Go read that book, then come back and ask me that question.' Well, I never went back to her after I read the book because that was the answer. That book had a profound impact on my life. In our growing-up years, we had the musical drive of Jim Stewart, and we had the spiritual drive of Estelle Axton. And all of us came through that."

This was an environment that suited Al Bell. "Al would call his friend in Detroit, and call his friend in LA," says Steve. "He knew a lot of the disc jockeys, and he communicated with these guys. They all liked to know what was going on." Bell was not only promoting, he was exploring. "They would share this information," Steve continues, "and then we would have production meetings. We started doing that every Monday morning, early, before sessions would start. We'd sit down and talk about what the trends were. A lot of times, we'd play stuff we had recorded the week before, and get everybody's feelings about it." Al was cultivating communication, within the building and beyond its walls.

"Al was exclusively in promotion to begin with," Jim says. "He traveled almost constantly. He had to build relationships. He was on the road seventy-five percent of the time in the first couple years. When we hired other promotion men, he began spending more time at the company." The persuasive magic that Al worked over the radio and telephone was ever more powerful in person.

Al had a way of seeing the best in everything. Motown wasn't competition, it was complementary. "Motown was the wind beneath our wings," he explains. "Berry Gordy was a master of taking soul music and giving it the cosmopolitan flavor, great melodies, great rhythms that were immediately accepted by the European-Americans. It made them more comfortable at the radio level and retail with African-Americans." With a dedicated promotions man—and not just anyone, but the formidable Al Bell—Stax was ready to knock on, and knock down, many a door.

11. KINGS AND QUEENS OF SOUL
1965–1966

A PROMOTIONS MAN needs records to promote, and the timing of Al Bell's arrival was serendipitous. As he was settling in, the studio was delivering great material: an artistic breakthrough by Otis Redding; a Mad Lads hit that Al could peddle in the Northeast, where his connections were solid and fresh; and the establishment of a style by Sam and Dave. Stax had been releasing great records all along, but with Al on staff dedicated to getting airplay, he made his heavenly explosion a reality.

By the summer of 1965, Otis was on a hot streak. "I've Been Loving You Too Long" had begun creeping up the charts less than a month after its release. "Mr. Pitiful" had just slipped off the charts, but not off the DJs' turntables. Each of his previous singles had hit the pop charts, sometimes each side charting separately as a hit. Fortunately for Stax, as Al Bell signed on, so did Otis, reupping his contract for another five years. Why not? Jim had just re-signed with Atlantic, solidifying that relationship. Otis got an improved royalty rate—5 percent when previously he'd had 3 percent. There was a living to be made as a successful recording artist, but the fast money and the bigger money came through performance fees.

Living the dream, Otis wore out the road, taking his thirteen-piece band everywhere he could get a gig. Hit records drew more people to the shows, getting him into bigger clubs, allowing him to command higher fees. But every night he was in the studio meant he was not getting a gig fee, and it was becoming harder to get him to swing through Stax. Finally, with enough planning, a session was squeezed into his summer '65 schedule: He'd arrive and polish some material with Steve Cropper the first day, then they'd hit the studio to record as much as they could in about twenty-four hours; after a nap, he'd fly out to his next gig. The intention was to complete an album, which would be his third. Albums were a way to repackage established hits, surrounding them with misses and studio extras; profit margins were higher on albums, so record labels liked to get them out such as the hits allowed—and "I've Been Loving You Too Long" was providing an opportunity.

For reasons lost to history, the days Otis could get off the road fell on a Friday and Saturday, meaning he would miss the weekend gig opportunities and several of the Stax band would have to break during the marathon session to make their gigs. The task was monumental, and Jim asked Atlantic's Tom Dowd to come help him engineer. "I got a call midweek," says Tom, " 'Can you be here by Friday at noontime?' And I said, 'Yeah, sure, what's happening?' And they said, 'We gotta make an album with Otis but he's got a gig on Sunday.' So I got to the studio and it was done in a day and a night, and then Otis was gone!"

The session—an all-nighter with horns, vocals, and full band being recorded live and without overdubs—resulted in one of the greatest soul music albums ever recorded, *Otis Blue*. It's a telling snapshot of where Otis, Stax, and soul music found themselves in July 1965. Half a year earlier, Sam Cooke had been murdered in Los Angeles, and Redding— whose raw and gritty style was very different from the smooth and suave

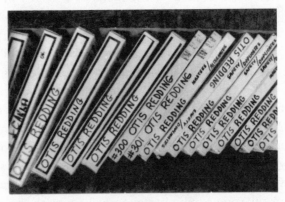

(Photograph by Don Nix/Courtesy of the Oklahoma Museum of Popular Culture, Steve Todoroff Collection)

sounds of Cooke—pays tribute to the man and his influence, recording three of his songs, including a solemn and moving take on "A Change Is Gonna Come." Defining soul music's breadth—the album's subtitle is *Otis Redding Sings Soul*—he renders a blues from B.B. King; a funked-up take on the traditional "Down in the Valley" ("Oh, man," says Duck Dunn about that one, "he took a song and just kicked your ass with it"); a gritty take on the Rolling Stones' "Satisfaction" (a reciprocation for their cutting his "That's How Strong My Love Is"—and a reach for that elusive white audience); a pared-down Memphis arrangement of Motown's "My Girl"; and, for the home team, William Bell's "You Don't Miss Your Water." The album is jarring in its intensity. "Old Man Trouble" opens, the guitar immediate and doleful—No, no, no, it can't be this sad—and the horns hit—Yes, yes, yes, it will be this sad, and Otis pleads on our behalf such that we'd want no one else pleading for us.

And then there is "Respect." "Respect" is one of Otis Redding's greatest songs, and a perfect example of Al Jackson's leadership in the studio. Drums are often considered a group's anchor, but in this case, the drums are the grand marshal. The song starts as a 4/4 pounding, and the band, the singer, the horns—everyone's chugging along to keep up with the drummer. By the song's end, you can almost feel the group's effort to maintain Al's pace. His fills are battle cries, announcing the emphatic moments. At the song's end, it's a duet between drums and vocalist, the band serenading them. "Respect" belies the notion that the Memphis groove was just behind the beat; sometimes it may have been ("Last Night" comes to mind), but sometimes it was way ahead. The groove was where Al Jackson wanted it to be.

Otis's manager, Phil Walden, was just being discharged from the military and he came straight to Memphis to see Otis in the studio. "While Phil was gone," says Dowd, "Otis had become a successful artist. Phil came to Memphis and Joe Galkin ran out to the airport. It was Saturday, we were about seven or eight songs done, and Phil was standing there in uniform with his discharge ribbons on and he's saying, 'Ah cain't believe it!' Ha ha . . . *Boom! Poof!* Next! We knocked off the whole album in a day and a night." Joe Galkin arranged for Jim to cut Otis in on the publishing, and Phil established a publishing company for Otis—and himself—using the Stax model of nomenclature (Redding-Walden) to form Redwal; "Respect" was the first song they published, which paid dividends in 1967 when Aretha Franklin took her version of the song to number one on the pop charts. Also riding along was Stax's publishing company, East Music, and Galkin's publishing company, Time; so on "Respect," for example, every publishing penny that came in was split three ways, with each company then paying the writer half. (The standard publishing deal split the money fifty-fifty between the publishing company and the writer; if a writer had enough clout to have his own company, he got more of the pot; many who didn't know about publishing got less, or none.) The publisher nearly always got paid.

Otis Blue gave Al Bell plenty of material to promote. Three singles hit the top five of the R&B charts—"I've Been Loving You Too Long," "Respect," and "Satisfaction." The album hit number seventy-five on the pop charts, and if it didn't sell enough at once to burst higher, it sold steadily, present on the album chart for thirty-four weeks.

Otis slept a bit when the session was done, then shot out to his next gig. He'd burn up the road, expanding his popularity for the next half year, returning to Stax in early November 1965 to record another masterpiece, the Al Jackson–led, Duck Dunn–fueled, inspired-horns-afire "I Can't Turn You Loose." Opening with Duck's slinky, hip-shaking bass riff, the part doubled by Steve's guitar, Al joins hot on their heels, pounding the drums like a raging child, the horns playing what has to be one of their greatest-ever get-up-on-your-feet riffs—and that's just in the song's first five seconds. It never lets up, nearly three minutes of propulsion, and is neck and neck with "Respect" for the greatest dance song Otis ever recorded, the greatest drumming Al Jackson ever delivered.

The gigs were paying off for Otis. He bought 270 acres outside Macon, naming it the Big O Ranch, and built a beautiful twelve-room home for his family there. In an effort to see more of his wife and three kids, he bought a small plane. But mostly he stayed on the road, playing the gigs, with Phil Walden angling for that pop crossover, booking him into Los Angeles's Whisky a Go Go club for a three-day run in the spring of 1966. The hottest club on the famed Sunset Strip, it had clientele accustomed to rock and folk-rock bands—the Byrds, Johnny Rivers, the Doors—and if soul music was something they'd heard of, it was distant, exotic, unfamiliar. Otis's reputation was powerful enough to attract a full house for the first night, but the audience's lack of response to the MC's opening exhortations was evidence of the bridge to be crossed. When Otis took the stage, instincts kicked in and the West Coast whites couldn't help but groove to the good tunes. Seven sets over three nights were packed. Pioneering producer Phil Spector invited Otis to his house; Bob Dylan came backstage with an acetate of "Just Like a Woman," a song he wanted Otis to record. (Otis later told Phil Walden it had too many words.) "His gig at the Whisky a Go Go was probably the most exciting thing that rock-worn room has ever harbored," wrote *Los Angeles Times* critic Pete Johnson. "He was a magic singer with an unquenchable store of energy and a great flittering band. Crowds never sat still when he was onstage nor could they stay quiet when he asked them for a response, because he gave them too much to leave them strangers."

In late 1966, Otis made his first visit to Europe. *Otis Blue* had hit the top of the European charts, indicating a strong welcome awaited. Further, breaking into Europe could be a way to the hearts of America's white audience; the British Invasion of new music was in full swing. Phil booked ten days, including an incendiary TV appearance on *Ready, Steady, Go!*, and the payoff came pretty quick, with famed San Francisco promoter Bill Graham showing up on Phil Walden's Georgia doorstep to invite Otis for three nights at the Fillmore. "Every artist in [San Francisco] asked to open for Otis," Graham writes in his autobiography. "The first night, it was the Grateful Dead. Janis Joplin came at three in the afternoon the day of the first show to make sure that she'd be in front. To this day, no musician ever got *everybody* out to see them the way he did."

As Otis's popularity spread, he brought Stax with him. "Otis was growing in record sales and public acceptance," Al says from the front lines. "Otis was becoming our standard-bearer. The world was beginning to view Stax as Otis Redding, and when they heard Stax music, they heard Otis Redding."

◆ ◆ ◆

ONE GROUP AT Stax that stood out from the others was the Mad Lads. Instead of the gritty soul tradition, they were four male singers influenced by the smooth vocal harmonies of the Philadelphia and Baltimore doo-wop groups. This sound didn't interest Jim very much, but Estelle liked the guys and, never dissuaded by the tension with her brother, she encouraged them. "Estelle had been trying to persuade Jim to cultivate a group of male vocalists that could rival this spectacular harmony coming off the East Coast," says Deanie. Singer William C. Brown worked in her record shop; he and John Gary Williams, John Phillips, and Julius Green were always around there singing. "I named them the Mad Lads," says Deanie, "because that is what they were: energetic and all over the place." Mrs. Axton suggested she and Deanie collaborate on a song for them. "She

Deanie Parker and Al Jackson Jr. (Deanie Parker Collection)

brought a book of poems one day, told me, 'Read some of these poems, they're so simple.' Estelle loved a simple message. She loved love songs—I think she was a romantic at heart. She wrote the first verse and titled it 'I Want Someone.' Then I wrote the melody and we finished it. Then, she says, 'Now let's get the Mad Lads.'"

"I Want Someone" features vibrato-heavy instruments—you can't tell if it's a guitar or an organ, and it sounds like it's floating to the top of a fish tank in bursts of bubbles. (It's Isaac on the organ, at Packy's suggestion. "Packy said, 'I hear a sound like Shep and the Limelites,'" says Packy's friend Johnny Keyes. "He said, 'Can you do that on the organ?'") The vocals knit a fabric made of blues, pop, and church, handing off lines to horns, or harmonizing with them. "We taught the Mad Lads that song and produced that record," Deanie continues. "It became a big hit. She made her point to Jim, and I was thrilled to be a part of another one of her little enterprises." Al Bell used "I Want Someone" and also the group's "Don't Have to Shop Around" to insinuate them with his cohorts in Philadelphia, Baltimore, Washington, New York, and Boston. Once in these markets with the Mad Lads, Al would have plenty more to offer.

Estelle's ongoing battles with Jim were not shouting matches (well, rarely so), and were not usually bitter. "It was productive competition," Deanie says. "It was a family at Stax, and Jim and Estelle played a major role in that. And we were extensions of their philosophies."

In addition to vocal groups, Estelle wanted the company to put out more blues. While soul music had decidedly become the new sound of young African-American society, blues remained a very popular seller in the record store. Jim, however, saw no sizable market for straight blues. When Albert King came strolling into Estelle's record shop, she approached him . . . like a spider to a fly. "I'd been selling blues records on other artists and I had to do a lot of talking to the people in the back to get them interested in doing blues, because they just couldn't see a real blues record selling." "Laundromat Blues" hit number twenty-nine on the R&B charts, and Albert King became a member of the Stax family. Al Bell liked blues, and he knew the jocks who still played it.

Jim's conservative nature cost the company a couple opportunities (though the payoff would only be clear in retrospect). In Autumn 1966, Jerry Wexler called Jim with a proposal, one of those alternate realities that leaves the mind boggled: He'd just picked up the contract on a young singer who had pipes but who lacked direction. She'd put out eight albums on Columbia and had enjoyed a little chart action; Wexler wondered if Jim would like to buy Aretha Franklin's contract from him. "I had such respect for Booker T. and the MG's and all the guys," Jerry says. "I thought they would do a hell of a job on her. I said, 'There's only one thing, there's a twenty-five-thousand-dollar advance.'" Jim had opened the purse a bit to hire Al Bell, but that purse quickly snapped shut. "Jim said he'd pass." Wexler pauses, then adds, "Thank you, Jesus."

"I didn't want to spend that kind of money for an act," says Jim. "Aretha Franklin wasn't selling then. Jerry took a gamble. I could have signed Gladys Knight for five grand even earlier, but it's against my principle. Why should I pay five grand? I could cut an album for five grand. I had never paid an artist to sign a contract. Front money was not even a word in my vocabulary. In retrospect, I should have been a little more receptive in those areas."

Fortunately, another Stax act was about to break out and enjoy a stellar run for the next couple years. Sam and Dave's "I Take What I Want" hadn't charted, but their performance excited their songwriters, Isaac Hayes and David Porter, whose synchronicity was just starting to hum. "There's a gospel tune, 'You don't know like I know, what the lord has done for me,'" says Isaac with a grin. "I said, 'What if I turned this around? 'You don't know like I know, what that woman has done for me.'" So David and I commenced, I did the horn arrangements on it, brought in Wayne Jackson with a flugelhorn—fat sound. *Bam!*" Converting a church song, Isaac and David had the blues singing in praise of earthly delights. Sam and Dave corralled that holy energy and with Al Bell now promoting records at Stax, "You Don't Know" went to number-seven R&B and hit the pop charts too. It was their first of eight consecutive singles that would land in the R&B top twenty; half of those landed in the top five, two of which were number one.

That hit ignited the songwriting team of Hayes and Porter. "We wrote for practically everybody on the label," Isaac continues. "It was a good time for Stax, like a family. During the summer months in midafternoon when we were sweltering and sweating and toiling—the studio didn't have air-conditioning—we'd knock off and go downtown to the Lorraine Motel, chill out and hit the pool. Bailey, the proprietor, would fry some chicken and we'd lay back until about seven in the evening, then go back to work again. In wintertime we'd freeze to death. We had one heater on the wall, and we'd all crowd around it and that's where the ideas came from. It was a loose kind of working thing, and the ideas and creativity were just flowing."

Isaac describes a fluidity between their lives and their art, a collaboration that gushed: "Carla Thomas's 'B-A-B-Y'—I got that title from my

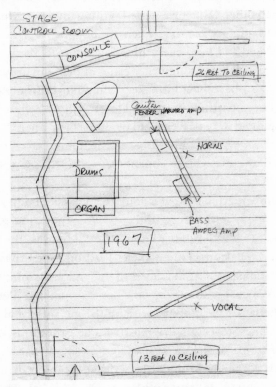

A later configuration of the recording setup. (Drawing by Steve Cropper/Courtesy of René Wu)

second wife, she was calling me 'baby' a lot." He goes on. "One day David and I were tired, went home, and David's wife at the time, he sat in the easy chair, pondering and toiling, and she said, 'What's wrong? Is something wrong with my baby?' David jumped up and he rang me. 'I got it, I got it.' Tired after a whole day's work, he got that inspiration and fired me up, came to my house and we wrote 'When Something Is Wrong with My Baby.' Sam and Dave came in—another hit record!"

The songwriters' success came right on time for Jim. The label was accumulating talented singers, and his concern was that they have good songs. "We began developing writing teams," he says. "Homer Banks, Bettye Crutcher, Raymond Jackson, and others. David Porter was in charge of developing the writing teams. David was never jealous, and he'd give everything he had. He was not worried about the competition. We had workshops, bringing writers in, working with them. The company really concentrated on that writing staff."

"You have to have that burning desire to achieve," advises Isaac, "regardless of the odds or the circumstances. We came from humble beginnings, to put it mildly, and we stuck through it until something happened. We pushed each other. When we started writing hit songs, we both bought Cadillac El Dorados. Same day. Then we bought Rivieras, after that a convertible. David and I did everything together."

Another new artist and songwriter came in the door around this time, and he would also become a hitmaker. Eddie Floyd, from Montgomery, Alabama, had been partners in a record label with Al Bell in Washington, DC, and had visited Stax to write and demo records when Al began making the treks from Washington. "I get to Memphis," says Eddie, "and it's a little theater, and everybody contributes to putting songs together. It was perfect."

Steve remembers Al making it a point that he meet Eddie. "Al Bell saw the potential in me," says Steve, "and said, 'You know, I've got a guy that you could cowrite with.' I didn't know who Eddie was. But when Eddie told me about the Falcons, I knew them. [Wilson Pickett had been in the Falcons with Eddie.] We sat in a hotel room, and we just hit it off."

"They made a deal with me to come down something like every other month," Eddie says, "write songs with all the guys. But I always wanted to record." While Steve was driving to Eddie's room just off from the pool at the Lorraine Motel, he saw a Coca-Cola billboard, and the two, later joined by Wayne Jackson, set to writing. The soft drink's motto at the time was "Things go better with Coke." Unable to shake that from their minds, they made it their own, and "Things Get Better" became Eddie Floyd's first release as an artist on Stax.

◆ ◆ ◆

EDDIE'S OLD BANDMATE Wilson Pickett returned to Stax in December of 1965. Before that, in the wake of Pickett's first visit, Atlantic had sent down Don Covay, a soul singer they'd recently signed but had been unable to break. At Stax in June of 1965, Covay's sessions resulted in two of the strongest outings of his career, "See Saw" and "Sookie Sookie," both stone soul classics.

The music was good, but the vibe wasn't; Covay rubbed the players wrong, and that amplified the imbalance in the relationship with Atlantic that Jim was feeling. Big sales meant big money—for Atlantic. When Pickett came back, he was ever more full of bravado and his own self. He'd been difficult enough to get along with before he was a star; now "Midnight Hour" had become a huge hit. "Wilson grew up in the street," says Steve, "and he carried that with him."

Musically, it was a match made in soul heaven, but Pickett was no angel. Two songs were cut on Pickett's first day back—"634-5789" and "99 and a Half Won't Do," the first going to number one, the second to number thirteen—but tension ripped the session apart. When the band went outside, cooling their heels away from the man of fire, he walked out to try and buy their affection, offering each $100 if they'd come back inside and cut with him. Their self-respect cost more than that, and Pickett was spurned, leading Jim Stewart to phone Wexler and tell him, though the arrangement seemed promising, not to send any more of Atlantic's stars to Stax to cut the greatest songs of their careers. "The guys shut that door," says Jim. "They said, 'Don't bring that asshole down here again. We don't have to put up with that crap.' The guys loved working with Tom Dowd and Jerry Wexler. They just didn't want to be subjected to Wilson."

There were many labels around the South and across the country that would have been shocked at Stax's spurning of Atlantic. All the small producers in garages and storefronts across America were trying to get their music heard, to make the kind of alliance that Stax had fallen into with Atlantic, and they'd have put up with jerks, conceit, and pomposity to do it. One such producer was Rick Hall and his FAME Studio, 150 miles southeast of Memphis in the even more remote town of Muscle Shoals, Alabama. "Pickett did have a corrosive personality with a lot of people," says Wexler. "So I had discovered this new way of making records and now Stax barred the door. But Joe Galkin [the Atlantic promotions man who'd told Wexler about Rufus and Carla and who'd found Otis] told me about FAME and Rick Hall. Wilson Pickett was the first artist I brought to Muscle Shoals. The records we made there, which Chips Moman had a lot to do with, are the gutbucket, finest, swinging, cooking tracks of any records that I ever made. 'Land of 1,000 Dances,' 'Mustang Sally,' 'Soul Dance Number Three'—those are my platonic ideal of great R&B tracks."

It was a windfall for FAME, but the whole experience of recording Atlantic's artists had proved beneficial for Stax as well. "When Wilson Pickett was placed on our doorstep," says Al Bell, "it became clear to me that these people in New York that I respected and held in high esteem— the great Atlantic Records—thought enough of us that if they sent someone like Wilson Pickett to Memphis to get this gritty, gutsy, raw sound and feel that was coming out of Stax, that there had to be something very important and profound about what we were doing. To me, it validated Stax and its sound."

12. UNUSUAL SUCCESS
1966

JIM STEWART HAD never taken a producer's credit for his work at Stax. There wasn't much room on a single to designate a producer, and when albums came out, his credit read, SUPERVISION: JIM STEWART. Many times he had produced, and many times he'd stayed out of the way, knowing when these talented kids didn't need his input. He usually engineered the recording, and if things moved in a direction he didn't like, he'd make it known. Part of Stax's success was based on everyone contributing ideas. "There was a lot of creativity in those days," says Jim. "Total involvement from everybody. There was no greed factor, and no limits to the input that we gave."

Early in 1966, Isaac Hayes and David Porter were working on material for an upcoming Sam and Dave session. Isaac and David had become Stax's custodians of Sam and Dave, writing and producing nearly all of their material. The two sets of partners fed off each other, the ideas between the four providing inspiration and vigor.

Sam and Dave weren't harmonizers, they were combatants, each vocal line a thrust and parry, goosing the other to reach further, jump higher, and dance harder. In the studio, David coached the vocalists while Isaac arranged the band. David pushed them higher in their registers—it was a harder reach, and he liked hearing that extra effort in their voices.

L–R: Jim Stewart (partial), Duck Dunn (shorts), Gene "Bowlegs" Miller (seated), Andrew Love, Floyd Newman, Wayne Jackson, Eddie Floyd's back, Al Jackson (drums, rear), unidentified background, Isaac Hayes (piano), Mildred Pratcher Steve Cropper. (Promotional photo by API Photographers/Earlie Biles Collection)

"There was not a musical chart there," says Sam, who had previously worked with bands that read their parts off charts written before the session. "Isaac would voice that stuff with the piano. 'This is what I want the horns to do, this is what Sam and Dave's gonna do—' He would voice everything. I would go, 'God, this guy!'—'cause I'm not accustomed to seeing that."

"Sometimes David and I would sleep all night under the piano," says Isaac, "and we'd be awakened the next morning by the secretary. 'What are you *doing* here?'" There were other places Isaac preferred to sleep, and this night, working late in preparation for Sam and Dave, Isaac, a ladies' man, had a date waiting—at home, for him. But he and David were committed to their responsibilities and knew that most songs are not born without labor, and ideas have to be nurtured until the heart is revealed and the body can be built around it. It was late, no one else was in the building, and David, pacing the studio, retired for a bathroom respite. He walked up the sloped floor, went through the old theater doors, and was sitting on the toilet, listening to Isaac noodle on the piano. Inspiration can be elusive, the ideas being—as the term indicates—breathed into a person. And as Isaac moved his hands on the black and whites, David's ears perked up. He could hear form taking shape.

"I finally struck a groove," says Isaac, "and it's taking David forever! I said, 'David! C'mon man, I got something.'"

David had heard Isaac's progress, but he had his own business to finish. He hollered back from the stall, "Hold on, I'm coming."

Isaac continued with the chords, but in a moment his concentration was broken by a commotion from the back of the room. "That's it! That's it!" David ran in yelling, one hand holding his pants halfway up, the other one waving wildly. "Hold on, I'm coming! That's it!" It would be the chorus, and title, to Sam and Dave's breakout song.

They developed a basic structure, and Isaac had a horn riff he'd put on tape a couple weeks earlier, an idea too good not to have on hand. He'd called together the horn section so he wouldn't forget it. He pulled the tape and it fit their new song, heroic like the cavalry's arrival. At the next day's session, they built the parts quickly. For the rhythm David refer-enced the funky hit out of New Orleans, Lee Dorsey's "Get Out of My Life Woman." That proved a good starting point for Al Jackson. Isaac's horn part became a central riff. Steve dug into his James Brown trick bag for a funky guitar part, and the result was a surefire hit that shot up the R&B charts all the way to the number-one position. Penned as a love song, this piece transcends romance and becomes a cultural message with civil rights overtones, urging unity among African-Americans, remind-ing that help is always nearby—and on the way:

> Don't you ever, be sad
> Lean on me, when times are bad
> When the day comes, and you're down
> In a river of trouble, and about to drown
> Hold on, I'm coming
> Hold on, I'm coming

"That was the chemistry," says Sam. "Sam and Dave, Hayes and Porter. Just like the chemistry between Berry Gordy and Motown and between Michael Jackson and Quincy Jones. Hayes—I believed in whatever he said. His mouth, to me, was a bible."

"Isaac would be playing piano," says Duck, "and David would be behind

Listening to a Sam and Dave playback in the control room. The Altec Voice of the Theater mono speaker is to the right. L–R: Sam Moore, Isaac Hayes, Andrew Love, Wayne Jackson, Dave Prater, Jim Stewart, Steve Cropper. (Promotional photo by API Photographers/Earlie Biles Collection)

the [sound] screen, almost like a band director. He'd tell them which line to sing when. David was great with that."

"When it came to laying down the vocals," David Porter told the Smithsonian Institution, "I'm on one side of the mike, Sam and Dave are on the other, and I'd direct them, like a choir. One hand: you hold it, you do the ad-lib. Take the hand up: you do the ad-lib up high. Take the hand down: ad-lib lower. Laying down the vocals was orchestrated and developed at the mike."

"Porter was tough—oh, he was tough," says Sam. "He wanted hit records. And I'm lazy, I'm the first to admit that I'm very lazy. I don't want to sing all up in the ceiling—I visualize being Frank Sinatra, or Nat King Cole, Sam Cooke. And he would change keys on me. He challenged me a lot." Sam got sound advice from Jim Stewart as well. "'You're trying to compete with Motown,' he told me. 'Stop. Motown's vision is pop. You are raw soul. Let's concentrate on that.'"

Sam, with some exceptions, did not like the songs they were being given at Stax—even after they started hitting. He still heard himself as a crooner and balladeer. And when he was feeling down about the material, he'd voice his concerns where everyone at Stax went to disburden themselves: the Satellite Record Shop counter. "Estelle—it was her money that started the company, and she always stood up behind the counter at Satellite. I'd say, 'Miz Axton, I don't like that song.' She'd say, 'Sam, you and Dave stick with it son, that's a good song.' I'd go back in the studio, I'd focus on what she'd say. Goddogit if it didn't work out like she said."

"Hold On" was released mid-March, 1966, and it was the kind of powerful, catchy, and exciting song that made Al Bell's promotion job both more exciting and more difficult—giving him that many new disc jockeys to reach out to. Three weeks later, it hit the R&B charts, where it would stay for twenty weeks, working its way to number one in mid-June; it peaked at number twenty-one on the pop charts at the same time, a song of the summer. They got better TV appearances, broke into wider— and wealthier—audiences. Sam and Dave were becoming mainstream artists.

This expanded fan base—the dreamed-of crossover success—was further evidenced by sales of their first album recorded at Stax. Where most of the market had been singles so far, Al Bell saw not only the growing commercial trend toward albums, but also the higher profitability in their sale; they were more expensive to create and produce, but their higher price allowed a significant profit margin. Riding on the back

Estelle Axton outside the Satellite Record Shop. (Stax Museum of American Soul Music/Photograph by Jonas Bernholm)

of their hit single, their album *Hold On I'm Coming* proved to be the breakthrough for Stax's album sales. In all the company's years through 1965, they'd released only eight albums—on the Stax and Volt labels combined. After Al Bell arrived, in 1966 alone they released eleven albums, and Sam and Dave's *Hold On* went to number one on the R&B album sales chart.

Albums were good business, as Al would demonstrate over the years to come. "The albums were generating more revenue than the singles," he explains. "There were times when we'd sell a hundred thousand albums, and at the end of the year, that adds up to serious cash flow. If they were retailing at $6.98, then our wholesale was three and a half dollars or so per unit. So one hundred thousand units is three hundred and fifty thousand dollars. We were generating cash. We had obligations with writers, producers, and publishers, and our fixed costs, and general administrative expenses. But we had the gross revenue coming in, because we had hit records."

Beyond his promotional abilities, Al was becoming a dynamic personality within the company. When the MG's became frustrated with Jim, Al would step in; Jim's stoic pursuit for perfection drove even his most loyal employees to irritation. Sam and Dave leaned on Al in the same way. "Jim recorded almost all of our hits, but Jim and I had our differences," says Sam. "I had a big mouth. Jim had no personality. He depended on Steve Cropper. I'm saying, 'Steve Cropper's mouth ain't no damn prayer book.' I was called on the carpet to keep my mouth shut. And Al became the man between Jim and myself. Al Bell became a spiritual adviser. One time we were supposed to perform in Atlanta for the National Association of Television and Radio Announcers. I was upset with Jim Stewart and Al talked to me, said, 'You can be upset, but don't take it out on the people in Atlanta.' Stax did a good job promoting. And over the years, Jim and I turned out to be good friends. His sister—there was nothing I wouldn't do for her."

◆ ◆ ◆

THE FAMILY FEELING still dominated, but in the solidifying hierarchy, there was no place for Packy. In the wake of the "Hole in the Wall" success, the Magnificent Montague, the LA DJ and promoter, matched Packy with Johnny Keyes, a vocalist, conga player, songwriter, and laid-back African-American hipster from Chicago. They formed a band and a deep friendship, and the Packers toured behind the single, ultimately winding down in Memphis. There, any friend of Packy's was instantly adored by Estelle, so Johnny found himself with a job at the record store, and a new mentor—Estelle—who was paying for an apartment he shared with Packy near Stax. "Packy would go home every now and then, but he preferred to stay in South Memphis with black people," Johnny says. "She didn't fight it. And she believed in me and my talent. She'd say, 'Johnny, when you write something, look through a magazine and you'll come across some phrases you might be able to use.' She said, 'I've found that records sell when you ask a question. Will you still love me tomorrow?' I said, 'Ahh.'"

JOHNNY KEYES

Johnny Keyes, who became Packy Axton's best friend. (University of Memphis Libraries/Special Collections)

Johnny wrote songs for Stax's East/Memphis publishing. He and Packy cowrote "Double Up" with Estelle's employee Homer Banks, and it had an appeal to Sam and Dave who, in a recording frenzy, were working on their second album of 1966; they wanted to call it *Double Dynamite*, so Johnny's song had thematic appeal. "Miz Axton had told us, 'If you give them that tune without getting publishing, I'm through with both of you," says Johnny. "She said, 'I'll stop paying your rent, I won't back you in anything you do, you'll no longer be able to borrow money from my cash register.' She said all bets would be off. David Porter said, 'We're gonna cut it and we'll start rehearsing the tune.' I told him we needed to have half of the publishing and he said he'd talk to Jim Stewart.

"So Sam and Dave are rehearsing 'Double Up,' I'm elated. David comes back and said, 'We don't split publishing.' I said, 'Yes you do, East Publishing splits with Otis's publishing company, Redwal.' He said, 'No publishing, but we'll make it a single from the album.' That would have boosted our money as writers. But then I could hear Miz Axton's voice in my ear—'All bets are off if you don't get the publishing.' I held my ground. All of a sudden they said, 'Stop rehearsing the song, the deal is off.'" Sam and Dave had to abandon the song, but Estelle didn't leave Johnny in a lurch. She had him teach the song to Clarence "C.L. Blast" Lewis, a solid Memphis soul singer. She booked time at Ardent Studios, an up-and-coming facility in town (they'd installed the same recording console as Stax, with an eye toward getting their overflow work). C.L.'s

"Double Up" came out on Stax and didn't chart, but Keyes and Axton still had their rent paid.

◆ ◆ ◆

THOUGH STAX HAD all these records on the charts, they were still a provincial company. Songs may have been played in the Northeast, Midwest, and down South, but the Stax personnel recorded them in Memphis, mailed them out from Memphis, and read about them while they sat in their Memphis office. So when the phone rang in the spring of 1966 and the crackly voice on the other end said it was England calling, they wondered if it was a joke. Their credulity was further tested when the caller identified himself as Brian Epstein, manager of the Beatles. He'd gotten their phone number from Jerry Wexler. The Beatles would be touring the US that year and, as their December 1965 album *Rubber Soul* indicated, they were grooving to the sounds of sweet southern soul. (The song "Drive My Car" lifted the bass line from Otis's "Respect." "That's my one *la-di-da*," says the ever-humble Duck Dunn.) The Beatles were at new heights of popularity, and bursting creatively, working toward their *Sgt. Pepper* breakthrough the following year.

In March of 1966, the Beatles' manager was in Memphis, surveying the landscape, with Estelle as his host. She placed him in the luxury downtown hotel, the Rivermont, and suggested the Beatles could stay there too; touring politicos were often put up there. (Elvis, meanwhile, offered Graceland.) Estelle's son-in-law worked for the Memphis police, and his responsibilities included traffic detail, so she assured Epstein that the Beatles would have no trouble moving through town. A plan was developing.

"One day Miz Axton came to us," says Johnny Keyes, "and she said, 'Don't spread this around, but the Beatles are coming to Memphis.' Everybody told somebody, 'The Beatles are coming, don't tell anybody.' And soon everybody knew." Johnny remembers girls coming into the record shop, and hysterical, offering money for information, trying to buy the dress the secretary would wear when the Beatles came through the door. "It was wild, man," he says. "Nobody knew, but everybody did."

"They wanted to record at Stax so bad," says Don Nix, who later befriended George Harrison. "They had the whole thing all laid out, were gonna land a helicopter on the roof. But word leaked out."

On the front page of the March 31 morning newspaper, just below the article KLANSMAN CHIEF TO GIVE SELF UP, is the headline BEATLES TO RECORD HERE. In the article, Brian Epstein's visit is acknowledged, and Estelle announces their April 9 arrival, explaining they were drawn by the sounds of

Otis, Carla, Rufus, the MG's, and others. She confirms an album and a single are planned—Jim will produce, Steve will arrange, and Tom Dowd will come down from Atlantic to supervise. The Beatles, yes, but the newspaper realized that readers may not be familiar with the studio that has drawn their attention. So the article ends with an explanation for the general public who, familiar with the Beatles, may not know this world-renowned studio in their hometown: that "has had unusual success with Negro artists."

Once fans had official confirmation of where to be on what day, the Beatles had to cancel; Beatlemania was still in full swing. The album *Revolver* would be recorded in London, and its songs are full of soul possibility. The horns and vocal style on "Got to Get You into My Life" are the most obvious paean to the American soul sound, but the dark funk of "Taxman" and the bright punch of "Good Day Sunshine" would also have been right at home in Memphis.

The Beatles had not called Motown in Detroit, and while the African-American label in the North continued to dominate Stax in sales, it did not dominate in soul. The Beatles canceled, but artists from Elton John to Janis Joplin and the Monkees all came through. Stax was setting the bar for grit and feeling in commercial music.

◆◆◆

Even by 1966, it was difficult for an integrated group to drink a cup of coffee in public, much less dine formally or casually in Memphis. Usually, establishments that catered to African-Americans were more welcoming to mixed groups and to visiting whites. The Lorraine Motel's small restaurant and swimming pool were always hospitable, the prices were reasonable, and that was where Stax would usually host its guests. "When I'd come to Memphis, I stayed at the Lorraine," says Eddie Floyd. "And that's where we would write songs. Mr. Bailey, who owned the motel, he didn't care about the noise and he liked having us around."

"Anytime you went to the Lorraine," remembers Mavis Staples, who traveled often through the South with her gospel-singing family, the Staple Singers, "it was like a reunion. Bobby 'Blue' Bland, Little Junior Parker, Joe Hinton—everyone stayed at the Lorraine Motel. Mr. Bailey and his wife and daughter [the motel was named for the daughter] had a nice restaurant there, and it was just the motel for blacks in Memphis. That was home away from home."

"We used their dining room for our meeting hall and we swam in their pool," says Booker T. Jones. "We ate there on a regular basis. The Lorraine Motel was an institution for us."

Eddie Floyd (Photograph by API Photographers/
API Collection)

"When I was writing songs with Eddie Floyd," says Steve, "Mr. Bailey would give us the honeymoon suite if he didn't have it booked. It was plush red velvet everywhere, a big room, and it was great."

Eddie's "Knock on Wood" was written at the Lorraine. "Steve and I were trying to write a track for Otis Redding," says Eddie. "We're sitting at the Lorraine in the summer. It's storming, there's lightning, and we're trying to come up with a song. Steve's strumming, and I had an idea for a line: knock on wood. Steve had the idea about the rabbit foot for good luck, and stepping over those cracks in the sidewalk, black cats, all that. Then I told him the story of when I was a kid in Montgomery, Alabama, when it was storming big like that, thunder and lightning, we used to hide under the bed, and we'd be frightened. He said, 'That's it, that's it!' "

"Wayne Jackson was playing in West Memphis, and I called him on a break," says Steve, "said, 'We've got a great song, when you get off your gig, come by the Lorraine and help me with the horn arrangements because I want to cut this tomorrow morning.' "

This wasn't the first time Wayne had received such a call. "I'd go to the Lorraine, sit on the edge of the bed, and there Steve'd be with a guitar and a singer," says Wayne. "I'd use a mute so that I wouldn't wake people. I'd play the little horn lines that they were talking about, or try something else. We'd work until everybody was tired. I could remember the lines till the morning, and in the studio we'd have a song to show everybody."

"The next morning," says Steve, "we worked it up with the band. Hour or two later, we had it cut."

Eddie credits Al Jackson with making the song a hit. "He said, 'Let me put something in there.'" Eddie laughs. "And he put in a break where everyone stops and he hits the drum, like knocking on the door. Everybody laughed, but that's what makes it. If he hadn't did that, I'm convinced it wouldn't have been a hit."

"Knock on Wood" was cut as a demo for Otis Redding, but once done, it didn't sound like Otis's style. So Stax released it, and with Al Bell promoting it, Eddie's demo hit the number-one spot on the R&B charts and became a top-forty pop hit.

◆◆◆

HITS CREATED A cash flow, with money for the songwriters and the label based on numbers of copies sold, and money for the artists based on radio play (and the reward of better-paying gigs). But the musicians who backed the artist were paid per session, union scale, whether the song hit or missed. (Often their pay was considerably less, what the union termed "demo scale"—fifteen dollars—with the remaining fifty to come if the song were actually released.) At studios in New York and Los Angeles, union rules stipulated that sessions were three hours and it was expected that four songs could be cut in that time. Musicians arrived, were given sheet music, and they played the part as written. At Stax, a song might be sketched out, as "Knock on Wood" was, or it might develop in the studio and need to be rehearsed over time. "We might spend a month working on four, five, six artists and records," says Steve, "trying to get a hit single on them." The pay wouldn't come until the recording session did.

The studio stars kept their club dates because they needed regular income. When Steve phoned Wayne for help with "Knock on Wood," Wayne was working a nightclub gig into the wee hours. He had a wife and kids at home. He was selling vacuum cleaners door-to-door in the daytime, catnapping in his car. Most of these musicians, cutting hit after hit after hit, were scrounging to make a living. Al Jackson was in the clubs at night. Booker, recently resettled in Memphis after college, was taking club gigs. And most of these players were feeding young families, too.

Duck Dunn, who was playing on all the hits, was still working days at King Records and nights at the Rebel Room or Hernando's Hideaway, in addition to sessions—just to make ends meet. "I'd work till two in the morning on the bandstand," says Duck, "then stop on the way home to see Al Jackson till four and then be at King Records at eight. My wife used to take a broom and poke me to wake me up. I went out and did *Shindig!* and I left [my wife] June and my son Jeff with fifty dollars. I'm doing Hollywood TV and we're living off peanut butter, eating Kentucky Fried Chicken."

Al Bell was increasingly aware of their struggles to make a living. He saw the yawning, the bags under the eyes. "Finally," Duck continues, "Al Bell says, 'We need to put these guys on salary.' Man, it relieved me from working till two in the morning. That's one reason I respect Al so much—he took me out of my nighttime job and made me a studio musician."

After giving them $125 a week, Al took the incentives even further by spearheading the move to form a production pool, a pot of royalty money to be equally shared by the six key players responsible for most of the sessions and hits. With his track record of success, Al held some sway with Jim, and he convinced him of the benefits. "The MG's became the group that backed everybody," says Al. "Whether it was Albert King with his blues, or Carla Thomas with her pop, or William Bell—they adapted to whomever it was that came in the studio. And Isaac and David were doing most of the writing and lots of the producing." Stax was being paid a royalty from Atlantic of about 15 percent, and Al arranged for a sliver of that money to be divided equally between the four MG's and Hayes and Porter. "It was the fairest way to give them a producer's revenue," Al says. The more hits they made, the more these six core players would earn.

"Al made Booker T. & the MG's and David and Isaac part of the company," says Duck. "And what can I say? Here's a gift that saved my life."

The production pool resulted in a new distribution of duties, with each key player assuming responsibility for certain artists, and each being made a company vice president. Steve had Eddie and Otis. Al Jackson had Albert King and a few others; often he and Duck shared. Booker had William Bell, later Albert King—and there was fluidity within the designations. Thereafter, all the albums and many of the singles included a producer's credit.

While generous, this also further compartmentalized a very collaborative organization. If one player were designated as producer, would the others feel as free to introduce suggestions? Or would that be stepping on toes? Or contributing with no reward? Suddenly there were proprietary concerns and a new layer of politics. "In my mind that was one of the things that began to break down the Stax structure," says Booker. "I was vice president of something and I had an office. But I wasn't feeling it." No one was bemoaning the better money, but the new emphasis on individual profit introduced weeds into the garden.

13. FATBACK CACCIATORE
1967

STAX STOOD TALL as a symbol of opportunity, a beacon in the neighborhood, the glow from the ascending stars ensconcing nearby residents. Deanie Parker, who had enlisted local kids into her Stax-Volt Fan Club, hired them for small change to help get mass mailings packed and ready. In the label's conference room, they'd be stuffing envelopes, the excited chatter audible through much of the building. William Bell, Rufus Thomas, Carla—artists would stop in and encourage the kids, thank them for helping. And Stax's light shone brighter.

There was one group of African-American teenagers who had penetrated the studio doors earlier, and gotten in deeper, than the others: the Bar-Kays. "Every spare chance we got," says bassist James Alexander, "we'd go down to Stax to watch various people play." After performing at Booker T. Washington High School, they got a nightclub gig across the Mississippi River in West Memphis—even though they weren't old enough to be inside. They'd recently met the white keyboardist Ronnie Caldwell, also a high school student, and become an integrated band. "It was pretty unusual at that time to integrate," James continues, "and the Bar-Kays and Booker T. & the MG's were two of the first groups around here to do it."

Originally named the Impalas after the car that got them to gigs, they

Signing the charter for the Stax-Volt Fan Club, surrounded by kids from the Soulsville neighborhood. L–R: Deanie Parker, Al Bell, Jim Stewart, Julian Bond. (Deanie Parker Collection)

rechristened themselves the Bar-Kays; it was inspired by a Bacardi Rum billboard with letters missing, and it evoked Stax's Mar-Keys. They played Willie Mitchell's hit "20-75," Junior Walker's "Shotgun," and the funky, Latin-tinged "Watermelon Man." They covered Ray Charles and even worked up a couple Beatles tunes, "I Want to Hold Your Hand" and an original take on "Michelle." "We wanted to be a band," explains James, "but we wanted to act like a vocal group, doing steps like the Temptations." They could back a vocalist or carry a set with just their instruments, their energy drawing the audience from their seats—a good time for the band, the dancers and listeners, and soon for the club owners. Sometimes, they'd get calls for sessions. Ben Cauley had recently played trumpet on Carla Thomas's "B-A-B-Y" and several Rufus Thomas songs.

There's a difference between playing a club and making a recording, and when the Bar-Kays auditioned for Steve Cropper on a Saturday morning, Steve didn't think their cover songs showed promise. James Alexander remembers him saying, "I just don't think you all got what it takes." Undeterred, the Bar-Kays practiced harder.

"Soul Finger," the song that would establish them upon its spring 1967 release, grew from their club gig. They were working at the Hippodrome on Beale Street, among the top-tier clubs on what was still the South's African-American Main Street. Too young to be in the club, too good not be there, they were vamping at the end of another song and fell into a musical pattern that made them all take notice. "When it was done, nobody said anything," James remembers. "We looked at each other like, There's something to this. We ain't thinking this could be the start of a record or anything but we don't know what it was, because we're still young."

They came back and auditioned again for Steve. They'd worked up an instrumental titled "Don't Do That," a horn-and-guitar exchange with a popping snare drum that was getting hot in the clubs. Perhaps Steve's ear had become tired or his patience had worn thin by the steady flow of auditions; he still didn't hear it. "When we were leaving the studio, Jim Stewart saw us and said, 'Why are you guys up here?' We're feeling kind of low, and we said, 'We were just auditioning for Steve Cropper.' He said, 'I'll tell you what. I want you to come back up here on Sunday and audition for me.'"

When they played their original for Jim, he was impressed. He was also attracted by their youth; Estelle had been hounding him to consider creating a new studio band, both to give the MG's a break and to infuse new ideas into the scene. Trumpeter Ben Cauley remembers that Jim stepped away from the studio for a moment, and while he was gone, they returned to the groove they'd stumbled onto while vamping at the Hippodrome. "I'll never forget it," Ben says. "He came back and said, 'Fellas, what's that? Do it again.' We played and he said, 'Let's cut it right now.'"

The song needed an introduction, and Jim needed to set audio levels for recording. "He ran up into the control room and said to run it down," James says. "It wasn't a big elaborate studio—just a little recording board, he turned a few knobs. You didn't even have a talkback button, you'd send hand signals. Ben came up with this nursery rhyme horn lick, Jim gave us a signal to play it from the top, and when we recorded it, we had 'Soul Finger.'"

Well, they had most of it. Jim played it at the staff meeting that Monday morning, and David Porter suggested putting teenage party sounds on it. "David told us to find some kids and have them come to Stax after classes," James says. "He went to the College Street Sundry, across from Stax, and bought a case of the short Cokes in the little green bottle. The deal was if all these people hollered and screamed and shouted on our record, you get a free Coca-Cola." Porter set up a mike in the studio and

James Alexander, bassist in the Bar-Kays. (Stax Museum of American Soul Music)

recorded the kids while copying the master track onto a new tape—the overdubbing process at the time. He cued them when to shout "soul finger" and gave the song a party atmosphere.

The record was released in April of '67 on Stax's Volt subsidiary, most of the band still in high school. The flip side was another instrumental, this one written by Cropper and Booker T. Jones, featuring Jones on harmonica. The song was named "Knucklehead" in honor of James Alexander. "My nickname was Knuck, which comes from Knucklehead Smith [the name of a ventriloquist's sidekick from a late-1950s TV program]. I was always slow to learn my part, and when Isaac and David would be teaching us stuff, they had to keep going over it with me."

The single creeped, then leaped to national attention, with "Soul Finger" hitting number three on the national R&B charts within two months, and a whopping number seventeen on the pop charts. This affirmation of their talent led to more after-school work for the boys, the kind that didn't require shoe polish or carrying other stars' clothes to the dry cleaners. "After the MG's were getting really busy, I started filling in for Duck Dunn," James says. "Duck wanted to be on the golf course, and he'd call me." Other Bar-Kays also began to get studio experience. The family feeling was revivified: The kids had grown, a new generation was coming up.

◆ ◆ ◆

It had been a thrilling realization the previous year that the Beatles had wanted to come to Stax. It made all at the label aware of the range their radiance had reached. Now, in 1967, plans grew for the label to send a group of artists to England and across Europe. Many at Stax had never been outside Memphis's Shelby County. Europe was a distant place that had been discussed briefly in geography classes long ago, where people spoke in languages that couldn't be understood; they lived in castles and ate snails.

The tour grew out of Otis's previous visit abroad. Audience reception had been fantastic, and the visit's problems were minor—Otis said the lemonade came syrupy and with small bubbles in it, and the food was weird, but the band found a fast-food chain with burgers recognizable enough to eat before each show. The promoters reached out to Phil Walden, Otis's manager, to discuss a return, perhaps on a larger scale. Phil brought the idea to Jim, who discussed it with Al Bell. Otis had been planning a break from the road and he'd broken up his band; perhaps the MG's could back him. Al liked big ideas, and in short order a Stax Revue was lined up: The MG's would anchor as the house band, the horns would receive separate billing as the Mar-Keys, and the lineup would include Otis, Sam and Dave, Eddie Floyd, and Carla Thomas, though she'd have to depart early to fulfill some previously arranged US obligations. The bill also included Arthur Conley, a fellow Georgia artist that Otis had signed to a record label he was developing, an enterprise with Joe Galkin, Jotis Records (derived from the usual christening pattern, "Joe" and "Otis"). Conley broke big, going to number two on both Pop and R&B with "Sweet Soul Music," penned and produced (at FAME Studio in Muscle Shoals) by Otis. William Bell, invited, was already committed to dates in the US. Rufus Thomas was not asked along, which he felt was unjust; Stax said the final lineup was dictated by EMI, their distributor abroad, who knew which artists would be popular. "Otis," Al Bell says, "was opening doors for all of us at Stax."

Though the MG's had recently gone onto salary at Stax, the horns had not, and they were still rushing from sessions to make their fifteen-dollar gigs. Wayne Jackson was working at Hernando's Hideway, what he calls "a redneck joint," alongside saxman Joe Arnold, who was also enlisted for Europe. They went to the club's owner to arrange time off and he told them if they left, they couldn't come back. "I really was worried about that, too," says Wayne, " 'cause I was working there seven nights a week and I needed that fifteen dollars." But the lure of travel was too great; as far as they knew, they'd never get to Europe again. Fortunately, they quickly had no regrets: "That door closed and other doors opened," says Wayne, "and we walked right on through, kept on going."

BOOKER T. JONES

(Earlie Biles Collection)

New thresholds beckoned the moment they disembarked. Crowds at the London airport were holding signs and cheering their arrival. The hubbub continued as they realized that the Beatles had sent their Bentley limousines to transport them from the airport to the hotel. "Maybe," saxman Andrew Love remembers musing, "they like us over here."

The tour ran from March 17 to April 9, 1967, beginning and ending in London, with stops throughout England and in Paris, Oslo, Stockholm, Copenhagen, and the Netherlands. The executives at Stax, wanting to make the most out of the trip, decided to record several of the shows;

DONALD "DUCK" DUNN

(Earlie Biles Collection)

Atlantic liked that, and Tom Dowd was enlisted—he and Jim developed a solid working relationship in the studio. The bands flew over first, allowing them to recuperate before the gigs began. "I flew with the bands," says Tom, "and then I flew back to escort Jim Stewart and Al Bell to Europe because they'd never flown across the ocean and they were skittish about it." The night of his return, Tom recorded the first London show. "They had their chops and it didn't matter where they were in the world."

STEVE CROPPER

(Earlie Biles Collection)

Before the first public show at the Finsbury Park Astoria, there was a private show for invited guests at the Bag O'Nails, a small London club. "Paul McCartney was there," Carla says. The Beatles were working on *Sgt. Pepper*, and he'd taken a break to come hear his colleagues live. "He stayed through the whole night. It was a real intimate place. He came back and introduced himself. And we all sat at a table and talked to him. It was a mutual admiration society."

The entourage traveled on a bus, playing packed concerts to enthusiastic response, and sightseeing informally. Wayne Jackson and Duck Dunn acquired home movie cameras and began rolling film as soon as the plane got above the clouds; there were lots of things they'd never seen before. "When I was a little bitty girl," Carla continues, "it was almost as if the Lord spoke to me and said, 'You're going to be doing a lot of traveling.' I thought I would be in the air force or something. I had no idea that I would be traveling as a singer." The downside to traveling, like Otis had warned, was that the food in Europe was not what they were accustomed to. "All I could eat was boiled eggs and baked potatoes," says Duck. "The rest of it was just horrible. The lettuce was like wet newspapers. It was a great time, but it was also the longest weeks of my life." At an English lunch one day, Duck summoned all the foreign words he could muster from the fancier menus he'd seen in Memphis restaurants and told the waiter that he'd like an order of "fatback cacciatore." Communication gap, soul style.

"I always compare it to what happened when the Beatles first came to the States and they had all these screaming teenagers rushing them," says Steve. "That's what happened for us."

"The barriers, the people standing outside the theaters waiting to see the show," affirms Eddie Floyd. "And we were nervous, didn't know whether the Europeans are going to like the show. But we know the music and so we put the music on, and they liked the music."

In fact, they *loved* the music. Prior to their arrival, radio stations had Stax in heavy rotation—the latest music, and the already classic songs like "Green Onions" and "Last Night." The band would hit nightclubs when they had the chance, and Steve immediately noticed that the records' bass sounds hit harder—the European mastering and pressing drew out more bottom, making them more danceable.

And at the shows, the audiences couldn't be held in their seats. Carla had them dancing to "B-A-B-Y" and won their hearts with her version of the Beatles' "Yesterday." Arthur Conley became the new artist to watch, his "Sweet Soul Music" an irresistible battle cry. Eddie Floyd, Sam and Dave, and Otis Redding presented the problems that every promoter embraces—each one is dynamic enough to close the show, so what order should they go in? The artists hadn't toured as a group and most had not seen how the others performed. The results were eye-opening to everyone. Otis, having been to Europe, had to climax, and Eddie preceded the duet because they were double dynamite. They were so explosive that they became a problem for Otis Redding. "We came on and we broke out," says Sam Moore. "Whoa! We were like mad animals. We went at them, singing and sweating and twisting and turning and spinning and—and the European people went crazy. They just went crazy."

Sam and Dave ended their set with "Hold On, I'm Coming," and the energy that song drew from the audience could never be anticipated. "Sam and Dave got these people going," says Steve, "got them dancing and they'd run through the aisles."

The Stax Revue was taking the Europeans to church, or as near as most of the audience would get to a Mississippi Baptist congregation. "They had to get a mop out there to wipe some of Sam and Dave's blood and guts off the stage," recounts Wayne Jackson, mostly figuratively. "They were just slopping in their own sweat. Their clothes were wringing wet. We were wringing wet. One of them would just faint, fall out, they'd drag him offstage. And then Sam would say good night . . . and here they come, back out and starting again. They had everybody just in pandemonium. And Otis would stand over there on the side, watching." More than once, the crowds got so out of control that security interrupted Sam and Dave's set to restore calm, threatening to forbid their return to the stage—for the safety of all concerned.

The problem for Otis Redding was that he had to follow them and, unless he wanted to be upstaged, he had to outdo them. Otis was a recording artist who understood the dynamics of a song, but as a performer, he was just learning about stage movement. "Up to this point, Otis had been like Sam Cooke and Jesse Velvet," says Al Bell, "a great balladeer, standing at the microphone, and he'd sing and move the audience, 'cause he had that passion and that tear in his voice." Otis didn't dance like James Brown. From his place at the center microphone, he'd sing with feeling, make eye contact with the audience, twist his upper body, and stomp his feet—but he rarely left that center stage. Watching Sam and Dave from behind the curtain, he knew he'd have to add extra oomph.

"Otis is standing in the wings and he's nervous," Al Jackson told an interviewer in the early 1970s. "From the time we started, from the Mar-Keys to Arthur Conley on down, that whole show didn't lighten up. He's seeing that reception that Sam and Dave is getting and he ain't digging this at all. And so he got ready to get out there. The cat introducing him says 'O-T—' I'm sitting there just as ready as he is and when the host says, 'Otis Redding' I go 'One, two, three—' and Otis transformed. I didn't believe it. When he hit that stage he had a smile on his face and he was there, all man. 'Here I am.' He'd grab that mike and that's all he'd do for that whole forty-five minutes was prowl that stage. I used to sit there and wonder how he did it. That son of a bitch was all man."

Al Bell saw the same transformation. "He was just like a thoroughbred racehorse waiting for the bell," he says. "When Sam and Dave finished, Otis Redding broke from behind that stage and grabbed the microphone, and he started going from one end of the stage to the other. I couldn't believe what was going on—the energy that I had never seen before!" Once, after following Sam and Dave, Otis was heard to mutter, "I never want to have to follow those motherfuckers again."

In addition to the battles on the stage, there was some in-fighting off the stage. To everyone's surprise, Otis got better lodging than they did; some of the shows were even billed as the Otis Redding Show instead of the Stax-Volt Revue. Another simmering tension came to a head, this one between Steve and Al Bell—once so close they'd written songs together. Steve, who had wielded authority at Stax long before Al arrived, saw that Al was exuding a new confidence. Indeed, Stax's sales had risen dramatically since his arrival, and their prominence—now on two continents—was largely attributable to his promotional work. A show-down seemed inevitable. It occurred in Al Bell's hotel room, where a tour meeting had been called. "Some things were said," says Steve. "There were bad feelings that I never, ever got over." Al coveted the clout that Steve had as the label's A&R director, the ability to sign new artists. The sensitivities of what transpired behind closed doors remain raw decades later, and details are not discussed. "All of a sudden, I wasn't A&R director anymore," says Steve. "I was still a member of the band. I was still making the same money. But I had no stick. My stick was taken away and given to Al Bell."

That summer, Al was promoted to executive vice president. Other changes transpired after they got home. Wayne and Andrew were finally put on salary; if the rhythm section was getting proper treatment, why not the horns? But the biggest changes were in self-perception. Having been exposed to the wider world, they realized the impact of the place they'd carved in it. "Europe changed everybody's perception of themselves," says Steve. "That Stax-Volt tour gave us a new insight to what the world really thought of us, 'cause we didn't think outside the block we lived on. But all of a sudden, we got a sense that the whole world is listening to what we're doing."

"The tour was certainly enlightening for all of us," Jim Stewart under-states, "a watershed moment. We were no longer the funky little com-pany on McLemore Avenue. What can we do to enhance our position in this world market? We began to become more business oriented, looking for larger margins. It was like the light flashed on and now we were deal-ing with a different level. It's mind-boggling."

"The world to me at that time was the United States of America," says Booker. "The European tour was like the Indians meeting Columbus, a huge eye-opener."

"It was amazing to have all-white audiences, standing room only, and to be treated by the bellhops or attendants at the hotels and other people like stars," says Al Bell. "We hadn't felt that or experienced that before." This sense of respect that he felt proved transformative, both on a per-sonal level and on his goals for the company. Coming from a land where his skin color often obscured his worth, Al was recalibrated by strangers treating him as a whole man, a citizen of value. "Although the music came from an integrated group of people, Europeans viewed it as blacks's music, as a music that came from a culture. I realized, The world says this is a legitimate, authentic music, and it should be respected and appreciated as a music of that black peoples' culture. That's what I felt and received and understood in Europe. And that caused me to move to another level in my thinking of how we would promote and market our product in America.

His determination as a record promoter was rejuvenated, fortified. "We hadn't been getting our records into many of the larger stores that catered primarily to whites. But I became very aggressive and demanding with respect to that. Europe let me know that the sales potential is out there. And that sales potential justifies us making that kind of investment into our product, even though, at that point, the industry was not enthusiastically positioning our product. I didn't stop. I mean, I just didn't stop. Don't tell me, 'No, it can't be done.' I see it. I was on the kill to take Stax and those artists to that level of appreciation in this country."

Their horizons widened, deepened. They'd flown on a plane now, and their thoughts, goals, and visions soared like never before. They had experienced their own power, seen and felt the response they summoned. Otis was undeniable as a superstar in the making, Sam and Dave too. The potential everyone felt was unbounded, the possibilities overwhelming.

14. WHITE CARNATIONS
1967–1968

THIS WAS A prolific period for Stax, the success fueling the fires of creativity. There were hits from house regulars: William Bell—"Never Like This Before," "Everybody Loves a Winner," and "Eloise, Hang On In There"; from Booker T. & the MG's—"My Sweet Potato," "Booker Loo," "Hip Hug Her," "Slim Jenkins' Place," and "Groovin'" (released by the MG's before the original by the Rascals, because Tom Dowd shared an Atlantic test pressing with them, and they cut it on the spot); Carla recorded one of her career highlights, "B-A-B-Y," and also hit with her Otis duet, "Tramp," a session that proved so much fun they recorded a whole album together, *The King and Queen of Soul.*

Otis's hits included "My Lover's Prayer," "Fa-Fa-Fa-Fa-Fa (Sad Song)," and his innovative take on "Try a Little Tenderness," transforming a standard into a truly personal vision. "Tenderness" dates to the 1930s, and had been covered by Bing Crosby and Nina Simone, among many. Phil Walden suggested the song, and before Otis played Phil his version, he told Phil, "It's a brand-new song now." Sam and Dave's "I Can't Stand Up," a less shouted, more nuanced vocal, was another in their run (a bigger hit abroad than in the USA), this one written by Stax's Homer Banks and Allen Jones, a break from the duo's Hayes and Porter hits.

Newly arrived Albert King, after making his presence known with

"Laundromat Blues," released classics "Crosscut Saw" and "Born Under a Bad Sign." Eddie Floyd hit again with "Raise Your Hand," Mable John announced her arrival with "Your Good Thing (Is About to End)" and "Same Time, Same Place," and Johnnie Taylor got comfortable, hitting with "I Got to Love Somebody's Baby," "Little Bluebird," and "Ain't That Lovin' You (for More Reasons Than One)."

Stax expanded its publishing offices, taking over the neighboring bay to the west after the TV-repair service closed. David Porter was growing a team, and now they had a place with their own piano, where the business of writing and publishing could be managed. The glory spread beyond the artists. *Record World* magazine named Jim Stewart its outstanding record producer of 1967, and in early 1968, Jim announced an expansion into St. Louis, taking over office space and a studio there. He told *Billboard* that Stax was eyeing studio space in Atlanta too.

◆ ◆ ◆

THE THRILL OF the European tour was still hanging like a garland around the musicians when another call came, this time from the West. Promoters in California were planning the first rock and roll festival, modeled on successful jazz and folk festivals. Organizers in Monterey wanted Otis to help round out a lineup that included established artists performing alongside relatively unknown British rock acts, upcoming psychedelic artists, and blues, jazz, and country artists. Jimi Hendrix, Janis Joplin, and the Who are among those who jump-started their careers at the Monterey Pop Festival. Otis was the only southern soul act invited, but one of the festival organizers, Andrew Oldham, who managed the Rolling Stones, was intent on exposing the Haight-Ashbury hipsters to this artist who had so strongly influenced his group. Any doubts about the show's potential were assuaged by the adamant endorsement of Jerry Wexler. Otis was still without a band and the MG's were committed to the studio, but they—and Jim Stewart—knew the West Coast exposure could be really helpful, so they happily obliged; the horns too. Everyone got their tour suits dry-cleaned and prepared to go West for the June 17, 1967, appearance. They were given the honor of closing the Saturday night of the festival.

Otis met the MG's and Mar-Keys there a day early, time enough to get refreshed and to review their show. "We had an afternoon rehearsal without amplifiers in a hotel room," says Duck, "just trying to remember what we'd done in Europe." The festival was in full swing, and Monterey was like a rainbow commune, an eye-opening, mind-blowing experience from the moment they arrived. "I stepped on the street in Monterey and it changed my life," Booker says, describing the place that won his heart and would eventually draw him West to settle. "It was our first announcement that something new was happening in the United States. I had never seen people dress like that. For the first time I saw restaurants giving food for free. People were sharing hotel rooms and disregarding money. No police in the streets. Coming out of Memphis, it was a shock. History was changing at that moment, and we knew it."

"We'd seen hippies on television," says Wayne, "but we hadn't been around them, with the babies and flowers and headbands and doing all that love, dove, peace thing."

"The aroma," says Steve, referring to the prevalence of marijuana, "we weren't exposed to any of that yet. We were just little choirboys from Memphis." The cherubs found themselves at the dawning of the age of Aquarius. More than two years before Woodstock, this was the loudest announcement yet to mainstream America that there was more to rock and soul than girls screaming at the Beatles. Duck would promptly adopt the fashion, letting his hair and sideburns grow, getting a wide-brimmed hat and bell-bottoms. "There were fifty thousand people there," says Wayne. "The biggest crowd we'd ever seen—three times bigger than my hometown. And they were all hippies."

On show day, the choirboys watched and waited. The Electric Flag, Moby Grape, Hugh Masekela—California was even further from Memphis than they imagined. Their set was to begin after the Jefferson Airplane, who were hot with the recent singles "Somebody to Love" and "White Rabbit." By then, the show's schedule had fallen behind, and a light rain was beginning. The plan had been to give the hippies a proper soul revue, with the MG's warming up the crowd, then the horns joining them for a couple songs; a ramp-up to star time with Otis Redding. Festival organizers got in Otis's manager's ear, suggesting they cut the warm-up and go directly to the main event; Phil Walden didn't want to lose the crowd, and he bore down hard on the band to give up their set. When the Airplane finished, the rain caused a fifteen-minute delay and the tension backstage thickened. The audience, meanwhile, found the drizzle refreshing; the original plan held.

The MG's walked out wearing green mohair suits and Beatle boots, and in that audience at that time, *they* were the freaks: No one else looked like that. "We were doing our steps," says Wayne, "and we must have looked like a lounge act." Nothing may have looked right, but something was definitely working.

"Booker T. & the MG's took the stage with their little amps," says Jerry Wexler. "All day there'd been wild uninhibited rock and roll and volume with twenty-foot Marshall amps—all the wrong things about rock and roll. And when the audience heard the real thing, they made the right responses. Next thing you know, you could hear the band and the groove. I found out one thing that night: When you got a loud crowd, play soft."

Filmmaker D.A. Pennebaker, the documentarian responsible for Bob Dylan's *Don't Look Back*, was there with a camera crew, and his film *Monterey Pop* (and the subsequent DVD of the entire Stax set) documents the crowd's reaction. After the warm-up there's a quick and low-key introduction from Tommy Smothers of the folk-comedy act the Smothers Brothers, and the audience reacts with mild applause. The horns play a galloping fanfare and Otis hustles onstage, his blue mohair suit contrasting with the band's matched green. Behind them is a thirty-foot psychedelic display of swirls and strobing blobs. Moments into the first verse of "Shake," the Sam Cooke song performed at a trillion miles per hour, half the band drops out, leaving just Otis, Al Jackson, and Duck Dunn to carry the song—and they drive it, hauling the tens of thousands of people with them. Every audience likes dynamics, and Otis was winning them over. Aretha had just made a pop hit with her version of Otis's "Respect," and he next let the audience know where the song originated.

Catching his breath before the ballad—everyone needed a ballad after that fiery romp—he chatted with the audience, Booker's organ quietly evoking prayer time at the neighborhood church. Introducing a "soulful number," Otis asks, "This is the love crowd, right? We all love each other, don't we?" They assure him it is and they do. He can hear them, but he's not satisfied. "Am I right?" he screams, and they scream back at him affirmatively. "Let me hear you say 'Yeah,' then!" And he hears them, a pregnant pause following, organ notes falling, a hole opening in the sky and the music outlining God's face. It's only a few seconds, but it's a world, too, and then Otis eases in: "I've been—" and he takes a breath, maybe two. It's as if he's finished his sentence. Subject, verb. The past tense is made present by the next words, framed by breaths, "loving you"—and the guitar begins to rise—"too lo-o-ng"—another breath—"to stop now." As fast as the other songs were, this one is that much slower. Did we rock your socks off? (Let me hear you say Yeah!) Well, now we're going to wrench your heart. (Yeah!) The horns stair-step up, soon to be answered by Booker's cascade down. Every note Steve plays is distinct—there's that much space. The verse is punctuated by three staccato notes, the whole band together, and Otis's body flails on each note. As if the song could get more intense, Otis shares the intimacy of the group with the masses by casually turning toward the drummer and, totally unplanned, interrupts the song (without it feeling like an interruption) and says, "Can we do that one more time, Al, just like that?" and without pause or hesitation—the band is that tight—they give Otis three more notes. Each one fires like a rifle, and he flails and wails, then asks twice more to do it again—oh, oh, oh—and then eases into the rest of the song. It's showmanship, it's artistry, it's love and affection, and that night in Monterey, California, it was contagious. The Love Generation caught Otis Redding.

They were living the crossover moment, the cultural connection between the insular southerners and progressive America—the white, record-buying hippies and the deep soul of Redding and the MG's. He followed with a reinterpretation of the Rolling Stones' "Satisfaction" that was familiar enough to keep the audience comfortable but also distinctly his own; the lead-guitar riff was played by the horns. The set and the night closed with "Try a Little Tenderness" rising from a ballad to a full-on soul maelstrom—"I don't want to go but I have to go y'all"—and when he leaves, the heavens open, a destiny manifest, a new audience that will leave the show and seek his records. Louis Armstrong crossed over, Sammy Davis Jr. crossed over, Sam Cooke crossed over, and finally, great God almighty, Otis Redding was reaching that fabled shore.

"After that," says Jim Stewart, "especially on the West Coast, his sales mushroomed." Otis's career had been a steady and constant ascension, a fire that continuously grew in both light and heat. Finally, it was raging.

Zelma Redding, Otis's widow, recollects him standing in the doorway after he made his way home. "He said, 'You just can't believe what happened.' He said, 'I blew them away.'" Zelma laughs. "Monterey was a highlight. Him walking in that door and looking with those big eyes, saying, 'I killed them.' He just knew he was on the right path."

◆ ◆ ◆

SAM AND DAVE were also walking that path. Since hitting with "Hold On, I'm Coming," the duo had released "Said I Wasn't Gonna Tell Nobody," "You Got Me Hummin'," and "When Something Is Wrong with My Baby," all written by Isaac Hayes and David Porter and all top-ten R&B hits. From the European tour, their live version of Sam Cooke's "Soothe Me" also hit the charts. They performed nearly three hundred shows a year, carrying a band that would soon grow to sixteen pieces—mostly horn players whose energetic moves with their gleaming instruments became solar flares radiating from these two stars. They were widely known as the greatest live act of all time.

Songwriters Hayes and Porter were also on an astral plane, merged into a single identity. Their songs seemed pulled from the ether wholly formed for listening enjoyment, but their channeling of the ordinary to create something extraordinary was in fact a laborious process requiring dedication, discernment, and discipline. "It's amazing how one little spark will ignite," Isaac says, explaining how they wrote the duo's next timeless hit. "'Soul Man' was written when there was a lot of racial unrest in this country. There was uprising in various cities, people burning buildings—Watts, Detroit. So I was watching TV and one of the news commentators said, 'If the black businesses write *soul* on the building, the rioters will bypass it,' and I thought about the night of the Passover in the Bible, blood of the lamb on the door, the firstborn is spared. And I realized the word *soul* keeps them from burning up their establishments. Wow, soul. Soul. Soul man. 'David, I got one!' So we started working on it and came up with 'Soul Man.'"

Released in August of 1967, the song opens with Steve playing a

The Sam and Dave Orchestra, widely known in the late 1960s as the greatest live act of all time. (Photograph by Jack Robinson/Jack Robinson Archive/The Conde Nast Archive)

Isaac Hayes (far right) and David Porter (next to him), in front of Stax, February 1968. L–R: Booker T. Jones, Ronnie Stoots, Bonnie Bramlett, Al Jackson Jr. (looking down), Duck Dunn, Delaney Bramlett, Steve Cropper (obscured). (Photograph by Don Nix/Courtesy of the Oklahoma Museum of Popular Culture, Steve Todoroff Collection)

(deceptively) simple two-string guitar lick, backed by a tambourine beat. But that restraint gives way to a playful horn line. As Sam's lead vocal kicks in, he's nearly growling, singing of a daring love rescue. Each part is perfectly placed as the song progresses, a carousel of leads and hooks, none battling the other, each a support when not in the spotlight. The horns have applied all they've learned from Otis, alternating between complicated but catchy lines and bedrock foundations for the other instruments. Steve injects such exciting bluesy slide-guitar parts that Sam Moore can't contain himself during one of the choruses and, seeing him create these sounds by moving his Zippo lighter along the strings, Sam hollers out, "Play it, Steve!" Play it he does, they all do, all the way to the number-one spot on the R&B charts (where it stayed for seven weeks) and to number two on the pop charts. Race riots were occurring in Boston, New York, Chicago, and cities large and small across the country. "When 'Soul Man' becomes a national number one record," wrote *Rolling Stone* magazine at the time, "it indicates that a much more earthy, low-down kind of soul is beginning to get to white America."

◆ ◆ ◆

ON THE HEELS of Monterey, Otis was ready to tour again, his management eager to capitalize on his success. The MG's were tethered to the studio, and he needed a band. He'd been hearing of the MG's protégés, the kids they'd been training and who'd had their own hit, but it wasn't till that spring that he got to hear them. On a visit to Memphis, he went with Carla Thomas and some other Stax artists to Beale Street, where the Bar-Kays were playing at the Hippodrome. "The Bar-Kays were doing their thing," recalls Carla. "We were all sitting at the table, and Otis said, 'Listen to those little boys!' He called them 'little boys.' 'Listen to those little boys! My goodness, they sound like tenfold.'"

The Bar-Kays could play the hits of the day as well as their own material (they were nearly done recording their first album, a mix of originals and cover songs). Guests began sitting in with the band, and Otis leapt at the opportunity. "When Otis got up there and we started playing behind him," says James Alexander, "he kept looking back. We were just teenagers, we had all this energy—boundless energy. And when we finished our performance, he just kept saying, 'I like this band.'" He mentioned going on the road, an idea that appealed to these "little boys" much more than attending school. "He said he would get us a tutor so we could travel and be his band," James continues, "but our parents banded together and said, 'We're not going to let these kids go until they finish high school.' At that

Otis Redding

time, all of the Bar-Kays except for me were in the twelfth grade. I was in the eleventh grade. And it was very clear that we was going to end up playing with Otis Redding."

"Oh, Otis loved those kids so much," says Zelma. "One of the reasons for getting a new, bigger plane was so the Bar-Kays could tour with him and he could get them home on Sunday night or Monday morning so they could go to school. They was his babies. That's exactly what the Bar-Kays were. And they had so much talent."

Four of the five Bar-Kays threw their high school graduation caps in the air and then all of them, including rising senior James Alexander, boarded a plane that very night bound for New York and a series of gigs at the Apollo. They'd had no rehearsal; Otis had told them which records to learn, and in the dressing room before the first show, they discussed the gig. "The night of graduation," says James, "we took a flight to New York—a group of guys that have never been no more than a fifty-mile radius in all directions of Memphis, Tennessee. That whole thing that Stevie Wonder says—'skyscrapers and everything'—we're just looking all around." The bill had other soul stars on it, and between sets of the whole revue, the Apollo ran a feature film. "The Apollo audience is tough," James continues. "They had four or five shows a day, starting from like twelve forty-five [in the afternoon]. We didn't have but one uniform at the time, so we would wear that uniform all day. Parents would drop their kids in the morning and there wasn't no such thing as turning over the house. You'd ask the crowd, 'How y'all doing this evening?' Nobody would respond. If somebody has been there since a quarter to one, they might answer, 'When you going to change clothes?' We were there for ten days, and before we left, we won them over."

"The last day at the Apollo, we did one of the best shows of my life," says trumpeter Ben Cauley. "As the group played, Otis called James Brown onto the bandstand, and we were doing 'Papa's Got a Brand New Bag.' We was playing some stuff there that I couldn't explain to you. But Otis was stepping, James was stepping, and we started stepping right with them. 'One thing's for sure,' Otis said, 'I don't care if y'all are stepping because y'all be playing your behinds off!' We were in full bloom. Whatever we needed, it just opened up."

That summer, Otis toured heavily with the Bar-Kays. He'd upgraded to a twin-engine Beechcraft private plane; it held eight people, but they were a ten-person entourage: Otis, the pilot, two valets, and six Bar-Kays. They worked out a rotation system. "When we got to each city," explains James Alexander, "we would always rent two vehicles. The two not on the private plane would drop the group at the hangar, then return the rental vehicles and take a commercial flight." They played all over the continent, including a show at the Expo '67 World's Fair in Montreal, Canada, on July 4, and a week in San Francisco at the Basin Street West that James recalls as among their best gigs. The Bar-Kays pushed Otis hard; he'd been developing a serious hoarseness, and it worsened. When a doctor found polyps on his vocal cords, surgery was required. The operation would risk that he'd never sing again, but if he didn't have it, he was guaranteed to lose his voice. Some of the Bar-Kays had enrolled for the fall semester of college in Memphis, so there was a natural break around Labor Day. The convalescence required six weeks of total silence, and Otis decided to throw a last party. He was having a swimming pool installed at the Big O Ranch, so he planned a huge gathering there for Labor Day weekend. He set up a stage and featured Sam and Dave, Arthur Conley, the Bar-Kays, and others. They cooked five pigs and two cows, and guests arrived on buses from Atlanta. Otis didn't perform, worn out by the summer's travels, but he was a gracious host. "He was so tired he was just sitting there out in the middle of the front yard," Zelma said. "He spoke to everybody but he just couldn't move."

For the first time in this constant climb for success, Otis would have a few weeks off. His children were five, four, and three, and he'd taste bonding time with them. He'd have quiet time with Zelma, from whom he'd grown distant by the constant travel. And he'd have time with his thoughts—to be creative, to reflect on where he'd come from and where he was going. He was twenty-six, and the past five years had been a blur. He'd be able to consider his relationships: with his manager, with his record company, with his wife. After Labor Day, he went under the knife, and the Bar-Kays went back to school.

◆ ◆ ◆

OTIS WOULDN'T KNOW the surgery's results until six weeks had passed. If he tested his voice, he could do irreparable damage. Strict silence, doctor's orders. He couldn't even shout for joy when the October issue of the British magazine *Melody Maker* named him top male vocalist; he'd dethroned Elvis from the position the King had held for ten years. In the quiet, he wrote new material. Instead of having to snatch an hour after sound check, or pull out the guitar before going to bed, he could really focus on songwriting. "He dissected the *Sgt. Pepper* album," says manager

Phil Walden. "I'd get him Bob Dylan albums and stuff like that. It made him much more conscious of the importance of lyrics."

When he returned to the doctor, the results were very good indeed. Given clearance to resume his career, his voice quickly regained strength. With a mixture of excitement and trepidation, he booked time at Stax for the end of November and beginning of December, more than two weeks—time enough to polish some songs with Steve Cropper and to record a batch of new material.

"Otis was so busy on the road we could hardly get time to do any sessions with him," says Jim. This booking was going to be different.

"Otis called me from the airport," Steve remembers. He'd just landed in Memphis, and he was excited. "He was coming in to write, and then we were gonna set up the sessions based on what we'd written. He said, 'I gotta show you this song.' He said, 'I'm coming right down the studio.'" When he walked in, he told Steve to get his "guh-tar" (as he pronounced it); Steve kept an acoustic Gibson B-25 at the studio. Otis wrote songs in open tuning, so Steve tuned to open E. "He started singing this 'Dock of the Bay,'" says Steve. "He had the intro and most of the first verse. I helped him with, I think, 'I left my home in Georgia, headed for the Frisco bay,' and then I wrote the bridge with him."

They quickly recorded the song. (Steve remembers doing it early in the sessions; Jim says it was the very last song.) "We had been trying to find something that Otis could sing that would be a crossover hit," Steve continues. "We tried ballads, from 'A Change Is Gonna Come' to 'Try a Little Tenderness.' We came close, but we didn't really have that record that leaves rhythm and blues and starts going up the pop charts, being played by popular demand. The day we recorded 'Dock of the Bay,' we looked at each other and said, 'This is our hit, we got it.'"

Jim Stewart, harking back to his first session with Otis, wasn't terribly impressed by "Dock of the Bay." The song was unusual for Otis, and didn't strike Jim like "I've Been Loving You Too Long" or "Try a Little Tenderness."

In fact, "Dock of the Bay" has none of the trademark Otis Redding characteristics. There's not the rambunctious energy, there's no growling vocals, it's not a ballad that aches. Rather, it's introspective and contemplative, a sudden synthesis of the Beatles and Bob Dylan by a soul singer. He'd been captivated by *Sgt. Pepper*—but the song is hardly derivative of the Beatles. It conveys a new worldliness, an ability to present the ultimate sophistication, which is simplicity. It's a leap in the way that Otis's first session was, when he went from imitating Little Richard to establishing his own ballad style, walking through a door he hadn't previously the confidence, nor the artistic development, to enter.

During those couple weeks in Memphis, Otis recorded and sang, sang and recorded. "Hard to Handle" hit the tape. They cut the Five Royales' "Tell the Truth," Zelma's "I've Got Dreams to Remember," the propulsive "Love Man." Things kept getting better. "Before the operation, he couldn't sing all night," Steve explains. "His voice would break up. But after, he just kept going. We were up till six one morning." His post-surgery voice sounded so much stronger and warmer that they dug up multitrack tapes from prior sessions and replaced the older vocals. Over the two weeks, they cut nearly four albums' worth of material.

On Friday, December 8, they took a break. That weekend, Otis was to perform three shows with the Bar-Kays—Nashville, Cleveland, and then Madison, Wisconsin—and the MG's (with David Porter on vocals) were going out Saturday to play Indiana State University. "Otis stuck his head in the studio before leaving," says Steve, "and said, 'See ya on Monday.'"

Otis's Friday-night gig in Nashville ended early, so at his suggestion they left for Cleveland right away, giving them a chance to catch a bit of the O'Jays and the Temptations at Leo's Casino, the same Cleveland club they were booked into. It was a treat for the band. They did the *Upbeat* TV show that afternoon and when they played Saturday night, "It was just unbelievable," says James, "the crowd response was just unbelievable."

On Sunday, James Alexander and roadie Carl Sims dropped the band at the hangar. It was midday in Cleveland and cold. Ben Cauley remembers that Carl Cunningham asked for the plane to be turned on so the cabin could warm up. The attendant "told us he couldn't crank it up because the battery was kind of low," says Ben. "He said he'd rather have the pilot do it. We looked at each other, as young fellows do, and said, 'The battery's low?' Five minutes after that it got started—but we were still thinking about that. Then we took off going to Madison with no problems."

There were no direct flights to Madison, so James and Carl caught a plane to Milwaukee. Otis's pilot would shuttle them to Madison for the 6:30 gig, the first of two at the club that night. In Milwaukee, they waited, and they waited some more. "This was not like them," says James. "We started calling around and calling around. We called the hangar and couldn't find them. Two or three hours passed and we still didn't know anything."

The private plane's flight had gone smoothly enough that most of the guys were catching a nap. The pilot was given clearance to land at 3:25

P.M., four miles from Madison. Visibility was hampered by low cloud cover, dense at one hundred feet. "We were three minutes from landing," says Ben Cauley, "and then it crashed. I remember waking up because I couldn't breathe. The engines sounded real loud and I had a funny spinning sensation of falling through space. I thought the plane had hit an air pocket. [Saxman] Phalon was sitting next to me and said, 'What's that, man?' And he looked out the window. Now, what he saw, I couldn't tell you, but I do remember, he says, 'Oh no.' And I turned to say something to him, but I couldn't because I couldn't breathe. I unbuckled my seatbelt. I was going to tell them to do the same thing, but I wasn't fast enough. I'm bumping around. Mentally, I wanted to tell them to. But I had done mine. This may have saved my life."

The low battery was affecting the instrument panel and perhaps the engines, while the pilot's judgment was hampered by the clouds and his inexperience in cold weather, the temperature intensified by the bitter lake below. A Lake Monona resident heard the peculiar engine sound, so loud and low, and stepped outside to see the plane appear through the cloud cover—and and dive headlong into the water. He called authorities. They would arrive in seventeen minutes. Upon impact, the plane's fuselage ripped open, ejecting Cauley and the others.

Otis was seated in the front, next to the pilot. He'd become an airplane enthusiast, and after some informal training, the pilot sometimes let him fly. But he'd stayed up late with the other guys, and he was also taking a nap. "Otis was sitting directly in front of me in the copilot's seat," Ben continues. "I didn't hear him say a word. Didn't see him do a thing. The next thing I remember is bobbing up in the water holding onto this cushion. I was on top of all this water. And then I saw Phalon coming up after me, and Ronnie, and some of the cats come up—Carl [Cunningham], I saw Carl. And I said, 'What in the world are we doing?' At that time, my mind was really fogged up. And the only thing I could think was, We're in the wrong place. We're in the wrong place. I'll never forget that.

"I was in the water about a good twenty minutes. And I was cold out there. I had on my winter shoes and I remember my right shoe was on. And I had my trench coat on. And, I was bleeding in my head, I didn't realize that. And I was cold. I was shaking. I saw little bits of ice floating around in the water.

"I was the only one who couldn't swim. I was holding the airplane seat in my hand. Do you know, I lost it in the water, the airplane seat? I saw Ronnie come out. I'll never forget that. Ronnie came up and he was hol-

The fateful Friday, December 8, 1967. As the Bar-Kays prepare to leave Memphis for what will be their final tour, drummer Carl Cunningham (far left) laughs with neighborhood friends. One carries his gig clothes, dry cleaned. (Photograph by Don Nix/Courtesy of the Oklahoma Museum of Popular Culture, Steve Todoroff Collection)

lering for help. And I was saying, 'Ronnie, hold on man. I'm trying to get over to you.' I was trying to get to him, and the more I tried to get to him, this airplane seat was slipping out my hand. And then finally, it slipped out of my hand and at that point, I said, 'Oh no.' I knew I was next because I didn't have nothing, and then another seat cushion came straight to me.

"I saw Carl come out of the water. He didn't say anything. I saw [Otis's valet] Matt come up on the other side. And then, for a while, nobody was there. They had floated away or drowned. And, I felt like—I knew I was next." Cauley remembers that he'd begun slipping into the water, fighting to stay afloat, the chaotic and panicked efforts of a drowning man. "I laid there one time and then I came back up and said, 'I'm all right.'" He'd been in the water for seventeen minutes, his body moments from severe hypothermia, and when he felt like he was going down for the last time, "Someone just lifted me up. When they got me aboard the boat, I couldn't talk at all. I saw them bringing the others in and that's when I stopped talking. When they got Jimmy—just think about it, what I saw. I tightened up. I could not talk. I said, 'What is this?' But I couldn't talk." The images in his head are dreamlike, a nightmare of confusion and shock. "There was this thing over all our heads, including me too. They didn't want me to see what really had happened. And I was trying to get to them to help them, to see if everything was all right. And they just kept constantly pushing me back down, told me to lay down. 'Are you all right?' And I said, 'I'm all right.'"

Ben, husband and father to a nine-month-old, was taken to a hospital. "I remember the coroner told the nurse and two of the doctors to stay around my bedside because I was in shock. I didn't know what shock was. But I knew how I was feeling. I couldn't talk. And I was scared because Jimmy and them was gone. And when I came back around, I realized what really happened to me." What really happened was that the dead bodies of guitarist Jimmy King and pilot Dick Fraser had been pulled from the lake, and there was a frantic search for the others as nightfall closed in. He remembers, "I kept asking, 'Are they all right?' And this guy just looked at me and said, 'Well, son, you're the only one alive.' Once he said that, I couldn't talk. I'd never been that way before in my life. I was shaking all over."

James Alexander and Carl Sims were still waiting for their ride to the gig. "Then some authorities came to Milwaukee to pick us up," says James, "and they said, 'The plane went down.' They didn't have any details other than the plane had gone down." Slowly, more information came in. First they were told that everyone had died, and then later that Ben had survived. "We got to Madison, we went to talk to—to see Ben in the hospital and he was in a state of shock. He was just laying there with his eyes open. He didn't really know he was there at that point."

James Alexander, seventeen years old, had the grisly task of identifying the bodies. "I was numb," he says. "That Sunday night, late, we identified two people. Just a strange thing to do, especially when all these guys were your friends and you grew up with them, and then here you have to go and identify them in a morgue. That's tough."

Jim Stewart got a call that Sunday evening from Joe Galkin, the traveling promotions man who'd brought Otis to his attention a short five and a half years earlier. Galkin told him to turn on the television, and Jim absorbed the news with the rest of the world. He remembered that last session, and an unusual feeling he'd had. "I had gone to my office," Jim says, "and I knew Otis was getting ready to leave. I had the feeling that I must tell Otis good-bye. I had never felt that way before. Otis would come in and everything would be hectic and then he'd leave and I'd never think anything about it. I don't know if you believe in premonitions, but if you listen to the lyrics on 'Dock of the Bay,' it's kind of scary if you relate that to the events that happened. And I was never able to say good-bye."

The MG's were trapped by the weather in the Indianapolis airport. "We had missed our connection," Steve remembers. "There was an icy runway. And I know we made the comment that if we could get a hold of Otis's pilot, he'd come get us out of here. David Porter called home to let his wife know. We didn't all want to spend the same dime, so he was going to ask his wife to call our wives. And he came back, just—'What's wrong?' And he'd just found out. His wife heard on the radio that Otis's plane had gone down."

"We had just come from a wedding of one of our very good friends," says Carla Thomas. "We had gotten home and we were jiving and joking about it. And we just happened to turn on the TV, and we were in this elated mood. And then they said, 'Bulletin.' Just, *boom*. 'Plane belonging to Otis Redding . . .' And I knew that the kids were with him. They were traveling together. And, what I did? I just put my hands in my ear. I didn't even hear the rest of it. Mother and I were in there together, so after the bulletin went off, I looked at her. She looked at me. And I said, 'What did they say?' I wanted to get it secondhand. And then she told me."

"I was in the kitchen, the phone rang," says Wayne Jackson. It was his horn partner, Andrew Love, calling. "He said, 'Did you hear about Otis?' When you hear those words, you know something really bad's happened. I said, 'No. I hadn't been listening to the radio today.' And he said, 'They're all gone.' I said, 'What do you mean, "gone"?' He said, 'They're gone. They all went in the lake up in Wisconsin.' And we stood there, just silence, nothing but static in the air."

Silence. Static. "And that's the way I thought my life would be with no Otis in it. He was such a predominant force in our lives and we'd learned so much about being energetic and having a great time, the joy that you feel playing music with him. It was really hard to get a hold of the fact that he was gone and would never be back."

Jimmy King, age eighteen. Guitarist.

Carl Cunningham, age eighteen. Drummer.

Phalon Jones, age nineteen. Saxophonist.

Ronnie Caldwell, age nineteen. Organist.

Matthew Kelly, age seventeen. Valet.

Richard Fraser, age twenty-six. Pilot.

Otis Redding, age twenty-six. Star.

Nashville, Tennessee 37203

A Newspaper With A Constructive Policy

MEMPHIS WORLD

VOLUME 36, NUMBER 25

MEMPHIS, TENNESSEE, SATURDAY, DECEMBER 16, 1967

Mourning Bar-Kays

MEMPHIS IN TEARS!

Magicians Whip Fisk, Play Bucs

Plane Crash Shocks

THE BAR-KAYS — Five of The Bar-Kays in this photograph were aboard Otis Redding's plane which crashed Sunday in a lake near Madison, Wis. Killed were Phalon Jones (bottom, center), tenor sax; Carl Cunningham (middle, center), drummer; Ronnie Caldwell (top, left), organist; Jimmy King (top, center), guitarist and leader, and Matthew Kelly, drummer, not pictured. Ben Cauley (bottom, left), trumpet player, was the only survivor, and James Alexander (right), bass player, was not aboard the craft.

ONE IS "MISS LeMOYNE" — Yes, one of coeds is the new "Miss LeMoyne College"

❖ ❖ ❖

SUCH A TRAGEDY brings out the crass essence of a commercial enterprise like a record label. Steve remembers, "We got a call from Atlantic saying, 'We've got to rush something out immediately. What have you got?' And I immediately said, 'We need to put our hit out.' The difficulty was not the fact that it had to be done real quick. The difficulty was—they hadn't even found Otis's body yet." Cropper threw himself into the project, a way to block all other thoughts from his mind. He added electric guitar, seagulls, and the sound of waves. He went in early and mixed all night. "I handed it to a flight attendant, who flew it to New York and handed it to a representative from Atlantic. Trying to work on something like that when you don't even know where one of your closest friends is is difficult."

Otis's body wasn't found until later on Monday, when Carl Cunningham was also retrieved. The ongoing search was hampered by the chill of the water. "Police skin divers said they were unable to remain in the 30–40 degree water longer than fifteen minutes at maximum," *Sepia* magazine reported. When Otis was brought up, he was still buckled into his seat, his eyes closed. "He looked," said a witness, "as if he was taking a nap." Four thousand five hundred people overflowed the Macon Municipal Auditorium's three thousand seats for Otis's funeral. The hour-long service was quiet and solemn. Joe Simon sang "Jesus Keep Me Near the Cross," and midway through, Zelma broke down, wailing and stamping her feet in sorrow. Decorum was broken only when James Brown exited the building, mobbed by teenagers who pounced on his car; when it tried to follow the hearse, their weight caused the tires to spin, blue smoke rising. Otis was buried at the Big O Ranch, in view of his kitchen window.

The funerals for Cunningham, King, and Kelly were held together on Sunday the seventeenth, a week after the crash. Aptly, a heavy rain descended from a gloomy Memphis sky. Nearly three thousand mourners filled Clayborn Temple AME Church, and the speakers included Estelle Axton and the principal of Booker T. Washington High School who said, "We are witnessing a phenomenon of life, in which the evening sun of their lives has gone down while it is still morning." During the service, word spread that divers had just found Phalon Jones. The line of cars leading to the cemetery ran over a mile long. The four African-American Bar-Kays are buried alongside each other at New Park Cemetery. Ronnie Caldwell, whose body was not recovered until Wednesday, was buried on the twenty-second in a family plot.

"That next week I went to Stax," says Cauley, where a wreath of white carnations hung on the door. "It was like going back home, because we put so much into Stax. It was part of us. We used to sit on the floor many nights and practice, rehearse and play shows together. And Miz Axton was there with us. Miz Axton was like our mama. The Bar-Kays could do no wrong because of Miz Axton. She came in and hugged me."

"Otis was not only an artist, he was a dear friend," says Jim. "He stayed at my home many times when he would come to town. It was a great loss, so much talent that we never got to explore. He was just beginning."

"Everybody was walking around staring at their feet for two months after that," says Marvell Thomas. "There was true sadness at that place. I didn't know Otis nearly as well as a lot of the other people did, but I certainly felt his loss. You would walk in the door—Stax was usually a happy, peppy place, there was conversations in the hallways and songwriters over here and a demo going—that all stopped. It was quiet like a mausoleum. Everybody was very sad and very introspective. And strictly from a business standpoint, Stax Records lost its biggest act. So they felt it psychologically, emotionally, and in their pocketbook."

"About a month or two after the plane crash," remembers Don Nix, "here comes a UPS truck with all these boxes. They were all warped and somebody come dumped them in the lobby. It was Carl's drums. They'd been at the bottom of that lake all that time. And everybody just sighed. We were getting over it, and I remember how that made me feel. 'Cause everyone was friends—a neighborhood. It was guys that cared about each other."

15. "BORN UNDER A BAD SIGN"
1968

AFTER THE LOSS of someone close, we seek solace in the familiar, comfort among others with whom we share similar bonds. Routine actions, longtime friends—the heightened appreciation for the mundane—these come into high relief. Assessing its new, bleaker world, Stax sought the balm of the ordinary but found instead yet more encroaching change.

Stax Records was an independent record company, its home in Memphis, its owners and staff in the same building as the studio, as the mailing room, as the retail record store. But to get the records into the stores, Stax was under the Atlantic Records umbrella. Stax found the talent and made the recordings, shipping the master tapes to New York; there, Atlantic pressed and distributed the recordings, keeping the lion's share for its expenses and its effort, paying a royalty to Stax. Atlantic was older and larger than Stax and the other independents it had similar deals with; it had earlier faced the same retail problem, and it conquered that by creating a distribution network: If stores could come to Atlantic and order not only Atlantic's product but also those of other independent record labels—Dial with hitmaker Joe Tex; T-Neck with the Isley Brothers; Moonglow with the Righteous Brothers—then the smaller labels could have a shot at competing with Warner Bros., with Columbia, with RCA. Stax, then, was its own entity, but its arms and reach were through its association with Atlantic.

By the middle of the 1960s, the business world in America was rumbling toward conglomerates. Big corporations were buying big companies to become more massive, making it harder for the independent companies to find sunlight and grow. Warner Bros. had just been purchased by Seven Arts, and the new company (that would soon sell to a corporation built from New Jersey's commercial parking lots) was buying Atlantic Records for breakfast. Offered $17.5 million in late 1967, Jerry Wexler and Ahmet Ertegun couldn't resist selling. And as part of the deal, they would continue to run the company. From out of the sky fell a little piece of heaven.

But their nirvana was another's hell. First Stax negotiated with Atlantic. Jim, Estelle, and Al even flew to New York to discuss joining Atlantic in the Warner deal. "What Jerry offered me was an insult for the company," says Jim. "We were supplying Atlantic with a lot of hit records. A lot of hits. We were a big portion of their 1967 sales. That's why I was totally astounded when they came to me with some ridiculous offer." Jerry had become a mentor to Jim, making the situation that much harder for Jim to accept. "I took it as a personal thing. You realize how many millions of dollars we've run through that company since 1960. Seven years, and their total outlay of money from 1960 through '67, their cost to get that deal, was five thousand dollars. From there on they never had one penny invested, not even in production costs. They were using our money all during that period of time."

Jim went to Warner Bros. directly, but the offers were still meager, and he'd have been foolish to accept them. Fortunately, Jim had an escape: At Jim's request, the 1965 contract had a key-man clause. That meant that Jim trusted Wexler, and if ever Wexler divested his Atlantic stock, Jim could choose to terminate the relationship. The sale to Warner triggered the key-man clause, and Jim—with Estelle and input from Al Bell and other key figures—had six months to find a new company to ally with.

And then more bad news came in. "Of course, there was a contract," says Wexler, quickly adding, "and it turned out that there was a clause whereby we owned the masters."

A "clause whereby we owned the masters" meant that Stax owned nothing. It meant that all right, title, and interest in the records belonged to Atlantic, including any rights of reproduction, with Stax having no ownership, no control, and due only about a 15 percent royalty. It meant that Atlantic owned everything that it distributed for Stax—even though it said "Stax" on the label, even though Stax had paid all the money associated with those recordings and Atlantic had paid none and was at risk for not a single penny, and even though Jim and Estelle had operated for years believing their work was their own. Suddenly they were tenants of their destiny; they were sharecroppers, with nothing to show for their labor but a promise. The contract that Jim signed in 1965, formalizing the handshake, actually did not formalize the handshake but rather it slipped handcuffs on him, establishing an entirely new relationship, a very good one for Atlantic and a very bad one for Stax.

Wexler, well-spoken and widely read, a degree in journalism, continues, "I didn't know this. I never read contracts. I trusted my lawyers. And when I protest about this, people think, Well, here's a record executive who stole this thing from these poor people and he's copping out. I didn't know it. And when we were severing from Stax, it came to my notice that we had ownership of the masters. We were being bought by the Warner complex. I went to [the Warner head], I said, 'I want to give these people their masters back.' I said, 'It was just a dirty trick played on them.' They said, 'No way, this is corporate property.' Now, whether or not Jim Stewart and Cropper and the people down there believed it ultimately, to this day, I don't know."

"Jerry and I operated under a gentleman's agreement until '65," says Jim. "I had not read the fine print in the distribution agreement. In '65, I allowed that to get by me. So, I suddenly realized that I'm in the record business and it's all not peaches and cream. I love Jerry, but we had a serious, serious argument." The clause that Jim had not noticed and never read was almost exactly halfway through the thirteen-page contract. With as much information on one side of the clause as on the other, one might say it was buried—the clause that indicated Jim agreed to "sell, assign, and transfer . . . the entire right, title and interest in and to each of such masters and to each of the performances embodied thereon." Elsewhere, the contract had another clause, this one making the agreement retroactive to include every record that Atlantic had ever distributed for Stax. Consequent discussions were both over the phone and in New York; Jim remembers Ahmet present in Jerry's office "to smooth things over when things got rough."

It was corporate homicide—polite, sterile, and deadly. It also clarified the low offers Jim received from both Atlantic and Warner Bros.; if they knew they owned the masters, they wouldn't need to bid high. The news about Stax's loss was delivered to Jim by Jerry well into their negotiation. By not revealing the information earlier, and with the clock ticking for

Stax having to find a new distribution arrangement, Wexler was heaping injury upon insult, making their situation dire.

"Oh, they were aghast," Jerry says. "I said, 'I'm really distressed. Believe me, I didn't know it.' How could I expect them to believe me? It really is one of the worst things that ever happened—abuse in the record business. They made the masters, they paid for them under contract, and my clever New York lawyer winkled the masters away to our benefit and not my knowledge. 'What's wrong with you, Wexler? Don't you read your contracts?' No." (The fact against which Jerry doth protest so much spilled forth within the first couple minutes of my conversation with him, responding to my inquiry how he, in New York, had heard of Stax.)

Reeling from the loss of the catalog—not yet able to comprehend it, to absorb and react to it—Stax got more bad news from their longtime pals at Atlantic: Sam and Dave, who had been vying with Otis as Stax's leading act, were being yanked back to Atlantic. Since Otis's death, they had assumed the label's lead position. Their latest single, "I Thank You," was bold in its spare arrangement, emblematic of the new generation finding its own voice. Their albums had come out on Stax, their royalty had been paid by Stax, all of their creative decisions had been made by, with, and at Stax. But Wexler claimed that when he'd first brought the act to Stax, they were signed to Atlantic and had only ever been loaned to Stax. "We gave them Sam and Dave on lease," Wexler explains. "When the deal broke with Stax, Jim had no cognizance of that. And I said, 'Hey, since you're leaving, Sam and Dave will come back to us.' He was aghast, had no idea."

"Sam and Dave at Stax was a family thing," says Sam. "That chemistry works. And when you separate that nucleus between those four people—Sam and Dave, Hayes and Porter—something happens. It wasn't going to work. So, when they broke that mold, it all went downhill. Jerry had us down in Muscle Shoals, Alabama, but he couldn't pull the magic off, he really couldn't." Sam and Dave never had another hit.

Atlantic's failure would be no consolation. It was one bad deed after another. "We said, 'Wait a minute,'" says Steve. "'That's not what you said, and that's not what you implied,' but then they go, 'Well, yeah, but the paper [contract] says this.' Well, there didn't need to be any paper in the first place. And when you were told one thing and then later, it becomes something else—it was bad business and got kind of ugly. We'd contributed a lot of success to [Atlantic] since the early sixties. We all felt that we deserved a little bit better. It's called trusting somebody. And the world has been built on trust and when somebody goes back on their word, then hey, it's pretty devastating."

◆ ◆ ◆

THE DEVASTATION WAS just beginning. They'd lost Otis and they'd lost Sam and Dave. They'd lost every record they'd ever released. And in April of 1968, Martin Luther King stood on the balcony of the Lorraine Motel, the Stax home away from home, and took an assassin's bullet. Nothing in Memphis would ever be the same.

Events leading to Dr. King's assassination began on January 30, 1968, when a superintendent in the Department of Public Works sent home twenty-two African-American sewer workers during a morning rain. "They cut the crew and 'fore the crew leaves the barn," said one of the men, "the sun would be shining pretty, but still us go home. White men worked shine, rain, sleet, or snow." The next day, T.O. Jones—the former garbageman who'd dedicated himself to forming a union—held the twenty-two sewer workers and demanded the men receive a full day's pay, not the compensation pay of two hours (less than two dollars). The commissioner agreed to review the department's rainy-day policy, and the men returned to work.

The next day, February 1, an AFSCME field representative flew to Memphis, meeting with the commissioner to ask, on behalf of the sewer and sanitation workers, for more: a written grievance procedure and a union-dues checkoff (the option to pay union dues directly from the department). Later that afternoon, during a driving rain, two sanitation workers took refuge in a truck's hull, riding where the garbage was thrown in; there wasn't enough room for a whole crew to get in the truck's cab. A shovel slipped while the truck was en route, causing the crusher to engage. The driver heard the packing engine turn on and quickly halted, running outside to mash the stop button. A woman at her kitchen table saw the truck, then heard the screams. "It was horrible," she told the newspaper. "[One worker] was standing there on the end of the truck and suddenly it looked like the big thing [the crusher] just swallowed him." This make of vehicle had been purchased by Commissioner Loeb in the 1950s, and the workers had insisted many times that it was unsafe. Two workers, Echol Cole and Robert Walker, were crushed to death.

Henry Loeb had been reelected mayor and sworn in the prior month. He'd been hearing—and not heeding—the sanitation department's complaints for more than a decade. Loeb, who'd received 90 percent of the white vote, gave the families of the recently deceased garbagemen a month's pay (less than $200) plus $500 toward the burial expenses of $900. The city had failed to maintain its trucks, and shrugged at the consequent ruin; each family was immediately destitute. Then payday came, Friday, February 9, and the twenty-two sewer workers found no increased compensation despite their returning to work. More deaf ears and delaying tactics. (Jones later observed that the whole strike could possibly have been averted for less than forty-four dollars, two additional hours of pay to the twenty-two men.) Finally, it was too much.

On Sunday, February 11, nearly one thousand sanitation department employees overflowed a meeting hall and vented their anger. T.O. Jones led the assembly and organized the basic grievances: These men were making less than seventy dollars per week, and forced to work overtime with no compensation; the equipment was faulty and dangerous; they wanted union representation without fear of being fired; they wanted a restroom, and showers, and uniforms; they wanted to be able to advance in the department, and they wanted an acceptable wage on rain days.

The head of Public Works would concede nothing, and refused to even come address the assembled men. No strike was called, but the next morning, Abraham Lincoln's birthday, about 1,150 of Public Works' 1,300 employees refused to work; many who did work quickly returned. There was no picket line, no leaflets, no union organization, and no strategy; this was a wildcat strike, and there was only anger and the determined will for justice.

AFSCME representatives scrambled to town, including Jesse Epps, who would soon move there to lead the AFSCME local. Mayor Loeb's term was the first for a new form of government, switching from the good ole boys' club of the mayor and four at-large commissioners to a mayor and thirteen-member city council. Racial progress was kept at bay by composing the council of only seven district representatives, with the six others "at-large." Blacks, who composed 40 percent of the city, had tried to negotiate ten districts with three at-large and were stymied; they were able to place only three representatives on the council. Loeb assumed that AFSCME perceived Memphis as weak during this transition period and had provoked the situation as a way to swoop in; there was no substantiation for such an opinion then, and none has ever turned up. When Loeb told an assembly of workers that striking was against the law—"This you can't do!" he barked at them—the response was laughter. He stormed out, and AFSCME's Epps later said, "That was the first time in the history of Loeb's life that he was no longer the master. There was

Mayor Henry Loeb, left, addresses striking sanitation workers, Memphis, 1968. (University of Memphis Libraries/Special Collections)

an insurrection among the slaves . . . And he just drew the line." The Staple Singers, who were about to sign to Stax, would voice the sentiment of these and all African-American workers with a song from their first Stax album, "When Will We Be Paid (for the Work We've Done)."

"The garbagemen were a part of the fabric of the society," explains Booker T. Jones. "My father always taught me to shake their hands and say hello to them. Know who they are. They were closely interwoven into the African-American community. So their fight was everybody's fight."

"Mayor Loeb's attitude was, 'The hell with 'em!' " says Marvell Thomas. "People were tolerant of each other, even if they weren't all that trustful. But Loeb was so intractable that he made a chasm between the black and white communities."

The strike was national news before the arrival of Dr. King. Mayor Loeb, entrenched, stated to his associates, "I'll never be known as the mayor who signed a contract with a Negro union."

Despite constant attempts at negotiation, the striking workers found City Hall obstinate. Within two weeks, there was a police confrontation

March 1968, Main Street, Memphis. Police spray mace on a sanitation worker's march. (University of Memphis Libraries/Special Collections)

involving mace (a newly introduced chemical weapon). Within a month, the mayor requested that the National Guard begin riot drills. Recommendations for resolution from the state legislature were ignored. The newspaper claimed that scabs were mitigating the strike, but when Dr. King paid a first visit, seventeen thousand people came out to hear him say, "Whenever you are engaged in work that serves humanity and is for the building of humanity, it has dignity and it has worth . . . You are reminding the nation that it is a crime for people to live in this rich nation and receive starvation wages."

"Really, Dr. King was preaching what we were about inside of Stax," says Al Bell, who had worked and studied with Dr. King since the late 1950s, "where you judge a person by the content of their character rather than the color of their skin. And looking forward to the day when, as he said, his little black child and the little white child could walk down the streets together, hand in hand. Well, we were living that inside of Stax Records."

"Pops heard Dr. King speaking," Mavis Staples explains, referring to her father. "We'd been all over singing our gospel. We were in Montgomery, Alabama, one Sunday, so all of us went to Dr. King's eleven o'clock service, Dexter Avenue Baptist Church [before he moved to Atlanta]. Pops talked to Dr. King for a while and when we got back to the hotel, he called us to his room and he said, 'I really like this man's message, and if he can preach it, we can sing it.' And that was the beginning of our freedom songs. When we signed with Stax, 1968, we were singing message songs. We made that transition from strictly gospel to protest songs, freedom songs. And it seemed that Dr. King was getting the world together."

The strikers began daily marches down Main Street. They wore signs, some stating the painfully simple I AM A MAN, a fact that the city government, for years and decades, seemed intent on ignoring. These marches were not led by bullhorns, nor by chanting, protests, or group song. These marches were silent. To the sound of their own hushed footsteps, hundreds of African-American men and women traversed the length of Main Street, from Clayborn Temple to City Hall and back. (My father worked on the twelfth floor of a building on Main; his office overlooked the street. In 1968, he brought my brother and me to his office, had us open the window and look down. The image seared. The silence roared.)

On March 28, Dr. King's peaceful march was violently disbanded by police. Stores were looted and Larry Payne, a sixteen-year-old black child, was killed by a policeman's shotgun blast. Tanks, armored cars, and rifle-bearing National Guardsmen filled the streets of downtown Memphis. King, intending to negate the violence with a peaceful march, planned another stand in early April. By March 29, President Johnson got involved; Loeb rebuffed him.

Young Larry Payne was buried on April 2, his funeral amplified by the hundreds of supporters and by the raging emotions. The following day, Dr. King spoke at Clayborn Temple. There'd been death threats, serious enough that each time the window's shutters clanged against the building, Dr. King and his associates reacted with a jolt. The shutters were finally locked in place. He spoke of "difficult days ahead," then said, "I've looked over. And I've seen the Promised Land. I may not get there with you. But I want you to know tonight, that we, as a people, will get to the Promised Land!"

The next evening, in Memphis, at the Lorraine Motel, Dr. Martin Luther King was shot dead by a single bullet.

"It wasn't just that it happened in Memphis," says Booker. "He was shot at the Lorraine Motel and the Lorraine Motel was where we had our meetings on Monday morning. We used their dining room for our meeting hall and the Lorraine Motel was the place where Steve Cropper and

The day after Martin Luther King was assassinated, Mayor Henry Loeb greets a coalition of Memphis ministers with an outstretched hand. At his feet, he has a shotgun at the ready. (*Commercial Appeal*/Photograph by Robert Williams)

Eddie Floyd wrote 'Knock on Wood.' We ate there on a regular basis. It was an institution for us. And so it couldn't have been any closer had he been shot at 926 McLemore [Stax's address]."

There was rioting across the nation. Windows on Beale Street and Main Street were smashed, businesses looted and destroyed. Fires were set. But the National Guard had been withdrawn from Memphis only two days earlier, and they were easily recalled. Several artists appealed for calm on the radio, Isaac Hayes, David Porter, Rufus Thomas, and William Bell among them.

The day after the murder, Mayor Loeb held a large meeting with ministers and clergy from across the city. There is a photograph of him extending his hand to shake and make peace with men of God who had come in large number to his office. The photograph is taken from behind Loeb at his desk, and at his feet, he has stashed a shotgun. The hand may be extended, but the weapon is at the ready.

"It was the type of thing that happened and then you—you can't see a solution," says Booker. "There's no solution. There's no arrest that would help. There's no way to fix it."

Jesse Jackson had the same thought, and his solution was to not become derailed. "We were determined not to let one bullet kill the whole movement," he says. "Right after Dr. King was killed, we determined to focus on *what* killed him, not just *who* killed him in sick society. And it was a mad struggle for identity. We had lost our leadership. The ship had lost its rudder. And I remember we regrouped and kept going to Washington with the Poor People's Campaign. We didn't spend a lot of time, frankly, in Memphis trying to find the killer."

"As a testament to how the neighborhood valued Stax Records," says William Bell, "a lot of the places were either broken into or burned—everything around this neighborhood. Stax was left standing and untouched."

"Jim, Steve, and two or three others loaded up the tapes we had in the back," explains Estelle Axton, "because those tapes were a lot of investment. They put them in the trunk of the car. We closed our business, I closed the shop. We stayed closed, the shop and the studio, for about a week, because we wanted to respect the people. We didn't know who thought what and what would happen, so we just closed our doors and never knew whether the building would be damaged—but it wasn't. We were protected because the people in the neighborhood, they respected us enough to not harm a place that talent out of their community was using."

"They were burning down the buildings next to us," says Jim. "They burned the laundry across the street, all kinds of things, but by that time, people understood that we were a good effect on the community."

"When Martin Luther King was killed," says Rufus Thomas, "that changed conditions in the whole world, and especially in Memphis. The death of Martin—the whole complexion of everything changed."

Windswept.

Sideswiped.

President Johnson sent James Reynolds, his undersecretary of labor for labor-management relations, as a special emissary to settle the strike, calling him often to find out why talks dragged on. Twelve more days passed, filled with sorrow and anger; humiliating and bitter days as the pharoah's heart hardened. Reynolds finally negotiated for the dues checkoff to come indirectly from a federal credit union; he negotiated for Loeb to pass to the city council the task of recognizing the union, relieving him of the burden of responsibility, and also accountability. When the city balked at the last minute on the pay raises, an anonymous businessman donated $60,000 dedicated to their pay. On April 16, a memorandum of understanding was ratified between the two sides: The City of Memphis recognized the sanitation department employees as men. They recognized their union, gave them a written grievance procedure, agreed to end discrimination on the basis of race, and improved their working conditions. The terms were quickly ratified by the men inside the Clayborn Temple. T.O. Jones sat on the dais up front, and while others leaped in the air and shouted with joy, he leaned forward, his forehead cupped in his bent arm, weeping quietly.

It was a resolution, but the future was uncertain. "That horrible occasion turned everything around," says Wexler. "That was the end of rhythm and blues in the South."

"The heart has a lot to do with the success," says Jim, "and I think the death of Otis took a lot of heart out of Stax. It was never quite the same afterwards. Then Dr. King was killed. I still love records and music, but that was just a pure time. We were such an emotional group, everybody was so involved. The company was the studio, and it was recording, and it was songs, everybody going to the control room and just going crazy with excitement. After that, something happened."

Less than a decade earlier, Jim Stewart had known no African-Americans on a personal basis. He'd had no success in the music business, save for gigs in smoky bars between night classes in law. He narrowly missed going under, rescued by his older sister. Since then, every victory had been hard won, every loss personal. But from their corner on McLemore, they'd reached the whole wide world.

The death of Otis and the Bar-Kays dimmed their soul. The pillaging by Atlantic tore at their self-respect. The assassination of Martin Luther King choked their heart. In a state of shock, Stax was a body going cold.

PART 2
INDEPENDENCE

16. "SOUL LIMBO"
1968

THE ASSASSIN'S GUNSHOT detonated an explosion nationwide. More than a hundred cities broke into riots—Chicago, Washington, DC, Detroit, Los Angeles. American blacks were daily reminded of the institutional bias against them—Kansas City, Baltimore, Cincinnati, Tallahassee, Raleigh, North Carolina—and the eruptions spread. For five days, from coast to coast, the anger ran rampant. There was arson, looting, and untold injuries. More than twenty thousand people were arrested; forty were killed. Many cities called out the National Guard. President Johnson ordered four thousand troops into the nation's capital.

In Memphis, the riot had occurred at Dr. King's march the previous week. After the assassination, tanks that had just rolled out of Memphis were called back, positioning themselves on streets normally busy with automobiles. There was occasional unrest, some scattered fires and gunshots, but mostly the shock and awe produced a stunned silence. Blood from the minister of peace stained a Memphis balcony, and decades later stains the city still. Relations between the races in Memphis remain a festering wound, never quite scarred over, unable to fully heal.

"After those losses, not only Dr. King but also Otis and the Bar-Kays," says Jim Stewart, "it brings reality into focus, the reality of living together

Memphis, late March 1968, before Dr. King was assassinated. (University of Memphis Libraries/Special Collections)

in this divided city. It was difficult for the employees, the African-Americans, for me. Relationships were stressed. What can I say to our people? It changed the company."

At Stax, in the gloom of its three-way misery, Al Bell was struck by a thought. "What hit me with Dr. King's death," Al says, "was that it was time to start moving with economic empowerment." The response to powerlessness, he realized, could be an assumption of power. Like the fighter rising from the mat, Al shook off the daze, felt the engines fire. "What I had in mind as a businessperson was to go into the marketplace with strength." As a child, Al had worked for his father, landscaping, sent out with the burly workers to fell trees. "My father used to tell me, 'Keep up,' and he put me out there with the rest of the men. And if I didn't keep up, I'd be reprimanded that evening when I got home. So this situation at Stax was just another battle for me."

In the years since Al's stay with Dr. King in Georgia, a growing faction within the movement sought to bring strength back to the community by supporting locally owned businesses, enriching and empowering the people and places where one lived, instead of distant or absent landlords and owners. Support the neighborhood, and build out from there. The natural extension was locating leaders who could advocate for local needs in politics. The name given to this movement brought fear to the hearts of the established white leadership: Black Power. In 1966, SNCC, the Student Nonviolent Coordinating Committee, in its first published statement on Black Power, defined the effort: "When the Negro community is able to control local office and negotiate with other groups from a position of organized strength, the possibility of meaningful political alliances on specific issues will be increased." Further, they contrasted it with what it's not: "SNCC proposes that it is now time for the black freedom movement to stop pandering to the fears and anxieties of the white middle class in the attempt to earn its 'good-will,' and to return to the ghetto to organize these communities to control themselves."

Stax, however unintentionally, had essentially done just that—tuned in to its immediate environment, lifting the neighborhood with itself. Though integrated and white-owned, Stax had become an example of Black Power's potential. "Because of segregation," says Al, "we African-Americans were doing what every other ethnic group had done in America: We had our own hotels, our own banks, our own insurance companies, and et cetera. And I recognized at an early age that that economic base is what caused others to be mainstreamed. Your Italian bankers dealt with Korean bankers and Chinese bankers and Greek bankers. If our banks had been allowed to grow, then we would have been able to relate to the other banks in this country. But that was cut off. We got programmed into saying, 'Two, four, six, eight, we want to integrate.' That stopped what progress we were making."

Al's vision of a capitalized African-American populace could be realized at Stax. Stax had made music the third-largest industry in Memphis, generating $100 million in the local economy. "Forefront in my mind," says Al, "was to take this natural resource that we have, which is music, and turn it into something that becomes an economic generator that enables us to build a power base." Amid the fury and passion that roiled within his city and his own being, Al Bell was finding a way to create opportunity. "Otis was dead, Sam and Dave gone, our catalog was gone, and the industry was saying, 'Stax Records is dead,' and 'It's impossible for Stax to come back from that.' Well, I refused to accept that. And I persuaded others that we could go forward from here." He had experienced Atlantic Records release conferences, conventions of their wholesale distributors, "and I would watch Jerry Wexler, so eloquent, the passion, how he related to all of the music. It was personal with him."

Al conceived a huge promotions event—the simultaneous release of about thirty albums and thirty singles to create an instant catalog. A sales conference that would draw the industry to Memphis. It could be so big it would run two weekends, not one. It could spawn a TV special. Cooking inside Al Bell was nothing less than an industry-wide soul explosion to premiere the new Stax Records. At the Atlantic conferences, "you would walk away with the feeling of Atlantic, who also distributed Atco, Stax, Volt, and all these other labels—as the premier independent record company. And they would sell several million dollars' worth of product. I knew we had to present ourselves as viable and formidable with these independent wholesale buyers." It would be high-tech, high-class, a clear statement that Stax, far from dead, was thinking grandly, spending lavishly, a key player in the music industry. Once it had some new recordings.

"Al Bell is a very spiritual person, perhaps whose real calling was to be a minister," says Rev. Jesse Jackson, who met Al in Memphis shortly after Dr. King's assassination. "Al's mantra is, 'Let not your heart be troubled. No matter how difficult circumstances are, let not your heart be troubled.' It is a way of saying that we have to be survivors. Al is a dream maker, an odds buster."

Dream maker. Not Dr. King's dream, but Al Bell's American dream: middle-class status for *everyone*. "To get from where I came from in Arkansas to where I was at that point in time," says Al, "was a fight. Nothing but a constant fight." He envisioned an expanding Stax Records. The more people it employed, the more who would rise from struggle to prosperity. A soul explosion would put the company back to work, would up the odds for a hit, would quickly establish catalog sales. But first, needing material fast, Al went to the vault; Atlantic owned everything they'd released, but not what was unreleased. He found a Booker T. & the MG's track and gave it to Terry Manning, a young engineer at nearby Ardent Studios, where Stax would send its overflow work. Terry added marimbas to give it a new shine, an infectious effect leading to an appropriate title: "Soul Limbo." Stax hired a sales manager, Ewell Roussell, who'd worked for the regional distributor of Stax, Atlantic, and other labels, and Roussell began assembling a sales force. They'd make this a hit.

"We were angry," says Jim Stewart, invigorated by Al and ready to prove himself to Wexler. "Those first records, we were so damn determined." Released in May 1968 while Stax was still sorting out its future, "Soul Limbo" shot to the top-ten R&B, top-twenty pop, running arm in

Studio A, 1968. L–R: James Alexander, Steve Cropper, Al Jackson (rear), Eddie Floyd (back to camera), Homer Banks, Booker T. Jones. (Photograph by Jonas Bernholm)

arm with the simultaneous Stax release of Eddie Floyd's "I've Never Found a Girl" (featuring Booker's gorgeous string arrangements), reaching number-two R&B and pop top forty. The pulse was strengtening.

◆ ◆ ◆

THESE HITS LET Stax catch its breath and, before embarking on the soul explosion, it turned to a more immediate threat. Soulsville, the neighborhood around Stax, had changed with the riots. There'd always been an underlying poverty, but it was never as dominant as the sense of community that defined the place. Now that poverty was made manifest. After the March riots, many looted businesses did not reopen. Windows and doors were boarded up and stayed that way. Quietly, a fear crept through. What once bustled now felt busted. "We had to be more security conscious," says Jim. "Up until that time, anybody could walk through our doors and we'd stop and listen. After the assassination, the community was totally disrupted. We had to increase security. I mean, this is not what the company is about."

While vandals had wreaked havoc on absentee landlords throughout Soulsville, they'd respected the Stax facility. But that symbol of pride became, to some, an isolated prosperity, and it provoked a smoldering resentment. One gang—a couple thugs really—saw the fancy cars and the big-name stars going in and out of 926. McLemore, and they wanted a piece of the profits. In the shadows of Dr. King's murder, strong-arms fed on the undercurrent of trepidation, extorting small businessmen: *Pay us to be protected—from us.*

These toughs monitored the parking lot across the street from Stax, and when musicians parked where they'd been parking for years, these thugs hassled and hustled, thieving even words from the legitimate movement. "For the cause," they hissed. "The cause" implied a political purpose and a moral obligation, and instead of nickel-and-diming, the demands were higher. Ten bucks. Twenty. Your life. For the cause. Steve and Duck got hit, so did others. "I was threatened," says Booker T. Jones. "People trying to extort money from me, threatening to kidnap me." Threats continued, and the men began walking the ladies to their cars after work.

The horn players bought small weapons, and others did too. "It got pretty intense around there," says Duck. "Al sent me to West Memphis, Arkansas. I bought five thiry-eight pistols. He said, 'Anybody gives you any shit, pull the trigger.'" (Duck adds quickly, "Shit, I didn't shoot nobody. Well, I maybe ought to have, but I wouldn't have the guts to do it. I'd probably get shot.")

"It was a continuous problem," says Jim of the neighborhood antagonists. "I even went to the FBI. 'Too bad' was the way he put it. 'You're over there on McLemore Avenue, what are you doing over there anyway?' That kind of mentality. So we decided, 'Okay, if you're not going to take care of the problem we're going to have to take care of it ourselves.'"

Stax brought in someone who was not uncomfortable with either end of a gun. He'd fire a pistol and stare at a gun barrel with equal equanimity. "Johnny Baylor was a New York street hustler," says Jim. "We brought Johnny in, Al knew him from somewhere. He came in essentially as a security man."

"Johnny Baylor, firstly, was a very personal friend of mine, someone I knew long before he ever set foot in Memphis, Tennessee," says Al, who would soon also carry a gun. They met when Al was starting his small label in Washington, DC. "Johnny came from Alabama, and moved at an early age with his family to Harlem in New York. Johnny defended himself on the streets, and in life. He was a boxer, he worked in Sugar Ray Robinson's corner. Johnny was also involved in the recorded music business."

Johnny Baylor went *bang* when he entered a room. He wore fine suits, tailored. He cut clean and sharp as a blade. Baylor favored sunglasses. If you couldn't see his eyes, you could feel them, the pupils shooting stilet-

Meet Johnny Baylor (right, sunglasses). Isaac Hayes is second from left. (Stax Museum of American Soul Music)

tos. One associate said, "Whenever he was in the room, you felt uncomfortable, and he cultured that. That was part of his weaponry."

He'd served with the Rangers in the army, Special Ops, the cold killers. Regimentation suited his personality, and he mastered it, first in lockstep among the corps, later as a street capo. "You ever heard of the Black Mafia?" asks Randy Stewart, a boxer turned record promoter who would later work for Stax and knew Johnny from Sugar Ray Robinson's Harlem barbershop. "Johnny Baylor come out of that territory. Johnny was a good person, but he didn't take no shit. I saw those guys shooting guns down One-hundred-twenty-fifth Street. They were for real."

Baylor's right-hand fist was Dino Woodard, a Memphis boy born and raised, who'd met Baylor through Sugar Ray Robinson. Sugar Ray, a champion boxer, was a Harlem hero and entrepreneur whose domain included a barbershop where boxers and musicians congregated, where Baylor learned to drink a daily cup of beef blood with a raw egg in it—to build strength. Dino, who'd come to New York in the radiant glow of

Golden Gloves, wound up in the training ring with Ray, who was, Dino says simply, "the greatest fighter pound for pound." Dino was a fighter who could keep Ray interested, who could take a beating and give one too. ("Dino was built like a wall," says Duck.) Dino was slower than a champ, couldn't read his opponent quickly enough, but he lumbered with awesome power out of the ring, he would be all smiles and fun until Johnny's order came to flip the switch. Fun Dino gone, mean Dino here. Dino was also known by his favorite catchphrase—"Boom," or the more complex "Boom boom"—which, depending on its emphasis, its sentence placement, or the hand gestures that accompanied it, could have as many meanings as there are varieties of explosions. Dino made an excellent lieutenant in Baylor's small army.

> *When I get to heaven, St. Peter's gonna say*
> *How'd you earn your living, how'd you earn your pay*
> *I will reply with a whole lot of anger*
> *Earned my pay as an Airborne Ranger*
> *Living my life full of danger*

"If you run into him in a fistfight or something like that," says Dino of Baylor, "he would come out on top, because of his experience in the Rangers and knowing about ammunition. There were—there may have been some guns around. And we were fortunate, I guess, to keep from getting arrested. But how he would do it, boom, that's another thing. He was just a good guy who really wanted African-Americans to be all right." Johnny Baylor wanted no more compromises. He had high ideals and low—but effective—means to achieve them. Baylor was always on the attack, whether shaking hands with businessmen or threatening punks. Each moment of every day was about accruing and maintaining power.

Baylor was invited to Memphis by Al's valet, Mac Guy. Busy growing a company, Al hired Guy to help with the mundane activities: Mac drove Al's kids to school, ran errands for him and his wife, Lydia, was a messenger for Al at the office. "Mac and I had a great relationship. And he was close with Johnny Baylor. So when Mac realized that these black guys on the street were threatening me at Stax," says Al, "Mac called Johnny Baylor and the next thing I knew, Johnny Baylor was in Memphis and asking me, 'Dick'—we called each other Dick—'What's going on, Dick?' I was surprised to see him there."

The harassment problem could be solved quickly and easily by Johnny

Baylor. But Baylor was a man who breathed control if he breathed at all, and having Johnny Baylor around to solve problems could, Al knew with the immediacy of Johnny's presence, lead to new problems. Such, however, were the issues and the times. "Some want to make Stax appear, with Johnny Baylor moving into our environment, to be gangsters or something like that, because Johnny had a gun." But the gun, Al points out, is an American institution, a tool employed often by the white majority. "I resist all that gangster talk, and in many instances it pisses me off, because in America, the gun is how European-Americans established a footprint and dominance in this country. The National Rifle Association is one of the most influential organizations in America. In the South, we're not real southerners if we don't have a shotgun, let alone the other weapons that we carry."

Johnny only carried a gun because he would use it. "Johnny and I were able to go out and meet the head of the gang that was challenging the artists," Dino Woodard states. "We let them know that, hey, they cannot bother the artists because it disturbed the mentality of the mind. They cannot work. They cannot record properly. We let them know that there wasn't gonna be any more robberies." Dino slips into quiet reflection: "A lot of people are not thinking about death, even though they are hollering and challenging people. We let them know that even though they did have guns, we were ready to die for our rights, for Stax artists, and the protection of Al Bell. Stax was accumulating jobs for African-American people and we wasn't gonna have the challenge from them. Boom. When we faced them, they could see that we was serious. It's do or die."

"Johnny had a rather clear-cut and well-defined conversation with the thugs," says Al, "and I think they clearly understood, for after that discussion, we ceased to have problems from them."

With the street problem swept away—a trifle to Baylor, really—Johnny Baylor looked around and liked what he saw. One of his sidelines was a record label, Koko, a nod to his favorite boxing moment—the KO, or knockout. Among the few artists he represented was the handsome and mellifluous vocalist Luther Ingram, who would later deliver one of the great love songs of the 1970s, "If Loving You Is Wrong (I Don't Wanna Be Right)." There was legitimate business he could have with Stax beyond the continued security issues in which he could assist.

"Johnny Baylor was a very smart guy," says Rev. Jesse Jackson. "Very streetwise, very savvy. A lot of the kind of street elements that you have to deal with in the record business—Baylor was fit for the task and was loyal. He made a big contribution to the Stax development." Baylor took a suite in a Memphis Holiday Inn, but kept his apartment in New York City.

◆ ◆ ◆

WITH THE IMMEDIATE environment cleaned up, a few records out, and the business engines firing, the Stax executives could turn their eyes to the farther horizon. "Our contract had run out with Atlantic Records and so it was up for sale to somebody or we'd have to go independent," says Estelle. "We didn't think we could handle it independently. It takes a lot of money to be independent." Atlantic had carried a lot of the financial risk—floating the pressing-plant fees, for example, or waiting for the slow payments from distributors. Independent labels could be easily caught short of cash, finding themselves suddenly vulnerable to takeover. "You have to think about your competitors out there," Estelle continues. "They're going to swallow you up if they can."

"I had a rude awakening at that point in the record business," says Jim. "I decided, 'What the hell have I been working for all these years?' I had made no money up to that point, putting everything back into the company. I might as well get something out of it. We were looking for capital gains, basically."

After they'd decided not to be sold with Atlantic to Warner Bros., Stax sought a new patron. They'd engaged in discussions with a variety of larger labels and companies, but nothing had developed. "We needed money to operate," says Al Bell. "And I had a dear friend who really became our angel, a gentleman by the name of Clarence Avant. He was a master salesperson, but more importantly, he was respected throughout the big-business world, particularly in the entertainment world. I spoke to him about our situation, and Clarence knew Charlie Bluhdorn at Gulf & Western. So Clarence took this little company that had no master tape catalog, this little company that had lost its flagship artist, this little company that no one believed could be raised from the dead, and sold that company to Gulf & Western for us."

Gulf & Western Industries, which began in Michigan manufacturing automobile parts, had become one of the earliest and largest conglomerates of the new business era. By the late 1960s, its holdings included the Kayser-Roth clothing manufacturers (owners of the Miss Universe pageant), New Jersey Zinc, sugar plantations in the Dominican Republic, a financial services company, and Consolidated Cigars. At the time of the Stax purchase,

G&W was also negotiating with Armour & Co., one of America's largest meatpackers, and Allis & Chambers, an international leader in industrial manufacturing. "Their gross sales in 1967," says Jim, "were equivalent to that of the entire recording industry, in excess of seven hundred million dollars." In 1967, G&W purchased the Paramount Pictures movie studio, which itself was a mini-empire; among its holdings were Famous Music, one of the oldest music publishing companies, and Dot Records, a label that was home to Pat Boone, a giant in 1950s pop music.

PARAMOUNT TO BUY THE STAX COMPLEX was the May 1968 headline in *Billboard*, and the article explained, "Jim Stewart . . . will continue to helm the Stax/Volt companies reporting directly to Arnold D. Burk, Paramount Pictures vice-president in charge of music operations . . . Burk added that no changes in the distribution setup of Stax is contemplated and that Stax would continue to be handled mostly by independent distributors." Paramount recognized that Stax had, during its tenure with Atlantic, created a successful, working apparatus that was best not disturbed; Gulf & Western would provide the operating capital for Stax to continue doing what it did best. "Gulf & Western were trying to expand their record division," Jim confirms. "We were selling our stock, but we were going to maintain the company's operations." Jim anticipated a barely perceptible change. "There was no transition," he says. "I just picked up the phone and said to the distributor, 'You won't be paying Atlantic next month, you'll be paying us.'" Stax in Memphis would report to Paramount in California; Paramount to Gulf & Western in New York City.

Gulf & Western gave Stax over $4 million. Less than a quarter of that was cash; some was common stock in Gulf & Western, and lots of it was in convertible debentures that could be redeemed only after a specified period of time. These debentures were issued to Stax, and the value and the return on the debentures were based on Stax's net revenues; in other words, the better Stax did as a company, the more money it received. The company's attorney Seymour Rosenberg did not learn of the deal until after its conclusion, and he was not impressed: "In essence, Gulf & Western bought Stax with Stax's own money. They paid them out of profits. If there wasn't any profits there wouldn't have been any payment."

The Gulf & Western sale restored a stability to Stax, relieving them of the financial pressures that came with the loss of their catalog, and the loss of hitmakers Otis Redding and Sam and Dave. "Gulf & Western were a very large company and we thought they would give us the visibility that we needed," says Jim. "Like the kid that leaves home, we didn't have that big Atlantic machine to protect us. And we didn't have the capital to be on our own. Under that sale, we became more or less a division of Paramount Pictures. Paramount—we're talking big time."

Not that Stax was small potatoes, and Paramount quickly capitalized on its latest acquisition, hiring Booker T. Jones to score an upcoming film, *Up Tight*. The film by Jules Dassin, who'd made the provocative movie *Never on Sunday*, was an updated version of a 1935 John Ford film, *The Informer*, a story of betrayal and emotional disintegration. Dassin changed the setting from Dublin and the Irish Republican Army to Cleveland, Ohio, and an African-American gang. Preceding the "blaxploitation" genre by several years, *Up Tight* was a serious movie on a low budget, and Booker, twenty-three years old, gave it his all. He began post-production work in Hollywood, then moved with the production to Paris, France (witnessing there the May 1968 uprisings). In the City of Light, looking at the River Seine, he came up with a melody. Far from his usual location, he could easily stretch out. The MG's joined him there to record the soundtrack. "DJs liked the records to be two minutes and thirty seconds," Booker says. "And 'Time Is Tight' is double that. We were starting to disregard radio's restrictions. But Bob Dylan was doing that too, and some others." Paris was good for inspiration, but the recording facility was not up to the MG's standards. After laying down the movie's soundtrack, the band returned to Stax to re-record the soundtrack album. "Time Is Tight" became one of their most enduring hits, reaching the top ten of both the pop and R&B charts. The song moves in fuguelike parts—a slow, melancholy meditation on the organ, a choogling guitar section that is funky and danceable, then back to the melancholia, as if someone has broken from a fever dream of exuberance to realize, alas, the euphoria and intensity at that temperature could not endure.

Others around Stax could see that this alliance with the movie studio might prove fruitful; both Carla Thomas and William Bell began taking acting lessons. Eddie Floyd, perhaps with an eye toward Gulf & Western's origins, took up drag racing.

◆ ◆ ◆

WHILE THERE WERE portents of change at Stax with this new relationship, the nation's racial relationships seemed immalleable. Racism still held sway in 1968. Though President Johnson had passed the Civil Rights Act four years earlier and one could point to concrete changes all about—bus seating, bathrooms, water fountains, and dining rooms were open to anyone anywhere (by law and, slowly but increasingly, by custom)—it was also easy to see how little had changed. The Memphis Police Department reviewed the sanitation strike when it was over and determined that Memphis had been the object of "outside provocation." They ignored the facts and instead suggested that AFSCME had riled up the workers and instigated the strike. The department's response was to buy more helicopters, mace, and riot helmets.

The civil rights movement lurched forward with its leader gone. Rev. Ralph Abernathy took charge of the SCLC, and a month after Dr. King's assassination, thousands of impoverished blacks, Latinos, Native Americans, and others began a march from diverse places in the South to Washington, actualizing Dr. King's Poor People's Campaign. The intention was to widen the movement's base, breaking beyond race issues to economics, but unity proved elusive. Though thousands converged and built a camp on the National Mall, their effort was undermined by infighting and disagreement. Living conditions were difficult, and morale was hit hard when Senator Robert Kennedy was assassinated on June 6. Less than three weeks later, police routed the encampment with tear gas, and the protestors departed, their goals unfulfilled.

When Stax artists discuss race, nearly all call Stax an "oasis"—the same word recurs in interview after interview. Did those social problems not exist, or did the continued success serve to mask them? "Things changed because of King's assassination," Steve says. "I can tell you that prior to that, there was never ever any color that came through the doors. Didn't happen. And after that, it was never the same."

It never was the same, but everyone had always seen color. The beauty was that till then, no one had cared. The anger that followed the assassination made people care. With the veil of innocence lifted, race emerged in ways it hadn't before. Al Jackson suddenly gave Duck the cold treatment. "It was tense," says Duck. "I turned around to Al and said, 'Al, I got to get this off my chest.' I said, 'You won't talk to me. Tell me what's wrong?' And he told me another musician accused me of being racist. I said, 'Al, if that's the truth, God strike me dead today.' And he looked at me. He called me Dundy Dunn Dunn. He says, 'Dundy Dunn Dunn, what more can I ask?'" Duck shakes his head. "The n-word. I didn't allow that word in my house. I worked with Booker and Al and I couldn't handle that word. And I think I even changed my mother and my father about that. I really do."

◆ ◆ ◆

AFTER DR. KING'S murder, there was conflicting opinion among civil rights groups about how best to proceed. The failure of the Poor People's

Campaign heightened those tensions. "Nonviolence has died with King's death," Eldridge Cleaver, a Black Panther activist, declared. The armed revolution seemed to be at hand. In the summer of 1968, at the annual meeting of the National Association of Television and Radio Announcers (NATRA), activism was everywhere. NATRA's convention drew a racially mixed crowd including record company presidents, promotions men, songwriters, and others associated with music, but the organization was established as a forum for African-American broadcasters, and that remained its core. The 1968 theme was "The New Breed's New Image Creates Self Determination and Pride," which meant, according to Executive Secretary Del Shields, "this loosely is our translation of Black Power and Soul Power."

Trouble was brewing well before the group convened in mid-August. A month prior, a venue change was announced in *Jet*, one of the nation's leading magazines directed at a black audience. According to the magazine, the "plush Marco Polo Hotel reportedly made a 'last-minute' demand that the National Assn. of TV and Radio Announcers (NATRA) post a $25,000 bond in advance of the group's annual convention . . . to cover property damages and unpaid accounts that might accrue during the predominantly Negro group's affair . . . A $10,000 offer to Marco Polo was rejected." The event relocated and NATRA stated its intention "to file suit . . . charging the establishment with rank discrimination."

The president of NATRA, E. Rodney Jones, a prominent DJ in Chicago, told *Billboard* that the group planned to address "the nation's problems on a sociological level. Many who expect to attend are hopeful that even more deejays will lend their efforts to easing tensions." By the time the convention rolled around, a subset of the more radical-minded activists had formed, calling themselves the Fair Play Committee. Two of its members were Johnny Baylor and Dino Woodard. Exactly what happened at the Miami convention is disputed—various reports indicate Marshall Sehorn, the white partner of black New Orleans producer and musician Allen Toussaint, was pistol-whipped; or that Phil Walden, Otis's white manager, received death threats; or that Jerry Wexler was accused of stealing from Aretha Franklin and his effigy was hung in the hotel lobby. The pernicious mood extended onto, and emanated from, the dais, where speakers riled and goaded the crowd.

"There was a changing racial climate throughout the country," says Jim. "But nobody ever came to me and said, 'Get out of the record business or we'll blow you away.' Nobody threatened me. Al was like a buffer.

They couldn't destroy Stax without destroying one of their own. I never had any confrontations."

Jerry Wexler was not so lucky. "That infamous convention in Miami was a big turning point," he says. "A certain element thought that it was gonna be their time to actually take possession of the record companies and the radio stations. And the emcee was whipping them up. 'It's your time, boys. Go and grab it.' I'm sitting there to receive an award for Aretha Franklin when King Curtis got me and said, 'You're out of here right now.' He said somebody was coming after me—a part of this irredentist movement, they were gonna off me. It was one of those moments when the surge of Black Power infected the whole record business." Southern soul wasn't over, but it was a time for new sounds, and under new authority.

At Stax, the front door—long the symbol of the studio's connection to the neighborhood, and through which had walked, uninvited, several of its biggest stars—was locked. A twelve-foot cyclone fence was installed around the parking lot, and a guard was stationed at the back gate to monitor who entered, preventing that uninvited future star from popping in to announce him or herself. The open-door policy was effectively terminated.

A short eight years earlier, Wayne Jackson and some other kids were pulling seats out of the theater. Now a company stood there. "The family feeling that we had," says Wayne, "that fraternity of young guys who couldn't even conceive of a job that much fun, and Otis Redding and all that we did—suddenly was gone. There were people with guns in the house. That really put a cold towel on the party. It wasn't any fun to go there. They put the big fences up and a guard: Fort Stax."

17. A STEP OFF THE CURB
1968

HAVING INSTIGATED THE successful sale, Al Bell was wielding new power in the company, and he took a deep breath, still clearing the path toward the soul explosion. One hurdle he'd always faced was the perception of Stax as too southern—what the DJs called 'Bama music, short for Alabama. "Many African-Americans looked down their nose at blues as too raw and rural," says Al. They heard that influence in Stax and he heard that said as a criticism of Stax. "So there came a time of diversification that I started looking for what I called cross-fertilization—a merger between Stax, with this raw, gritty, gutsy soul, and Motown and its contemporary, sophisticated, polished soul. When I was a DJ on the radio, I played Stax, and I played Motown—so why shouldn't we have a company here that reflects the sum total of black music? The idea wasn't to lose the centerpiece but to broaden the music that's considered black music. In my mind, I needed to deal with somebody in Detroit." Through a Detroit disc jockey with Memphis roots, Al was introduced to Don Davis, a guitarist who'd played at Motown before breaking away with his own studio, United, and record label. Al first brought Davis to Memphis in 1967 to produce Carla Thomas, who wanted to establish herself as a cabaret singer. Carla had begun performing as an innocent, sexy teenager; her photo shoots toyed with a coquettish appeal. She'd since had soul hits, matched Otis Redding in gritty duets, and blossomed into a college-educated, beautiful woman. But Carla wanted to be a voice; she had a pop sensibility and, like Dionne Warwick, she wanted to make believers of the adult cabaret and ballad crowd.

"We had a new producer to come," says Carla. "Don Davis—that's when I could tell a whole big difference in the music. He brought a Detroit style, and he was accustomed to that Detroit full sound, and he brought in different writers, which made a big difference." Davis's first record with Carla was "Pick Up the Pieces," which he cowrote. The sound is decidedly different from what might be termed standard Stax fare, with its heavy strings and vibraphone; even the horn section sounds more like a pops symphony than a soul record. And it was recorded Detroit style, meaning Carla recorded her part to a finished musical track, not with a band. To sing to the track, she had to wear headphones, a new device at Stax but common at most major studios. The song became a top-twenty R&B hit, and set a sonic template for "Where Do I Go," an even more fully realized production.

The experiment with Carla a success, Al gave Don Davis more duties. Al believed there was untapped appeal in Johnnie Taylor, and wanted Davis to expand his audience. "I knew Johnnie could be in that arena with Marvin Gaye," says Al, "if he was produced in that fashion." When Davis expressed an interest in Taylor, Al leapt at the notion; Hayes and Porter had been producing him, and so had Cropper and Al Jackson. Johnnie's voice was warm and wistful, attractive enough to be steadily hovering just inside the R&B top forty, but unable to find that breakout song or style. Seeking material, Davis rummaged the discard stack and found "Who's Making Love," cowritten by new Stax writers Homer Banks (a longtime clerk in Estelle's store), Raymond Jackson, and Bettye Crutcher, a song that had been pitched to and rejected by the producer's pool.

"Everybody knew that Johnnie Taylor was a talent," says Bettye Crutcher, whose first song, "Somebody's Been Sleeping in My Bed," had been recorded by Taylor the previous year. "But they just were not getting him right. So Homer Banks had started a song. He's the kind of guy who would come up with a line. They're looking at somebody's girl, and Homer goes, 'Well, who's making love to your lady—while you're out making love?' And I said, 'You really got to tell this story in a way that women are going to listen to it.' And so the song gave the guy a thought that his girlfriend might be playing with somebody else while he's out. And Don Davis recognized that. He said, 'I want this to be an anthem for women.' And I would have guys who would stop me and say, 'Why did you write a song like that? You had me going back home, checking to see if my wife was leaving with somebody!'"

"Who's Making Love" is a bold statement, more overtly sexual than anything Stax had done, and musically it fulfilled Al's vision: Rooted in gospel—listen to this preacher of love shout ecstatically in the first few bars—it has a sophisticated sound that takes Stax into yet more new and fresh territory. In spirit, it captures the humor, the fun, the love that permeated so much Stax material, but its drive and modernity draw heavily from the northern polish. "We had a ball working with Don Davis," says Steve Cropper. "'Who's Making Love' is one of the most fun sessions I ever played on. In the old days, there was one guitar player because we couldn't afford but one—or Jim didn't think he could afford but one. That had three guitars on it. Raymond Jackson, one of the song's writers, and Don Davis played and, at the end, Don knew it was a great take and he laughed so hard he fell backwards out of the chair." Later, Isaac Hayes came in and helped with the song's horn lines, an inside view of Memphis work that thrilled the Detroiter to witness.

"'Who's Making Love' was a step off the curb for all of us," says trumpeter Wayne Jackson, "because it was such a sexually charged song. It was perfect for Johnnie Taylor, because he's so good looking. People started fighting when they heard him sing, 'cause their girlfriends started lifting that dress, and Johnny'd be on the stage and just destroy all of them."

"The popular broadcast media was not ready to accept 'Who's Making Love' at that point," says Jim. "This was an ongoing battle all through the sixties and early seventies. Pop stations said, 'It's too funky,' but we knew they meant, 'It's too black.' They wouldn't admit they didn't play black records. They didn't consider Motown black records, but Stax was black. 'Who's Making Love' sold close to half a million copies before we could get it onto pop radio."

"After they had recorded it," Al remembers, "they were saying, 'Well, we can't release that. That's a little too risqué.' What are you talking about, 'too risqué'? This is an automatic record here. It sells itself." Indeed, "Who's Making Love" became the biggest-selling song yet in the company's history, hitting two million in sales (the first million within six weeks of its release), rising to the top of the R&B charts and the top five of the pop charts—a thrilling finish to a year full of turmoil.

On the tails of "Who's Making Love," Davis released another Taylor hit, "Take Care of Your Homework," calling again on writers Crutcher, Jackson, and Banks, shooting to R&B number two and entering the pop

1968. L–R: Yoko Ono, John Lennon, and Bettye Crutcher. "I was receiving a BMI Award in New York and John Lennon was receiving one too [for 'Hey Jude']," says Bettye, cowriter of Johnnie Taylor's "Who's Making Love." "I wanted so much to meet him, but I found that he wanted to meet me. I bet I was ten feet tall when I left that presentation. It said that somebody was listening to what I wrote." (Stax Museum of American Soul Music)

top twenty. Davis had Johnnie singing from his hips, and they had a groove on: Taylor went on to have eleven singles in a row produced by Davis, none of which placed lower than number thirteen on the R&B chart (most were in the top five), and all of which hit the pop Hot 100 (most within the top forty). Johnnie Taylor became a bona fide R&B triumph, steadily selling hundreds of thousands of records, generating considerable cash flow for the company. His success was emblematic of the new Stax approach. Instead of being grounded in a core group in a single place, Davis would record different parts of a song in several cities—basic tracks might be Memphis, strings might be Detroit, horns could be Muscle Shoals; then he'd bring the tape to Dallas, where Johnny lived, to overdub his vocals. The final mix could be yet elsewhere. Don Davis took the Mad Lads to Philadelphia, and the new girl group the Goodees to Detroit. And when Davis worked next with Carla Thomas, he returned her to the R&B top ten after a long absence with a title that was true to its word, "I Like What You're Doing to Me."

Al Bell, left, and Johnnie Taylor, with Johnnie's gold record for "Who's Making Love."
"The finger snap signaled a change," says Al. "*Pow.* This was the company that's
moving." (Bettye Crutcher Collection)

Davis's success was exactly the blend of new and old, of Memphis and
Detroit, that Al had envisioned, and its phenomenal sales affirmed his
sense of the future. Production duties at Stax had been changing as Jim
found himself with less time to spend in the studio and more demands to
run the business. Hiring and firing. Corporate and conglomerate paperwork. Overseeing the growing staff. At one time, a single's release could
be anticipated by the way Jim danced in the control room when it was
being recorded, but now Jim was rarely in the control room and the dancing he did was from meeting to meeting. Don Davis was given more

authority over production at Stax—even though his own studio was in Detroit, as was his permanent residence.

"Hits are not made by one person," Don Davis told a reporter. "Every step is part of a critical process, and sometimes you need some outside help. That's why Stax is great. Everybody helps everybody else. Togetherness is happening."

This togetherness, however, was a bit of an illusion. Before Gulf & Western, it was a Memphis-centric company. Producers, writers, artists, and staff—with the notable exceptions of Otis Redding and Sam and Dave, everyone at Stax was from Memphis, and most of the stars had risen with the company. Instead of promoting from within, in a classic corporate-style move the expert was brought in from outside. Don Davis had his own way of doing things, resulting in creations decidedly different from the Stax hits. And he'd manufactured this new success without relying on the studio's A-team musicians—the MG's—nor the A-team writers, Hayes and Porter. "The fact that Don hadn't been there long, and was from Detroit," says Bettye Crutcher, "this made Don look like he was catching up to Hayes and Porter." The old order—the Big Six—felt assaulted. They'd been the core of hits at Stax until now.

Promoting Davis may have suited Bell's vision of the future, but in this present tense, it was met with considerable dubiousness and resistance. "I was troubled like hell when they brought in Don Davis," says the usually unflappable Deanie Parker. "If you have a house and you want to redecorate, would you hold on to some valuable pieces or throw everything out and start all over? Would I throw out your favorite chair? How would that make you feel? People were pissed off. I understood that Al Bell was trying to diversify, but I also know there is a way to go about diversification. You don't throw out the gold for this new material that's not tested, that's uniquely different from our primary product."

Steve Cropper was also among those rankled by Don Davis's ascension, exacerbating his already strained relationship with Al. "By [the 1967 tour in] Europe, things were building up between Steve and Al," says Jim. "I had to step in between, be the mediator. Steve had been my right-hand man, I took everything to him—all my conversations and lunches would be with Steve. When Bell came in, it was Bell and Stewart. We worked at the same desk for a long time. We had our disagreements, but Al and I were a good team. I did what I thought was best for the company. I was running no popularity contest. It didn't occur to me if it would make Steve mad."

"Don Davis made more money in two years than I've made in all my life probably," says Duck Dunn, getting directly to the core of the issue. "That's not his fault. That's my fault." The burgeoning discontent was about the money: The production pool allowed the core six players to share in each other's successes. Davis had been invited to Stax, offered the use of the studio's key players from the pool, but unlike everyone else, his royalties were his own. "When Al Bell or Isaac and David or myself go to Muscle Shoals or Detroit or Chicago and record other sessions, that's one thing," says Steve. "But when you come in-house and use the same players in the same format and the same everything that we've always done, and walk away and not share—well, that's where the business difficulty came from. We're not just gonna give something away that we sat here for years building."

Don Davis was promoted to head the company's A&R department—to sign artists and determine the musical direction, and the production pool was disbanded; royalties would go to the song's producer and no longer be shared. Stax was gaining strength, but the configuration, the mood, and the feeling were different. "We could have had the best of both," says Deanie, "what we had and then also Don. What was wrong was we were not given an opportunity to buy in to the need for diversification."

"I had Gulf & Western and all these details," says Jim. "Sales people, promotion people. The company had grown. I couldn't go to the studio every day and solve these people's problems like I had before. Six guys, eight people—you can do that. The company had grown beyond them. They didn't grow with it." Community and communion gave way to the individual and a cold efficiency. If this guy wasn't going to share, that one wasn't either. Producers still worked as individuals and in pairs, the MG's continued to record together—for themselves and behind others—but the family illusion fell away, exposing a hierarchy of individuals, a business.

18. THE INSPIRER
1968–1969

THE WHIR OF activity sounded like a resurrection, but deep within, there was an insurrection. Al Bell's influence had grown with his vision. Since his arrival three short years earlier, his thermometer had sparked sales, his enthusiasm had boosted morale, his energy had lit fires beneath everyone.

Almost everyone.

Al Bell's ascent was directly related to Estelle Axton's descent. The relationship had begun amicably. Indeed, Estelle was a fervent supporter of bringing Al into the fold. Estelle and Jim had never seen eye to eye, and that had clearly served the company well; her hunches had proven correct time and again, and the differences between her and Jim had established dual creative spaces—the studio and the record shop—and given the artists plenty of room. Al Bell brought a bigger vision for the company, and gradually he'd won more and more of Jim's attention, and his trust.

Al Bell wanted to build a "total record company." He wanted to continue to cultivate artists as Stax had always done, but also to become a major force in distribution. He knew that the wider and deeper a company's penetration into the market, the greater the sales potential. By signing smaller labels for distribution, he would add heft to his enterprise, raise the company's chances for being involved in hits, and help those labels that wouldn't otherwise have access—empowering a middle class for small record labels. He believed in more and bigger, establishing Birdees Music, another publishing company, another Stax arm that might catch a hit. His total record company could, someday, have its own pressing plant, be a promotions giant, employ a major sales force. He could see this conglomerate age, connecting the music industry with film and television: Once Stax was distributing records, it could easily distribute other products—films, and especially videocassettes, in formats just appearing on the trade's horizon. It could finance those shows, pay itself by including songs from its own publishing companies, and usher its stars to the silver screen. Columbia Records, an example of a total record company, had once been a small label itself, gradually enlarging its web to become the industry's giant, with powers and interests across many media platforms. So Al signed Arch Records out of St. Louis for distribution, followed soon by Weis Records out of Chicago; he established new distribution for Stax in Canada, England, and France. He sought labels the way he sought talent.

As Al grew the company, he eyed the record store's real estate. The cash flow it had once provided continued to trickle in with the neighborhood purchases of seventy-nine- and ninety-nine-cent singles. But Al was interested in sales beyond the neighborhood and in purchases greater than a buck. He could read the national trend toward album sales and could count the difference it would make in the company's bottom line. In 1967, the Beatles had released *Sgt. Pepper*, and artists began to conceive the LP not as a collection of singles but as a new form of artistic statement. So Al wanted to put teams in place that would help generate more albums, more labels, more hits. He could build a lot of offices where the record store tallied its ninety-nine-cent sales.

When Estelle was asked to relinquish her domain, she could read the writing on the wall. "They wanted the space," she says. "I had a woman's intuition. I could feel things before they did happen. They didn't want me around." Estelle had become something as radical as the racial activists: a female executive wielding power in a world perceived as not her own. She did not have the same authority as her brother but she exerted the same influence. She got records released, she made decisions about cash flow and salaries and affected the course of business. She held her head high and moved the Satellite Record Shop from the Stax complex to a building across the street. "My shop had become one of the biggest in this part of the country. I had the R&B market sewed up. I reported sales to

Billboard for their charts, and *Billboard* never knew that the Satellite Record Shop was the front end of Stax Records. Every week they called me for my [top sales] list. There was always a Stax record [in my report] that was busting out." Despite her store's contributions beyond finances—as a training ground, as a research facility, as a lounge, and as an escape from the studio—her achievements were now considered quaint. This was the cusp of a new decade—new technologies, new horizons. Recorders with sixteen tracks were coming on the market. Televisions were broadcasting in color. Man was about to walk on the moon! Her notions of research were outmoded; real research was going to be done by a new hire, John Smith, an Arkansas native and cousin of Al Bell's. To pinpoint which songs would be hits, he would helm the company's Department of Statistics and Market Analysis.

Jim did not support his sister. He'd always be the little brother, and they both would always be strong-willed. Al had a dominant personality too, but there was not the sibling hierarchy, the life history between them. "We kept the record shop open until it became a nuisance factor," Jim says, referring to the valuable space it occupied that could be offices. "We had to close it." (Some employees recall her space being replaced by a decorative fountain.) Soon after relocating, she sold the store to Packy's good friend Johnny Keyes. Johnny kept his day job at a record distributor and Packy managed the store. It quickly went out of business.

Estelle was given an office in the back near Jim's, though if it was presented as a promotion or sign of respect, she knew better. She'd been assigned publicity duties, but Stax already had a director of publicity in her protégé Deanie Parker. Besides, Estelle didn't want an executive office, she wanted to keep her hands dirty with hard work. "I couldn't sit in that office and do nothing," she says, so she looked for practical ways to help. "I straightened out the mail room because it was a mess. They were getting half the records back because they hadn't kept the addresses up to date." Undeterred, she dove into what needed doing.

Before signing the Gulf & Western deal, Jim approached Estelle about fulfilling a lingering obligation they'd discussed in 1965. "Jim and I owned fifty-fifty stock for the publishing and record company," says Estelle. "Just before this deal went down, Jim came to me and said, I think we should give Al Bell twenty percent off the top. I said, 'That's not right. The only way I will sign anything to give away twenty percent is for you to give Steve ten percent and Al ten percent.' I knew that Steve had worked there longer than Al had, and had helped develop that company to where we'd gotten."

"It was for service," Jim says of the financial rearrangment, "work well done. It wasn't a gift."

"That turned Al Bell against me," Estelle continues. "Al Bell had by this time gotten in so tight with the blacks, you could see division—both in the company and outside. I could feel it and could see it, how he would have meetings with some of the blacks and no white was allowed, and this had begun to build up. After Gulf & Western came in, Stax became a conglomerate. Jim and Al were going to get a salary, seventy-five thousand dollars apiece, and they weren't going to give me anything. I said, 'This is not going to work. All this stock I'm going to get, I can't sell them for a term, so what am I going to live on?' I demanded twenty-five thousand dollars a year. And to this day I'm sorry I didn't ask for fifty."

He'd helped land the deal, and power shifted to Al from Estelle. "Instead of being a creative world that we lived in with great songs, great music, camaraderie and all of that, the outside business world trickled into Stax," says Al. Then, summoning a complacent chivalry, he continues, "And as days would pass, I remember it having a really profound effect on Miz Axton's attitude and her spirit. We're talking about major Wall Street corporations and how their decisions and their thinking impacted with us and interfered, and in some instances, prohibited us from doing the things that Miz Axton and Jim enjoyed the most about this business, which was the creative aspect. And she really wanted out from under that. So we made arrangements to buy Mrs. Estelle Axton's interest, which would allow her to do whatever it is she chose to do with the rest of her life. It'd just gotten to a point where it wasn't fun to her anymore."

Jim found himself caught between his sister and his partner. "I had a decision to make," says Jim, "a very hard decision to make. It involved family versus the company—a very hard choice. Al and my sister did not get along and it had gotten to the point where Al was ready to leave. In the end I made the decision that more people's livelihoods were at stake than just mine and asked my sister to step down."

Estelle had risked her home for the company (essentially also risking her marriage) and had as much heart, muscle, and love in the place as anyone. Her commitment was beyond question, and however anyone wanted to frame her departure, she damn sure wasn't going to fold her cards and walk away, was not going to assume the role of the powerless woman. So each side lawyered up. Jim hired Seymour Rosenberg, the trumpet-playing attorney whom he'd first encountered when Chips Moman sued him for royalties after leaving Stax. "Jim told me one time that he didn't like me," laughs Rosenberg, "and that the only reason he wanted me to be his lawyer was he didn't want me on the other side. I took it as a compliment."

Talks dragged on until the summer of 1969, and finally all parties hunkered down in a suite in the Holiday Inn Rivermont, the city's finest hotel. There were two bedrooms connected by a living room, Jim and his lawyer to one side, Estelle and hers to the other. Representatives from the conglomerate occupied the neutral ground. "We had a big bar in the main room and the Gulf & Western people stayed there and had drinks," explains Rosenberg. "We went back and forth and back and forth and I said, 'We're gonna stay here till we make a deal.'" When the smoke cleared, Al Bell and Jim were partners, and Lady A was to receive, according to the July 17, 1969, Redistribution of Earn-Out Agreement, "$490,000 to be paid at the rate of ninety percent of the first debentures used under said agreement until the total amount is reached." She was a wealthy woman who proceeded to sink her buyout money into a large apartment complex that served her well, and she also collected a $25,000 annual salary for the next five years; in return, she signed a five-year non-compete agreement.

Estelle Axton, May 1968.
(*Commercial Appeal*/Photograph by Jim McKnight)

"I decided to take my money and run," she says. "But I had to wait five years before I could get back in. I couldn't have a record shop, I couldn't have anything that had to do with music."

There was no grand crescendo, no weepy string arrangement as Lady A made for the door. She had only good wishes for all the friends she was leaving behind, and could exit knowing she'd ignited the sparks that burned so brightly throughout that building. She'd affected the course of American popular music, could point to lasting hits that wouldn't have existed but for her. Lives had been changed because of her work—hers, her brother's, her son's, a real family affair. Purse on her arm, smartly dressed and with a Parliament cigarette between her fingers, her head was held high as she exited the company she'd helped make.

"Estelle was an inspirer," says Booker. "She had a great sense of humor. She just loved music, loved people. She was always bringing us up there, having us listen to records. She kept us in touch with the music industry. I doubt if there would have ever been a Stax Records without Estelle Axton. She encouraged the entire Stax roster from her little perch behind the counter. She could've just as well been sitting in Las Vegas winning a jackpot to see the joy on her face when we made records."

"Estelle Axton mentored all of us, and encouraged us to pursue our dreams, our professional wishes," says Deanie Parker. "She was an unusual woman, a natural entrepreneur. She didn't have formal training in marketing, in sales, or in promotion, but she had more common sense than twenty people put together. She was thinking and operating very professionally—a woman in a man's world, a white man's world."

She'd done more than pick hits. A nurturer, she'd fostered a sense of family, even organizing care packages for Stax employees serving in Vietnam. William C. Brown, John Gary Williams, William Bell, and others all said that those packages fired their spirits, kept them connected with a distant place close to their hearts. "When she left, we were begging her to come back," says William Bell. " 'Oh, no, our mother has left!' When the artists were down, she could talk you back. You'd come to the record shop when you couldn't get a song right and she'd say, 'It's going to be all right, just go back and do this and do that.' And it was like magic. And when she left, the magic was gone. Many artists said, 'This building will never be the same,' and it was never the same again."

19. THE SOUL EXPLOSION
1968–1969

A L BELL ROLLED up his sleeves. "Hit records are the number one thing on our list," he said in a magazine article at the time. "Soul music has grown from a particular market to become the new music of the nation," and he set about making "product [that] is appealing to and accepted by the masses in America."

Jim Stewart was fully on board with Al's vision. "This is a corporate change," Jim explained. "We are certainly proud of our R&B background . . . but now we will merchandise to the mass market. The racks [department stores and drug stores that had racks in a particular area devoted to records] historically have been hesitant to put out 'black product' . . . Finally they began realizing they were losing sales."

Through music, and through the company behind the music, Al could realize the essence of the Black Power platform. Stax could appeal to all people of all races in all places, and bring more jobs—good jobs, high-paying jobs—back home. But he needed a catalog. "I wanted to get as many hit records as possible into the marketplace," says Al. "Then, we'd bring all of these distributors in and let them know that we are a formidable, independent record company. And the window of time to get this done was just a few months. They said that can't be done, it's impossible. So I got together with Steve Cropper and Isaac Hayes, [producer] Rick

Hall and the guys in Muscle Shoals, Alabama, Don Davis and his studio in Detroit, and we had productions going on in all of those places at the same time. And I was busy, back and forth on the phone, pumping everybody up and just driving, driving, driving."

Al's visionary soul explosion could be made a reality. One compilation album even took that name, *Soul Explosion*, and the 1969 sales conference, though unnamed, has become known to many as just that: the soul explosion. Thirty singles would accompany what became twenty-eight albums, all created in about eight months. Al Bell signed jazz greats Sonny Stitt and Maynard Ferguson and was seeking a fresh comedian. The studio upgraded its recorder to an eight-track. That made room to establish Studio B, smaller than the A room and using the older gear—but busy. Soon, a C studio was built near the publishing office, a demo studio for writers. There was so much traffic and demand that a chalkboard was put outside of studio A to reserve time, and the three rooms were booked all hours of the day, all days of the week.

Stax took over the whole block of buildings. The staff had rapidly expanded: The sales force included Herb Kole, who brought nearly two decades of experience, including a stint as Atlantic's East Coast sales manager. Bernard Roberson, an African-American, was named national R&B promotions director, and other promotions men were hired. A New York publicity firm was retained to work with Deanie Parker; New York lawyers were hired, and so were California graphic artists. "They'd knock all the walls out," says Don Nix, "and they'd rebuilt. It was just one big maze of offices and hallways."

"Stax was an architectural nightmare," recalls one visitor, who was buzzed in from the lobby, which was decorated in lavender and purple. "The lavender carpeting instantly changed to deep, deep green. I'd never seen such a clash in my life, until we walked down the hall, and the carpeting suddenly changed to bright red. The color scheme at Stax was shocking."

The company's fresh start was emblematized by a new logo. The stack of spinning records had worn thin, and Al and Jim had discussions with Paramount's art department about an emblem to indicate their new direction, their return to the game, their instant catalog. Paramount delivered: the snapping fingers. "The finger snap signaled a change," says Al. "*Pow.* This was the company that's moving."

When working the deal between Stax and Gulf & Western, Al had not been shy about his needs. "In addition to getting stock in the sale," he explains, "we had budgets to operate the company. They understood the need, from a business standpoint, of having a catalog. Built in to those budgets was the cost for putting together that sales presentation."

"What Al Bell did was to galvanize the creative force of that organization," reflects Deanie Parker. "He had the writers writing. He had the producers producing back-to-back marathon recording sessions. Of course Jim was a part of it, but Al Bell was the motivating factor. It was like a tornado. I'm serious—like a tornado. We all had a common goal and that was the restoration of that organization."

"It was somewhat contradictory to my spending philosophy up to that point," says Jim. "But I'd had a rude awakening when we terminated with Atlantic Records. It's not a bed of roses out here. *Survival* is the word. You've got to take a stand, and make your presence felt in the industry."

The soul explosion included a foundational change in emphasis. Stax releases through the Atlantic years had relied on the MG's, which gave a consistency to the label's sound, an identity. A Stax release could usually be identified with just a few seconds of play; the music was always unique to the song, but it had readily identifiable characteristics and feel.

No more. The new Stax sound was the sound of hits, whether recorded at McLemore or a foreign land, whether produced by Stax or simply licensed by them for distribution and made by people in other cities that no one at Stax had ever met. If the song appealed to Al's DJ instincts, Stax wanted it. What Stax sought was no longer about identity, it was about opportunity.

The rush of work kept Jim too busy to engineer sessions, so Ron Capone was hired away from another studio to oversee production. Shocked by how fast and loose the work was being done, he quickly recognized the shortage of production staff. Others were hired and Capone organized weekly Saturday-morning training sessions, designed not only to give a chance for improvement to employees like William Brown from the mail room and night watchman Henry Bush (each of whom would soon engineer hits), but also to establish a sense of basic standards for all the sessions produced at Stax.

Duck Dunn remembers being swept up in the moment. "Al Bell missed his calling," smiles Duck. "He should have been a preacher. He could put you in the palm of his hand. He did it to me, he did it to everyone. I mean, the man was incredible: 'Lord gonna bless you.' Al Bell became God in rhythm and blues. He said, 'We're gonna take this company, and we're gonna turn it into a multimillion-dollar thing.' And he did it. With Jim."

"The timing was perfect," says Deanie. "Jim needed an Al Bell. Stax

Records needed an Al Bell. So Al had a series of meetings and he explained what the situation was—how we'd lost our catalog but we're gonna move on and it's gonna be bigger and it's gonna be better than it was when we first started. And we were all young and naïve and energetic, and certainly our love for Stax Records was unquestionable, so we said, 'Let's do it.'"

In concept, the soul explosion idea was brilliant. In execution, however, the effort was almost brutal. The "factory" was going to up its output by more than tenfold. "The market was changing toward albums," says Steve. "Where we would spend months working on four, five, six artists and singles trying to get a hit on them, all of a sudden I'm working on four, five, six *albums*—ten times as much. The fatigue of the in-house songwriters, producers, and players trying to keep up with the demand was just overwhelming. It was wearing us out."

Combined with the increased workload was a new system of office procedures dictated by the distant corporate headquarters. New York instructed Los Angeles to instruct Memphis: time management, product quotas, and the like. "I didn't like the new situation," says Booker. "We were getting memos as to what time to have the sessions and at one point they had us operating in shifts. That whole concept was so foreign to me. Three shifts with Stax? We started as a company that had trouble getting the drummer to the studio by noon. It wasn't the same company. It wasn't the same at all." This malaise that Booker felt from the conditions was also expressed in the art. "There was an absence of the spirit in the music," he continues. "The music was coming from a different place. There was a feeling like mass production, a factory or assembly line feeling. I think the arrangements lost their sensitivity."

"The profit and the amount of record sales increased greatly," says Steve. "The record company had a lot of hits and a lot of chart action. But I think the quality started deteriorating. And a lot of records had been farmed out to other studios, to other producers, to other musicians that didn't have the Stax seal of approval. It's like a great shirt company farming out to some other country to make their shirts and they wear out after three weeks. They're not the same shirt anymore."

As the engine revved higher in preparation for the soul explosion, the company released a steady stream of singles, many of which sold well and landed on the charts. Jimmy Hughes stole away from Muscle Shoals and, under the guidance of Al Jackson, he hit with "I Like Everything About You." Linda Lyndell put the sultry "What a Man" on the charts, the Mad Lads (also produced by Al Jackson) hit with "So Nice," and the Soul Children's debut, "Give 'Em Love," placed well. (Isaac and David created the Soul Children to replace Sam and Dave, using two men and two women to create high-energy songs.) William Bell and Booker T. Jones wrote "Private Number" for vocalist Judy Clay, and Bell's demo was so good it wound up as a duet with her, made all the more lush by Jones's restrained guitar playing and his beautiful string arrangement. "Private Number" is classic soul timelessly updated; if there's less raw funk and juke-joint dirt floor, it is a song built on that same foundation. William Bell was certainly on a roll, releasing three more singles before the sales meeting, all of which landed on the charts, including another duet with Clay.

Money kept coming in, and Stax had no problem spending it. With the vast building to fill, the six vice presidents—each of the MG's and Hayes and Porter—got their own offices. There was an expanded space for the publishing company. Jim and Al each redecorated their offices. Jim's looked like the Memphis retreat for *Playboy*'s Hugh Hefner. He put in slick wood paneling, sleek modern furniture, a TV set built into the wall. Would you like a drink? Step over to the leopard-skin bar and feast your eyes on the sumptuous supine woman in the black velvet painting while the highballs are shaken. His former bank loan customers would have been amazed that this hepster dwelled inside the straitlaced man who'd sat across the loan desk from them. Al Bell's office was upstairs—the old projection room. "We called it 'the bird's nest,'" says the Bar-Kays' new drummer, Willie Hall. "You go up these steps, a little narrow hall, and it was this little room with a great stereo system, some great speakers, a tape machine to play what you'd just recorded. You go in there man, and Al, he'd be up dancing, and he'd say, 'Have you heard this? Let me show you this. You got to hear this.' He would put on songs from Stevie Wonder or the Jackson Five and he would encourage us to try to get those type of productive ideas and production feels. Every time you saw Al, he was moving at a hundred plus."

Al moved into a large house on the city's prominent North Parkway thoroughfare. Steve bought a house in the expanding eastern suburbs (his doorbell played "Green Onions"). Jim spent nearly a quarter million dollars on a new home, ten thousand square feet sitting on more than fifty acres, just outside Memphis. He installed four swimming pools, a tennis court, a bathhouse, a party house, and a guesthouse. In December 1968, he threw a lavish Christmas party there. "He had this house that I could not believe," says Don Nix, who remembered the Jim Stewart who had squeezed all the manual labor from the hapless Mar-Keys when they were building the studio. "Janis Joplin was there. They had a trout stream running through the living room. I said, 'Look at ole Jim. He's having himself a good time,' and I was glad to see it.'"

"Those parties were huge affairs," says Jim's niece Doris, Estelle's daughter. "Jim went through a period where he was king of the hill. Mother wouldn't go to the parties, but they continued to see each other at their parents' house in Middleton, for Christmas and Thanksgiving. My mother was hurt, but there was never any not-speaking. She was able to be cordial and carry on." In his big spread, Jim feted Julian Bond and Dick Gregory, bringing in African-American leaders from Atlanta, Chicago, and Memphis. Stax was working every front it could, affirming its vitality, announcing its expansive future.

The company's success, noted Jim, was rooted in his partnership. "Because of my background as a banker and businessman, I'm considered a conservative, while Al Bell, a wheeler and dealer, is just the opposite. He's liberal," Jim wrote in a magazine piece. "Here we are, two opposites with the same goals. Put us together and you have perfect equilibrium . . . If we've done nothing more, we've shown the world that people of different colors, origins, and convictions can be as one, working together towards the same goal. Because we've learned how to live and work together at Stax Records, we've reaped many material benefits. But, most of all, we've acquired peace of mind. When hate and resentment break out all over the nation, we pull our blinds and display a sign that reads 'Look What We've Done—TOGETHER.'"

◆◆◆

AL BELL WAS on a signing spree, building a wide and diverse roster. His inspiration was the Vee-Jay label, an indie from Chicago founded by two African-Americans, Vivian Carter and Jimmy Bracken (it went bankrupt in 1966). "I aspired to have a label that was as diverse as Vee-Jay," Al explains. "They had soul music: Jerry Butler and the Impressions. They had blues: Jimmy Reed, Memphis Slim. They had gospel: the Staple Singers, the Swan Silvertones. They had pop: Gene Chandler with 'The Duke of Earl,' and they had the Beatles before Capitol exercised its option."

Early in 1969, Pervis Staples brought a young Chicago gospel group to Stax. The Hutchinson Sunbeams, three sisters, wanted to go secular, and Pervis convinced them to do like the Staple Singers and join Stax. "We're trying to carry a freedom message," Pervis said, explaining that the move from gospel to pop didn't have to be as radical as some feared. "One reason we changed our way of singing from straight gospel to this new style is 'cause we want to reach more people. And it's for sure we wouldn't have gotten to all the concert halls we've played so far as a pure gospel group." The Hutchinson Sunbeams changed their name to the Emotions, and with "So I Can Love You," a classic Hayes and Porter soul-drenched production, they landed a top-five R&B hit the first time out, crossing over to the pop top forty.

In February, Stax shone at the 1969 Grammy Awards, the nominations including Johnnie Taylor (who'd performed the previous month at President Nixon's inaugural ball), the Staple Singers, Sam and Dave, and writers Bettye Crutcher, Raymond Jackson, and Homer Banks; Otis Redding won Best R&B Vocal Performance for "Dock of the Bay," and he and Steve Cropper won as writers for Best R&B Song.

New label distribution deals were announced, more in-house labels were created—Hip, for pop acts, and Enterprise, a jazz and catchall label named for the galaxy-traveling spaceship on Al's favorite TV show, *Star Trek*. The hubbub of activity and the accompanying expenditures were so astonishing that Gulf & Western sent representatives from Paramount to see what its new subsidiary was doing. "Almost immediately there was some friction between the executives at Paramount and us," Jim remembers. "They wanted to control the company, basically."

"One day in my office on Chelsea Avenue, a bad part of town," says attorney Seymour Rosenberg, "this little fat guy and a young guy buzzed my door. I thought maybe they were criminal clients and so I let 'em in and the little fat guy says, 'Do you know who I am?' and I laughed and said, 'No.' He says, 'I'm the president of Paramount Records.' I said, 'Well great. What are you doing here?' 'Nobody's at Stax Records we can talk to. They said you were their lawyer.' I had a good laugh over that. Here's a guy making a quarter of a million a year and he's gotta come to a six-hundred-dollar-a-month lawyer to find out what's going on with the company he owns. I don't think Paramount knew what Stax was doing and Stax didn't care what Paramount was doing."

The relationship with Atlantic had been organic—built from shared sensibilities; between Paramount/Gulf & Western and Stax, it was just business. Stax could have been auto parts, pet food, or baby wear. "Atlantic loved the music," explains William Bell. "I don't think Gulf & Western understood it, or understood some disc jockey down in Monroe, Louisiana, how to get to him or how to even talk to him."

"It was big fun until Paramount came along," says trumpeter Wayne Jackson. "They wanted us to be corporate. They sent people who drifted around the hallways, but they didn't stay around very long. We weren't the kind that they wanted to go out to dinner with. And they put up a time machine, *ka-toonk*, and a card with your name on it. You'd have to *ka-toonk* when you got there, *ka-toonk* when you went to lunch. They made us fill out time sheets, what you did each hour. After about a week of that, we started putting in, 'Eleven A.M., cheeseburger at Slim Jenkins's Joint. One o'clock went to studio and checked on Booker T. and the MG's. Nobody there, so back to Slim Jenkins's Joint.' We made up this long list of crap that the suits would have to read before they wrote the checks and I know it ate their shorts."

The suits from New York and Los Angeles might not have understood what was going on in Memphis, but they couldn't deny its success.

◆ ◆ ◆

WHILE STAX WAS piecing itself together, Memphis was furthering its civic segregation. Though fifteen years had passed since the Supreme Court had declared separate but equal schools unsatisfactory and illegal, Memphis and the rest of the nation had done little to act on it. Blacks students made up 54.5 percent of the total Memphis City Schools' 1969–1970 population, but there were no people of color in positions of authority at the school board. Schools on the largely black south and north sides of Memphis were in disrepair, were afforded only the outdated textbooks recently discarded by white schools, and were saddled with higher student-teacher ratios. The NAACP stepped up its efforts to foment change, demanding more meetings with city officials and demanding representation on the school board. Looking to the success of the sanitation workers in getting their point made, the NAACP began publicly discussing a student boycott. State and federal school funding was based on average daily attendance, and if great numbers of African-Americans began to miss school, it would hit the school board in their pocket.

Meanwhile, as the year since the sanitation strike's settlement was drawing to a close, so was the memorandum of understanding with the city. Though new discussions had begun in January 1969, no contract was agreed upon by April and, as if to spite the sanitation workers, the city took a unilateral action and passed a fiscal budget that did little to address the wage disagreement. Strike talk was renewed.

T.O. Jones, however, was no longer head of the local. Soon after the strike's end, the national AFSCME office hired him to help organize in Florida. But once there, he was fired. During his brief time away, his Memphis position had been taken by Jesse Epps, the national representative who'd been in Memphis for several months. The newspaper described Epps as "a short man who walks slightly stooped forward and

Jesse Epps, left, assumed leadership of the AFSCME union after
T.O. Jones. (University of Memphis Libraries/Special Collections)

usually has an examining, pensive look on his face as he pauses between
rapid-fire outbursts." Epps summoned the Public Works employees to
Clayborn Temple, scene of the previous year's meetings. Epps could excite a crowd, and eight hundred sanitation workers cheered him as he
shouted, "Strike come July 1!" and "War with Memphis!" He threatened
to bring Memphis to a "screeching economic halt" unless union demands
were met, including a raise of fifty cents an hour for all employees, which
would establish a two-dollar-per-hour minimum (hundreds were making much less). The city was countering with a $1.60 minimum, dismiss-
ing the fifty-cent raise as too expensive. The newspaper reported that city
council chairman Wyeth Chandler (who would soon be elected mayor)
and others "believe that meeting the union demands now would lead to
further demands which could not be met." On the plantation, the phrase-
ology for this thinking was more poetic: Give 'em an inch and they'll take
a mile.

By late May, when Stax was hosting its soul explosion, Epps led a
"spread the misery" campaign in an upscale white shopping center. His

followers intended to fill parking lots to prevent commerce; to fill shopping baskets and abandon them; to fill stores and not shop. Several businesses, seeing blacks amassed at the entryway, simply locked their doors and closed early. By mid-June, a strike looming in two weeks, the city announced that garbage trucks would be placed at central locations where citizens could dump their trash. Various other fail-safes were being planned when, with only days left, a settlement was reached. The city agreed to the two-dollar hourly minimum and conceded the direct dues checkoff (paying union dues from Public Works paychecks instead of indirectly through the credit union); the union gave the city a year to implement the raise, and extended the agreement's term for three years, having long insisted it be only for two. The sanitation workers ratified the agreement with jubilant cheers. While everyone was assembled, the union won an additional dollar per month per member, bringing members' total checkoff to six dollars per month; the additional dollar was designated for a community-action program in Memphis that Epps said "would work to feed hungry children and to give aid to the poor and those less fortunate than us."

◆ ◆ ◆

WHILE THE UNION fought the good fight, Stax fought for its life. Twenty-eight albums—about 280 songs. Working from the autumn of 1968 to the May 1969 soul explosion meant writing, recording, and mixing about one and a half releasable songs every day of the week, weekends included.

The pressure fell heaviest on Booker T. & the MG's. Though other studios were involved, Stax was still headquarters and they were still top dogs. In addition to playing, they were each producing other artists. Because they had to sleep, and since there was a new second studio inside the McLemore facility, Stax looked for another backing group it could rely on. Ben Cauley and James Alexander, the surviving original Bar-Kays, had sought solace in their music. Soon after the plane crash, they formed a new version of the band. The soul explosion gave them an opportunity to hone their chops.

"Me and James was around each other a whole lot," says Ben. "We had to go on, but we wanted a new thing." The group they put together was recognizable yet different. The two original members were in place, and a white cat (Ron Gorden) was on the organ, as before. One noticeable difference was that the group had two drummers, a nod to James Brown's current band; one was Roy Cunningham, brother to original Bar-Kay Carl Cunningham, and Willie Hall played a second kit.

926 East McLemore, July 1966. Notice Jim Stewart under the marquee. (Charles Okle)

L–R: Packy Axton, Don Nix, Steve Cropper, in front of Stax and Satellite, 1960 or 1961. (Photograph by Don Nix/Courtesy of the Oklahoma Museum of Popular Culture, Steve Todoroff Collection)

Early Mar-Keys gig. L–R: Unidentified, Donald "Duck" Dunn, Packy Axton (obscured), Don Nix, Wayne Jackson, Steve Cropper. (Photograph by Don Nix/Courtesy of the Oklahoma Museum of Popular Culture, Steve Todoroff Collection)

Steve Cropper, 1966. (Charles Okle)

Carla Thomas, 1966. The headboard is the one favored by Al Jackson, Homer
Banks, and others. (Photograph by API Photographers/API Collection)

Sam and Dave session, probably 1966. L–R: Al Jackson's back, Isaac Hayes,
Wayne Jackson's back, Sam Moore, Dave Prater, Duck Dunn, Steve Cropper,
Booker T. Jones. (Photograph by API Photographers/API Collection)

THE BAR-KAYS

Bar-Kays, Mach II, 1967 or 1968. L–R: Roy Cunningham, Ben Cauley, Harvey Henderson, Ron Gorden, Michael Toles (kneeling), James Alexander, Willie Hall. (Earlie Biles Collection)

The "We Three" songwriting team. L–R: Raymond Jackson, Bettye Crutcher, Homer Banks, probably late 1960s. (Photograph by Wayne E. Moore/Courtesy Bettye Crutcher Collection)

Sam and Dave session, probably 1967. Wayne Jackson foreground, Dave Prater (left) and Sam Moore, with Isaac Hayes at the piano. (Stax Museum of American Soul Music)

L–R: Jesse Jackson, Isaac Hayes, Al Bell. (Earlie Biles Collection)

An industry convention, probably 1971 or 1972. L–R: Al Bell (lower left), Leroy Little, Mack Guy, Dino Woodard, John Arnold, WMBM disc jockey Butterball (lower right), unknown. (Earlie Biles Collection)

Willie Hall, drummer for both the Bar-Kays and Isaac Hayes. (Earlie Biles Collection)

Isaac Hayes (left) and Stax artist John KaSandra.
(Earlie Biles Collection)

Estelle Axton, in the Fretone offices. (University of Memphis Libraries/Special Collections)

Isaac Hayes's office at Stax. (Earlie Biles Collection)

Isaac Hayes and the Cadillac that Stax gave him. (Deanie Parker Collection)

"Stax was very supportive of us," says James. "We was trying to operate real fast, to get back to recording right away." The new group's first single, "Copy Kat," was released in October 1968. Another came in March 1969, its title pretty much their motto: "Don't Stop Dancing (to the Music)," a hard-hitting funk breakdown that evokes King Curtis's "Memphis Soul Stew." It also introduces Larry Dodson, who'd joined the Bar-Kays as lead vocalist, adding further dimension to their act. The grooves caught the attention of Isaac Hayes.

Al had approached Isaac about making a solo record for the instant catalog. Isaac had made a jazz piano album at Al's behest a couple years earlier; this time, Isaac asked if he could record his own way. "Al said, 'Man, you got carte blanche. Do it however you want to do it,'" remembers Isaac. "I was under no format restrictions and I had total artistic freedom. There were twenty-seven other LPs to carry the load, so I felt no pressure."

Al had watched Isaac produce records and teach songs to artists, and he sensed a star quality not unlike that of Brook Benton and Billy Eckstine—major stars in their day. He knew Isaac was a flamboyant fashion man. "And that bald head," says Al. "Bald heads weren't popular back then, but from a marketing standpoint, we could probably do wonders with this guy—he's different." Being different—Al knew that's how you get records played.

The Bar-Kays had a regular gig and one day Isaac asked—well, told—the new band that he was going to sit in with them, and they should learn "By the Time I Get to Phoenix." A country hit by Glen Campbell the previous year (and more recently redone by Stax's Mad Lads), "Phoenix" had struck Isaac at first listen. "I thought, God, how this man must have loved this woman," says Isaac. "I went on the stage, there was a bunch of conversations going in the club, so I told James to hold that first chord and sustain it. 'Don't move, don't change, don't do anything.' And I started telling a story about the situation in the song. And the conversations started to subside. Upon the first note of the first verse, I had 'em. And when the song was done, people were crying. I'd touched them. Now, this place, the Tiki Club, was predominantly black. Across town was Club Le Ronde, a predominantly white club. I did the tune there the same way, and the response was the same."

Bar-Kays drummer Willie Hall, in his late teens, became close with Isaac, who was about a decade older. Willie had finished high school, and when his family moved to Detroit, he'd moved in with his aunt because he didn't want to break up the Bar-Kays. He remembers Isaac working up the song with the band. "Isaac was one hell of a womanizer," says Willie.

"With so many women, he had some problems. And a lot of the women had their own egos and personalities and problems, and that could spill over onto the rest of the guys. So, a lot of times we would be doing 'By the Time I Get to Phoenix,' people in the audience would be crying, Isaac would be crying, I'd be crying, the background singers would be crying—because we could relate to the situation."

Working during the wee hours of the night, Isaac developed four songs. "'By the Time I Get to Phoenix' was eighteen minutes and forty seconds long," he says. "We cut it live, right there in the studio. I felt what I had to say could not be said in two minutes and thirty seconds. I was all about feeling." More than half of the song was the spoken, moaning introduction, the story he'd begun telling in nightclubs to attract the audience's attention. The album was cut at Ardent Studios—Stax was already booked around the clock. Ardent had purchased the same recording console and tape machine that Stax had, and was drawing their overflow. "The terrifying thing was the length of Isaac's songs," says Ardent's owner and chief engineer John Fry. "A reel of tape ran for fifteen minutes, and Isaac's songs would run longer. We began splicing extra tape onto the reels. Even still, there were takes when I walked into the studio while they were playing and made circles in the air with my finger. They'd improvise an ending."

Isaac recorded the basic tracks in Memphis and then brought the tapes to Detroit, where arranger Dale Warren (often with Johnny Allen) wrote and recorded string parts. Isaac put his own stamp on another hit, the Bacharach-David song "Walk on By," which Dionne Warwick took to the top ten in 1964 (his version ran over twelve minutes), and also on "One Woman," a track recorded the previous year by the then-obscure vocalist Al Green; it was written by two of Memphis's premier backing vocalists, Charlie Chalmers and Sandra Rhodes. The final song was a collaboration between Isaac and Al Bell with the fanciful title "Hyperbolicsyllabicsesquedalymistic." Isaac explains, "We just wanted to tease people with all these syllables. The tune actually was talking about a beautiful affair that you had with this woman and you want an encore, a repeat." The title may be barely pronounceable, but the music is propulsive and grooving. Multilayered, there's tinkling piano notes on the high end, funky wah-wah guitar in the middle, and drumming on the low end that, just when its rhythm seems clear, defies expectations. Initially a challenge, the song trusts its audience, and sets off for territory not yet explored.

"Isaac was just cool as shit," says Willie Hall. "He was a great person, energetic, didn't do any drugs. He'd drink a little Lancers wine. And he

What a birthday party in 1968

Deanie Parker's birthday party, 1968. L–R: Cleotha Staples (rear), Deanie Parker, Pops Staples, Jo Bridges. (Deanie Parker Collection)

would look up in the top of his head, the third eye, trying to come up with an idea—*boom*, it would come—perfect."

"When I finished the album," Isaac remembers, "I played it for Jack Gibson—Jack the Rapper. He was a former DJ and a new Stax promotions man. And for Joe Medlin, the godfather of all promotions. I dragged them into the conference room and said, 'I want you all to listen to something.' When it was over they just sat there. 'Well?' I asked. One said, 'Ike, I never heard anything like it in my life. It's fantastic. But we don't know about you getting airplay because it's so long.'" But Isaac was seeking self-expression—he was leaving airplay to the other albums in the soul explosion.

◆ ◆ ◆

AL'S VISION OF a total record company embraced the expanding multimedia world. Nothing was too big. For starters: television. He enlisted WNEW in New York as a partner, creating a one-hour TV concert that beamed from the antenna atop the Empire State Building to all of New York and beyond, and was syndicated in markets including Washington, DC, San Francisco, Memphis, and Los Angeles. "Gettin' It All Together" featured Carla Thomas, Booker T. & the MG's, and, in a final effort before parting, Sam and Dave. The set list of classic hits, a tribute to Otis

Redding, and a group finale doing Motown were a calculated effort to reach a wide and new audience. "[The TV show] will introduce Stax artists to millions of new people and establish them as visual personalities," Al proclaimed in the company's new magazine, *Stax Fax*, its foray into the print medium. "The New York broadcast in April will also give our first major album release in May a terrific boost, and the subsequent prime-time broadcasts across the country will keep the excitement going."

Stax Fax was a magazine that Al delegated to Deanie Parker in the autumn of 1968, directed toward both industry personnel and the popular audience. Filled with pictures, it kept Stax on the coffee table when it wasn't on the turntable, and it quickly grew into a glossy format that included news stories germane to the contemporary African-American audience, opinion columns, and profiles on Stax artists and others, like Nina Simone and Florence Ballard, who were not associated with the label.

Busy with these big plans, Al needed an executive assistant, which he found in the African-American applicant Earlie Biles. She'd had training in secretarial science but knew nothing about the music business. "I was sitting there waiting," she says of her job interview, "and in comes Isaac Hayes—with no shirt, some thongs, and some orange-and-purple shorts. He was the first baldheaded black man I'd ever seen. I was introduced to Johnny Baylor as a producer. He looked like the typical gangster you saw on television. He was kind of scary to me. Dino came in with him, and he was the second person I saw with a bald head. But Johnny was very nice to me—except one time. I stood up from my desk to greet him and he touched my leg. I slapped him, and then I got really scared because I realized I slapped this— what looked like a thug. He said, 'Woo.' And I said, 'Don't ever do that again.' He said, 'Okay, okay.' And then a couple of weeks went by and he asked me to keep his gun for him. He wore kind of tight pants, and a short leather jacket, so I guess he couldn't hide his gun. I don't like guns, but I allowed him to put his gun in my drawer every time he came. And I learned to live with that." Earlie was twenty-one years old.

Earlie Biles came to Stax in 1968. (Stax Museum of American Soul Music)

The feel and smell of success that permeated the new Stax was buttressed by the company's friendly relations with its loan officer, Joe Harwell, who'd been working at the nearby branch of Union Planters National Bank since 1966. In the era of flower power and the burgeoning hippie movement, Joe was not your average straitlaced banker; not that he wore bell-bottoms and long hair, but he was comfortable around musicians and those whom mainstream society considered oddballs. "Mr. Harwell always did nice things for all the artists who would come in town," says Earlie. "Johnnie Taylor or Don Davis, if they had no ID and needed checks cashed, I would just phone Joe Harwell.' He supported all the Stax personnel very well."

"Joe was this personable guy that would be right at home on a used car lot," says one Stax employee. "He became a star at Union Planters. He would loan Stax a lot of money, and Stax would pay it back, and Harwell looked good. Whenever Stax needed money, he was ready for us."

"I'd get on the phone to Joe Harwell," says Duck. " 'Hey, it's Duck. I'd like to buy my wife a car.' Joe Harwell, he was so sweet. 'What kind of car you want?' 'Cadillac!' 'You work for Stax? Okay, it's done.'"

With friends like Joe Harwell, everyone could dress well, live in a nice home, and furnish it in the fashion of the day, driving to work in the car of their dreams. The songwriters for "Who's Making Love" drove matching canary-yellow Cadillacs with black roofs. Al Jackson drove a blue Lincoln Continental Mark III. Steve was in a purple Buick Riviera (among other cars). Duck had a custom yellow Excalibur. The newly fenced parking area outside McLemore looked like a million-dollar car lot, a bouquet of gas-guzzling success.

Keyboardist Steve Leigh, then known as Sandy Kay, came to Stax in 1969 from New York, where he'd been playing with a group named the Soul Survivors. "Raymond Jackson [songwriter on 'Who's Making Love'] brought me over to see Joe Harwell, and I opened a bank account at Union Planters Bank on Bellevue," he recalls. "Then Raymond brought me to a furniture store in Memphis, and with no more than his say-so, I had enough instant credit to buy thousands of dollars of furniture for the townhouse we rented. 'You work at Stax?' *Presto!* Credit! Just like that. The next day, all the furniture was delivered . . . A super king-size bed with the tufted velvet headboard and matching tufted velvet bench. It was exactly like Raymond's, but ours was blue and Raymond's was purple. Homer [Banks] had one, and Al Jackson did, too."

It was boom time. "The city opened itself up to us," says Willie Hall.

"You could borrow money if you wanted it," says Earlie. "Joe Harwell, he was the fix-it-all for everybody." By the time the soul explosion rolled around, everyone was living large.

◆ ◆ ◆

IF THE SOUL exploding sales conference had been a symphony, it would have been Beethoven's Ninth. It was a huge and glorious effort, interweaving the grand themes of salesmanship, civic responsibility, and the recording arts. It employed live performances, recordings, speeches, and a high-tech multiscreen slide show presentation with synchronized music. The future of Stax was riding on the success of the event. Its theme was, appropriately, "Gettin' It All Together." Had it failed, Gulf & Western would be hard-pressed to justify investing another cent in an organization that conceived such a folly. The company morale could not sustain a failure. Underlying the sales conference was the stark truth that this effort could sink them forever.

Stax booked all the meeting spaces at the city's high-end Rivermont Hotel, overlooking the Mississippi River. Guests were greeted by klieg lights outside, and inside by Deanie Parker and her staff, who presented them with weekend schedules that included tours of the Stax studios. The first weekend, May 16–18, 1969, was dedicated to the distributors and sales agents from across the country—those wholesalers who could purchase the records and get them to the public. The following weekend, a one-two punch, was for members of the press and those who could urge the customer to purchase the Stax material, including the all-important "rack jobbers"—the companies that filled the Sears, Woolworth's, and other non–music store racks with product. The rack jobbers reached the casual shopper who could be converted to an ardent fan. Great numbers of people were flown in at company expense. "We had *Billboard* and *Record World* and *Cash Box*," says Deanie. "*Rolling Stone* was there, *Playboy*, *Vanity Fair*, *Time*, *Jet*, the *New York Times*. Representatives from BMI, from advertising agencies, publishing companies, and film production companies. Writers came from papers in Massachusetts, Pennsylvania, and Connecticut. We brought in a lot of the ethnic publications. And people came in from England. We did all of the right things right, and it was very, very impressive." Artists performed their new material, including Booker T. & the MG's, Carla Thomas, the Staple Singers, William Bell, Albert King, and new rock and roll signees the Knowbody Else (who would later become Black Oak Arkansas).

The albums that comprised the staggering twenty-eight featured many Stax stalwarts. The MG's entry, *The Booker T. Set*, featured them inter-

Steve Cropper, left, speaks with Johnny Baylor at the May 1968 soul explosion sales meeting. (Stax Museum of American Soul Music)

preting eleven notable songs from the preceding year, from Sly Stone to the Beatles, the Doors to Herb Alpert. They'd been recently named Instrumental Group of the Year, 1968, by *Billboard*, and managed to squeeze in their own sessions while producing and backing other artists. "From the company's perspective, the MG's were meant to be the support band for Stax Records—always," Booker explains. "The band would be allowed to make some singles and to have some solo success, but not to the point that we could become separate from the studio. The records weren't given short shrift but the sessions and the opportunity to make the records were given short shrift. Booker T. & the MG's, we just scratched the surface of what we could've done. The music we were able to do stands on its own and I'm extremely proud of it. I just think we could've done a lot more."

The Bar-Kays cut their own album for the sales meeting, *Gotta Groove*. Ambitiously funky, they merged the traditional Stax instrumental with screaming rock and roll guitar, creating in songs like "Street Walker"—its blues harmonica dueling with the guitar's edginess—a tune that wouldn't be out of place on a Led Zeppelin album. Huge-sounding fuzz-guitar amps wail atop hard-driving drums. Their interpretation of the Beatles' "Yesterday" is cubist and rich, thrilling in its breadth; an embrace of life's possibilities. Booker says, "I thought the Bar-Kays were fully capable of taking over the Stax tradition."

The goal of twenty-eight albums was missed by one: Though there was an album cover for Rufus Thomas's *May I Have Your Ticket, Please?* there was no album inside—like getting a graduation envelope filled with a summer-school summons. Rufus was stung. There'd be no shindig were it not for Rufus Thomas and his family, less than a decade back and many a day since. His very spirit was woven into the company's fabric. Since "Walking the Dog" in 1963, he'd been on and off the lower reaches of the charts (despite great efforts like "Willy Nilly"), and the company couldn't manage to find time for finishing his record. But Rufus Thomas wore a frog costume on a Beale Street stage when he was five, and he'd been in showbiz long enough to know that if you kept them coming out, one would hit. He was the Clown Prince of Dance and the Funkiest Man Alive, and he remained professional all the way. He performed for the audiences, glad-handed the clients, and smiled his way through both weekends, despite the breach of faith. Instead of giving in to anger and resentment, he kept his eyes on the future. Indeed, he would soon demonstrate how much fun a third comeback could be.

The highlights of the convocation were the presentations. Each album was introduced with a multiscreen slide show, synchronized music, encouraging words from Jim and Al. With everyone gathered, Stax heralded its new emphasis on distribution, announcing a deal with soul star Jerry Butler and his Chicago-based company, Fountain Records. Interspersed among the business achievements were charitable announcements, including an educational program for the underprivileged called SAFEE—the Stax Association for Everybody's Education. "The day care centers would be for children whose parents cannot afford to pay to send them to preschools or other centers," Jim announced. "The trade school would furnish education for students through high school and for those who cannot afford to attend a college or university."

The meeting's keynote speaker was Julian Bond, who was then a state congressman in the Georgia House and a founding member of SNCC, for which he'd been communications director from 1961 to 1966. He hit strong notes of black separatism in his charged address, quoting a speech given 120 years earlier by the first African-American lawyer admitted to practice before the US Supreme Court, Dr. John S. Rock. But by the

Isaac Hayes.

conclusion, Bond was establishing a broader platform for community activism, unifying the room as young people capable of implementing change. This speech was clearly not your typical music industry rhetoric of sales, markets, and profits. But Julian Bond was there because the Stax that Al Bell envisioned was not your typical music industry company. Stax, a new Stax, was on the rise.

One published estimate calculated Stax's expenses for the two week-ends at a quarter million dollars. "It was awesome," remembers Al. "And like Atlantic, we had the sales forms there and the purchase orders and our wholesalers left purchasing product"—$2 million worth of product, according to *Billboard*. "With those twenty-seven albums at one time, folk began to forget that we didn't have a catalog. Out of that meeting was born Mavis as an individual artist, Isaac Hayes as a giant, and on and on. We came back from the dead not with the vintage Stax sound of Otis Redding and Sam and Dave. We came now as a diversified new company. And that positioned us in the record industry as a viable independent record company. It accelerated from that point forward."

20. A POT OF NECKBONES
1969–1970

A L BELL'S ALBUM avalanche would generate dollars, but it would be the singles that would snag the public's attention and direct them toward Stax's myriad album possibilities. Thirty singles were chosen from the albums, thirty shots at radio play and chart action. Eddie Floyd won favor with "Don't Tell Your Mama," its punctuated beat pushing it to the top twenty of the R&B charts, its string arrangement landing it on the Hot 100 pop charts. Johnnie Taylor continued his drive with "Testify," landing on both charts, and the MG's placed in the top forty of each chart with their take on Paul Simon's recent hit from the soundtrack to *The Graduate*, "Mrs. Robinson." Despite the emphasis on pairings—there were singles featuring Mavis with William Bell, and another with her and Eddie Floyd; one with Carla and William, one with Carla and Johnnie Taylor, and a fifth single featuring them all plus others—none of them landed on any charts. In fact, despite all the calculating, the biggest hit from the May '69 sales meeting wasn't released as a single until two months later because no real hopes had been pinned on it; it was, to some extent, filler, an easy album that would help boost the numbers, with no single pulled because nothing on Isaac Hayes's *Hot Buttered Soul* was less than five minutes long. The project was decidedly uncommercial: The album cover photo was an unusual angle on Isaac—a frame-filling shot from

Isaac's breakout record.

above of his bald head, the landscape dotted with vacant hair follicles. His face is obscured because he's looking down, conveying humility, even as the wide gold chain around his neck proclaims a voluptuous arrogance. And there's skin everywhere: black, beautiful skin.

Isaac was unlike anything else in popular music. He wasn't "the sound of young America," as Motown had been billing itself since the early 1960s, nor was he treading the soul territory he'd established as a writer and producer at Stax. This was a boudoir record. The pop song opens with a nearly nine-minute tale of lover's woe—a drumstick tick-tocks the hollow, forlorn sounds of the wood that surrounds the drum while Isaac's organ moans. The song's body is relatively brief, Ike and the Bar-Kays breaking into a symphonic, luscious passion so intense that it needs all the five minutes it takes to wind down to the song's postcoital fade. Immersed in the studio's possibilities, and his own, with instructions to do as he pleased, he'd opened a door that other singers hadn't seen, and legions followed him through it, fans and artists alike.

"I performed at the sales meeting," remembers Isaac Hayes. "David Porter and I did some Sam and Dave stuff, then I sang 'By the Time I Get to Phoenix,' and got a standing ovation. That's when the merchandisers were asking, 'Did you record that?' 'Oh, yes, we have it back there.' They picked it up and started checking it out. And *Hot Buttered Soul* took off." A single was rushed out when the album began garnering sales. DJs absorbed the edited "Phoenix," then made a hit of the B-side too, an edited "Walk on By." The album promptly hit four charts—R&B, pop, easy listening, and jazz; on the latter it spent nearly three quarters of a year moving between the top two spots. When *The Isaac Hayes Movement* was released the following year, *Hot Buttered Soul* was still in the jazz top ten, and those two albums were there to greet Hayes's *To Be Continued* when it came out in December 1970. Making the record to satisfy himself, Isaac reached everyone.

Besides Isaac, no one could have been more pleased than Al Bell. The soul explosion had been his perilous and expensive experiment. As tall as he stood and strong as he pushed for this massive product creation, Al must have considered the possibility of failure—awake in the middle of the night, alone on the long drives to see his parents in Arkansas. If the soul explosion had been a dud, Stax risked never recovering. But the effort had succeeded grandly, even without Isaac's ascension; his album was only a part of the convention's $2 million worth of orders. It was, however, his ongoing, accelerating sales that affirmed the event.

Into the vacuum created by the death of Otis Redding and the contractual snafu of Sam and Dave stepped Isaac Hayes. Stax no longer was a shadow of its former self, but was becoming a new, revitalized company, with a new star establishing a new look. And as the spotlight shone brighter, Isaac allowed it to illuminate more of him, bringing African-American cultural and social issues to the fore. Isaac established the market that would soon support socially driven concept albums from Marvin Gaye, Stevie Wonder, and Curtis Mayfield. Isaac gave the old label a new identity.

Stepping in front of the curtain required adjustment. A few weeks after the sales meeting, Isaac was performing his first concert—August 1969, the Masonic Temple in Detroit, with the Staple Singers as the opening act. Detroit DJ Wash Allen, originally from Memphis, had a midnight to six A.M. show, a time slot that allowed him to stretch out with album cuts instead of short singles. The DJ knew Isaac and liked his groove. He featured the album, and especially "Phoenix," on his show. "That was basically the way the whole damn thing got started," says Isaac's trumpet player and childhood friend Mickey Gregory, who stepped up to handle many of the growing duties that Isaac's sudden career was demanding. Isaac and Mickey had slept in cars together as children, shared the poverty, and Mickey had Isaac's back. "The first couple gigs were in Detroit. We flew up with some cats from the studio—Marvell Thomas and Allen Jones [they'd coproduced the record with Al Bell] and Bobby Manuel and Harold Beane."

The show sold out more than two weeks in advance, and Isaac, though already a music industry success, was nervous as a high school thespian.

"Do you think they'll like me?" he remembers asking backstage. He eased onto the stage and hit the first song—during which he realized that the microphone needed adjusting. "I started talking to the audience," he remembers. "I had a terry cloth floppy hat on and I was sweating. I took it off, exposing my head, and women screamed. *Ahhh—make a note of that, Ike.* The next song, we popped it and we just went on through and did a whole concert. And I got standing ovations. I learned something from that experience. I learned to communicate with the audience."

"I think we started at five grand for the night," says Mickey. "When the cat called back it was seventy-five hundred, and next time it was, 'Man, get me the string orchestra and about ten grand, pay all expenses and I *might* can get him to go.' The album went buck fucking wild—first time a black artist sold a million dollars' worth of albums—and after that it was on like a pot of neckbones."

No longer crafting the performances of others, Isaac assumed the spotlight. And he got good at it, real quick. He moved his organ from the side to center stage, leading the group instead of flanking them, and he settled into what he began to term "rapping"—not rhyming so much as talking intimately with the audience. He began to dress the part, again with a visionary intensity. "How Isaac combined colors was unbelievable, and absolutely unique," says Al, who could be describing Isaac's music as easily as his attire. "I don't know his rationale, his justification, but I have never seen anybody dressed like Isaac Hayes. He was out from the crowd by himself."

Isaac had been infusing personality into his work since well before "Soul Man," and he didn't wait long to add to his stage character. A man of fashion, he was aware of how much the spotlight made him sweat. "One day I was wearing rawhide onstage," he says. "Moccasins, my French rabbit bag—I'd been out to California and seen the hippies. But I was hot onstage all the time. And I would see James Brown and all those guys take their tie off and throw it back there and then the jacket. I thought, These guys come out sharp, so why do they want to get on stage and strip? I need something else. So this shop in Memphis gave me a chain outfit. It was a necklace and a belt. Then I saw Roy Cunningham, the drummer of the new Bar-Kays, he came out on stage with some tights on, being different. I thought, if Nureyev can do it, why can't I? I put those chains around my neck and around my waist, I had those boots on, and I was air-conditioned. And that was the look. The chains at one time represented bondage to black men, and now it was a symbol of power and influence. The chains, the bald head, beard, and shades—the television networks was taking it as a militant look. Anybody that speaks out and acts upon being suppressed, you become militant. Well, I was militant."

Militant was one reading. Carnal was another. Isaac unleashed a new male sexuality that made James Brown seem like a drag queen. Bare-chested, well muscled, skin-tight pants that bulged in all the right places, Isaac's deep voice sang softly, slowly, fully, about passion. The women swooned at his seductive manner. "Isaac was a big draw wherever he appeared," says Dino Woodard. "Big crowds. It wasn't just the women. Men, too, really dug his arrangements and the lyrics. He won across both ways. But women, hey, they was just, wow, crazy about him. Boom, screaming all the time."

Isaac spurned drugs and drunkenness, but he had a weak spot for women, and this role in the spotlight played to his vulnerabilities. "That was all he lived for," says lifelong friend Mickey Gregory. "Women. Nothing was more important to Isaac than women being attracted to him."

A *Jet* magazine cover story described his "physique like a Mandingo Daddy," and wrote of his fashion sense: "He may appear in cranberry colored tights, striped fur Eskimo boots, a buckskin or suede vest with beaded thongs naked to the waist; a zebra-like cloak, or a Russian, military-appearing cape, bright colored scarf, heavy fur or a big floppy hat. The colors are as striking as the designs: purples, yellows, pinks . . . Like a strutting, virile peacock, he takes the stage, ceremoniously sweeps off his hat and, with the klieg lights bouncing whitely from his shining head, executes an exaggerated bow to an exploding audience."

There was more to that explosion than the audience knew. In James Brown tradition, Isaac's MC was also his valet onstage—Randy Stewart. When Isaac would bow for Randy to remove his hat, there was a quick conversation. "He'd say, 'There's a pretty girl right there in the front seat,' " says Randy. "I'd say, 'What's she got on?' He'd tell me, and we'd send someone to get her, and she'd be backstage for him when he was done. Isaac was a woman freak. He had women all over Memphis. Get them a house, a car. Women, women, women."

Stax bet that Isaac's sensual image would sell on the West Coast, and they purchased a prominent corner billboard on a Hollywood stretch of Sunset Boulevard: Isaac's bald pate gleaming to the setting sun. "*Hot Buttered Soul* hit," says Bar-Kays drummer Willie Hall, "and we all started making money. The Bar-Kays opened the shows for Isaac, and then we backed him on his gigs."

Isaac's entourage increased with his popularity. Soon there were four

Isaac Hayes at a party. (Stax Museum of American Soul Music)

female backup singers, and Dale Warren was rehearsing string sections hired in each city. He had someone to sell programs (Randy Stewart), someone to run lights (Johnny Keyes) and sound (Henry "Creeper" Bush), someone to manage the band, someone else to manage Isaac. More musicians, more instruments. "All of a sudden, we were the shit," says Willie Hall. "I was about eighteen years old, fresh out of high school, and it was wonderful. We went from groupies to hired hookers. Everything was gorgeous."

◆◆◆

THE MOVE TO performing immersed Isaac in the world of scumbag promoters, people who would book the show with certain promises but were nowhere to be found when the show was over and it was their turn to deliver. Promoting shows and running clubs was a cash business and always attracted gangsters. You toughened up to play, hiring men mean enough to scare promoters, or you got eaten. "A lot of times we wouldn't get our money," says Johnny Keyes, Packy's friend who would eventually become Isaac's stage manager. "Guys would say, 'Man, we sorry, man. We got *some* of your money, but the Man got us again.'" After a few incidents of feeling helpless in his tights and chains, Isaac saw that other performers had brawn in their entourage and realized he needed a muscle man to enforce the deal. Money, girls, the spotlight? Johnny Baylor was up for that.

"Isaac did the show in Chicago at McCormick Hall," says Randy Stewart, who'd come from Sugar Ray's boxing camp to run Isaac's concessions. "When the show was over, the guy didn't have the money. Isaac would have to pay everything anyway. Johnny Baylor said, 'I'll get your money.' He went and kidnapped the guy, told the house, 'If you don't come up with the money, we'll kill the guy.' So the next time we went to Chicago, when we went to the dressing room, there was a wreath welcoming Isaac on his door."

"We tried to make sure that Isaac got his due," says Dino, Baylor's partner, "that he was promoted properly before we went into a city, and we tried to see that he received his pay. That there was no cheating, which promoters do."

Having Baylor was fighting fire with gunfire and would certainly protect Isaac. But Baylor's presence changed the tenor of the traveling cavalcade. "Johnny's whole deal was intimidation," says Marvell Thomas, who was playing keyboards in Isaac's band. "If he could whip

Aloha - Isaac Hayes Group

Isaac Hayes's road show in Hawaii. Isaac in rear with sunglasses and bald head. Johnny Baylor is next to him in the white hat. Johnny Keyes is next to Baylor. Dino Woodard toward the left, with handlebar mustache and lei. Randy Stewart, with sunglasses, next to Hayes. (Johnny Keyes Collection)

everybody into line, then he could have control. He threatened me with a gun one day, onstage, at a rehearsal in Chicago. I told him to either shoot me or go to hell and get away from me. Half of the Chicago Symphony Orchestra was in that pit. I called his bluff in front of enough witnesses to where he didn't feel comfortable blowing my brains out. But as a result of that little incident and Johnny's relationship with Isaac, Johnny spent a lot of time lobbying Isaac real hard to get me fired. And eventually, he did."

Guns were becoming commonplace. "You'd see Isaac and his entourage and they all wore these tight Italian suits, real sharp," says Joe Mulherin, a trumpet player who worked in Stax's publicity department, "but all of them had bulges coming out of the rear or side, depending on where they kept their pieces. A tailor could have resolved the issue, but no one seemed to mind."

Baylor was a brutal enforcer. Willie Hall remembers how Baylor dealt with one of his own team: "This guy had been stealing money from Isaac. He was supposed to pay the hotel bills and things like that, but it had been proven that he was buying his girlfriend things with the money and skimming off the top. They confronted him, and an argument broke out. I saw them drag him out of the room and take him to the hospital. The side of his face was closed up and, actually, they had to remove his eye. He wore a black patch after that." One beating or one firing of a weapon goes a long way toward cementing someone's reputation.

During one Christmas season, Isaac was asked by Jane Fonda to do a benefit performance in New York. The band was at the Holiday Inn on Fifty-seventh Street, and Isaac was at a fancy hotel not far away; Johnny and Dino were with him. The weather turned bad and after the gig, they were stuck in New York for a few days. The band was told to go easy on the room service and expenses at the hotel—there was no income from the gig. Word was duly disbursed. But a night without income was different for the star than it was for the crew, and some were dissatisfied with the mandated frugality. "About seven or eight of us were in a hotel room," says Willie Hall, "and Johnny Keyes decides to order steak for everybody, wine, and chocolate cake, everything. They brought it, and Johnny [Keyes] signed for it."

"Johnny Keyes had a room right down from mine," says Randy Stewart. "He's down there partying, got a big table, eating big steaks, drinking. Johnny Baylor had told the hotel if there's an issue to get in touch with them at the other hotel. So the hotel told [Baylor] they're ordering all this stuff, so Johnny called me." Randy explained the situation, and

Baylor asked for Johnny Keyes to come to the phone. Randy set down the receiver. "I told Johnny Keyes, 'Johnny Baylor and Isaac want to talk to you.' He come over to my room, phone still laying there, he said, 'What they talking about?' I said, 'They're talking about you ordering all that food and wine and whiskey.' Johnny Keyes said, 'Motherfuck Johnny Baylor.' He left. When Johnny Baylor heard that, he got pissed. And I heard this on the phone plain as day. [Baylor] said, 'Isaac, what do you think I should do?' Isaac said, 'Go kick his ass.'" Isaac was fully under Baylor's spell, reveling in the power. Baylor, the boxer, went to whip a skinny musician.

"They come over there and damn near killed him," Randy continues. "I was in my room watching TV. Willie Hall run in and jumped in the bed in the corner. I said, 'What's wrong with you?' He said, 'Man, they're down there killing him.' I went down there, Johnny Keyes was slumped in the chair, they were crushing him, crushing him. Benny Mabone, Isaac's valet, was standing in the door trembling. Johnny Baylor had those pistols raised over his head, said, 'Did he do anything to you? Go on over there and kick his ass too.' I got between Dino and Johnny Keyes, said, 'Don't hit this man no more.' Blood was everywhere."

"I thought they might kill him," says Willie. "I looked back and there were some guys in the band dragging Johnny Keyes down the hall, taking him to the hospital. This part of his jaw was way over here, and everybody was crying and upset. I ran like a little scared puppy. I'm like, Oh, my God, what have I gotten into? And Johnny called me and said, 'Hall, don't be afraid. We're not gonna hurt you. You're Skull's boy.' [They called Isaac 'Skull.'] And that became the order. From that point on, all the years that I knew Johnny Baylor, I could do no wrong in his eyesight."

Baylor next turned his attention to David Porter, who, witnessing the success of his longtime partner's performing career, was recording his own debut album and forming a band, the Soul Spacemen, with keyboardist Ronnie Williams. Isaac had agreed to produce it, but the time it took to agree and to actually be in the studio were proving two different commitments. Isaac put a good front on it all when asked about it by a reporter in 1970, saying, "It's true that we are getting apart because we have both evolved so much that we now must do our own things. But David and I are both very much together. We work together and we still compare ideas a lot to make each of us more aware of what is happening. I think that it is equally important to David and myself that we concentrate on both things. Being an artist is something that is in both of us—we were both singers before we got involved in these other things. But you can be sure that David and I will be together for a long while to come."

Such, however, was not Johnny Baylor's plan. "I think Johnny did pull a gun on David Porter," says Dino, "but he did it to let him know, to frighten him. Jealousies existed, because Johnny had become the mouthpiece for Isaac. So he and David got into an argument."

The partnership eroded. Isaac's name went on David's debut album as producer—which would help his old friend. But Isaac slipped into his own universe, and David assumed responsibility for the Emotions and the Soul Children, whom the two had been producing. After a couple years of missed appointments, Isaac did make time to squeeze out a single with David, a duet on both sides, each a love song of longing and reunion. The A-side was a propulsive take on the Homer Banks and Allen Jones song "Ain't That Lovin' You (for More Reasons Than One)," featuring a big Isaac Hayes horn arrangement; the flip was a version of the recent Bread hit "Baby I'm-a Want You." "I didn't like what was happening," says Jim. "I was looking at it from a business standpoint. We lost a great writing team. Why do we have to break up the writing team just because an artist is breaking? If you've got something successful going, it's okay to experiment, but why break up the success? Once those egos get that big, you can't control them."

Indeed, control seemed lost. "They put a gun up to David Porter's head and told him to stay away from Isaac," says Wayne Jackson. "Well, there went all those magical songs—gone. And that was the day that [saxophone partner] Andrew [Love] and I went to Jim and told him we'd like to be off the payroll if he didn't mind, so we could go on down the road." The two incorporated by the name everyone was calling them—the Memphis Horns—then doubled their prices and missed not a beat, freelancing for Stax and picking up sessions all over Memphis, Muscle Shoals, and elsewhere. "When we started, it was about family, and genius and Otis and the fun we were having—and now Paramount wants to know where we are every hour and there's guys walking around in the halls with guns? They had to search my horn case, me and Andrew both, going in the door and coming out. They weren't searching for fried chicken."

◆ ◆ ◆

"I GUESS IT was an explosion," says Steve Cropper. "Could have been an implosion, too."

Change was the status quo. A new promotion team was hired, including several guys who had been with Motown. They fanned out across the US, city to city, radio station to station, to see that Stax artists got quality airtime. Larry Shaw, a Chicago advertising man who'd made Afro

Sheen a household name, was lured to Stax by both Al Bell's philosophy of creating an African-American economic base and a very lucrative offer. A former speechwriter for Dr. King and onetime Motown employee, Junius Griffin, joined the staff—but didn't stay long, repulsed by the depth of Memphis's racism. Motown's comptroller Ed Pollack was brought from Detroit to Memphis. "I'd always heard that Stax artists were treated fairly and Motown artists were screwed," says Duck. "And what did Stax do? They go out and get Motown's comptroller. I told myself, 'Well, I'm about to get fucked.'" Changes occurred so fast, Stax couldn't even decide on a motto. With equal fanfare and sincerity it boasted that its mission was "Tell the truth with truthful music." And "Look what we have done together." Or was it "The Memphis Sound"? Or "The soul label for your swinging turntable"? One that lasted a while was "Where everything is everything."

Herb Kole, director of merchandising and marketing, announced the sale of one million albums just seven weeks after the 1969 sales meeting. Ewell Roussell, national sales manager for Stax, announced that during its first year with Gulf & Western, June 1, 1968, to June 1, 1969, Stax sold ten million singles through the thirty-two national distributors it worked with. Its business plan had called for selling 7.5 million singles by the third year of the merger. "We were challenging Atlantic right away with album sales," says Jim. "I don't think we were competition with Motown for singles, but we were outselling them for albums. We sold a million *Hot Buttered Soul* albums to a pure black audience, and that was unheard of."

"Profits increased greatly, which did what?" asks Steve, then answers himself: "It allowed us to have accountants, lawyers, more secretaries for everybody." There were upsides for artists too: "Better offices. Better distribution. Better promotion guys, because you could afford to pay the better guys."

"It was a gradual increase in personnel," says Earlie Biles, Al's secretary who was becoming his de facto traffic cop. The more people he hired, the more who sought his attention. "The staff was about ten people when I started, and then more people started coming in. It seemed like one day you looked up and there are all these people here. Like, you know, what are we doing?"

Al was hiring experts, working toward his vision of a total record company, his own Columbia, with involvement in multiple media, producing, promoting, and distributing. The breadth of the company grew so much that Al changed its name from the parochial Stax Records to the panoramic Stax Organization.

The Motown alumni brought a practical know-how for operating on a national, not regional, level. And Larry Shaw brought a pragmatism to Al's vision. "Larry Shaw kicked it up another level," says Joe Mulherin, from the publicity department. "His understanding of the practicalities meshed perfectly with Al's sense of vision and hype. Al could see the mansion on the hill, and Larry could see the path that led to it."

"Larry was an exceptionally bright man," says Rev. Jesse Jackson; Larry helped him establish Operation Breadbasket. "He had creative skills, but he was also a very socially conscious guy, an intellectual. Larry could put ideas on paper. He had this commitment and genius locked up and no place to go, trying to make his way in the white corporate world, which kept closing doors in his face. And Al spotted that talent and their spirits combined. Larry became the creative director and really much of the mental strength behind Stax as well. And Stax became an international platform for Larry to display his talents and skills."

Larry Shaw used national media to lock Stax deeper into the American consciousness. Applying the same techniques that had worked with Afro Sheen and also with his Newport cigarettes campaign, he grabbed the simplest of Al's mottos, "The Memphis Sound," and emblazoned it atop full-page album ads for the world to see—not only in industry magazines like *Billboard*, but in lifestyle magazines such as *Jet*, a weekly that was prominent in African-American households, and *Essence*, a fashion magazine launched in 1970 that quickly reached the burgeoning African-American middle class. Shaw understood that Al's vision needed more than indiscriminate immersion, and he placed ads in embattled and struggling publications, because he recognized that minor magazines buttressed the major ones. As Shaw explained to author Rob Bowman, they sought titles not just directed at African-Americans but also owned by African-Americans. "*Soul* magazine was a struggling publication," Shaw said. "We financed it on many occasions . . . We helped *Essence*. I would fly to any fledgling magazine that we thought would give us some value." Stax was building a community, a large-scale, national community that would operate alongside, but not be contingent upon, the established white corporate world.

Offices were built for the new hires, the studio was upgraded to sixteen tracks, and walls came and went like the set of a grand opera. Stax had eased, oozed, and broken into adjoining stores it had formerly frequented until, by late 1969, it had outgrown the entire building. McLemore, its spiritual home, was abuzz with activity, sometimes nonstop for days on end. To accommodate the growth, Stax rented office space nearer to the center of town, 98 N. Avalon, atop TJ's, Memphis's hippest nightclub.

Jim, Al, the administrative offices, accounting, promotions—everything but the creative staff, Deanie's publicity department, and the publishing company—departed McLemore. Stax was expanding, Stax was atomizing, and the family unit was splintering.

As Stax shed its old skin, it had trouble fitting into its new one. In mid-March 1970, Jim Stewart gathered the entire company for a speech, articulating the issues before them and attempting to inject familial DNA into the increasingly corporate body. "The year 1970 will be a year of truth," Jim read from his prepared remarks. "We may perhaps be put to the most crucial of all tests . . . SURVIVAL. [The capital letters are Jim's.] As I look back at the year 1969, I see a measure of success, and I see failure. The sales last year were greater than any period in the history of your company. Employees increased from 20 to over 60 in number, and we achieved our first gold album. We expanded our studio facilities. It was a year of many improvements and accomplishments . . . and yet, we failed. We failed to overcome our immaturities, we failed to overcome our jealousies, our prejudice, our mistrusts.

"WHO IS IT TO BLAME? Every day I hear this word 'BLAME' almost as much as the four-letter words. The Producers blame the Company for interfering with their creative efforts. The Promotion Department blames Producers for poor product. Producers blame Promotions for 'lack of air play.' The Sales Departments blame both Promotions and Product, while the Executives listened, nodded approval, and blamed each other . . . AND ALL THE WHILE THE RUMORS ROLL ON . . . . The M.G.S. were kicked out of the studio; the Blacks are taking over; the Whites are taking over; Al Bell is getting rid of Jim Stewart; Jim Stewart is taking power away from Al Bell."

Jim's candor underscores the dire state of the company's morale. He wasn't opposed to change—Jim was Al's champion; Jim recognized Al's capacity for vision, and Al relied on Jim's background in banking as well as his support and his musical ear. They were a team; *Stax Fax* described them as Mr. Inside (Jim, the more introverted) and Mr. Outside (Al, the extrovert)—ready to take the company into the future. But the instant catalog and the breakneck growth had cost the corps its old esprit. Jim's solution was a new workflow. He announced the promotion of four people to vice presidential rank—Don Davis, Ed Pollack, Junius Griffin, and Larry Shaw. Additionally, this "Board of Advisors" will "organize, plan, and direct the day to day operation of your company," Jim read. "They will initiate policy and procedure from the top echelon down through the departmental level and enforce same at all levels."

This corporate restructuring would prove to be the first of frequent changes in the ongoing effort to maintain a working flowchart for the growing company. Employee turnover was high—people didn't have the same allegiance to a corporation as they did to a family.

◆ ◆ ◆

ALLEGIANCES WERE BEING tested outside Stax as well. Much like the sanitation workers two years earlier, the NAACP finally got tired of trying to reason with city officials. They submitted to the Memphis Board of Education a list of fifteen demands, of which the most important were the resignation of two board members to be replaced by blacks; the hiring of more black teachers and supervisors; and an improved school lunch program. To make sure they were heard, the NAACP proceeded with a school boycott. In early October 1969, on the protest's first day, one third of the nearly 135,000 students were absent (slightly over half the total student body was black), with disturbances reported at several schools and a march on the education office. On the second day, a Monday, more than 65,000 students were absent. The board heeded its pockets and agreed to meet with the NAACP on Wednesday. There, they submitted a typed response to their demands. The NAACP stormed out of the meeting, its president telling the newspaper, "The answers that the board has given to our demands are vague, negative, utterly ridiculous and an insult to the intelligence of anyone concerned with education."

The NAACP representatives then took a meeting with Jesse Epps, the leader of AFSCME who'd taken up a new battle on behalf of about one thousand "non-supervisory" employees (orderlies, janitors, some nursing staff) at St. Joseph's Hospital, a private facility. Though the hospital had willingly entered into talks with its employees and then the union, Epps was threatening and berating hospital officials in the press. St. Joseph's, feeling abused, broke off negotiations with Epps, and he responded with a picket line. The NAACP approached him about the school board; both saw strength in merging the issues. The newspaper headline read, NEW COALITION OF NEGRO GROUPS PLAN MASS MARCH AS FIRST STEP, and the article listed about ten groups who revealed their intention to "fight cooperatively against white racism wherever it is found," including by economic boycott. "The coalition," stated the article, "may represent the most potent expression of 'black power' in the civil rights movement in Memphis since the marches and sit-ins in 1959 and 1960 and the sanitation strike last year." One leader was quoted, "This is an all-out war in terms of keeping our money in our pockets," and another said, "We can no longer talk about separate issues in racial problems. All issues overlap—politics, unemployment, housing, poverty, education."

The call for missing school was formalized as Black Mondays, and the second week, nearly half of the city's student body was absent. Hospital employees and students marched down Main Street to a city council meeting but were denied a platform to speak. Epps announced plans for more "spread the misery" campaigns, but the hospital board remained adamant, and the school board was unyielding. The following Monday, nearly two thousand city workers joined the Black Monday picket, crippling garbage collection among other city services.

A month into the Black Mondays, and a month into the hospital picket, a march turned violent, or the police did—each side blamed the other—and tear gas was used to disperse the crowd. Many leaders were arrested, including Epps, the SCLC's Rev. Ralph Abernathy, and Rev. Ezekiel Bell, president of the Memphis branch of the NAACP. In a sign that nerves were wearing thin, a group of seventeen religious, service, and educational organizations released a statement that they were "weary of existing from crisis to crisis that are never truly resolved" and pleaded with the city to settle the grievances with justice. In fact, there were signs that the AFSCME hospital strike was weakening, as the hospital reported about 85 percent of its staff at work, and pointed out that its wages and employee benefits exceeded those of any institution represented by AFSCME in the city. When the school board conceded to implementing changes, including the appointment of two interim black advisers "who will have the privilege of attending all private and public meetings of the board," half of the NAACP leaders supported the decision and half decried it, resulting in the resignation of the local president and a public split among its members. Nonetheless, the highest number yet missed school when the Black Mondays were continued.

The City of Memphis proceeded on two fronts: First, it passed an ordinance restricting "parades" as a way to control the protest marches; one of the three black city councilmen said, "I think it is bad wisdom along with bad timing. The necessity for this type of ordinance was only spawned out of the city's reaction to the Negro protest movement." Second, feeling the economic pain of school boycotts, the school board filed a $10 million suit against several of the groups and their leaders; their suit alleged that the "dominant purpose" of the school boycotts "was to aid and abet the union in its controversy with St. Joseph Hospital." The suit brought a close to the school boycotts, with the NAACP having gains to show; Epps felt abandoned by them, and the hospital protest limped along until the day after

Christmas, when employees returned to work, having gained nothing. Asked if the union had lost the strike, Epps declared they'd lost nothing, adding, "When you are poor, you have nothing to start with." It was, however, a blow to the union, which had seemed all-powerful. In a few months, Epps would be terminated altogether when T.O. Jones led a group that asked for an accounting of the additional dollar the men were donating to help the poor. No program had ever been initiated, and an audit revealed about $100,000 in misused funds, including payment of closing costs on Epps's private home. Epps retired from AFSCME. Jones was not brought back, but stable leadership arrived, and AFSCME remains the major force in Memphis labor to this day. Conflicts in the school system, however, were far from over. The pursuit of justice and equality was going to make national headlines, and result in renewed civic disorder.

◆◆◆

IN APRIL OF 1970, Tim Whitsett began working at Stax. From Jackson, Mississippi, Whitsett was a young bandleader who'd sent demos to various production companies, including the Robert Stigwood Organization in New York. Stigwood managed Eric Clapton's Cream and the Bee Gees. Stax's Don Davis heard Tim Whitsett's demos in Stigwood's New York office and invited Whitsett to bring his band to Memphis. At that point, there was no longer any band to bring, so Whitsett arrived as a songwriter. While settling in, he mentioned his interest in copyright law and publishing, a shuffling of papers that can lead to longtime and significant income. "I'd been there about two days," Whitsett says, "and Don said, 'You look like an executive, how'd you like to run our publishing house?' So I wound up running East/Memphis Music. You walk down the McLemore hall on that green carpet that makes you not walk straight, then open my office where the carpet was bright Christmas red. Then we decided to build a demo studio there and move me down an office, and I wound up with the green carpet like everyone else. But it was still plush enough, and people would come in and say, 'Wow,' and then ask me for some money as a publishing advance."

Whitsett had cut his chops listening to the Stax hits and playing them at dances with his band. He was surprised that recent employees didn't know what he knew: The names, faces, and histories of the Stax artists. The heart of Stax may have been the old-school players—Eddie Floyd, William Bell, Deanie Parker, Steve, Duck, Al, Booker, and others—but the new influx had no idea who the old school was. A generation had moved in, with different ideas and new goals. "There was a point," says

Tim Whitsett, East/Memphis Publishing. (Phillip Rauls collection)

Tim, "when you looked around the hallways and wondered, Who are these people? And you would hear whispers: Do you know how much he's being paid? Some guy you never saw before. And you didn't know what he did." That point—when the newbies don't know the forebears and everyone's wondering who everyone else is—is perhaps the full realization of the corporation: A mind with no memory in a body with no soul. Al was giving more people more paychecks, and they were able to leave their jobs with their time cards at the—*ka-toonk*—time clock. They didn't bring home the worry, or dwell upon problem solving while preparing dinner. Al, however, left at the end of each long day with two briefcases, papers overflowing. Earlie, who soon moved next door to Al's family, would see his office light on until the wee hours of the morning. The burden had shifted, from many shoulders to just a few.

◆ ◆ ◆

WITH ALL THE success they'd had at Stax, the MG's had become known for their work as producers as well as backing musicians, and they were regularly sought by non-Stax artists. Simon and Garfunkel, after hearing the MG's interpretation of their "Mrs. Robinson," invited the quartet to back them on their next recording. "We did get the offer to do 'Bridge over Troubled Water,'" says Steve. "Booker told me they had already sent him a demo to prepare for the session. And when whoever was handling the Stax business got a hold of the whole idea, they didn't feel like the percentages were right and they said, 'You can't use our band unless we get so-and-so.' And Simon's people said, 'We're not gonna pay so-and-so so we'll just do it otherwise.'" It didn't end there. "I was getting offers from big artists," Steve continues. "And I was getting offers to do movie scores, and Booker was getting offered all these artists. And we were told that we couldn't do it as long as we were salaried at Stax."

At the same time their outside production work was being constrained, the MG's felt insecure about their in-house work. During the sales convention preparation, Stax had relied ever more on the new Bar-Kays. Younger, and with fewer family obligations, the kids were open to the myriad opportunities. "I could see us very soon being benched and having to move over for somebody else," Steve says, "and we weren't very happy with that."

The opportunities, the Bar-Kays were finding out (like the MG's already knew), were a mixed blessing. "Stax never intended for the Bar-Kays to be an act," says bassist James Alexander, echoing a sentiment previously expressed by Booker. "In the back of the company's mind, they wanted us to be the second string to Booker T. & the MG's. The company started using different producers who used our rhythm section. We were young, and fearless, so we weren't afraid to try stuff. But when we're backing up Albert King, the Emotions, Johnnie Taylor, Isaac Hayes, and everything that Duck doesn't play on, there's no time to concentrate on our own thing." When there wasn't time to conentrate on Isaac's thing either, Michael Toles, Ben Cauley, and Willie Hall left the Bar-Kays for the road with Isaac and his new band, the Movement.

For Booker, as much as the studio constraints and the in-house politics were an issue, he was most upset about the business, specifically the band's royalty arrangement. Everyone had been innocent when "Green Onions" had become a hit, and the agreement they'd made then was outmoded. Otis's agreement had been renegotiated, new artists being signed were given a better, more modern royalty deal, but the company would not budge from its deal with the MG's. "I wanted the studio to update our business arrangement and I wanted them to support us creatively," says Booker. "But they never did meet my terms. Instead of getting together with the guys and suggesting that we all get out of there together, I took off for California. I was very young. I didn't do it the way it should've been done." He'd never forgotten the way California felt when he'd arrived in Monterey; cooperative, respectful feelings that Memphis had never come close to replicating. Booker picked up work promptly upon his Los Angeles arrival, recording on Stephen Stills's first solo album, then employing Stills to play lead guitar on recordings Booker was producing for a new artist, Bill Withers. Booker's work led to a gold record and a Grammy Award for Withers's song "Ain't No Sunshine." California was going to be okay.

Booker left in the summer of 1969, followed by Steve in the fall of 1970. The band didn't break up, and in fact they would continue to record for the label, but the departure of these two players shook the company's foundation. Jim attributes the disenchantment from longtime Stax employees to the company's growing pains. "Al was executive vice president and you had to come up through the channels to get to me," he says. "I guess Steve and the guys felt like I'd put a stumbling block between them and me. They felt alienated. And I felt really bad about losing that group. Bell and I disagreed about the value of that particular production team. Bell and Al Jackson didn't get along. Bell and Cropper didn't get along. So the stage was set for a split as Bell became more in charge of productions. The MG's had splintered, Isaac became an artist, and that took him away from production for other acts. It's part of the problems of growth."

Early in 1970, Booker flew back to Memphis to record with the MG's. He arrived with the idea for *McLemore Avenue*, their reinterpretation of the Beatles' *Abbey Road* (including an album cover homage). Steve, however, was in a New York studio producing the Detroit-based Dramatics for Stax's California parent, Paramount; he made a later trip to California to record his guitar parts. "It was a tenacious struggle to get that music recorded," says Booker. "Stax had become more corporate and they didn't see the need, but I thought the Beatles had made an album that would change the face of music." *McLemore Avenue* is an exciting rearrangement of *Abbey Road*, mostly instrumental, deeply soulful.

Steve had a harder time leaving Stax, perhaps because his business ties were more entwined. To get out of his existing agreement, Cropper had to give up his stake in Stax's publishing (worth about $100,000); he had to commit to a two-year exclusive writing contract with Stax's publishing company; he had to produce several recordings for Stax at his new studio; and, instead of announcing his departure from Stax, he had to agree that Stax could announce he'd been promoted to a new vice president's position. On September 20, 1970, Steve signed on the dotted line, established

Trans Maximus Inc. a few miles from College and McLemore, produced records by Eddie Floyd and Eric Mercury for Stax, and was hired independently to make records for Jeff Beck, Poco, and Tower of Power. Not that leaving the company made him—or them—happy. "We were all family and it's tough to break up a family. I just felt like if they were gonna continue business the way they were, that it was gonna head for disaster at some point."

◆◆◆

IN THE WAKE of Isaac's hit, more R&B hits kept coming: the Soul Children hit the top ten with "The Sweeter He Is"; Eddie Floyd went top forty with "Why Is the Wine Sweeter"; Johnnie Taylor hit number four with "Love Bones"; the Emotions hit the top forty with "Stealing Love"—all of these also hit the pop charts, and this list is just for latter 1969. Rufus Thomas also made his comeback then, releasing "Do the Funky Chicken," which went to number-five R&B and number-twenty-eight pop.

Another Stax-associated artist established himself in early 1970—Luther Ingram. Luther was Johnny Baylor's artist, signed to Baylor's Koko label that Stax distributed. Baylor, well before coming to Memphis, had hired Luther in New York as a songwriter, and soon made him an artist. They tried a variety of styles before falling into the soul ballad groove with a version of the Allen Jones and Homer Banks song that had been a hit for Johnnie Taylor, "Ain't That Lovin' You (for More Reasons Than One)." Luther took it to the top-ten R&B and close to pop's top forty. "Johnny was a hell of a record producer," says Isaac's friend and trumpet player Mickey Gregory. "If he had spent as much time producing as he did trying to be a badass, he would have been recognized as a great producer." With this record, Baylor knew he'd found something: Luther's was a bedroom voice, a between-the-sheets crooner. In that style, Baylor would soon coax from Luther one of the decade's biggest hits.

The hits came from good airplay, and the good response from radio still grew from Al's connections. "Al Bell was the one who was making it happen," reports Johnny Keyes, who did not return to Isaac's entourage and instead traveled as a promotions man for Stax. "His was the name that you heard. You didn't really think of Jim Stewart as much. So the face changed." In late 1969, Al was named Record Executive of the Year by the Radio Program Conference; the following year, NATRA named him Man of the Year, and he was on *Ebony* magazine's list of 100 Most Influential Blacks in the United States.

Jim had grown his hair long and taken to the loud fashion of the day.

National Association of Television and Radio Announcers, 1970. L–R: Dino Woodard, Jack "the Rapper" Gibson, Harold Burnside, Al Bell, John Smith (rear), Mack Guy, and JoJo Samuels. (Stax Museum of American Soul Music)

He'd thrown big parties and tasted the high life. The clothes he could do, but the spotlight didn't suit him. "I didn't like the hoopla, the glitter, the limousines and the jets, the parties," Jim says. "That was Bell's forte."

Despite Stax's phenomenal comeback and its ongoing show of strength, Gulf & Western continued to insert itself into the business. "They wanted to gain some kind of creative control," says Jim. "More and more they wanted to become involved in the day-to-day operations and at one point wanted to move the company to the West Coast. We said no."

Soon after, Gulf & Western announced its intention to consolidate its record label holdings and distribution under the Dot Records imprint; that is, they wanted to fold Stax and merge it with Dot, which was pushing easy listening artists like Billy Vaughn and Anita Kerr. "We saw that as a death knell," says Jim. During his travels, Al Bell had seen warehouses full of Dot releases, and retail shelves lacking them, so he had no interest in being caught up in a system that couldn't get records to the stores. "I fought the consolidation," Al says. "I was called in and questioned about not being cooperative, and they had been told that I had spent this inordinate amount of money producing *Hot Buttered Soul* with these four tracks on it and that that wasn't industry standard. And they said I had given monies to Isaac Hayes, and that I should not have been doing that. Finally I said, 'Jim, let's see if we can't buy this company back and get out of Gulf & Western because this isn't gonna work.' And Jim was supportive. By that time, that stock they'd paid us with was toilet paper." Indeed, after a period of sustained growth since 1961, the US gross domestic product dropped, and for about a year from December 1969 unemployment grew and inflation rose. As an economic recession spread across the nation, the value of the stock payments diminished.

At a *Billboard* industry conference in Majorca, Spain, Al learned that the Deutsche Grammophon company, the industry leader in classical music, had an interest in exploring popular music. "Our sales numbers were very impressive," Al explains, "and Deutsche Grammophon made available to us a loan that was almost enough for us to acquire Stax back from Gulf & Western. For doing that, we would give them exclusive rights to international representation of Stax, and a minority interest in the company. The other dollars, which was about a million dollars, we were able to secure through Union Planters National Bank. We'd been banking all of this time with them and they were enjoying our successes."

The buyback was not consummated until July 24, 1970, terminating the two-year relationship. "I went to Charlie Bluhdorn at Gulf & Western and told him we wanted to buy the company back," says Al. "He said, 'Buy the company back? Public companies don't do that.' I said, 'Yeah, but we want to buy the company back.' And we finally persuaded him to do it—I think it was $4.5 million that he wanted."

"It cost us a million dollars over and above what they'd put in," says Jim, "plus the product they made money off of while they were in. They'd paid us in stock, and some cash. We paid them cash. Stax was prospering." The deal returned to them not only the Stax company but also the publishing companies, including East/Memphis and Birdees Music—the latter acquisitions meaning a sudden avalanche of work for Tim Whitsett, the publishing administrator. "Boxes started arriving of all of our copyrights, which Famous Music, a part of Paramount and Gulf & Western, had been looking after," says Tim. "I was appalled at how many songs hadn't been copyrighted, how many songs didn't have contracts, how many songs weren't registered with performing-rights societies. So we had to hire some staff and we poured ourselves into trying to get all the files straightened out."

The two deals—Deutsche Grammophon and Union Planters Bank—both had important ramifications. During Bell's visit to Germany, he saw that Philips, Deutsche Grammophon's parent company, was developing videocassettes, an innovation that would change not only home movies but, more important, how films were distributed. "I saw an opportunity to get involved in motion picture production," says Al, "because I had motion pictures on my mind. With them as a minority stockholder, it would be easier to talk about other ventures that would allow us to expand even further into the marketplace." In this world before home video, when movies had little life after their theatrical run, Al had glimpsed the future: People would collect movies like they collected records, and Stax could produce these movies and reach a ready audience through their established distribution system. With solid money and solid manufacturing innovations, Deutsche Grammophon was an attractive partner indeed.

The bank loan, larger than any of Stax's previous single-deal loans, had been amortized over a couple years, but due to Isaac Hayes's runaway success and the steady flow of hits from others, Stax paid it off in five months. "It freaked them out," says Al, "I mean it freaked them out. We were growing so rapidly."

"The bank," says Joe Harwell, Stax's representative at Union Planters, "had previously considered the music business a bunch of long-haired hippies who shot up dope all the time. But after that, they saw it as a source of great potential profit."

"From that point forward," Al continues, "every time we'd turn around, we were getting calls from Union Planters National Bank, wanting to know if we needed any money. I was getting many invitations to eat in the executive dining room with the president of the bank.

"We bought the company back from Gulf & Western, and continued to operate it as an independent, freestanding record company, and the curve kept on going up. We kept generating more and more revenue, kept daring to be different and kept defying what they said couldn't be done."

21. SHAFT
1971–1972

Isaac Hayes shot to fame like an express elevator to the penthouse floor. He released two albums in 1970, *The Isaac Hayes Movement* and *To Be Continued*, each built like *Hot Buttered Soul*—two songs on each side, with Ike's extended, intimate raps gliding listeners into his velvety world. Both raced up the charts.

The Isaac Hayes Movement came out in March and spent six weeks at the number-one spot on the soul chart; it stayed on the chart nearly the whole rest of the year, falling off just in time for the December release of *To Be Continued*, which ran to the top. *Movement* spent a year and a half on the *Billboard* 200 album chart and featured a version of the Jerry Butler song "I Stand Accused" as its single, which proved popular among both soul and pop audiences. The album art finds Isaac relishing his newfound star status. The cover opens to reveal a vertical centerfold of Isaac, shirt-less, wearing thick gold chains around his neck and waist. His arms are forward and down, as if he's lifting something, or someone. The light-ing is dramatic, he's wearing dark shades, and it's all so supercool that it trumps the back cover shot of him seated, draped in a matching multilay-ered zebra-striped outfit with a high collar and zebra cap. Isaac Hayes, song interpreter. Mellow and mature, intimate and warm. Dance? The horizontal dance, *ma cherie*. The next album, *To Be Continued*, hit the top of the soul and jazz album charts, and fell just shy of the pop top ten. "Isaac became a major artist, selling gold, then platinum, and double platinum," says his drummer Willie Hall. "Everywhere you went, you'd read about Isaac. You turn the radio on, every station, you'd hear his material. It was wonderful. Everybody had money to spend. I managed to take my family out of the ghetto and buy our first home. Things were really good."

Though Isaac had established himself first as a songwriter, none of these three albums featured any of his own songs. (He'd cowritten "Hyperbolic . . . " and by *To Be Continued*, he'd begun naming his long introductions, which allowed him to collect a publishing royalty on them.) The lack of original material followed the termination of his songwriting partnership—Isaac had always taken care of the music, David handled the lyrics. Without David, Isaac could maneuver other people's words, he could rearrange established hits—but he wasn't writing new songs. "I try to express myself in music," he told a journalist in 1970, putting a positive spin on it. "I generally prefer to do covers of other songs. I like to change the arrangement and do big productions, taking the songs into a completely different world."

Another world was, in fact, opening up for Isaac. The MGM movie studio was facing a slump at the box office, and before bellying up, they were willing to take inexpensive gambles, such as throwing half a million dollars at a movie that could wring a few bucks from the neglected African-American audience. The recent release of *Sweet Sweetback's Baadasssss Song*, saturated in black pride, had summoned an untapped market demographic. It opened with text on screen: "This film is dedicated to all the Brothers and Sisters who had enough of the Man." Filmmaker Melvin Van Peebles had funded and made the show himself, producing, directing, editing, and starring—among other roles. When the Chicago band Earth, Wind & Fire recorded the soundtrack, they had yet to release their first album and were totally unknown. With no promotion budget, Van Peebles approached Stax about pre-releasing the soundtrack; their promotional prowess in the black community was established, and he knew that a soundtrack would readily appeal to the company's expansive nature. (Additionally, vocalist Maurice White was from the same Memphis housing project where David Porter had grown up, so he had an in.) Three months after Stax's album release, the movie premiered. In addition to its sex scenes, part of the movie's appeal is that Sweetback survives the Man's manhunt—he outsmarts Whitey and escapes. As word spread, big crowds came to the theaters. Stax was ahead of that game; Al Bell arranged with the Detroit theater owner where it first screened to sell the soundtrack in the lobby, and he shipped three hundred albums. More were ordered the next day. "Many theater owners were hesitant about our suggestions to make albums available in the lobbies," says Al, "until they discovered how profitable it could be."

When MGM was designing its African-American pitch for *Shaft*, it too reached out to Stax. Isaac recalls MGM's concept: "A movie targeted at the black consumer market to have a black director, black leading actor, black editor, black composer. And I was asked to do the music." He'd always wanted to be on the screen, and this role seemed right for him: "A private dick who's a sex machine to all the chicks," as Isaac would soon write in the theme song. He said he'd commit to the music if he were allowed a screen audition. Isaac soon learned that the lead had gone to Richard Roundtree, a model who'd become prominent touring with the Fashion Fair promoted by *Ebony* magazine. The twenty-eight-year-old Hayes expressed his disappointment—but agreed to honor his musical commitment.

Some weeks later, the director Gordon Parks called. Parks was a revered fashion photographer, known also for turning his camera—still pictures and film—on African-American life. *Shaft* was his foray into bigger movies. He told Isaac he was sending him a few scenes to score. No one called them a test, but Isaac knew that if he didn't get it right, the job would vanish. "Gordon Parks knew I'd never done a soundtrack so they handled me with kid gloves," he says. "And I appreciated that. Gordon said to me, 'Shaft is always roving, always moving. Your music should depict that—something to capture his personality. His being. He's a cool dude too. But he's tough. You got to put all that in your music.'"

Willie Hall recalls being introduced to the project. "We're in the studio recording with Isaac," Willie says of the Bar-Kays. "We'd work through the night, and Isaac's in and out of the studio constantly—taking phone calls, doing business. Isaac even had a phone in his car—back when that took up nearly all of his trunk. He comes back from a break, and he and Al Bell wheeled this machine in. They didn't have the big video screen back then, so we all were squeezed in, trying to look in this little machine that you could see the footage through [a Moviola]. Everything was hush-hush and we see Richard Roundtree coming up out of the subway, walking down Broadway. Isaac said, 'I got a surprise for you all. We're gonna do a soundtrack to this movie.' Everybody went, 'Wow'— but we have no clue of what the procedure is gonna be." Lester Snell, keyboardist, remembers that the next question by all was, "How much will we get paid?"

Hayes was ready for the challenge. Soundtracks worked toward his strength—music and drama; he'd not need a lyricist. He told Willie to note the tempo of the characters walking. "He said, 'I want you to play sixteenths on the high hat to that tempo,'" Willie continues. "So they rolled the machine over to me, and I play the high hat. The tempo of his steps is where we got the tempo of the song from." Hall begins making the cymbal sounds, the classic cymbal sounds, that open the *Shaft* theme song.

They set to work. The title theme's trademark wah-wah guitar sound was accidental. "When I play rhythm, I will put a lot of drum beats with it," says guitarist Charles "Skip" Pitts. For *Shaft*, "I was checking my pedals. I tested my overdrive, my reverb, the Maestro box, and then I started in with the wah-wah. Isaac stopped everything and said, 'Skip, what is that you're playing?' I said, 'I'm just tuning up.' He said, 'Keep playing that G octave.'" Set to Willie's sixteenth notes, they had the makings of something good.

"Within two hours we had the arrangement for the main title," says Isaac. "The next piece of footage was the montage through Harlem. Did the music to that in about an hour and a half. It would become 'Soulsville.' The third piece was the love scene. I wrote that in about an hour, which later became 'Ellie's Love Theme.'" Isaac flew to New York, to Gordon Parks's East Side apartment overlooking the UN headquarters. "I had the tapes under my arm. Gordon was cooking some lamb chops, man it smelled so good in there. And he teased me because I liked apple butter instead of mint jelly with lamb chops. I'm a country boy, what do you want?" After dining, they put the footage on the Moviola and the tapes on the deck. Gordon watched. "He said, 'Okay, you can go to Hollywood now and start on the film.' Just like that."

It was a learning experience for everybody. Excited, their lack of experience fed their innovation.

"We were gigging every weekend on the East Coast," says Lester Snell. "We'd fly east and gig Friday, Saturday, Sunday, fly back Sunday night to be on set Monday morning. MGM put us on a schedule: Be on set at nine and work till five every afternoon. Just like a job. We had six weeks to do the movie—compose fifteen songs, rehearse them, lay out according to soundtrack, and then record. And still gig on weekends. It was a killer."

"That whole adventure was exciting," says Willie. "Skip and Michael and myself, we used to get in trouble on the studio lot because they had these bicycles you use to get from one area to the other. We'd be turning the corner, we're running over folks, man, people in costumes would be falling, they'd call and report us. 'Hey, man, you got to keep those niggers out of the way, they're running over everybody.' But we had a lot of fun and they loved us."

Gordon Parks stayed abreast of their progress. In a "making of *Shaft*" short movie, Parks, chewing a toothpick, listens intently as they play him a draft of the title song. "When Shaft pops up out of that subway," Parks tells Isaac, "that's when it should really come on and carry him all the way through Times Square right to his first encounter with a newspaperman. And that should be a driving, savage beat so we're right with him all the time."

When the recording dates arrived, it was a collision of cultures. "They set aside four days for us," Isaac explains. "The first two days was for the rhythm, the third was for the sweetening—horns, strings, all the miscellaneous instruments, and the fourth day was for vocals. So we walked on the soundstage, they had our music stands set up and everything. We're getting comfortable and the engineer said, 'Where are your charts?' 'What charts? We ain't got no charts, man.' 'You don't have charts!' I saw terror in this man's eyes. I said, 'Just roll the film, man.' Everybody had their own little private notes that they'd written down. This is head-arranging at its finest! Guy rolled the film, the swipe went across the screen, the first music cue came, *bam*! We hit it. I called, 'Next!' We played reel after reel. Next cue. Next cue. And we knocked 'em out. That first day we finished an hour and ten minutes ahead of schedule and had done both days work. The engineer said, 'I have to tell you guys I thought this was going to be a disaster. How'd you guys remember all that with no charts?' I says, 'We work in a studio, man. We've been doing this for years.'"

"We recorded the whole thing in three days," says Lester Snell. "They were amazed we could do it that quick, because they really didn't believe we could do it at all."

On the third and final day, Isaac was being driven to work with his three beautiful backup singers. Much as he wanted to concentrate on them, he was distracted; he'd just learned that for a song to be nominated for the Academy Award for Best Song, it needed lyrics. So he soaked in their vibe as he jotted the song's conversational lyrics on a piece of paper, not quite done even as they entered the lot. "Who is the man . . . Just talking 'bout Shaft . . ."

Isaac Hayes, backstage, with some of the Bar–Kays. L–R: Harvey Henderson, Winston Stewart, Isaac Hayes, Larry Dodson, James Alexander.

Everyone was excited by the results. But the standards in Hollywood were different from the standards in Memphis; MGM was a film-score factory, and this project was a low-budget toss-off. Isaac and the Bar-Kays—they were making art. MGM used what it paid for in the film, but when they returned to Memphis, Isaac and the Bar-Kays re-recorded the whole thing at Stax. The musical performances are better, the fidelity is higher, the arrangements are tighter. When inclined, Isaac extended a song longer than what the movie called for—he'd made MGM's soundtrack, now he was making his record.

And soon he'd be setting new records, as the *Shaft* album, released with the movie in July 1971, became his most successful album in a string of highly successful releases. It won three Grammy Awards and took home an Oscar for Best Music—Original Song. The album—the double album—became Stax's best-selling album ever and helped the film re-coup more than twenty-six times its investment. At the Academy Awards ceremony, Isaac—a ladies' man, sex symbol, and now pop star—brought as his date the woman who was the most significant in his life: his grand-mother who had raised him. He performed the theme song on the tele-cast, and then returned to her side to await the award announcement. "My grandmother was cool, but I was trembling," he told *Ebony* maga-zine. "I felt an enormous weight on my shoulders. There was a lot riding on that Oscar—not so much for me as for the brothers across the country. I didn't want to let them down."

After his success, other popular black musicians were offered film scores, including Curtis Mayfield (*Superfly*), Marvin Gaye (*Trouble Man*), Donny Hathaway (*Come Back Charleston Blue*), Willie Hutch (*The Mack*), James Brown (*Black Caesar*), and Bobby Womack (*Across 110th Street*). "A major film with a black director, a black star and sound by a black composer is an enormous source of pride to the black community," Al Bell told *Billboard*. "Since music is usually an integral part of these movies, soundtrack albums have a ready-made market if you know how to reach the people." Having converted theater lobbies to record stores, Al knew how to reach people.

Most important, the soundtrack was an expansion of Isaac's palette. His three prior albums had adhered to the same formula, and by the third, the formula was becoming stale; they seemed redundant, self-indulgent. The nearly twelve-minute version of "The Look of Love" from *To Be Continued*, originally recorded by Dusty Springfield in 1967, finds Isaac losing himself to heavily reverberating moans and grunts. (Granted, however, that the instrumental section of the song has been heavily sampled.) But *Shaft* featured all original material in a new and totally different direction,

Isaac Hayes in the lobby of the Memphis airport, returning from the Academy Awards, Oscar in hand. (University of Memphis Libraries/Special Collections)

and indicated a giant step forward in his art and career. *Shaft* relied on new sounds—the wah-wah—and it shifted to rhythms more aggressive than those emanating from the black church, essentially demarcating the end of the southern soul era and establishing a gateway to 1970s funk.

◆◆◆

A FEW MONTHS after *Shaft*'s release, the racial conflict in Memphis broke wide open. There were four days of rioting, three deaths, untold injuries, arson, and looting. The fury began with a pickup truck driver afraid to stop for the police. Three African-American friends led police and sheriff's deputies on a high-speed chase. When captured at a roadblock, seventeen-year-old Elton Hayes (no relation to Isaac) was beaten to death by eight policemen and sheriff's deputies. (One of the deputies was African-American.) The police announced the teen was killed when his truck overturned, but the morning paper ran a photo of the truck showing no significant damage; an autopsy revealed his skull had been crushed. His friends told of police beating them with billy clubs, and

October 1971, anger over the killing of Elton Hayes. Sweet Willie Wine, center, with beard, leader of the black militant group the Invaders, rallies a crowd. (University of Memphis Libraries/Special Collections)

described Elton's face when he was placed on a stretcher as looking like red Jell-O.

The fatal beating and the attempted cover-up led to four days of rampaging violence and destruction across the city. "These officers are riding the streets like it was duck hunting season and they were enjoying it," Isaac Hayes complained in the city's largest newspaper. "They're tearing down everything we are building."

Isaac, along with Deanie Parker, Rufus Thomas, James Alexander, and several others from Stax, was among the community leaders who met with Mayor Loeb and then took to the streets and the airwaves (WDIA) to restore order. After the meeting, Isaac said, "A miracle has happened in Memphis. The mayor and chief of police have joined with the black community." A curfew for the night was lifted and a benefit at the Mid-South Coliseum featuring Isaac was allowed to proceed.

The state attorney general promised a full investigation. Indeed, eight of the police and deputies were indicted, but the trial was another meeting of the good ole boys' club; all were acquitted.

As one trial ended, another began, this time in the schools. An April 1971 Supreme Court ruling (*Swann v. Charlotte-Mecklenburg Board of Education*) led to what opponents termed "forced busing," the transporting of black and white kids from their neighborhoods to schools across town. The object: to achieve a racial balance in student bodies and a semblance of fairness in accessibility to facilities.

White Memphis was angry, afraid, and defiant. In response to busing, a coalition formed, Citizens Against Busing. They held rallies and whipped up dissent. CAB, as the group became known, set out not only to stop busing but also to pass a constitutional amendment prohibiting federal court jurisdiction over public schools and to establish staggered terms for Supreme Court justices. Henry Loeb and Wyeth Chandler (who would succeed Loeb as mayor) were among the politicians supporting the group, with Loeb calling busing "reprehensible" and Chandler calling it "monstrous." State and federal congressmen joined CAB's rallies; a Tennessee senator in Washington, DC, took up older legislation that "would guarantee the rights of all children to full and equal access to neighborhood schools without being treated as members of a race." The senator did not add that the schools in the CAB neighborhoods were solid, and the schools in the black neighborhoods were crumbling. Many of the black schools had leaky roofs, unstable stairs, missing windows, and other structural deficiencies; few, if any, had air-conditioning. Such institutional disparity and legislated unfairness had long existed. Racially restrictive residential covenants—"no blacks allowed" in certain neighborhoods—had been Memphis law and enforced until early 1970, two years after the Fair Housing Act made such covenants illegal, more than twenty years since the Supreme Court said they were unconstitutional.

The school desegregation fight was making it evident that the majority of white Memphians clung to these discriminatory beliefs, proudly. Calm was restored after Elton Hayes's killing, but the tension over busing was just beginning.

◆ ◆ ◆

STAX WAS A sanctuary from the pervading hostility, but also a war room for its own ongoing expansion. The broad demand for *Shaft* opened doors through which Al Bell could ship other albums, increasing his access to the white market. The nearby Ardent Studios, where Stax sent much of its overflow work, was restarting its own label, Ardent Records, and Stax agreed to distribute them. Ardent had a promising young power pop band, Big Star, and Stax wanted to establish them nationally. "We were ginning money at that time," says Al. "We had hit records—like great apples falling off a tree. And we were selling albums—the albums were generating more revenue than the singles. We'd sell a hundred thousand albums on an artist, which wasn't much to some companies, but we'd sell hundred thousand after hundred thousand after hundred thousand. That's serious cash flow."

Just talkin' 'bout . . . Jim Stewart, with *Shaft* album and mandala, 1972. (Photograph by Tom Busler/*Commercial Appeal*)

The Bar-Kays remained consistent sellers and also consistent innovators. Their post-Otis incarnation—Bar-Kays Mach II, as they sometimes called themselves—always had a theatrical flair: Onstage they moved with coordinated chaos, ready for a party; their outfits were out there on an Isaac Hayes orbit; their music was brash, careering through styles, with dynamic changes that could propel a dance floor. Their 1971 album *Black Rock* opens with a nearly nine-minute interpretation of Aretha Franklin's "Baby I Love You." They filter it through Jimi Hendrix, but with soul horns. They remake Isaac and David's Sam and Dave hit "You Don't Know Like I Know," playing it like one of the aggressively cross-fertilizing late-sixties California bands—maybe Spirit or Moby Grape—part hippies, part jazz cats, part hard rockers. The single "Montego Bay" didn't chart, but the album did. A Bar-Kays album is like flipping a radio dial, landing only on the best songs.

The Bar-Kays weren't the only successes. Since the start of 1971, Stax had placed another wallop of chart singles—Isaac Hayes's edited version of "The Look of Love" and his "Never Can Say Goodbye," the Emotions' "You Make Me Want to Love You," Margie Joseph's "Stop! In the Name of Love," Johnnie Taylor's "I Don't Wanna Lose You" and "Hijackin' Love," the Staple Singers' "You've Got to Earn It," Rufus Thomas's "The World Is Round" and "The Breakdown," and the Newcomers' "Pin the Tail on the Donkey"—all these before summer was over.

So Al Bell had reason to be emboldened. He was achieving these huge sales with a distribution system that he, his salesmen, and marketers had built by themselves. It was independent distributors working with independent record companies, following independent rules. "Al Bell was a visionary," says James Douglass, one of several young salesmen hired by Al to fan out across the US and promote records. Al made sure his team was groomed, dressed in a jacket and tie, and he trained them in the basics of respectfulness. " 'Yes sir,' 'no sir,' stand until they ask you to sit," James explains. He had no background in the music industry and remembers his training in promotions as quite basic: "Al would have four, five, six releases for us to take out. Hopefully there'd be an Isaac Hayes in there. Al would present the records to the promotions guys, suggesting where they might be hot because of similar action there. I began to set up appointments with DJs to tell them about our product. Al used this word, *defuse*. He'd say, 'Defuse any situation out there.' "

The situations that needed defusing usually concerned money. "I go to some big DJ with several records and he says, 'I like this one here, can I get into it?' " James explains. New to the game, he wasn't immediately sure what was being asked. "I said, 'Into it, like what?' He tells me, 'See the distributor and he'll tell you.' I know if I go back to Al, he's going to say, 'Defuse it. Figure out the cracks, and figure out how to stuff the cracks.' I realized going to the independent distributor was the thing to do. He might say, 'When Stax mails in the next batch of records, tell them a station is doing a Stax weekend. Send me extras, but don't drill 'em.' " Promotional records were differentiated from commercial stock by a drill hole in the album cover's corner; shipping not-drilled records that were indicated on the paperwork as promotional was as good as cash for the distributor. "We'd ship in so much above what they order, and they'd give extra to the DJ and my hands stayed clean," James explains. The slush money, in other words, was covered by product that the distributor could sell at full price, and that the supplier—Stax—could write off as promotional. A DJ could receive them free and wholesale them to a store; a distributor could make a profit on them that might cover a loan they'd made on Stax's behalf. "Promotional" records with no drill holes allowed for creative accounting.

As the 1970s progressed, the record business got ever more crooked, harking back to the days of pay-for-play. "I wouldn't give DJs money," James says, "but if I were filling my gas tank, I'd fill theirs too. If we ate together, I'd buy. With my expense money, I'd take the DJ's wife to the grocery store. Al said, 'It's not payola, it's pride-ola.' They changed the name of our job to marketing. We didn't do no marketing. Promotion guys are promoting money. One station ran a Miss Black pageant. The guy couldn't meet payments, asked me to call Al. If I did, I knew Earlie would say, 'Mr. Bell don't have time to deal with that kind of mess.' I went to the independent distributor. Defuse it."

In early 1972, a *Washington Post* investigative reporter, Jack Anderson, exposed "the gangster-like world" in which James Douglass was finding himself immersed. NEW DISC JOCKEY PAYOLA UNCOVERED was the headline, and the series of articles documented how radio personnel "across the country are provided with free vacations, prostitutes, cash and cars as payoffs for song plugging." In other words, disc jockeys would play your records more often if you compensated them. (Soon, some wouldn't play your record *unless* you paid them.) The investigation revealed that record companies, large and small, indies and majors, "furnished wholesale lots of free records to so-called 'R&B' jockeys and programmers. They, in turn, sell the records cut-rate to record stores, pocket the profit and boom their benefactors' records over the airwaves." The issue—as always—was the money and how to hide it. Record retail was largely a cash business, and following the money becomes increasingly difficult, especially because promotional records often substituted for cash.

Anderson's next headline dug deeper: DISC JOCKEY PLAY-FOR-DRUGS OUTLINED. Some of the record companies were digging into deeper netherworlds. James Douglass remembers the first time he saw cocaine, which was making its way onto the American street in the early 1970s. He'd been working his way into larger markets and was visiting a distributor in Philadelphia. "I knock. 'Who the fuck is it?' 'James Douglass from Stax.'

'Come on in, shut the door.'" James entered and sat across from the program director. "I'd never seen a rock of cocaine before," James continues. "He had a razor blade and he was shaving off of it. Another record company's promotion guy had just left. 'Did Al send me anything?' 'No sir.' 'You're new. You been to the record shops yet?' 'No sir.' 'Get your ass down there, work them record shops, when you got product in the market, come back and let me know, I'll bust all your records.'" Things were getting ever more complicated. The night DJ saw the better clothes that the daytime DJ wore, or the bigger car that the distributor drove; everyone's demands rose. "Man," sighs James, "I just came to represent the company."

Distribution was a circuitous and rickety operation that had been thriving for years when Anderson exposed its crookedness; despite its effectiveness, it left Al dissatisfied. "The product was not getting into the larger stores that catered primarily to whites," he says, "and I became very aggressive and demanding with respect to that." He conceived a venture in the Chicago market that was not only about the sales it would achieve, but also about documenting those sales. Al's broad vision encompassed the meta-view; he would create a presentation about the success of the Chicago campaign that he could use to wedge his way into other prominent markets. Thus was born the Stax Sound in Chi-Town, a promotion in August 1971 (a month after *Shaft* hit theaters) that coordinated with the Sears home office and the many Sears stores in the Chicago area. "They put our entire catalog in all of their stores, and we came in with an advertising and marketing campaign—print, television, and radio," says Al. "We even hired some beautiful models and had them in front of all of the Sears stores wearing the little sash that Miss America wears, and it said STAX SOUND IN CHI-TOWN."

Chicago was not a random choice. The Great Migration had moved a huge population of southern black people to Chicago since the early 1900s; blues had begun in the Mississippi Delta (all roads there lead to Memphis) and become electric in Chicago. The cultures were related. As well, Chicago was home to Jesse Jackson's Operation PUSH, and since their meeting soon after Dr. King's assassination, Al and Rev. Jackson had grown increasingly close, a vision shared. The previous year, Al even initiated a new subsidiary, the Respect label, to release Rev. Jackson's first album, *I Am Somebody*, which included his outstanding title-track sermon and incantation Respect would soon add other spoken-word-oriented releases. The Chicago ties were many. "As it turned out," Al says, "one of my homeboys, E. Rodney Jones, born in Arkansas like me, was at Chicago radio station WVON. I had a deep relationship with several other great personality jocks there, and it dawned on me, instead of us going all over the place trying to get things done, let's build a base in Chicago. Let's get more involved with Johnson Publications [*Ebony, Jet*] and Operation PUSH—deal with Chicago like we're in Chicago."

Stax began sending talent—Isaac Hayes, the Staple Singers, and seven others—to the Operation PUSH Chicago Black Expo, a trade show and convention. Their performances were filmed, and thus able to be exploited long after the applause died down. "Al Bell never was just the record guy," says Rev. Jackson. "Al saw the vision. Many people see our artists through a keyhole, Al saw them through a door."

Al understood the moment—any moment—as a piece in an ever-expanding puzzle; the more assiduously he tried to see the limits, the bigger he knew the puzzle could get. While the success of Stax Sound in Chi-Town would prove the broad commercial potential of his label and result in increased sales, its long-term use would be through its repurposing. He hired an agency to professionally document the program and its results, creating an elaborately bound presentation. Was this a beautiful package to lie on the coffee table for guests waiting in his office? No. The images

Stax in Chicago. L–R: Jim Stewart, Jesse Jackson, Lydia Bell, Al Bell, Emily Hayes, Isaac Hayes. (Stax Museum of American Soul Music)

became slides accompanying his speech entitled "Black Is Beautiful . . . Business." He would soon present the speech at the 1972 National Association of Recording Merchandisers convention, where it became a powerful statement about the drive and success of an independent company.

After Al fit Chicago onto his expanding puzzle, he looked for more pieces. "We were able to move out from Chicago toward New York and Los Angeles and surrounding geographic areas," Al waxes. "We were looking toward getting into the state of New York—actually that triangle of New York, Philadelphia, and Boston. We'd captured the mid-Atlantic, which was Washington, DC, Virginia, and Maryland. We knew Rocky G and Frankie Crocker at WWRL in New York, and if we could get our artists into the Apollo, we could capture New York, meaning not just radio, but the consumers in New York. It was generally known in the industry that Los Angeles is gonna be the last place where you can get your product exposed." No worries: Al was cooking up a blockbuster-sized idea for Los Angeles.

◆◆◆

ON THE HOME front, a new problem had arisen. Deutsche Grammophon, which owned a piece of Stax, was so enjoying its taste of popular music that it wanted more. In mid-1971, the label purchased James Brown's recording contract and back catalog. Between James Brown and Stax, all they saw was hits and high sales, so they instigated an expansion of their own label, Polydor. "They began to want to exercise some influence on us and on our business decisions," says Al. "And the discussions arose once again about us consolidating our distribution." Stax had an interconnected web of independent distributors that Deutsche Grammophon saw as a peculiar and clunky arrangement. Despite the setup's obvious success, Deutsche Grammophon wanted to align Stax with a corporate distributor. While a corporate distributor might help Al get into the chains he sought, he feared losing the control he currently had; putting Deutsche Grammophon between himself and the product delivery created too great a distance. "The relationship," says Al, "grew uncomfortable."

"I told them that we wanted out of the deal," Al continues, "and they were irritated by that. The audacity! 'You little old fella from Memphis backwater Tennessee'—Philips, which owned Deutsche Grammophon, controlled the sockets that the light bulbs went in, and the energy throughout your home, so—'who do you think you are?'" Extended conversations ensued—"Somewhere in there I may have become an irritant, because of my persistence"—and finally Al was given a number: It would cost

$4.8 million to buy back Deutsche Grammophon's equity in Stax. "Nearly half of that came from cash that we had in the bank, and the other came from a $2.5 million loan from Union Planters Bank," says Al. Union Planters National Bank had helped them buy back their stock from Gulf & Western; payoff had gone very smoothly—ahead of schedule, even—so acquiring the new loan was easy.

The deal was settled that cool November of 1971 in the back bungalows of the Beverly Hills Hotel. "I walked rather proudly through the Polo Lounge," says Al, "and on back to the bungalows. And I politely put that cashier's check on the table and closed that deal with the gentleman, freeing us from the international distribution as well as purchasing back their equity interest in the company." Stax's 1971 gross income, according to court documents, was just short of $17 million. That's a heap of sales accumulated at wholesale rates of about fifty cents per single and $2.50 for albums. Stax was, for the first time since it had become a national concern, entirely independent, able to determine its destiny, keep its profits, set its own course.

22. BALANCE SHEETS AND BALANCING ACTS
1971–1972

Isaac Hayes, with his fourth hit album in a row, was fueling the Stax inferno. That November of 1971 when Stax paid off Deutsche Grammophon, the "*Shaft*" single hit number one on the pop charts. *Shaft* raged across the US—in theaters, on turntables, as a cultural phenomenon. Isaac was on daytime TV, nighttime TV—fashion talk, movie talk, music. His clothes, his chains, his bald head, his female dancer's bald head, the traveling orchestra: He was a phenomenon.

In Isaac's camp, in Isaac's glow, was his penumbra, Johnny Baylor. A heat radiated between them until that heat became a fever, a fever dream, and then a nightmare. "It got kind of rough around there," says Willie Hall. "There was pistol play, there were shots being fired in the building." At Stax, Baylor was running Isaac's camp, his words always in Isaac's ear. Baylor's artist, Luther Ingram, was opening for Isaac's concerts, using Isaac's band and singing in a style not dissimilar; Johnny even signed Isaac's shaved-headed female dancer, Helen Washington, to his Koko label. Johnny's key responsibility was handling Isaac's money, and when an important week of gigs at the Apollo came up short, there was nearly a bloodbath in the halls of Stax.

"When *Shaft* was coming out," Randy Stewart explains, "I went to New York, made a deal at the Apollo Theater. The money would be split seventy-thirty for us, because they couldn't have guaranteed us what we needed. While I was there, I had another meeting. We took ten thousand dollars and put it somewhere so *Shaft* would be number one when we got to New York City." They bought airplay and ratings, he's saying, so they'd be able to sell out all of their shows. It wasn't legal, but it was par for the day, industry-wide, and it worked. It was how you got records played.

"At the Apollo, we filled every seat in there every day for a week, several times a day," Randy continues. "Isaac was looking for big money." But when Dino brought the Apollo payment to Isaac, it seemed light. Trouble had been brewing anyway—Johnny was intense company and Isaac wanted some air. He accused Johnny of bringing him short pay. "I know they hadn't stolen the money," says Randy. "We paid Luther nine thousand dollars as opening act, ten thousand went for the number one at the radio station. I had papers to show Isaac." But this split, once begun, couldn't be stopped. "When we got back home," says Randy, "Isaac said that Johnny had stolen his money."

Dino remembers the incident, and believes Isaac was misled. "Some of Isaac's friends had misquoted some figures to Isaac," says Dino, "and he felt that something was going wrong with the financing. But certain people wanted Johnny out, because they wanted that position that Johnny had with Isaac. And to get that position next to Isaac, they had to, boom, come up with something that wasn't really true. And that put a space between Johnny and Isaac." Baylor didn't take such accusations well, and neither did he intend to simply walk away, or be pushed, from a star he felt he'd created. Baylor was top gun, and he was angry.

Mickey Gregory, who'd grown up with Isaac and, in addition to playing trumpet for him, had always been a trusted player in Isaac's organization, was looking out for his old friend. "I was never one of Dr. King's nonviolent Negroes," says Mickey. "I was the only one with the exception of Isaac that the sheriff's department would give a permit to tote a pistol—though I wasn't the only one toting a pistol." Mickey was tipped off by a woman friend whom Isaac had dated, now keeping company with Johnny, that Johnny was going to come to Stax with guns and that he intended to keep his job. "She gave me a vague warning that something was going to go down at the studio," says Mickey. "I didn't know if Johnny was supposed to kill Isaac, kidnap him, whup him, or whatever. But I did know that he was coming to the studio to do something, and I had that situation covered. I was in a beauty shop across McLemore from his office with an AR-15 [semi-automatic rifle]. I had the guards posi-

Isaac Hayes's trumpet player and childhood friend Mickey
Gregory, right, early 1970s, with a Houston concert promoter.
(Mickey Gregory Collection)

tioned. Everybody was doing whatever the fuck I said to. Wasn't nothing
going to happen—to Isaac."

"The night before," says engineer Larry Nix, "I was working late
in the copy room, making a little overtime. It was very unusual because
there was nobody in the building. Every hour the guard would come
through. Just me and him. The next morning I'm in studio A and everybody's talking to each other, asking, 'What went on?' It turned out that
nobody worked because they'd heard the Johnny Baylor confrontation
with Isaac was supposed to go down then. I didn't know because I always
steered *waaay* clear of Johnny Baylor." Just as people were sighing with
relief, the security guard rushed into the studio and told them to lock the
door, that Baylor was on the lot. "I took off to tell my wife, who was
working in the publishing office," Larry continues. "When I crossed the
hall, I looked down and there's Isaac's guys on one side of the wall, Johnny's guys on the other, staring at each other. You could hear Isaac and
Johnny going at it in Isaac's office. Johnny's saying, 'You can't fire me!'

And it was loud, you could hear them all over the building. I closed the door in the publishing office and I'm thinking how the walls are so temporary, if someone shoots, it'll go from one end of the building to the other."

In more than one account, each camp had guns drawn on the other, or at the ready, and the mess about to be made would require more than just the night janitors to clean up. The confrontation in Isaac's office got so bad, the threats so loud and so harsh, that someone, elsewhere in the building, called the police. Isaac's office had a door that opened onto McLemore, and that's where the police came. "The cops arrived outside," Larry continues, "and all at once Isaac's hallway door flies open. There were sawed-off shotguns, pistols, and these guys were stuffing them everywhere." Isaac didn't invite the cops in, but he came to the door, showed that he was all right, and admitted that there was indeed an argument going on but that it was a "family discussion." He put the cops at their ease, and they left. Isaac could have ratted out Baylor then and there; if he'd let the cops in, they'd have found guns, they might have found other illegalities—but Isaac protected Baylor, defused the situation.

"They stuck them pistols up there in different places before talking to the police," says Randy Stewart. "Police came, Isaac lied, said ain't nothing wrong. The police left. Johnny took a records box, put the pistols in there, sealed it up like a box of records, had me take it to Johnny's girl's house. I walked right on by the police with that records box. That was the end of that, and that was the end of Johnny and Isaac. It was all over between them."

While Johnny Baylor was very effective in increasing Stax's debt collection, and thereby its cash flow, every victory was also a loss of power from elsewhere, from Al or Jim. Was Johnny Baylor good to have around? Did the benefits outweigh the detriments? The showdown in Isaac's office, the threat of guns so close to—pointed at—the company's biggest star, one might conclude this is an opportunity for reassessment, for termination of the relationship. A threat to slay the company's star moneymaker should be the last threat before an employee is shown the door.

Not strongman Johnny Baylor. In 1972 in Memphis, Tennessee, at Stax Records, following an armed in-office showdown, Johnny Baylor was promoted. Instead of dismissing him, Al Bell assigned him to the promotions department, to the job of raising the company's profile through more radio play and more prominent display at retail locations. Al needed the company looking its best on paper because he was once again about to seek an investor: Jim had informed Al that he was ready to cash out.

Jim was looking at the business and it just didn't look like fun. Gargantuan corporate power struggles, absentee overlords mandating minor internal procedures, the threat of Wild West shoot-'em-ups in the hallways—this was a long way from, gee whiz, the good old days of 1957 or even 1967. He could grow his hair long and wear wide lapels, but now people were smoking marijuana in the building, there was talk of cocaine. The conglomerate world was ever consolidating. Instead of big labels nipping at smaller ones, unrelated companies were gathered under big umbrellas. Wexler sold out to Warner Bros., but the following year Warner was bought by the Kinney Parking Company. Wasn't Gulf & Western originally an auto parts manufacturer? The business was less and less about "record men," people with ears who could pick or create hits. How long since Jim had been transformed like when he'd first heard Ray Charles? He looked admiringly at his sister's exit. Riding out to his estate, Jim would pass near her apartment complex, and it must have given him pause. Having crossed into his early forties, he was newly aware of time ticking. He was hearing his exit cue.

The company was in a good place. Al had just broken the barrier with Sears. He was riding *Shaft*; his eyes were nationwide. He could put Isaac Hayes, Johnnie Taylor, the Staple Singers inside Camelot, Hastings, Peaches—the new world of record chains inside every mall being built coast to coast. Jim, however, was a fighter growing weary. His career in music was resembling his banking tenure. "I spent two years doing nothing but negotiating, back and forth from New York to California," he says. "I hardly went to the studio. It drained me, mentally. I spent one whole summer in New York trying to get out of Gulf & Western and get the money to pay them off. We gave them a profit. Then we borrowed money from Deutsche Grammophon and the bank. The bank was paid back three million dollars in six months' time, that's how much money we made. Deutsche Grammophon, we had to pay them back plus about a million dollars profit. A lot of bad decisions were made. All the profits were going to other companies. And the company was being neglected because Bell and I were tending to these deals. I decided I wanted to get out once and for all. I wanted to go back to the studio and have some fun again. I told Bell, 'I want to sell the company but I don't want stock, I don't want paper, I want cash.'"

"Jim said to me, 'I want to get some money out of this operation,'" Al recalls. "So I had the responsibility, once again, of trying to sell the company." He met with ready interest from RCA. "Elvis was alive at that time. I'm meeting with Rocco Laginestra, president of RCA Records. They offered us fifteen million dollars in RCA stock and I went back and told Jim about this great deal." Al laughs as he remembers Jim's response. "And Jim said, 'Oh yeah?' He said, 'Man, I don't want no more stock. I want cash money.' I said, 'But RCA is a blue-chip company.' He says, 'I don't care who it is, Al. I don't want anybody's stock: I want cash money.'"

Generating an offer that would let Al buy out Jim with cash would take time and require assistance. There was really only one person Al could enlist to make that happen. So Al leaned on the lean-on man: Johnny Baylor. While traveling with Isaac Hayes, Baylor's team had visited radio stations to take advantage of promotional opportunities. "They used to walk in the radio station, they'd lift the arm off that record while it's play-ing, put theirs on," says Randy Stewart, from Isaac's entourage. "Wasn't nobody going to argue with them."

"We were on tour and Johnny Baylor had sent some of his guys out to pay some disc jockeys in Birmingham," says Isaac's drummer Willie Hall. "These guys were no fools. They stayed around in Birmingham the rest of that day to make sure that the jocks lived up to their agreement. These disc jockeys man, some of them were dogs, money-hungry clowns. They were gangsters themselves. But that was the order of the day then—disc jockeys getting their arms broken and their face beat in for taking payola and not playing records."

Al and Johnny struck a deal that, in short, had them both betting on the future: I'll gladly pay you Tuesday for a hit record today. Al wanted a strong cash flow so he could command the best price for Jim's buyout. To push the company's earnings higher, "I went to my dear friend Johnny Baylor," says Al, "and explained, 'I need you to take your team and go out and promote the Stax product.' I said, 'I can't pay you for that. But what I'll do is, I'll take on the distribution of your label, and the manufacturing part of it, and that gives you compensation.'" That is, Al explains, "I didn't want to create any additional expense for the company while I'm out trying to sell it." In return for Baylor doing this promotions work, and for fronting the pay and expenses to his team, Al would assume the costs of Baylor's record label and would agree to pay him later if their work paid off. Al and Baylor shared an economic philosophy, even if their means were different. "Those guys were on top of taking Isaac Hayes's product to another level," Al says. "And their motivation was different. The others were salaried employees, but in this particular case, there was a lot of black pride involved in what we were doing."

"Johnny Baylor's perspective," says Dino, "was to see an African-American—boom—out there in the front. He wanted Al Bell to really be out there. And he would do anything that he had to to see that Al Bell would be all right."

There was a financial risk for Johnny—Al was not going to provide any immediate income. But money clung to Johnny. "The devil was with Johnny Baylor," says Randy Stewart, "because he had money all kind of ways." None of the ways were obvious, but the money was.

Johnny Baylor became the face of Stax Records in the field. He'd follow behind James Douglass and the other promo men who paid visits to stations, the good cops who greased the turntables with money. Baylor's team, the bad cops, would hit a town and you could almost hear his crew's boots in lockstep as they fanned out to radio, retail, and distribution centers. Johnny Baylor would take a hotel room, and everyone his team came in contact with was told to reach him there. In a day, they'd make their presence known—word about Johnny would spread quickly. Retailers moved Stax product to the front of the store, gave it a big display; jocks played the newest Stax releases, giving them an extra spin. When one of Baylor's team showed up, he'd be greeted with nervous smiles: "Hey f-f-fellas, you're in town?"

Now here's the kicker: Baylor would keep the hotel room for several days, maybe a week. DJs and store managers would phone the Holiday Inn, ask for his room. "I'm sorry sir, he's not answering." Thinking he's still in town, they'd keep on pushing the Stax product, figuring Baylor's pushing the presets on his car radio, and he's someone you want to keep finger-snapping happy. In fact, Baylor and the gang may have already moved on to the next town, taken another hotel room for a week, started intimidating another city's DJs and distributors. The Stax product received the extra push until the desk clerk said he's checked out. Baylor could keep a whole region on its toes, Stax product everywhere.

"Other companies who had already established themselves in the recording industry were doing the same thing—getting airplay by any means necessary," says Dino. "The top artists were selling millions of records, and some of that stuff is oopy-doopy stuff. But American music comes from gospel music, R&B, and jazz, so we felt that we deserved to be heard. We would meet the music directors and take up a little bit of their time to explain about R&B music. It was the way that we approached people, let them know that the African-American music needed to be heard."

"Dino was an ex-boxer and he promoted records," says Seymour Rosenberg, the Stax attorney. "He would open a briefcase and inside it was mounted a revolver. He would say, 'Boom!' and close it back up and, miraculously, his records got played."

In addition to promoting at radio and retail, Baylor's team collected on delinquent accounts, especially independent distributors who never wanted to let go of a dollar. "You gotta pay up," says Dino. "Boom. There's no getting around. A lot of distributors were holding back on the pay. And, well, we wanted to make sure that they paid now. There was some run-ins from time to time, and we got challenged a lot, so we had to really push our way through to those companies."

"They kept Stax floating," says Randy Stewart. "They were going to bring some money back. If you owe somebody and you're not paying, there's another way of getting it." Randy declined to give details, only to imply that fists and guns had a way of making distributors locate money they'd been unable to find earlier in the conversation.

As Baylor settled into his work in the field, he suggested Al bring in another industry veteran, Hymie Weiss, whose experience and analytical eye would help them increase the sales numbers. "Hymie Weiss was a gentleman, a friend like no other," says Al. "He'd had hits in the 1950s with Arthur Prysock. Hymie would fly from New York, stay at the Holiday Inn Central, run the sales department, and then fly back on the weekend."

"I was the payola king of New York," Weiss later bragged. "Payola was the greatest thing in the world. You didn't have to go out to dinner with someone and kiss their ass. Just pay them, here's the money, play the record, *fuck you*." One of his Stax associates remembered Weiss as the guy who could buy a million records for a million bucks. The distribution of them might not have been clean, the sales may not all be accounted for, but the money spent, the generator whirred, and the cash register went *ka-ching*. Jim wanted out, but to get top dollar he'd wait for Al to make sure the company was moving lots of product, generating lots of income, attracting top dollar.

◆ ◆ ◆

THE SUCCESS OF the *Shaft* soundtrack would not seem to be a source of complaint. Yet Baylor quickly noticed a funny thing happening in distribution: Sometimes stores returned more copies than they'd ordered. He brought the news to Al. An ironic by-product to success: "We were growing so large, until it allowed for people to commit white-collar crimes," Al explains. "You don't have that happening in small, nothing companies."

Pirating. That's different from bootlegging (bootlegs are unofficial recordings released through unofficial means), different from forgeries (attempts to copy album art and musical content). Pirating requires insiders to cheat, insiders at the label, at the pressing plant, or on a delivery truck—someone who could access or create great quantities of the genuine article. Industry-wide, pirating was estimated to account for 10 percent of product on the market—the equivalent of what is often a small company's profit margin. "We estimate that some 800,000 pirated copies of *Shaft* found their way onto the market in the States," Stax corporate management consultant Adam Oliphant told an industry publication. "That's something like 40 per cent [of the product accounted for]." Oliphant explained the pirate's methods: "There is the straight-forward theft of legitimate product. This can occur within a pressing plant, the press operative working on the principle of 'one for the company, one for me' and then getting the records out of the factory and onto the market with the collusion of a shipping clerk, a security guard and a trucker or, where independent pressing plants are employed, the management themselves may fiddle their clients by over-pressing. Once these records get into the shops they are virtually impossible to detect."

Stax was ready to pay high dollars to solve this high-dollar problem, and their New York law office led them to Norman Jaspan & Associates, an investigative firm that also advised Ford Motors. Al liked keeping such company. Jaspan sent in undercover operatives, and Stax bought infrared detection for shipping supervision, marking their boxes so that their representatives in the field could carry a special device to authenticate their product. "On a weekly basis I would get the reports," says Al, "not at the office but at home." Jaspan beefed up the studio's security, creating a guard station and adding a vault that required two keys.

In November 1971, while *Shaft* was massive, two Stax executives who'd been at the company barely two years were fired. Ewell Roussell, vice president of sales, and Herbert Kole, vice president of merchandising and marketing, were accused of piracy. Both had access to the master tapes and connections at the pressing plants for records and art, and Stax alleged that they'd manufactured illegal albums and sold them for profit—about $380,000 profit. They'd also forced a kickback from local and national photographers hired for album covers and promotional shots—another $26,000. "Jim and I decided not to prosecute them," says Al. "'Go your way, we don't want to send you through these kind of problems. You got family, kids.' We were supposed to turn them in to the bonding company, the bonding company would have given us our money back, and then the bonding company could have caused them to be prosecuted. We let them go, and several other people, at that point in time." Stax settled with the insurance for a tenth of what they'd lost.

(For his part, Ewell Roussell claimed not only innocence but also vindication, saying, "I lost my sales position at Stax Records because of something somebody else did, completely without my knowledge. Stax, through Jim Stewart, acknowledged by letter to me that pressure from its fidelity bond company caused my release and not any implication of me by the investigations. I still have that letter. The newspaper quotes have said that I received money from alleged kickbacks. I did not receive one cent and did not know of any such scheme until after my release. The bond company settled its claim with Herbert Kolesky [Kole], who had been my superior at Stax. They never even approached me about any claim because it was clear to them that they had no claim against me.")

"Al was too compassionate," says his assistant Earlie Biles. "A lot of people he brought in took advantage of him and the situation, because we grew so fast. He was bringing people in who had expertise in certain areas, but these people brought their own people in, their own ideas. We didn't have policies and procedures in place, so they would all run to Al Bell for whatever they wanted. When they couldn't get through me to see him, they would wait in the parking lot. They missed him there, they'd go to his house." Earlie and her husband, living next to Al's house, chased down the people who tried to get to Al by throwing pebbles at his window during the night. "The chain of command was broken."

One casualty of that broken chain was Don Davis. In the various shufflings, he bounced from head of A&R back to staff producer and, despite all the Johnnie Taylor hits, wound up out the door. "Don came in my office a few months after he'd hired me," says Tim Whitsett, "and said, 'I've just been canned and I'm on my way back to Detroit.'"

To the consumer—to anyone on the outside—Stax appeared to be thriving. Despite Booker T. Jones and Steve Cropper having left the Stax payroll, the MG's were still recording together, and their single "Melting Pot," in early 1971, from the album of the same name, had fared well on both the R&B and the pop charts. However, the tensions between the group and the Stax staff were so high that the band recorded in New York, far from their McLemore home. A new direction, "Melting Pot" is more jazz-influenced than the band's prior work, looser within its defined structure, a greater sense of impromptu jamming. (It remains a favorite for contemporary samplers.) This single and album would prove to be their last work on Stax—Duck and Al Jackson would release an album and single in late 1973 as the MG's, with no mention of Booker T., and without much success.

But Stax's original star was back on top: Rufus Thomas was enjoying hit after hit. In a slump since the mid-1960s, he'd teamed with newcomer Tom Nixon, a Detroit producer, and things clicked. "The Funky Chicken" went top ten in 1970, "(Do the) Push and Pull (Part 1)" went to number-one R&B and number-twenty-five pop, and "The Breakdown," released in July of 1971, was on its way to top-forty pop and number two on the R&B charts, with "Do the Funky Penguin" to chart before the year was out.

Stax continued to aggressively license material from outside sources. Jean Knight's hit "Mr. Big Stuff" had taken off in the middle of 1971. The song had come to the attention of Tim Whitsett when it arrived on a four-song tape from Malaco Studios in Jackson, Mississippi; they wanted Stax to license it and get it to the masses. Don Davis had rejected all the songs, but Tim thought three of them were really strong. After Stax declined their songs, the tiny struggling Malaco label released one itself. "Groove Me" hit the top of the soul charts and top-ten pop. With Davis gone, Whitsett had Stax reconsider the others. "We were being blessed and fortunate," says Al Bell. "I'm sitting in my office one day on Avalon, right across from Jim, and I'm hearing this bass slam through a wall. I said, 'Jesus Christ what a bass line. Poignant, poignant." He went to Jim's office, found out it was the relatively unknown Jean Knight doing a song called "Mr. Big Stuff." "I said, 'Man, we got to go to the street with this as fast as we possibly can.'" It went to number-one R&B and number-two pop. "It was," Al says, "like manna from heaven."

The Dramatics also hit big. They'd come to Stax through Don Davis in 1968, but departed after having no significant success. In 1971, they were re-signed on the strength of "Whatcha See Is Whatcha Get," made with Davis in Detroit. Stax leapt on the song, taking it to the top ten in both pop and R&B, and earning a gold record for a million sales before the year was out. Albert King was also on the make, with "Everybody Wants to Go to Heaven" from his *Lovejoy* album, a career highlight produced by onetime Mar-Key Don Nix. The Emotions, the gospel band brought from Chicago and given the pop patina, charted with "Show Me Now."

The Rance Allen Group was a gospel outfit that did not want to cross over, and Stax liked them so much, they created a new imprint, the Gospel Truth, just so they could sign them. "We tried to go to Motown, but Motown didn't do gospel at all," recalls Rance Allen. "The next step was Stax Records, and they didn't do gospel either. But Jim Stewart and Al Bell liked what they heard, and so they called my manager to tell him they were interested." No folly, Gospel Truth released three albums in 1971, and many more over the coming years.

Al Bell had taken over production of the Staple Singers from Steve Cropper well before Cropper's departure. He'd produced a couple records and enjoyed some success—"Heavy Makes You Happy (Sha-Na-Boom

1973, backstage at the Mid-South Coliseum. L–R: Eddie Floyd, Rance Allen, Johnnie Taylor, Rufus Thomas. (University of Memphis Libraries/Special Collections)

Boom)" from *The Staple Swingers* had gone top-forty pop and top-ten R&B—but for his third album with them, Al took the family to Muscle Shoals, Alabama. Muscle Shoals had become a notable recording center in 1961 when Rick Hall produced Arthur Alexander, whose songs were then cut by the Beatles and the Rolling Stones; Percy Sledge's "When a Man Loves a Woman" was recorded in Muscle Shoals, Wilson Pickett found more success there after leaving Stax, and the studios had developed top-notch house bands (on the Stax model). While preparing for the soul explosion, Stax developed a satellite relationship with the Muscle Shoals studios. By taking the Staples there, Al would be far from the office and not constantly distracted by phone calls. Plus, he says, producing at Stax was intimidating. "I don't know flat from sharp," he says. "I'm the other stuff." To the staff, he was the marketing guy, and he felt his lack of musical knowledge would lower their opinion of him; outside Stax, he could be just another client. Just another hit-making, star-making client. With the Staples in Muscle Shoals, he cut "Respect Yourself" and "I'll Take You There." To ensure he'd get the best efforts from the musicians, he made the unusual arrangement of paying them a royalty on sales.

"Respect Yourself" grew from a conversation between songwriter Mack Rice, who'd written Wilson Pickett's hit "Mustang Sally," and Luther Ingram, Johnny Baylor's artist. "When the administration moved out of the McLemore offices, they let everyone who was staying [the creative team] pick their offices," says Rice. "I picked Jim Stewart's office, man. It was plush, with long couches and zebra all over the floor. I felt like I was somebody then. So one day Luther Ingram and I was up there talking. One of us said, 'A guy got to respect himself out here to get anyplace.' It hit us the same time—that's a good title, 'Respect Yourself.' Luther went downstairs to see Isaac about something. I'm messing with my guitar and Luther—what are they doing so long? I started writing. It was like God just give me the words. About thirty minutes, I had the whole song wrote and Luther never came back.

"The next day I turned in the song to the publishing department, told the girl down there, 'When you see Luther, tell him to sign this contract.' Luther told her, 'I ain't did no song with Mack Rice.' She said, 'I had to almost beg him to sign it.' The song starts climbing the charts, Luther came to me and said, 'Hey, man, didn't I write some of that?' I said, 'No sir. I'm giving you ten percent of the song, though, 'cause one of us come up with the title.' "

The song jibed perfectly with the Staple Singers. "Pops would tell the songwriters," says Mavis about her father, " 'If you want to write for the Staples, read the headlines—we want to sing about what's happening in the world today.' So Mack said, 'Pops, I got one for you.' Pops heard it, said, 'Shoot, man, we could put that down.' " And they sure did.

Al, who'd been more occupied with business than songwriting, wrote "I'll Take You There." "My fourth oldest brother was murdered in North Little Rock, just as I was getting ready to go in the studio with the Staple Singers," he told a reporter. "I had nothing but deaths among my brothers. Paul, the one after me, was shot down and killed in Memphis. My youngest brother, Darnell, was murdered in North Little Rock. I couldn't come to grips with death." After leaving the Arkansas graveyard, his family broke bread at his parents' house. But Al got up and went outside, found himself pacing uncontrollably, the song welling up inside him, the sun heating him in his jacket as he walked. "My father had the relic of an old school bus under two oak trees," says Al. "He used that bus to haul cotton pickers, and it was a reminder to him how he moved from an eighth-grade education to being one of the leading landscaping contractors in Arkansas. I sat on the hood of that school bus and tried to deal with all the emotions I was feeling. All of a sudden—I cannot sing, I cannot dance, I cannot carry a tune in a vacuum-packed can—but I can feel and I can hear. Then I started singing the lyrics:

I know a place
Ain't nobody worried
Ain't nobody crying
And ain't no smiling faces
Lying to the races.
I'll take you there.

It wouldn't leave, it stayed there. I kept trying to write other verses, but I couldn't. Nothing worked. There was nothing left to say."

Al took that verse to Muscle Shoals, where Mavis ad-libbed with the group as they jammed on a riff. Muscle Shoals guitarist Jimmy Johnson had just returned from Jamaica and had a single of the reggae instrumental "The Liquidator" by the Harry J All Stars; bassist David Hood and drummer Roger Hawkins had recently completed a tour with the British rock band Traffic and had been listening to Bob Marley. Funky rhythms were in the air, and the band locked into a groove that sent Mavis improvising a call-and-response with the instruments. "Respect Yourself," released in latter 1971, went to number-two R&B and number-twelve pop, and "I'll Take You There," which wasn't released until the spring of 1972, went to number one on both charts. Baylor's troops on the street—promoting, enforcing, collecting—had no shortage of strong material to work with.

◆ ◆ ◆

AND THEN THERE was Isaac Hayes's *Black Moses* album, his second double album of the year, released while "Theme from *Shaft*" was still number one in the nation. The rare artist can churn out copious work at a rapid rate and maintain a high level of innovation. But Isaac Hayes was putting out music faster than the Beatles in their prime. *Black Moses* is not a bad record, but it doesn't move Hayes's career forward, and with the glut of his material in the marketplace, this album came off as stale.

The name "Black Moses" had first come from Dino Woodard. "Isaac was a great leader," he says, "And one time at the Apollo Theater their MC was late, and I introduced him as Black Moses. The audience was just overwhelmed."

Isaac initially found the name sacrilegious, but a *Jet* writer picked up on it, as did other MCs in their introductions. Stax capitalized on a growing trend. Larry Shaw, Stax's advertising and packaging chief (whose Stax work had already won several national awards), didn't like the record at all, and told writer Rob Bowman, "The music in there was of such poor quality, we had to sell the box it came in. We put an inordinate amount of money into that album jacket. It was to capture fully all the things about him that were not in the record. The record *was* the box." Shaw created a gatefold that unfurled in four directions, shaping into a cross four feet tall and three feet wide, with Isaac in an Egyptian-looking tunic, his arms outstretched, an all-enfolding embrace of his tribe.

Concurrent with the album's release was an antipiracy publicity storm. Having lost much profit to pirates with *Shaft*, Stax made its stance known through press releases, press conferences in New York, and filmed announcements for television. The label would be "utilizing ex-FBI operatives . . . [They] will institute close surveillance tactics at the fabricating plants, pressing operations, and known bootlegging operations throughout the U.S. FBI methods will be utilized in detecting and apprehending pirates."

Expecting big sales for *Black Moses*, Stax spared no expense. To its most influential people—DJs, radio station directors, owners of the largest distributors—Stax sent a space-age telephone, equal parts James Bond sleek and Daddy Mack pimpin': The size of a small tabletop, the device featured a clear plastic dome through which the phone's electronics were visible; the rotary-dial face protruded like a breast offering itself. The handset extended from the left side of the fine wood-grain box. It was sure to win favors, and likely helped important Stax supporters impress their dates.

Stax's excesses were growing. Another promotional phone came in a wood-and-leather case; lift the lid to reveal the phone ringing within. Elegant, futuristic. Stax gave away beautiful Bulova watches; a crystal desk set that evoked a lofty religious ceremony but was actually a sword-and-stone letter opener; a fine leather shoulder satchel embossed with the finger-snapping logo; a silver tea set. In addition, Shaw designed no end of everyday

Promotional telephone for the Isaac Hayes album
Black Moses. (Photograph by David Leonard)

giveaways: a package of playing cards, two decks side by side, one with the Stax logo on the back, the other with the Volt logo. Both also promote the Hip and Enterprise subsidiary labels (Hip was oriented toward white pop, and Enterprise was home to Isaac Hayes); the cards bear the motto: THE SOUND CENTER OF THE SOULAR SYSTEM MEMPHIS TN. There were Stax oven mitts, keychains, refrigerator magnets, and posters of all kinds.

Black Moses spent nearly two months at the top of the R&B album charts. Hayes's edited version of "Never Can Say Goodbye" reached number twenty-two on the pop charts, and the top five on the R&B. At the start of 1972, he was nominated for seven Grammy Awards and numerous other accolades. He seemed invincible, and it was a perfect time to negotiate a new contract. For several years there'd been talk about giving Isaac equity in the company, and while Al couldn't promise that at a time when he was trying to find a new partner, Al knew he'd never have a partner if Isaac got away. If this new contract were clothing, it would have fit only Isaac. Among numerous lavish perks, his new deal included a $26,000 gold-plated Cadillac, a leased house in a canyon near Hollywood, a very sweet royalty deal, and annual salaries totaling $55,000 for the administering of his publishing company and for himself as a producer—despite his production work having fallen off dramatically since he'd become an artist. Other than Billy Eckstine, Isaac had mostly just finished prior commitments with David Porter. Such outlandish payments were the price of keeping the Isaac Hayes generator humming.

Much like Hayes's contracts and his album, Stax had become outsize. The company's early-1970s phone directory had an intimidating two hundred names, many with multiple extensions. In the new Stax Organization, employees wandered the halls not knowing each other's names, even what their jobs were. Since the chain of operations had been initially revised in March 1970 by Jim Stewart, it had changed time and again. Problems were solved by hiring—a fixer, a specialist, a new department. "How are you gonna put a song on the turntable and statistically analyze it?" Deanie Parker asks of the department of statistical analysis. "It was getting crazy, just crazy." The magic wand is waved. A new department is created. Middle-class wage is granted. Plus five. The tally of Al's upwardly mobile employees rises.

"There was a lot of head games going on, political games as the company got bigger," says Jim, who was working on his exit. "I didn't like that, but there was no way I could stop it. You got a hundred and fifty, two hundred people, it's not like it's six people you can talk to every day. We were getting too big, the overhead was getting out of hand. At some point I felt that it was growing into a monster that could devour itself."

23. WATTSTAX
1972

S TAX ISSUED EMPLOYEE badges "like you worked at the Pentagon," says Duck Dunn. It was January 1972. "Good morning, Jim," and "What's up, Eddie?" were gone. A guard in uniform whom no one knew sat at the back door demanding proof that the person entering the building had reason to be there. When Duck forgot his badge and was refused entrance to the studio he'd helped build, he turned on his heels and went home.

"They was keeping me and Al Jackson there as a favor, or loyalty—that was the feeling," says Duck. "It wasn't because they really wanted us. I had an office there and about forty psychedelic San Francisco posters on the wall from when we played the Fillmore. I decorated it with some psychedelic curtains and I'd light incense." But Duck rarely went there. "I'd be there a few hours and I'd think, What in the hell am I doing here? If I'm not in there playing bass, why ain't I out on the golf course? But if you left, someone might stab you in the back and say, 'Duck ain't here.' And I didn't have the guts to walk out and say, 'Hey, do you need me to play bass? That's what I do. I don't talk on the phone to no damn radio station, I'm here to play bass.' Finally, somebody says to me, 'Hey, can we use your space?'" Duck was glad to relinquish it.

Engineer Larry Nix was struck by the ever-increasing surveillance and safety measures. Notably, it wasn't that they were afraid of being robbed, but rather fear they'd be framed so they could be taken down. They'd grown so large and were employing so many African-Americans that they knew resentment, hostility, and fear were roiling among Memphis business elite. "There was a paranoia," Larry says. "They were afraid someone would hide drugs in Stax, then try to bust them. My office had a special lock, and it had a motion detector. There was a *lot* of security."

The alienation grew. Men in suits appeared, carrying clipboards. "M.B.W.," says publishing head Tim Whitsett, explaining "management by walking around. You walk by somebody's office at ten o'clock in the morning and see if they're working. You come by at random times, then you begin to have some circumstantial evidence. So that becomes M.B.T.: management by terror. We should have had M.B.O.: management by objectives. We didn't have a real, structured management system."

A stack of beautiful, black leatherette notebooks arrived with the new year. The Stax logo was embossed in gold on the front, as was the title: *Field Representative's Policy Manual*. At last—a codified plan. But upon inspection, this hefty manual the length of a novella was more a description of intense corporate culture than a plan to organize the Stax Organization. It's like teaching teenagers to drive by giving them a NASCAR rule book. There are categories covering everything—payments, lunch time, inclement weather. Consider the statement in the category "Wage and Salary" under the subject "Salary Administration-Exempt cont'd," section number V-6.00, subsection (f), step (3), subsection (b) (in a book of approximately fifty *unnumbered* pages): "Dollars given <u>midpoint amounts</u> for performance as described in (4) and (5) are also uneconomical in that it retards motivation, lowers morale and increases turnover costs." Yes, that and having to read this manual.

"At that time we were trying to put in policies and procedures, and trying to get some control over who reported to whom, and who could do what," says Al's assistant, Earlie Biles. Among the departments created: Systems and Efficiency.

Earlie took time off from her work that summer to marry James Douglass (Isaac Hayes was his best man). They held their wedding in Rome, and Al had the company underwrite a number of round-trip flights so the couple could be married among friends—a trip, a treat, a dream, for everyone. A photo from the reception appeared in *Jet* magazine. "We shopped over there and everything," says Earlie, "came back and had our American Express bills due." She solved that pinch by a quick call to Joe Harwell at Union Planters National Bank.

Despite the rampant disorganization characterized—or caused—by continued reorganization, the hits couldn't be stopped, nor could the cash flow. Jean Knight had a top-twenty follow-up to "Mr. Big Stuff" with "You Think You're Hot Stuff." The Dramatics had another top-twenty hit, "Get Up and Get Down." The Bar-Kays and Little Milton each reached the top ten—with "Son of Shaft" and "That's What Love Will Make You Do"—and Johnnie Taylor came in at number twelve with "Standing In for Jody." Isaac kept his *Shaft* album moving with another single, the number-three hit "Do Your Thing." Albert King hit the top fifty with "Angel of Mercy." Don Davis sent Stax another Dramatics hit, "In the Rain," which shot to the tip-top of the soul charts for four weeks in a row and to number-five pop, and was followed two weeks later by the Staple Singers' "I'll Take You There," also spending a month at number one. Tim Whitsett developed a relationship with Frederick Knight, who was sending unsolicited song demos to various companies. Whitsett encouraged and coached him, urging him toward creating something more individual—all his material sounded like a modification of other hits. "He wrote 'I've Been Lonely for So Long,' where he sings in this pitiful little falsetto," says Tim. "He also sings in a low bass voice. He sent that to me, and I fell out of my chair because it just made you feel so good." The public agreed: R&B number eight, pop number twenty-seven. Seven of Stax's first eight singles in 1972 hit the top fifty; thirteen of the first eighteen singles; nearly half of their thirty-nine releases in the first half of 1972 were chart hits. Johnny Baylor's team was very good at what it did. The company purchased their longtime McLemore base on April 6, 1972, for $85,000. The mortgage was held by Union Planters National Bank, Joe Harwell, trustee.

◆ ◆ ◆

AL BELL HADN'T forgotten that Jim Stewart wanted out. But he was still raising the profile, enhancing the company's value. In 1972, Johnny Baylor found the song that would skyrocket his artist Luther Ingram to fame, and generate a heap of income for Stax. Luther was a songwriter and aspiring singer from near Jackson, Tennessee, about eighty miles east of Memphis. A tawny black man, Luther's complexion was bronzed by his Blackfoot Indian heritage. He was thin and lithe, with hair that konked close to his head. His face was angular and sharp, his eyes were stunningly amber, his smile revealed the disarming gap between his front teeth. He'd been raised in the Baptist church and sang with a gospel group that, after auditioning for Cincinnati's King Records (home to James Brown), went pop and was assigned Ike Turner as producer. Luther had made several recordings before

LUTHER INGRAM

he moved to New York, where he met Baylor in the mid-1960s. "When Johnny found Luther Ingram," says Dino, "he was really able to see that there was some extra talent there, extra voice, so he really strove to promote Luther."

Luther Ingram was what Baylor had been looking for. Johnny himself had the look and feel of a star. He saw nightclub singers in Sugar Ray's barbershop, and he felt the ladies and the men responding to them off the stage and on, and Johnny could almost taste the spotlight. But he wasn't a singer. "He wanted most of his life to sing," says Luther Ingram, "and he tried to do that through me."

Baylor could produce a flattened nose faster than a flattened note, and it was with a mixture of intimidation and aspiration for the spotlight that he would draw out his protégé in the recording studio. After Luther found his soul balladeer groove, Baylor tapped his Isaac Hayes connections, bringing Isaac's arrangers Dale Warren and Johnny Allen to write Luther's arrangements, and also using Isaac's backing vocalists. Even as Luther's hits began to mount, Baylor held off releasing an album on Luther until 1971's *I've Been Here All the Time*. "Johnny wanted to challenge Marvin Gaye," says Luther, "so he just waited until Marvin had released a lot of records." Luther's chart action improved (Willie Hall cowrote and coproduced some of his hits), but it wasn't until he stumbled onto an older Stax demo that his career was made. In 1970, Homer Banks and Raymond Jackson had cowritten a song with Carl Hampton for the Emotions. They recorded the song about infidelity and desire, but it was deemed too risqué for them and wasn't released. Another Stax artist (Veda Brown) had tried it, but it still didn't see the light of day.

"One day Luther Ingram was outside our office and heard the demo with me on it," says Homer Banks. "Next thing we knew, he'd cut it himself." Al Bell told Baylor he'd give him the publishing rights to the song: "Just stay on top of my product out here."

Baylor took Luther to Muscle Shoals to record in April 1972. It was the first time Luther met the musicians, but they synced quickly. The guitar sound is sinuous, like lovers sneaking to their secret hideaway. The organ, strings, and horns meld—lovers conjoined. It's not the classic church-based soul song, but neither is it a completely modern statement; the instruments are spare enough to let the emotion intensify, supporting Luther's plaintive perplexity: "If loving you is wrong," he pleads, "I don't want to be right."

Luther's song was cut in about half an hour, which is also how long Banks says it took to write. Baylor brought the tape back to Stax to have it mastered for release. "I was in the mastering room one day at lunchtime," says engineer Larry Nix, "and Johnny Baylor came in with Luther Ingram. Johnny was waving a German Luger and he walked up to me very quickly and pulled a reference disc [of 'If Loving You Is Wrong'] out of a sleeve and said, 'Did you do this?' My boss, had done it. He was at lunch. Johnny threw the record against the wall, pointed at the lathe, and said, 'Do you know how to do this?' I said, 'Sure.' Luther convinced Johnny to leave, and I went and got the master tape, started working on it. My boss came back, looked at my EQ settings, and says, 'You can't use that much EQ on there.' Luther stepped up and told him what had happened, said, 'Johnny Baylor is looking for you.' Not only did my boss turn and leave the building, he quit the company. I took the reference disc to WDIA [the city's leading black music radio station]. They'd play our tests on the air so we could hear how it'd sound. Jim would go to his Lincoln Continental and listen, someone else would go home with their hi-fi. On my ride back to Stax, I heard the DJ play it four times in a row. Johnny loved what I did, and from then on I was cutting masters at Stax."

"It would be scary to some people because Johnny felt that he would have to really put some force in there to push for products," says Dino. "He would sit in on different sessions sometimes that wasn't his artist, and then he would discuss things with Al Bell, what he felt was wrong and what was right, arrangements, and whatnot. He would push people to really do certain things to make sure that records were sold, and recorded right."

"One day, Johnny Baylor came into my office and shut the door," says Tim Whitsett, then executive vice president of the publishing companies. "He started cussing me out that all of Luther Ingram's songs were published by East/Memphis Music, Stax's publishing company, when they should be split with his company, Klondike. He wanted me to right then draw up the contracts giving fifty percent of all those copyrights to Klondike. I said, 'Johnny, I certainly can't do that without being asked by Mr. Bell or Mr. Stewart.' Johnny Baylor leaned back on my nice white leather sofa and opened his jacket. It seemed to me there were seven or eight guns and some bandoleers, but I think it was just one pearl-handled pistol. He

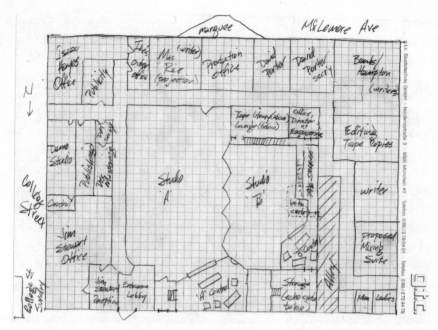

The layout of the Stax building, circa 1973, by engineer Dave Purple. Purple won a Grammy, Best Engineered Recording, for his work on "Theme from *Shaft*." (The Grammy was shared with Stax engineers Henry Bush and Ron Capone.) (Drawing by David Purple/Courtesy of René Wu)

said, 'I know where you live down in Jackson, Mississippi. I know where you live here in Memphis. I'm gonna leave you, and when I come back, I want those contracts.' I called Al Bell and he told me, 'Better go ahead and draw up those contracts.'" "If Loving You Is Wrong," promoted by Johnny Baylor, hit number one on the R&B charts and stayed at the top for four consecutive weeks. Within a few months, it sold so many copies that the master at the pressing plant wore out and a new one had to be made.

Baylor's ongoing success promoting the label fed Al's tendency toward expansiveness. If records were such a cinch, how hard could other media be? STAX IN TOTAL EXPANSION PLAN, read a February *Billboard* headline. Stax announced they were moving "into the Broadway play arena as major backers of 'The Selling of the President.'" Based on Joe McGinniss's best-selling book about the marketing of Richard Nixon's image in 1968, the play would open at Broadway's Shubert Theatre in late March. Stax put up over a third of the half-million-dollar backing, receiving in return the soundtrack rights, for which they "expect to be as successful . . . as we have with our recent motion picture soundtrack albums such as *Shaft*." Broadway, they announced, "is expected to be one of the numerous moves by this Company into the leisure-time areas."

The play closed after five performances—but such is the risk of every theatrical venture. Stax was undeterred, announcing it was putting $100,000 into the Melvin Van Peebles Broadway production of *Don't Play Us Cheap*; it ran for four and a half months at the Ethel Barrymore Theater and was nominated for two Tony Awards. Stax released the cast recording—as a double album.

Al Bell, Stax's chief executive officer by February 1972, quickly realized the inherent problem with a theatrical performance: Each night, there was a maximum number of people it could reach. Seating was limited, and viewers had to make a concerted effort to attend. Al had not forgotten the promise of home video that he'd seen at the Philips International offices, and he understood that the audience for a movie had an exponentially higher possibility for return than a play, especially a movie that could be turned into a home video and also broadcast on TV. "That's his beauty," says Wayne Jackson, the Mar-Keys trumpet player who'd cofounded the Memphis Horns. "Making movies appealed to Al Bell because it was bigger than records. When you talk bigger numbers, it's like fine-tuning his intellect. If you'd have said, 'Al, a billion dollars,' he would've lit up and shot out the roof like a rocket."

The expansion, even when it was successful, did not please everyone. "I was troubled by it, these layers and layers and layers," says Deanie Parker. "I always wanted to say, 'Why can't we be what we are? Why is all this ancillary stuff necessary?'"

◆◆◆

AL BELL WANTED an identity on the East and West Coasts as strong as he had across the South. He'd made inroads to the east, but the west . . . so distant, yet to be won. So he established an office there: Stax West, headed by concert promoter Forrest Hamilton, son of drummer Chico Hamilton. "We're still on this curve of trying to carry forth the resurrection and the ascension," says Al. "We really hadn't made our impact into Southern California, Los Angeles, Hollywood." Stax West suggested the company get more involved in the community, and the idea of helping the Watts Summer Festival caught some traction. This commemoration had begun in the wake of the 1967 Watts riots—also known as the Watts rebellion—which the Stax artists had witnessed when leaving Los Angeles after their "burn, baby, burn" appearance at the 5-4 Ballroom. A program honoring the memory of the thirty-four citizens killed had become an annual event, sometimes flourishing, sometimes not.

By sending a prominent artist to the festival, Stax would raise both its profile and the event's. Al began pondering the benefits of sending two artists—more always being better. Look what the Monterey Pop Festival had done for Otis, and for the MG's. The scope quickly grew large enough to shift locations from the Mafundi Institute in Watts to the much larger Will Rogers Park. In Memphis, meanwhile, the grassroots appeal attracted more artists, and when Isaac Hayes threw his weight behind it, the Watts project assumed magnitude. "Instead of just doing a concert," says Al, "we began to consider doing the entire Stax roster out there. We'd expose these artists to KGFJ, then the only black radio station in Los Angeles." The whole roster was tens of people, and would require a yet larger venue. No one's sure who thought of it, but when the idea was proposed to rent the Los Angeles Memorial Coliseum, where the Rams played football in front of a hundred thousand people, Al Bell leapt on it.

The Coliseum managers had never heard of the client knocking on their door. "We went to rent the stadium," Al says, "and the management there kind of laughed at us. 'You're some little record company from out of Memphis, Tennessee—who do you say these artists are?' They were laughing." But a rental is a rental, so the talk continued. "I said, 'We don't want LAPD at this concert, we want to be able to bring our own security.'" That task was overseen by Johnny Baylor and Melvin Van Peebles. "So we got the agreement signed and started organizing, started promoting." The Wattstax concert would be the culmination of the 1972 Watts Summer Festival where, for the price of a single US dollar, nationally lauded soul and gospel acts would perform from three in the afternoon until eleven at night. "The drums started beating louder and louder throughout Los Angeles, Hollywood, Beverly Hills, and Southern California," Al says. "We were promoting with door hangers and billboards and planes writing in the sky and planes pulling signs. Print media, television, radio—we were promoting the daylights out of this concert to where it looks like we may pack this stadium. That's when we got this panicked call—stadium management and law enforcement were concerned. We had to compromise on two points: The LAPD could be outside of the stadium, but not inside. Also, the Los Angeles Rams were going to play the next day and they were concerned about that turf. We had to jump through all kinds of hoops but we got turf insurance from Lloyds of London."

The idea of recording the event for an album release—a double album, might as well (and ultimately two double albums)—became obvious. And then the film possibility arose: They'd be in the moviemaking capital, and the Woodstock film and *Soul to Soul* had proven that concert films were a draw. Tip a domino, create a chain reaction. And like all Stax ideas, this wasn't all about dollars and sense. "I had preached that our music and our lyrics were a reflection of what goes on in our lives and our lifestyles," says Al. "And Larry Shaw [in charge of Stax advertising and a producer of the festival and the film] said, 'Then what we need to do is film this and allow it to become a mirror.'"

Larry Shaw at Wattstax. (Stax Museum of American Soul Music)

They brought in producer David Wolper, who'd been doing National Geographic specials since 1966 and had recently made Jacques Cousteau a household name. Wolper also produced Hollywood films, and to direct *Wattstax*, he brought in Mel Stuart; they'd just made *Willy Wonka and the Chocolate Factory* together. "We go and find the finest documentary producers in Hollywood, didn't care whether they were black or white," Al says. These two were white. "So once we got Wolper settled, we started seeking all of the black camerapersons through the union and otherwise in Southern California and hired all of them, and had a black camera crew integrated with the white cameramen." Stax was not missing the opportunity to help individuals who needed work, who needed a résumé booster. (Successful results were evident when, a month after handling the event, the African-American public relations firm the Edward Windsor Wright Corp. was hired by Columbia Records.)

The event also settled a corporate grievance. Schlitz beer, popular among black drinkers, had been targeted with a boycott by Jesse Jackson's Operation PUSH; in time for Wattstax, of which Jackson was one of the MCs, Schlitz signed a corporate covenant with PUSH promising that blacks would become 15 percent of its workforce, and that black businesses would receive 15 percent of the company's budget for advertising, construction, and insurance. Then Schlitz also agreed to sponsor Wattstax, allowing the revenues to go to the Watts Summer Festival and the other beneficiaries, which included the Martin Luther King Hospital in Watts, the Sickle Cell Anemia Foundation, Operation PUSH, and the Watts Labor Community and Action Committee. (A percentage of royalties from the film and albums also went to the Watts Summer Festival.) "If only one person steps through those turnstiles," Stax West's Hamilton said, "it represents one dollar of profits."

◆ ◆ ◆

ON THE TWENTIETH of August, 1972, the day dawned clear—which was important because the Coliseum was an open stadium, no roof. That morning, Al Bell saw all those empty seats and wondered how they could possibly fill it up. But promotion was his specialty. The morning kicked off with a parade through Watts, Stax stars riding in open Cadillac convertibles, waving and basking in the California clime, so unlike the swamp back home. Isaac Hayes was the grand marshal (it was his thirtieth birthday). He wore an African striped tunic, riding alongside Johnnie Taylor, Luther Ingram, and David Porter. The quartet was dashing and ebullient. Those citizens too tired to make it outside could tune in to Carla Thomas on Los Angeles radio. "I told them how Booker and all of us had been there right before the 1967 riots," she says, "and how we were so happy to be back and be a part of the rebuilding, instead of tearing something down."

Folks began arriving at the Coliseum, and there was clearly going to be a party. The clothes were radiant—a rainbow that beamed promise, that proclaimed the future, that reclaimed the present. What was bigger—the hats or the bell-bottoms? The Afros or the hoop earrings? Capacity was 92,000, but 112,000 people came through the turnstiles that day, said to be the largest single gathering of African-Americans in one place since the civil rights March on Washington in 1963. "I was thankful we packed the place," says Al, "because that weighed on my mind."

"When we played 'The Star Spangled Banner,'" Mel Stuart told a reporter, "I was surprised to see a whole audience sitting, talking, eating, or reading newspapers." Jesse Jackson grabbed their attention, connecting the event to the past and to Stax's appearance at the time of the riots, declaring, "We've gone from 'burn, baby, burn' to 'learn, baby, learn.'" He compelled the audience to join him in his exhortation, "I Am Somebody!" a powerful litany about the beauty and integrity of each single person (and also the title track from his debut album on the Stax subsidiary Respect Records). Stax artist Kim Weston began the gospel classic "Lift Every Voice and Sing," popularly known as the Black National Anthem. By then, Stuart observed, the crowd's attention was fixed on the stage, and nearly en masse they all rose, joining in the words. Front and center, Al Bell in a white suit and orange shirt, and Rev. Jackson in a flowing

"Lift Every Voice and Sing" at Wattstax. Jesse Jackson, left, and Al Bell. (Stax Museum of American Soul Music)

African shirt, lifted their right fists into the air, holding them there, clenched: the Black Power salute. Tens of thousands of fists joined. The crowd was paying attention now.

At that early moment in the show, it could already be declared a success. "Then, as now, if you were young and black (forget gifted) in this country, you were always looking for honorable terms to define yourself and your relationship to the society," Stokely Carmichael said of the times. "What in this 'white republic' truly represented you? With what or whom could you identify? And where did one look to find them? If one did not find these figures and values within one's immediate circles— family, friends, school, or church—you were not going to find them anywhere else, certainly not in the public media. Until the movement came along, we Africans—unless athletes or musicians—were rarely to be seen, except on the local news being accused of crimes." On that stage on that day, African-American leaders stood before their people, presenting a cornucopia of culture by, about, for, and policed by blacks (though little policing was needed).

"When Al and I had our fists extended," says Rev. Jesse Jackson, "we were proving that you could have this mass gathering of mostly blacks in Watts and it would be nonviolent. It was a resurrection, a kind of revival of hope and possibility and mass strength."

The convocation-cum-party began with the first thirteen acts performing only a single song each—the stage change sometimes taking longer than the musical performance. "It was almost like a doctor's surgery queue with the nurse yelling out 'next please' all the time," wrote one reviewer. "Thus, William Bell, Eddie Floyd, Ernie Hines, Jimmy Jones, Frederick Knight, Little Sonny, Debra Manning, Eric Mercury, Freddy Robinson, Lee Sain, Freddie Williamson, the Sons of Slum and the Newcomers simply didn't stand a chance." Maybe not a chance of winning over the crowd, but a great chance to appear in the movie, to introduce themselves to a potential fan base that was unfamiliar with them. "Frederick Knight looks good and I will look forward to witnessing his show," the same reviewer wrote, indicating a successfully whetted appetite.

Most of the more established stars performed for about twenty minutes. The Temprees won screams for their choreography, and the Soul Children livened up the place with "Hearsay," their strongest single (number-five R&B, pop top fifty) since signing with Stax four years earlier; Albert King doused the crowd in fiery blues. The Staple Singers made a surprise appearance, thanks indirectly to Richard Nixon. They'd been performing in Las Vegas as the opening act for Sammy Davis Jr. two shows a day. However, the day before Wattstax, Davis told the Staples that he'd be canceling his early show to make a campaign appearance for Richard Nixon; it became the day of his notorious presidential hug. The Staples made haste. "Pops called Al Bell," says Mavis, "said, 'Listen, man, we can make it to Wattstax.' And they got us there. We flew in, did our songs, stayed a while, and flew back to Las Vegas. That was the largest crowd any of us had ever seen." The Bar-Kays are captured in the film's full-color glory, giving a career-making performance of "Son of Shaft/Feel It." The original surviving members, James Alexander and Ben Cauley, had fully succeeded in their quest of being bigger, grander, funkier, more ostentatious, and musical—deeply, rhythmically, musical. Their outfits that day, all high-seventies outrageousness, included a white Afro wig the size of the Goodyear blimp. They move onstage like a rollercoaster thrill—unforgettable. The same way Elvis believed he had the extra energy of his dead twin, the Bar-Kays were given not only their own power, energy, and souls, but also all that of their brethren who had died so tragically.

Their latest album, *Do You See What I See*, was influenced by their work on *Shaft* but was decidedly its own. Fearless, each Bar-Kays album took them in a new direction, rooted in soul but pushing the boundaries, open-minded and thrilling.

For her set, Carla Thomas mixed past and present, reaching all the way back to "Gee Whiz," and also composing a new song "about myself and my God," she explained in her introduction to "I Have a God Who Loves." Standing tall in a maxi-dress of many colors and an outsize Afro, she sang in a voice so strong that the heavens would have no trouble tuning in. David Porter proved himself a performer of the first degree, not that it was in doubt; he'd mastered the stage long before he entered a recording studio. "His intro is superbly conceived," a concert reviewer wrote. "The band comes through with a dramatic and melodical opener, then two lithe young ladies come on stage and dance their way provocatively through a couple of minutes, all the time building up the climax before the man comes on." David arrived—his hip suit suave with a Latin tinge—and delivered a set both intimate and grand.

The day had drawn well into the night before the show's finale. There was disappointment backstage as the set changes and other delays inherent in such a massive event caused the cancellation of several key acts. Luther Ingram, Johnnie Taylor, the Emotions, Mel & Tim, and Little Milton all were ready, willing, and present, but there were not enough minutes in the day. Filming of some was rescheduled. Anticipation was high as MC Rev. Jesse Jackson revved up the crowd for the climax. While he spoke, a station wagon drove onto the field. Isaac Hayes had come from among the people, and he was still of the people; no limousine for him. He mounted the stage wearing his terry cloth hat, which Rev. Jackson made much ado about removing. When his shining pate was revealed, the crowd went wild, a cranial striptease. His set opened with two tracks from the *Shaft* soundtrack, the opening title and then "Soulsville," the latter introduced with, "You can say it's a mild form of protest. You can also say it's an informative tune because it tells about the situation in the ghetto. Now *we* know about it, but we're going to let the outside world know what's happening." He really hit his stride covering Bill Withers's "Ain't No Sunshine," the formula of spoken intro and extended jams hitting all the right grooves. Pianist Sidney Kirk plays a solo that captures Memphis's blues roots at its most polysyllabic and funky; Skip Pitts's guitar goes crazy, somewhere in the ether where the Bar-Kays meet heavy metal.

The day was notable for its lack of problems. Really, there was only one, and it was potentially riotous. Rufus Thomas took the stage at dusk in a pink outfit: cape, hot pants, shirt, and white knee-high go-go boots. He looked the hundred thousand people in the eye and asked them, with a model's reveal of his fashionable garb, "Ain't I'm clean?" The place exploded. His set included "The Funky Chicken," still hot from a year earlier, and as he exhorted the crowd to "get on up," they got on over, climbing the fence and turning the Rams' football field into a raucous dance party. Everyone was highstepping—except Al Bell, who immediately thought of the insurance policy. Randy Stewart and Larry Shaw got Rufus's ear, and at the song's end, the Funkiest Man Alive coaxed and cajoled the partiers back to their seats. "Don't jump the fence, it don't make no sense," Rufus chanted. "All power to folks that go to the stand," he incanted. It was crowd control at its finest, down to the very last straggler. The entire film sequence of Rufus sweet-talking the fans back to their seats is a lesson for police tactical units around the world.

The event—Jesse Jackson called it a public policy statement—was a grand success. "After the Watts riots, any time two black people got together, white America figured there was going to be a problem," says Al. "So it was a joyful, beautiful moment to see 112,000 of our people—from gang members sitting side by side to multiple generations of families—having a great time." For Stax, the West seemed about to be won: "An agreement has been reached between Stax and the Watts Summer Festival that will give us a three-to-five-year relationship with one another," explained a Watts Festival spokesperson. "So we're planning for the future even now."

◆ ◆ ◆

FINISHING THE CONCERT marked the beginning of Al's plans to commercially exploit the concert. However good the vibes on that August day, Al knew the impact would come from the event's documentation. He grasped the ephemeral nature of the present, and the permanence of a recording. Concert reviewers may have griped about the succession of acts and long set changes—but the album is fantastic and the movie is thrilling, and the crowd heard and seen is cheering, participatory, and wildly enthused. Integrated into the movie are some of the missed acts: Little Milton performing his hit "Walking the Backstreets and Crying," set evocatively at the Watts Towers; Johnnie Taylor in a swanky Hollywood club; and Luther Ingram on a soundstage made to look as if he were at the concert. When the first edit was done, director Mel Stuart was dissatisfied, describing the result as "a big newsreel of a concert." Absorbing Larry Shaw's idea of the film as a mirror, he suggested some verité shooting on the streets—

real-life images and commentary. The risk was deemed too high, and instead he found unknown actors who would be comfortable with the camera, and paid them to express their minds in various environments. The people are actors and the subjects are predetermined, but the situations are real, the lines impromptu, and it works splendidly.

Another edit was screened, and Stuart again expressed dissatisfaction. "We need somebody like the chorus in *Henry V*, and we need a comic person to do this, to express the feelings of the people in one person," he remembers telling the team. They sent him to see a young comic in Watts. He says, "I knew within three or four minutes that I was in the presence of a comic genius." Richard Pryor had yet to record his groundbreaking Stax album *That Nigger's Crazy*, but the film would prime his audience. Stuart set Pryor in a club environment, then pitched him words to riff from; his interludes are intimate, personal, universal, and hilarious. It was the perfect glue to hold the weaves together and to keep an edge on the film.

The movie was readied for release, but there was a last and surprising problem: MGM Films blocked the climax of Isaac performing "Theme from *Shaft*" and sued, citing "interference with contractual relationship, unfair competition, and misappropriation of rights." Meaning: Stax had used "Theme from *Shaft*" without asking MGM's permission, and now they were being held accountable. The footage was excised; Hayes and his band were flown to a Hollywood soundstage where the Wattstax look and feel were re-created, and they performed the new finale, "Rollin' Down the Mountainside," a song Isaac anticipated becoming his next hit. The cheat can't be noticed by most viewers, though as a climactic moment, the song pales against "*Shaft*." (In recent years, the original scene has been restored.)

The soundtrack—a double album—followed its own sequencing instead of mimicking the film—which itself was presented differently from the concert. The Staple Singers open with "Oh La De Da," a song that invites listeners to sing and dance along. Their second track encourages black self-esteem by rejecting that most insidious weapon of racism—self-hatred. "I Like the Things About Me (That I Used to Despise)" opens with these lyrics:

> *There was a time I wished my hair was fine*
> *And I do remember when I wished my lips were thin.*
> *Now, I wonder should I be surprised,*
> *I like the things about me that I once despised.*

Pops delivers the message that Isaac, in his chains and with his awards, emblematizes. Al, with these songs at the start of a four-sided journey, immediately establishes a "we," a unified group. "I Like the Things" is a call to self-reflection, an invitation to see how black people in America in 1972 on their march toward freedom are celebrating their culture. Creating this multimedia experience, Al is reformulating Americans as a larger, more inclusive, and certainly better-entertained civilization.

"The subtitle of *Wattstax* is 'The Living Word,'" says Al. "The Old Testament up and through the four gospels, Matthew, Mark, Luke, and John, is called 'the living word' by many people. We were presenting what I considered 'the living word' of African-American culture expressed through songs, our culture and our communication from slavery to the present." A coincident press release ties these efforts to Stax's grassroots intentions, quoting Al: "We work for the community, with the community. We see what is going on and we build to a position of strength to help out. Then we go work with every resource we can muster." The release continued, "For Al Bell, his own song 'I'll Take You There' is more than a lyric, it is a way of life, unwavering belief in the obligation of one man for his fellows—that's the way he has built the Stax Organization, and that is the way he intends to build upon it."

◆◆◆

THE BACKDROP OF the planning and execution of Wattstax was Memphis's reaction to plans for school integration. Busing, the nation's lead plan to bring white and black kids together, was complicated and divisive. Opposition arose not only between the races but also within each neighborhood community. Whites were afraid of their communities being infected by blacks, and the black communities—poorer, more fragile—were afraid of losing their children, their future.

Busing had been discussed as a plan for several years, but as it became more apparent that Memphis courts would force its implementation, the uproar against it increased. Taking a cue from the NAACP, the white group Citizens Against Busing planned a school boycott. The recently elected mayor, Wyeth Chandler, came to the rally and told an overflow audience of two thousand, "It is up to every citizen and certainly every parent whether or not your child is to be bused and whether it is this year or next, to stand together and stand together now." Of the schools' 145,000 students, nearly 53,000 were absent on the first day of the boycott—approximately 80 percent of the whites. The response was so successful that CAB called for the county schools to join the boycott the second day, and they did.

Despite the overwhelming community protest, the federal district judge held to the orders of the Supreme Court above him and, after assigning community panels and outside experts to convene, adopted a plan for busing in Memphis and set its implementation for January 1973, when school resumed after the winter break. In effect, this was the city finally complying with the Supreme Court's ruling two decades earlier in *Brown v. Board of Education*. Outraged whites held a massive rally, a funeral for busing where they actually buried a school bus in a grave; despite organizers' pleas, few stayed to help disinter the bus, as per city ordinance, and the photo in the newspaper of the remaining few struggling with the massive problem by lantern light became widely circulated and an evocative portrait of the struggles and myopia rapidly infecting the city.

This attempt to create equality in education was rife with problems. Busing removed the children from their communities, damaging their broader sense of home by placing them, for the better part of each school day, in a place far from, and quite unlike, home. For the black kids going to the white schools, this new location was often hostile, even dangerous; whatever teachers and school officials might do to create a smooth situation, the print and televised press were making it widely evident that new seeds planted there would find only arid conditions. Black students in white neighborhoods would have to learn survival techniques before they could learn the three R's.

When busing was implemented, tens of thousands of white Memphians did not do unto others as they would do unto themselves, and instead fled to the embrace of a pop-up school system where their children would not have to interact with blacks. Private schools boomed. Two years earlier, in 1971, there'd been 14,738 students in 54 private schools. In 1973, there were more than 33,000 in 90 private schools, and both of those numbers would grow. A new sports league was formed, the Memphis Christian Athletic Association. CAB ran from Baptist church to Baptist church, asking for the donation of Sunday-school buildings for the creation of a new CAB school system called Neighborhood Schools of Memphis. They opened with more than four thousand students. The public school population dropped from over 145,000 in 1971 to 119,000 in 1973, and it would drop further. The Board of Education's state and federal funding diminished with each student. The student racial balance shifted radically, reflecting the white flight, with the percentage of whites dropping from 46 percent to 32 percent, and it would continue further down.

The resistance to integration spread to real estate values, property taxes, and government income. Germantown, the wealthy white suburb to the east of Memphis, increased in population almost 500 percent over the next decade. Bartlett, another suburb with less money though also largely white, grew by 1,000 percent, with the black population of 248 representing less than 1.5 percent of the area's population. Over that same period of time, the black population in Memphis would increase by 27 percent in number, while the white population decreased by 12 percent. The white students who did participate in busing encountered little enmity upon their arrival in black neighborhoods. Much like black social venues that were always more welcoming to "others" than white ones were, black schools had smooth transitions with their new, but small, population of transplants.

◆◆◆

JIM STEWART, HIS fiddle gathering dust on his desk, sits in his Stax office. That fiddle—it's just wood and horsehair, but it's also the possibility of music, man's manipulation of his environment to create crystalline, pleasing beauty. It's within his grasp, but he never touches it. A reporter calls it "a memento to the past," but it is more than that, it's a living memory. One look at it and he's transported to a small smoky club, playing rags and breakdowns behind a steel-guitar player, couples on the dance floor with big smiles. He looks at it and Carla's "Gee Whiz" session comes to life, unlikely circumstances creating everlasting artistry. A glance and Jim escapes the soulless executive office. Running a company—whether it makes music, underwear, appliances, or is a bank like he'd fled from—is fundamentally the same exercise. Making music is different each time, different every day. Jim keeps the fiddle within reach, but he does not touch it, for fear the past, too, might shatter.

The white founder of the label, the co-owner, was absent from the Wattstax frenzy, absent from the film, soundtrack, and concert productions. "Stax being politically active was due to the times that we were in and Al's commitment to the black community," says Jim. "He felt like he should give something back to the community, and that the company would be rewarded, not necessarily financially. We were taking an active role to show that we were trying to do the right thing and we were concerned with civil rights. Wattstax was a project that he put together and I understood that he felt he needed to do that."

"Jim Stewart was still the president, and we all knew he was the president," says Earlie, Al's assistant. "He just let Al Bell do all the operations type of work, and also the creative side of it. I guess he saw how Stax was growing, and saw that Al Bell was the cause of it."

"Wattstax made me feel like I was on my way out," says Duck Dunn. "But I didn't particularly give a damn. Booker T. & the MG's had no clout—wasn't even there anymore, I wasn't invited to go. Let's just put it that way: I wasn't invited to go to Wattstax."

In the big picture, Wattstax proved the perfect component to complete the Stax groundswell. Isaac Hayes and the Staple Singers were pop music phenomena. Johnnie Taylor, Little Milton, Albert King—the whole roster just about—were black culture icons. Their strength in the marketplace had, like a raging forest fire, just jumped the canyon from music to movies. Jim wanted out, Al wanted to get further in. The success of Wattstax on so many levels finally made the company ripe for the sale Al and Jim wanted, for the premium price they wanted. A Stax press release at the time declared, "Bell is a diplomat without portfolio logging more air mileage than the most seasoned pilot."

"Al Bell was bigger than the label," says promo man James Douglass. "I'm saying, How big can this man be? You walk into a radio station, say 'Stax,' they say, 'Tell Al Bell I said hello.' It was a fever across the country."

In the autumn of 1972, the fever would spike.

24. THE SPIRIT OF MEMPHIS
1972–1974

A STRANGENESS SETTLED, like when the air turns green before a tornado. It's not something visible—air has no color—yet it's something that cannot be denied: Look outside and the air is green. Stax entered a period when the company seemed unbound by the laws of physics, freed from the material realm and alighting into the febrile ether. Construction and destruction skipped along together like twins at a park, lushness and desiccation, the concurrent growth and demise of the same organism.

After Wattstax, the Stax Organization was primed for buyers. The concert made Stax a household name, and the event's anticipated spin-offs were full of potential. The company's record sales were soaring—the Staple Singers, Isaac Hayes, Luther Ingram, Mel & Tim. The community efforts continued. Isaac Hayes, who'd formed his own charitable foundation in 1972, funded the Lorraine Village public housing for 250 low-income families in the US Virgin Islands (and hired a guitar player from there in the process). Beyond the philanthropy, there was opportunity: The Virgin Islands were selected because Stax's advertising director Larry Shaw was angling to gain the territory's public relations and tourism account. Why not? Stax's art department had all the facilities of an advertising agency, and it was the kind of diversification that innately appealed to Al. Ike's housing project—an $8 million enterprise that, according to newspaper accounts, he alone funded—put Stax squarely on the territory's map. The advertising deal fell through, but Stax recognized the gift in giving, and after Wattstax, the Isaac Hayes Foundation announced plans, in association with Al Bell and Stax-Volt Records, for "the construction and development of garden apartment communities in various parts of the United States [that] will house more than 20,000 people within the next five years." The cost of the plan was anticipated at $100 million. They were spending money outside of Memphis to build credibility on a national basis.

Who could resist such a package? Stax was a successful company, a culturally proactive generous organization. An appealing blend of art, philanthropy, and business: They created hit records, consistently introduced new stars, were able to create and execute events on a grand scale, and were adroit in a variety of media—they would enhance any team.

In March 1972, Clive Davis had been at the industry convention when Al Bell unveiled his multimedia presentation built from the Stax Sound in Chi-Town promotion. Clive Davis was the president of Columbia Records, which he'd made into the most successful record company in the world. (Columbia Records was a subsidiary of CBS, Inc., the industry giant with dominating television and radio divisions as well. Stax made its deal with Columbia Records, but the terms "Columbia" and "CBS" are used interchangeably by those quoted here.) Columbia Records had grown under Clive Davis to have twice the market share of RCA Records, its nearest competitor. Under Clive's stewardship since 1967, when he embraced rock and roll at the Monterey Pop Festival, his company's record sales rose from $170 million to $340 million. Their regional distribution system was fine-tuned, able to move millions of records in days—from nonexistent to fully packaged and spread across store shelves. Columbia ruled the pop world—Bob Dylan, Simon and Garfunkel, Barbra Streisand, Janis Joplin. Their classical division included Glenn Gould. Country—Johnny Cash, Tammy Wynette, Ray Price. Even jazz—Miles Davis, Duke Ellington, Charles Mingus. They were dominant in every category of music except for one: They could not crack the world of black pop.

In soul, R&B, and blues, even when Columbia had the talent, they didn't have the know-how. Aretha Franklin released nine albums and many singles during her seven years on Columbia, and she barely made waves. The moment she hit Atlantic, she went directly to the top of the charts. The Staple Singers had been on the label and Earth, Wind & Fire still were, and Columbia couldn't get traction. So Clive Davis listened intently to the well-dressed, articulate, commanding Al Bell, and was duly impressed by his visionary take on marketing, his aggressive ideas, and his success.

Recently, Davis had made inroads into the African-American music market. He'd signed a production deal with Philadelphia International Records, the newly formed label run by two hit-making producers, Kenny Gamble and Leon Huff. For much of 1971, he'd been negotiating with marketing whiz Logan Westbrooks, hiring him from his post of national R&B promotion director with Mercury Records in Chicago to join Columbia in New York as director of special markets ("special markets" being a euphemism for African-American music). Westbrooks, born and raised in Memphis (Dino Woodard was a classmate at Booker T. Washington High School), joined Columbia in November of 1971, by which time the label and Philadelphia International had enjoyed initial chart success with the Ebonys and Billy Paul; Westbrooks was charged with securing more and bigger hits. "Clive Davis, along with his VP of marketing Bruce Lundvall—they had the desire to dominate it all," says Logan. "They knew that there was green in the black marketplace."

Stax was making that green through their indie distribution patch- work. No longer with Gulf & Western, no longer with Deutsche Gram- mophon, Stax distribution was like a pieced-together jalopy that its mechanic—Al Bell—could drive like no one else; he had the knowledge of its nuances, knew how to get the most out of it.

Clive Davis sought Al Bell. "I talked to Clive about what I was trying to achieve with Stax," says Al, "and why, even though we had sold a tre- mendous amount of records, we were still having difficulty penetrating the white market. Clive wanted to penetrate deeper into the black market and the black community. CBS had the massive mass-merchandising ma- chine, and we had the diverse black product."

"Bell and the attorneys did the negotiation," says Jim. "I didn't get in- volved. He became chairman of Stax and the only director. He had all the power—which is the way I wanted it. All I wanted was my money. I never even read the agreement."

This contract that Jim didn't read was more beneficial to him than the one he'd not read with Atlantic. Columbia was loaning Stax $6 million for distribution rights; with that, Al would buy out Jim's ownership for $2.5 million up front and use the rest for operating capital. Jim would also be paid $62,500 per month from Stax for the next five years, and a final payment of $1.5 million on January 3, 1978. All told, he would receive more than $7.5 million for his stake. Union Planters, knowing what was good for Stax was good for them, agreed to subordinate its $1.7 million in loans to Stax so the CBS deal could go through. That was no issue; Stax had recently paid off its $2.5 million loan from the Deutsche Grammophon buyback and was among the bank's favored customers. To assure continuity, Jim's sale to Al was kept from the public. Jim agreed to keep his title, president, for five more years. No need to disturb distributors and other associates; their experience would be the same. No need to alarm Memphis's white business circles with news that one of the city's largest corporations was now black-owned. A change within, but from the outside, status quo.

The meeting of the minds, held at the Park Lane Hotel in Manhattan, went further than sharing expertise. Al requested, and Clive conceded, that their new deal be unique in this way: It would only cover distribution. It would not be a production deal like Stax had with Atlantic (or Philadelphia International had with Columbia), where Stax made the recordings, sent in the finished tape, and Atlantic did everything else. This deal would preserve all of the independence that Stax had established—its art department would make the covers, its pressing plant deals would remain in effect, its marketing and promotion men would still beat the pavement to drum up radio interest and to prepare shelf space. The difference would be how the records got to the stores: Stax would deliver all of its Stax, Volt, and Enterprise product to Columbia distribution centers instead of to their collage of indie distributors. The CBS branch distribution system was known for its effectiveness, able to respond to market demand, able to move tens of thousands of records into a region as soon as demand was felt. It was agile enough for Al to feel comfortable relinquishing the control he had over his present system. Through Columbia, Al would get records where he'd been trying for years to get them; in return, the demand for Stax product would lead Columbia to new accounts at the indie mom-and-pop outlets, giving Columbia an expressway to the heart of the African-American community.

Davis knew that access to Stax's small African-American retailers would be worth considerable money in the long term, and he was willing to pay for that by making considerably less money on this deal. Albums then retailed for $5.98; for this deal, Stax was paid $2.26 per sale by Columbia, while Columbia, as distributor, received around fifty cents. "We were responsible for manufacturing, financing all of the marketing of the product, and doing everything," says Al. "All they did was sell, ship, bill, and collect."

For Jim, the money and the relief from responsibilities were exactly what he wanted. "I wanted to be away from the promotion and the business aspect of the record business," says Jim, "to work in the studio on my own time whenever I felt like it." But Jim had become an outsider in his own studio. In early 1972, he'd had had a tiff with the engineers; he wanted to improve a Soul Children song by deleting a section, and the engineers thought what he was removing was exactly what would appeal to the coveted "white market." Levelheaded Jim lost his cool, reportedly stating, "I don't give a good God damn if we never sell another record to a white person." The bit stayed, but Jim didn't; it would be more than two years before he returned to the studio. Jim got his money, and Jim got out. He bought a vacation home in Miami on the intercontinental waterway; out back he kept the *Dream Boat*, a fifty-two-foot vessel with two bedrooms, and a young couple who maintained it. "When I get away from the studio, I want to be totally away from it," he says. "I prefer to get on my boat and head to the Florida Keys. No phones ringing, nobody to bother me." He liked getting way out in the water, where he couldn't see land, where telephones, aggressions, and problems couldn't reach. He kept his company title, but he stayed away from the McLemore studio and rarely showed up at the administrative offices. He was out.

Reaction to the deal at Columbia was less than warm. Bruce Lundvall, Columbia vice president of marketing, remembers Clive's early interest in Stax at a National Association of Recording Merchandisers convention. "I said we'd heard some things that weren't so savory," Lundvall explains. "I'd had a call from a rack jobber [a local distributor] in Washington, DC. He apparently had several very uncomfortable visits from Baylor and company. He said, 'They're criminals. If I was late with my payments, they'd send someone in with a gun and put it on the table.' We were being advised by a very loyal customer that these were not savory people, these enforcers. One would bring a record to a radio station. If the DJ didn't play it, the next guy would come in and he might give you a handshake more hearty than you would like. Breaking a hand, or threatening to kill somebody, is more persuasive than a hundred-dollar bill."

Lundvall and Logan Westbrooks, director of special markets, each remember a quickly assembled morning meeting at Columbia. "Johnny Baylor and his crew were there," Lundvall remembers. "I'd never met them. They were rough-and-tumble characters. We heard loud and clearly that we weren't any good at breaking records in the black marketplace. They said, 'Get the first single out, we'll get it on the radio immediately.' I was curious as to how they would do that. Dino hit the conference room table with his fist, said, 'Get it out now, *smack*, we'll get it on the air.'"

"There was resentment from the very beginning," says Westbrooks. "Every entity that came into CBS, the deal was the marketing and promotion as well as manufacturing and distribution. Here is a deal dumped on your lap that's for distribution only and you're told, 'Make it work.'"

On October 24, 1972, Stax got its $6 million. The proud indie label was in a distribution partnership with the world's largest record company. The coffers were full, ideas myriad. "So," says Al, "we were off to the races."

◆◆◆

NOVEMBER 1972, THE next month. Airline hijacking incidents had been on the rise for four years, and after domestic incidents early in 1972, the Nixon administration instituted airport security regulations. No longer would you be able to arrive late at the airport, kiss the wife good-bye, and dash madly to your gate. Cubans, Palestinians, bank robbers—those with an axe to grid or a gun to shoot were commandeering flights. The new regulations, set for early 1973, stipulated the x-raying of all carry-on baggage and the screening of all passengers. Then, on November 10, a Southern Airways flight originating in Memphis was hijacked out of Birmingham, Alabama, by three men who threatened to fly it into the nuclear reactor in Oak Ridge, Tennessee. It was the lead story in the Memphis morning paper on November 11, and a prominent headline the following day: HIJACKING INCREASES AIRPORT SECURITY. It was the nation's second hijacking within two weeks. An official was quoted as saying, "Now that [hijackers] have been run out of the larger terminals . . . they're going to seek out the smaller ones where there's less protection." A follow-up article was devoted specifically to the increased security of that particular flight: Memphis to Birmingham to Montgomery. Feature articles continued through the month.

On the morning of November 30, the Nixon administration issued an emergency measure requiring all of the nation's airports to provide policemen or armed guards to help intercept potential hijackers. That same morning, Johnny Baylor, apparently not a subscriber to the newspaper, entered the Memphis International Airport. As always, he was dressed impeccably in a suit, every hair in place. Destination: Birmingham. Airline: Southern Airways. He stood in the security line and, as his traveling companion Daryl Williams remembers, when asked to open the briefcase, Baylor obliged, but asked first to be taken aside. He lifted the hinged lid and revealed within neat stacks of green American bills totaling, it was later determined, more than $129,000. "When they saw that amount of money," says Daryl, "they checked the crime report to see if anything had been robbed or stolen. Nothing turned up." A search of Baylor's person revealed a check with his name on it. For half a million dollars. From the Stax Organization.

Johnny Baylor was interrogated by white men with close-cropped hair, skinny black ties, and plaid Bear Bryant Alabama Crimson Tide hats. He was carrying the money, Baylor explained, because the money was his. In Birmingham, he intended to deposit it with his mother. Banks? He didn't believe in them, thank you. "They allowed us to board the plane," Daryl says, "but they also contacted the Feds. Five agents boarded. Johnny spotted the guys, I wasn't aware of it." Johnny sent Daryl off the plane. "He told me to go home, he'd call me. Two got off with me and they tailed me home to see where I lived." The flight departed, Johnny Baylor and his money on board.

The Birmingham arrival, however, did not go smoothly. Like the ship carrying Jonah, the plane was stopped before reaching the gate. Men who shopped at the same haberdashery as the Memphis interrogators crossed the tarmac, intent on retrieving one man. Earlie Biles remembers getting a call from Baylor. "He just said he needed Al," she says, "and the way he told me he needed him, I found Al for him."

Al Bell dismisses the incident, explaining the monies as legitimate industry expenses, an acknowledgment of the always-and-still-shadowy world of industry promotions. (Stax's 1972 tax return would include a $111,000 line item for "miscellaneous," which the company comptroller later termed "cash transactions.") Before that flight, Al explains, "I called Johnny, and said, 'Johnny, I owe you some money.' He said, 'Yeah, you do, because I see this Luther ['If Loving You Is Wrong'] is selling out here. How much money you owe me?' I said, 'Johnny, right at a million dollars.' He said, 'Well, Dick, I better come in there and get my money.'" Baylor had asked for, and received, a royalty rate nearly triple the industry standard. "This was coming into the Christmas season, and he'd kept us alive while we negotiated with Columbia. It's time now for us to announce this Columbia deal, which I knew was gonna be a rough sell, based on how Columbia was perceived at black radio at that time. So I got Ed Pollack, who was the head of Stax's finance, to get fifty thousand dollars cash so we could get gifts for these disk jockeys, so when we announced that we got this deal with Columbia, these disc jockeys aren't pissed off at us. So Johnny had this check that I'd given him, and he had the cash to take on the trip and buy these gifts. In Birmingham, the FBI questioned him, found nothing wrong—'cause there was nothing wrong.

They call the IRS, so the IRS came, took the money." The IRS then filed a federal tax lien with the local registrar against Baylor for nearly $2 million. The attorney Baylor hired—Richard Z. Steinhaus—counted among his clients Kraft Foods and the Motion Picture Association of America. Soon after, Stax altered its books, changing the reason for the half-million-dollar check to Baylor from its original entry, "loan," to "royalty payment." Later it was changed again, to "promotional fee." These changes could be interpreted as Stax searching for a justification for the payments.

"It was *his* money," says Jim about Baylor, "what the hell is wrong with that? They blow up, assume it's drug money. That's bullshit. I happen to know it was his money."

Everything still sounded like hits, but the rhythm was amiss.

◆◆◆

As 1973 DAWNED, despite this recent crisis, the Stax Organization had a sunny outlook. A headline in *Billboard* announced, STAX CLOSES RECORD YEAR. They were sitting atop annual revenue in excess of $11 million (and efforts were under way by Baylor to reclaim his fees from the IRS). The year's end had showered them with an array of national awards, including the naming of Dino Woodard as Promotion Man of the Year and Luther Ingram as Most Promising Male Vocalist by the National Association of Television and Radio Announcers; Al Bell was given the National Pacesetter Award by the US Department of Commerce. In the immediate future, ready to ride wide on the Columbia distribution, were releases by the Staple Singers, Johnnie Taylor, Isaac Hayes, the Dramatics, and other hitmakers, as well as the national rollout of the *Wattstax* film and its double LP soundtrack.

"*Wattstax* is the company's spearhead for the young white market of middle America," Larry Shaw told *Billboard*. "Our radio spots and print ads for the album will refer to the movie, and then all the movie advertising will refer back to the music." Stax dedicated a quarter-million-dollar promotional budget to the project. Two hundred disc jockeys and radio programmers were flown to *Wattstax* film previews in four cities. There were posters and billboards. In February 1973, there were star-studded premieres in both Hollywood and New York. College students in Los Angeles entered an essay contest, competing for a $1,000 prize, writing on "The Black Experience in America." Media mogul Merv Griffin, with whom Stax had partnered on a TV taping at Caesar's Palace the previous December, devoted a whole episode of his TV show to Stax artists and *Wattstax*. "We did a promotional tour with that film," says Carla Thomas. "We went to different cities all over the country and up in Canada." Trailers hailed it as "A Soulful Expression of the Black Experience." The film's R rating for its language was utilized for promotion by Stax: "Rated R for 'Real.'"

The documentary had been a bold gamble, and it became a genius move. It promoted Stax generally, and branded it with community involvement particularly; it was good entertainment and good business. Coincident with the film's release, fifty stations broadcast a four-hour edited version of the concert. (In March, more being better, a six-hour version of the concert was made available.) Each major city's premiere benefited a local African–American charity, and Stax stars were present at most. "Black-oriented films have never had the lavish, old-Hollywood premiere before," Larry Shaw said. "And we feel it's important that *Wattstax* be presented with that kind of fanfare."

The film had a European premiere at the Cannes Film Festival, May 10, 1973, and earned rave reviews. European bookings commenced, help-

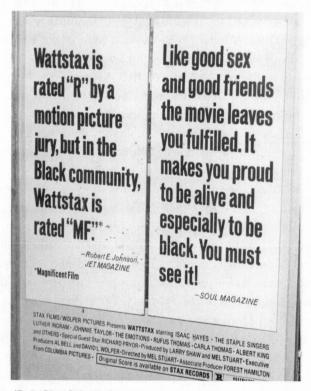

(Earlie Biles Collection)

ing the movie quickly earn nearly a million and a half dollars—a tidy profit in that. Larry Nix recounts a celebratory company picnic on rural land that Al owned: "They flew in Maine lobster for everybody."

Their community efforts continued unbounded. Isaac and the other artists performed numerous benefits on local, regional, and national levels. The infusion of young employees bursting with strident enthusiasm deepened the feeling of black pride that pulsed through the environment. "Whenever there was a black cause, Stax rose to the occasion," says Bar-Kays drummer Willie Hall. "Al Bell, Isaac Hayes—they made sure of that. Stax wasn't militant, but it was all black. Even though there was fortune being made at Stax, we were still having problems as a people. Whether it was homeless children, or something wrong happened to one black child across town, Stax always rose to the occasion."

"People read about what Al was doing at Stax and started coming in asking for support," says Earlie, Al's gatekeeper. "You name it, they came to Stax and they got monetary support." Roving solicitors left with checks for the Angela Davis Defense Fund, for local churches, for national political efforts.

As the community effort grew, Jim Stewart (from the sidelines) saw it interfering with the company's core mission. "My big problem with Bell was he was too much involved in politics and not enough in the record business," says Jim. "He was thinking it would add value to the company. Motown—they contribute, but you never hear of them personally getting involved in those kinds of things. They take away your attention from selling records."

"He never said no to anyone," says Earlie. "And that was my problem with him sometimes. 'How can we support everything that comes through the door?' And he would say, 'Well, this is a good cause, and this is.' He was a humanitarian, he thought it was great to be able to give back."

"Al was a sucker for any promoter that walked in his office," Jim continues. "Al didn't differentiate between color—anybody could hustle him. Motown survived because they recognized that the product keeps the company going, not their wheeling and dealing on the side. There was too much wheeling and dealing and not enough concentration on cutting records. Bell could draw, like flies to honey, the hustlers out there. They flocked to him."

"We were major contributors to the NAACP, the Urban League, to PUSH," lists Al, "the United Negro College Fund—the black colleges individually as well as the College Fund. We probably had 200 to 250 lifetime memberships in the NAACP. We were all over this country doing whatever was required for black people."

◆◆◆

REMEMBER WHEN YOU were a kid on a bike atop a really great hill, and you threw yourself into it, wide-eyed with pleasure and wonder as everything's whizzing by? Then there's a moment you can't pinpoint except in the past tense, that instant when control is lost, when you realize that your feet aren't on the pedals anymore, and you have no braking power. You can jump or ride it out, but either way you hope you don't get your teeth knocked out. One such moment came with the postman in February 1973: official correspondence from the Internal Revenue Service. The letter advised that the IRS, joined by their friends at the US Attorney's Office, were initiating an investigation of the Stax Organization. You look at the pedals—is there any way to regain control?

Another came in early April 1973, though this shock initially seemed to be a path toward safety. Stax was living large with its $6 million bride. Clive and Al were making it work. *Wattstax: The Living Word*—not a 45-RPM single, not a simple album, but a double album with all those increased profits—sold five hundred thousand copies within weeks of its release. A follow-up double album was in the works. Production and distribution are in the throes of romance. Now Stax's old-time used-to-be, Union Planters National Bank, wanted some loving too. The previous month, UP received Stax's payoff for a $1.75 million loan it had taken from the bank half a year earlier. Business as usual, UP issued Stax a new line of credit, a cool 1973 three million bucks. This time, because the record company was encumbered by its six million dollar Columbia obligation, Union Planters extended the money to the East/Memphis publishing company, Stax's cash cow. On the tenth of April, East/Memphis extended its hand and took half of that line of credit at once, a million and a half. Despite the scrutiny they were under, Stax wrote a check for one million dollars on that same day to Johnny Baylor—despite the scrutiny he was under. *Bump.* Two more checks were written to Baylor over the coming summer of '73; all told, beginning with the money found at the airport, he received more than $2.7 million over nine months.

Two million dollars doesn't just walk out of the room. It swaggers. "It's Johnny's," Al declares. "He could take it because it was his." However, in comparison, the annual salary for Al was $90,000, with the next highest being Ed Pollack, at less than half that. Other artists were selling in quantities similar to Luther Ingram, and their payments were not as high. Stax's finance officer later explained to investigators that Baylor was paid royalties on the basis of gross number of records shipped to distributors, not net number sold, and at an extraordinary royalty rate. "It was ridiculous," Jim says. "I told Bell, 'You can't afford to pay that.'"

Whizzz goes Johnnie Taylor as he releases "I Believe in You (You Believe in Me)" in May, going to the top of the R&B charts and to number eleven on the pop charts, selling in five easy months five hundred thousand copies to earn a gold record. *Whizzz* go the Staple Singers, following their first chart hit of the year with their second before the year's half done. The Soul Children, Veda Brown, and Stax stalwart William Bell all released charting records before the second half of the year. *Whoosh* is the sound of three loans totaling nearly $900,000, dating back less than eighteen months, being paid off by Stax to Union Planters.

But then there's the *crash* of the wheel coming off. On May 29, 1973, Clive Davis at Columbia Records, Al Bell's visionary partner, was escorted to the building's front door and unceremoniously dumped on the street. Fired. And then sued—for misuse of nearly $100,000 from company funds. The problem arose when Clive's director of artist relations, David Wynshaw, fell in with unsavory characters (mob associates) to perpetrate unsavory acts (heroin distribution); investigating Wynshaw's work with Clive, CBS learned it had unwittingly paid Clive's personal expenses: $54,000 to redecorate his Manhattan apartment, $20,000 for his son's bar mitzvah, and $13,000 to rent a summer house in Beverly Hills. On the stand, Clive's underling sang, revealing the company's secret annual budget of a quarter million dollars cash for radio "promotion," and he connected it directly to Stax and to Philadelphia International Records, Columbia's two African-American label partners. The IRS tore into Columbia, and the US Attorney's Office in Newark, New Jersey, instigated its national Project Sound investigation of payola, focusing on Philadelphia, Brooklyn, Los Angeles, and Memphis, seeking evidence of both financial payoffs and also gifts of cocaine and other drugs. (In addition to the US Attorney's Office, the Wynshaw case triggered two other national investigations: the Newark federal grand jury's payola probe and the Department of Justice's Newark Strike Force's organized crime study.)

Logan Westbrooks was watching this unraveling from the inside of Columbia. "Unfortunately for Al Bell and for Stax Records, the way the deal was cut, it was almost a personal thing between Al Bell and Clive Davis," Westbrooks explains. "They both had a dream. And they bought into each other's dream, and they knew exactly how they could make it work. But when Clive Davis was taken out of the picture, no one else at CBS had that vision of that dream. So consequently, Al Bell was just out there—drifting."

"It was not a deal that was enormously profitable for Columbia," says Al. "They made pennies and we were making dollars. I'm sure that was not too palatable from a corporate standpoint."

"For Columbia," says Westbrooks, "it's just a matter of business. The Stax deal became the responsibility of an executive named Jim Tyrell, vice president of sales. And Jim was strictly by the book. Black or white didn't make any difference, whatever the rule says, this is what Jim's going to do. [Jim Tyrell was African-American.] And that's the way he played it."

Al and Clive had never worked out the nuts and bolts. "When the new guys came in," says Al, "they looked and said, 'What is this?'"

A fundamental disagreement between the two corporations involved the deep pool of money used for co-op advertising. Co-op funds are a standard practice in advertising; retailers advertise particular brands and then recoup some or all of those costs from the brand. Columbia, for example, would underwrite a record chain's newspaper ads that featured Columbia product. Al understood that a hefty sum was available from Columbia's pool for the promotion of Stax product, and since Stax was overseeing its own marketing, he wanted that Columbia co-op money to administer. Jim Tyrell, on the other hand, had no intention of draining that money pool to Stax, and because he found the Stax deal too unusual, he set about bringing the relationship in line with the corporation's standard practice. The partners, thus, were at odds.

Further complicating the relationship was the existing stock in stores. Stax was handing over to Columbia a mom-and-pop market fully stocked, and expecting Columbia to open up the rack jobbers' market. But situating the new product line into its existing routine was going to take Columbia some time, under even the best of circumstances; and these circumstances were adverse. Stax, undeterred, continued manufacturing.

Three weeks after Clive Davis was fired, Memphis newspapers began reporting on various federal probes, criminal and civil, aimed at Stax. In an article entitled "Stax Probe Began After Cash Seized," the evening newspaper disclosed that Johnny Baylor "maintains an eighth-floor suite at the Holiday Inn-Central at 1837 Union, [and] also is said to occupy when in New York, a plush Stax apartment at 45 E. 89th St. [a block from Central Park, between Madison and Park Avenues]. Further, records in the Shelby County Register's Office show that on May 7 [1973] Stax transferred the deed to a $26,000 house at 872 W. Shelby Drive to [Dino] Woodard. The deed [was] signed by Alvertis Isbell (Al Bell), executive vice president of Stax." The flow of money was unusual, and there were no contracts that justified it. "It's just like the tip of the iceberg right now," said one attorney, "and it seems the iceberg is on the rise."

The waters were certainly troubled. Two years had passed since the Jaspan firm's undercover investigation that resulted in the firing of two Stax employees for piracy, Roussell and Kole. Now a judge was asking, Why would Stax settle such a large claim for ten cents on the dollar? Then another iceberg, a headline reading: STAX IS ACCUSED OF COVERING UP IN PAYOLA CASE. Why would seven Stax executives claim Fifth Amendment privileges when questioned by the IRS? The grand jury subpoena requested an explanation of all "the major activities of Stax, including the percentage of profit derived from each such activity, the structure of the company . . . and all performers, promoters or producers under contract to or presently in contract negotiations with the company." The Feds—both judge and grand jury—were bearing down.

◆◆◆

ICEBERGS NOTWITHSTANDING, THE *Titanic* of Stax, Isaac Hayes, continued on his course. In the spring he released *another* double LP (his third in a row), this one, *Live at the Sahara Tahoe*, quickly earning gold status for a million dollars in sales. It was support for Jim's notion: Sell what you know. Isaac had recorded away from Stax, out of Johnny Baylor's way, so it was reassuring when he returned to the Stax studio that summer. (He consented to booking his time around another Memphis artist who'd rented the facility, Elvis Presley.)

A new style of music was developing, creeping into the public's consciousness as it spread from New York dance clubs: disco. The music employed new technologies—early drum machines and synthesizers—but it was also shaped by Isaac's catalog, by his stretched-out grooves and repeated rhythms. In late 1973, Isaac released *Joy*, a single album of all original material that caught a new groove, blending some of the aggressive sounds of his movie work with his rich and mellow album sound. The songs still ran long—five on the album instead of ten, none shorter than six minutes, one longer than sixteen—and he continued to favor big productions with strings and intense arrangements. But he'd noticeably shifted his feel, riding atop the beat this time, a dance edge instead of all bedroom, all the time. The title track nicely loses itself to the rhythm, a dance trance, auguring the new style. In a matter of weeks, *Joy* was certified

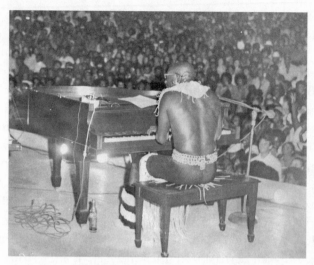

Isaac Hayes in performance. (University of Memphis Libraries/
Special Collections)

gold. Isaac was next coproducing, starring in, and scoring a new movie, and had made sure its soundtrack would be released on Stax. He was featured on the cover of *Ebony* in October 1973:

> Today he owns a Mercedes, two Jaguars, three chauffeur-driven limousines and a $26,000 sea blue, gold-plated Cadillac Eldorado he bought to put "pimpmobiles" out of business. Today he owns a townhouse in Washington D.C., a bungalow in Memphis, and a sprawling hilltop mansion in Los Angeles. "The money, the cars, all of it is just fringe, but Isaac Hayes is roots," he told *Ebony*. Under the auspices of Hot Buttered Soul, Ltd., he has hired more than 60 people—counting his agent, accountants, lawyers, business advisor, public relations personnel, bodyguards, gym and health coach, dancers, musicians, background singers, secretaries, valet, stage technicians and chauffeurs. "It takes a lot of patience to make yourself sit down and listen to some guy talk a lot of dull figures that are foreign to you. Absolute Greek. But you gotta keep in mind that it means economic power and a sound stable future. And it means that you're a link in that big chain so necessary for black progress and unity in this country. In short, it means taking care of your own."

Like Stax, Isaac carried a heavy payroll and many obligations. But if his success was supporting Stax, Stax's success could support him. Their relationship was symbiotic. The sales for *Joy* were good for everyone. He was the leading artist in a very strong roster. Chart hits kept coming from the Emotions, the Temprees, the Dramatics, the Soul Children; from long-time label artists Eddie Floyd, William Bell, Johnnie Taylor, the Staple Singers, and Albert King; and from newer signings Little Milton and Inez Foxx. There was additional growth in light of the Columbia deal. STAX EXPANDS WITH POP, C&W, GOSPEL RECORDS, announced a January 1974 newspaper story that boasted of not only new talent but also new staff to run the new pop-oriented departments. At 1973's end, Stax was ranked number five among black-owned and black-managed businesses, with sales estimated at $20 million. More artists! More employees! More ways to win!

As Al had envisioned, recordings were just a portion of the new Stax Organization's activities. STAX ANNOUNCES PLANS TO PRODUCE 4 MOVIES declared a February 1974 headline. The following month, news came that they were about to become the first black-owned company to own a pro sports franchise, with the intended purchase of Memphis's ABA basketball team.

Stax bought a church and its adjoining school facility just off Poplar Avenue, the city's main thoroughfare, as a new home for its corporate headquarters. "Banks were basically bricks-and-mortar oriented," Al explains. "They didn't understand the value of the masters and understood a little about the publishing. My charge as a businessperson was to start building a balance sheet that showed bricks and mortar." Union Planters funded the purchase; though they recognized there was not presently collateral, it was agreed that the upcoming renewal of Stax's foreign distribution deal with Polydor would produce more than enough money to accommodate the payoff.

"We got this church, and the school building with it," says Deanie Parker. "And tried to departmentalize. We really were bursting at the seams. I hadn't moved my publicity department to the Avalon offices, but I moved to the church—not wanting to go, but understanding that it was essential for us to become the Stax Organization."

Finally, in April 1974, Stax made good on the implied promise of the *Wattstax* movie, releasing Richard Pryor's first nationally available album, *That Nigger's Crazy*. The movie had primed audiences for this brash comic's talent, and the album lived up to the promise. The title, however, scared Columbia too much to touch it; Al created the Partee label and distributed it through the independent ties Stax had maintained with Respect, Gospel Truth, and other labels not under the Columbia deal. The reception was immediate, and warm, and Stax watched its new star, another album seller, on the rise.

◆ ◆ ◆

WITH ALL THIS activity, the McLemore studio, though just a few miles away, was sometimes a distant thought. And so perhaps it's not surprising how little reaction there was to Packy Axton's death in January 1974, a death foretold by the creases across his puffy face, by an old man's phlegmy laugh earned—hard-earned—well before its time. Packy was dead of cirrhosis at just thirty-two. Who on McLemore was left to mourn? His mom had left five years back, his uncle had sold out, his peers had dispersed.

"They used to call Packy 'the Spirit of Memphis,'" says Johnny Keyes, and he laughs with the memory. "Some would say, 'That name's already taken.' But no, *this*—Packy—*is* the spirit of Memphis."

On September 20, 1973, a few months before Packy died and a few months after her five-year ban from recording concluded, Estelle established Fretone Records (named for her children's last names, FREderick, and AxTON, the final "E" making it more musical). Estelle had money, and she says, "I had to prove to myself that I had sense enough to produce a hit record, to prove that a woman could do it too." She also needed to occupy Packy; he'd returned to Memphis from several years in California. Estelle bought a small house in an African-American neighborhood, established a studio in the basement, and put offices on the main floor. An important factor in the location was its proximity to her husband's favorite watering hole. After a quarter century in their one-thousand-square-foot house, she'd convinced Everett to move to the apartment complex she'd bought with her Stax money. It was several miles due north, but he still drank from his favorite bar stool at Berretta's Famous BBQ. "Mother would drop him off at Berretta's in the morning, go to Fretone and work all day, then go home around three fifteen and get him," says Doris. "By then he'd had enough. One beer every thirty minutes. If Mother couldn't pick him up, I would, and I'd send my daughter Amy in. 'Hey Granddad,' she'd say softly. He was extremely mellow but always on his feet."

"Packy used to say, 'Everett's going to die first,'" says Johnny, "'and by the time I get sick, medical science will fix it so I can have a new stomach.'"

Estelle's Fretone was another homegrown affair. She made Packy chief engineer, another opportunity for him to prove the mettle she knew he had. Johnny Keyes was staff writer, engineer, and promotions man. Daughter Doris ran the front office. "We'd stay at Fretone all night," says

Johnny. "It was ideal. I had the lyrics and some of the melody and he'd play his guitar. We'd put it together and he'd write the changes out. He always had a Tupperware cup. I'd say, 'Packy, why are you drinking that rotgut?' 'Hey, man, don't talk about my whiskey.'"

"Mother was off and running again," says Doris. "She spent all her money chasing that hit. I was trying to keep order in that place that had no order. It was an insane den of iniquity. Dark rooms, dirty old place, my kids running around—Amy was four or five, Adam [Doris's son], and Chuck [Packy's child that Estelle had been raising]. Amy's first memories of pot were over there. That's when I told Mother I was going back to being a wife and mother." The time at Fretone allowed Doris to relate to Packy as an adult. Yet "I never could get Packy to open up to me until the day before he died. He said, 'I was scared to go to the doctor, don't let that happen to you.' And he said, 'I want another chance.' But they couldn't get him well."

"Packy was sicker than he let on," says Johnny Keyes. "His body was slender, but his stomach grew, and we used to tease him about that. One particular night, I was in an office, writing, and Packy knocked, said, 'I'm going home, I don't feel well.' Next thing we know, he was at the hospital. His inside was tearing. It was his liver. I gave blood and I'd go see him, but he didn't have much to say."

Packy's condition startled his friends, though it was not unexpected. "You went to school with this guy since the fifth grade and you watch him turn into an old man in just a few years," says Don Nix. "I mean, thirty-two years old! It's tough to think about, but it was tough to watch. He was so full of life as a teenager, and he just became a shell. His mama got this doctor down from New York, got Packy through Christmas."

"Then one day I went up there, and he was his old self," says Johnny Keyes. "He said, 'I'll tell you what.' He said, 'I'm not drinking anymore. That's it.' And he said, 'You can have my Volkswagen Beetle while I'm in here.' He said Jim was by, and they had a good talk, made up and everything. He said, 'I guess I'll be getting out of here pretty soon.' His complexion was better, not blotched like it was before. I said, 'You had me worried there, boy.' And the next night, that was it, he was gone."

Packy died Sunday evening, January 20. The funeral was small, the day unseasonably warm. Johnny asked the funeral caravan to drive down McLemore Avenue, but a more direct route was taken. "He died, and everything changed," says Johnny. "That was her heart. That was Miz Axton's heart. They used to argue—my goodness they used to argue—so you know they loved each other. Yeah, that was her heart."

Packy had brought the Mar-Keys to the studio. Steve, Duck, Don, Wayne, and so many others would not have been exposed to the opportunity that shaped their lives, to their work in shaping America's soundtrack, had it not been for Packy. He'd linked them to his mother, to his uncle, and he'd set off a chain of reactions that was continuing long after his domino had fallen. In some ways, the world was only just catching up to Packy. The differences between the races had never bothered him, except for the close-minded attitude of his fellow Caucasians. Society was working to be more like Packy—in some ways. Despite all the connections he'd brought, he could never bridge the distance between his mother and his uncle. He was always the stick in his uncle's craw, the embodiment of the tension between the siblings. Now Packy's heart was stilled.

But on McLemore Avenue, in Stax's corporate offices in the former church, at the Columbia Records offices in distant Manhattan, the heart of Stax was pumping madly.

25. A VEXATION OF THE SPIRIT
1973–1974

UNION PLANTERS NATIONAL Bank was not in the music business, but it had become one of Stax's closest associates. "We had a great relationship with Union Planters," says Al Bell. "Matter of fact, we would keep a million dollars on deposit in a checking account just to provide additional funds for the bank instead of putting it in a certificate of deposit. It was that kind of working relationship."

The cash on hand must have been very helpful, assuming that the bank noticed. But they were a disorganized, improperly administrated institution. "Union Planters got very, very sloppy in its lending controls at the high, wide, and handsome age of the early seventies," says Wynn Smith, an attorney retained by the bank. Their problems extended from several areas, all of which might have been prevented by better oversight within the bank. In 1971, the bank expanded heavily into real estate loans, though it did little preparation or research, nor did it monitor how its new clients actually disbursed its funds. Further, says attorney Smith, "Union Planters had a project in the early seventies called 'Your Signature Is Your Collateral,' and they started going crazy making installment loans on automobiles. It was so easy to get a loan that people were coming from all over the country to buy very expensive Cadillacs, and then taking off with the Cadillacs and not paying the installment loans."

The inherent problems in the new ventures came to light when, in late 1973, interest rates began to rise nationally. At the same time, inflation was rising and so was unemployment, creating an economic recession that plagued the country until well into 1975. According to *The Turnaround*, a book written about the Union Planters fiasco (and its redemption), "The liability ledger of the bank was organized in such a manner that it was impossible to determine whether one loan was related to another. No employee of Union Planters knew what the bank's total exposure was." This description, the bank would soon find out, could also apply to Stax—not just regarding loans, but all bookkeeping.

The bank's situation got so far out of control that federal authorities took notice. UP's earnings dropped by half in the first nine months of 1973, with losses in the third quarter exceeding half a million dollars. By the end of 1973, UP's investment division was under investigation by the Securities and Exchange Commission. The threatening sound of sabers rattling in Washington was more compelling than Stax's nearby funk, and the bank focused on making a plan to save itself. Despite the frequent payoffs, Stax still owed UP close to $10 million, including an overdraft of nearly $1.7 million. Union Planters needed new collateral.

The record company was deep in hock, joined recently by the publishing company. There was no mistaking that the debts were high. But Stax's outlook was promising. The European distribution deal would soon be up for renewal, and Stax intended to hike its license fee. Isaac's *Two Tough Guys* soundtrack was imminent, sure to be a smash like all his albums were, maybe even bigger than *Shaft*, since he also starred in this movie. On its heels would be Isaac's soundtrack to the blaxploitation film *Truck Turner*. In the past five years, Isaac had released five albums that each did more than $2 million worth of business. The patterns indicated another welcome influx of money.

Jim contemplated the company's position from his fifty-six acres. It was very quiet there. He'd come from the country, and the dense trees on his estate reminded him of his childhood in Middleton. But the house did not. He could have fit perhaps every house from his hometown into the vast complex that was now the Stewart home. The old Capitol Theater would fit inside, and all the McLemore block he'd worked so hard to purchase. Jim, his wife, their three kids—it was like their own private country club. And it was quiet.

Jim would turn forty-three in a few months. He'd been mostly away from Stax the past year and a quarter. The pressures had greatly diminished, the constant thrumming of the business in his ears and eyes and brain had finally quelled. He'd missed much of his children's childhoods, and soon they'd be off on their own. This opulently feathered nest he'd finally built was soon to be empty. And quiet.

Music had made him independently wealthy. He'd collected, finally, on the years of long hours and hard work. He'd enriched Atlantic, he'd enriched Gulf & Western and Deutsche Grammophon. He'd stayed three more years after his sister left, and the company had mushroomed in size and success. His break with Stax came when they were thriving, and it made both them and him wealthy. Al wanted total control of the total record company, and he'd gotten it, and he'd received a swollen bank account courtesy of Columbia Records, who'd also swelled Jim's account. Whatever shape the company was now in, Jim was not responsible for it. He did not need to help.

Since retiring, when not in Florida, Jim mostly spent his days at home. He didn't use the tennis court much. The big pool's high diving board rarely rattled. Jim didn't often swim in any of the four pools. It was nice when the kids did, but even that was infrequent. He'd thrown big parties at the house, but that period had passed; big parties never really excited him. Living the dream was different from yearning for it. He could look at his many amenities on his many acres and say he had it all. Or he could consider how little these amenities meant to him and, soaking in everything around him, he could say he'd lost it all. Where was the challenge? Where was the grit that made the pearl?

Jim spent his money and time, both too plentiful, on jigsaw puzzles. Since leaving Stax, he was often at the family's expansive dining room table, alone. He'd open a thousand-piece jigsaw-puzzle box, turn the pieces faceup, separate the border pieces. Step by step, he'd assemble an image—a landscape, perhaps, pastoral and distant that he'd never visit. Completing it, he'd throw the pieces back into the box and open a new one. He was a builder, a producer, and what the hell was he supposed to produce by himself as he sat in the quiet and looked at the long, hushed second half of his life? Forty-three wasn't old. He had energy, he had ideas, vitality. And money.

In February 1974, unable to let go of the one great change he'd wrought upon the city and world, Jim pledged more than everything he had to the bank. He gave Union Planters a personal guaranty against the company's loans, putting up all he held, including the millions he'd recently collected, and all he was to receive. That is, if ever there were a problem, the bank would know that Jim's personal wealth was available to make up any financial insufficiency. (Though it's odd that the payments to cover the faltering company would come from the faltering company, Jim already held substantial assets. If Stax paid him no more money, he'd still be wealthy.) Jim was a family man, and one of his children was Stax. And even the child who grows up to spurn you, the baby you shaped and raised who morphs into something you don't like—you are forever attached. If that child needs you, you give your all for that child.

"I reacted with my heart instead of my head," he told writer Rob Bowman. "It was an emotional [decision], not a prudent, sensible one." After making the pledge, Jim promptly put nearly half a million dollars of his personal money into the company to help cover the operating costs. He was affirming his belief in the company's mission: with his heart, his soul, his wallet, and his children's future.

It was an epic move. Jim was a quiet man, conservative, and yet he'd been the one to alter the course of history, to create in a racist and stratified society a space both inclusive and collaborative. Like Superman, Jim turned society's tracks. A white country music fiddle player making his name in African-American soul music? If he'd asked anyone, they'd have said it was a stupid idea, it can't be done. If he'd reacted with his head, he'd have backed away. Stax grew despite logic and circumstances. Stax was not a "prudent, sensible" decision.

He placed all his chips on a single bet. He held nothing behind, no failsafe, no extra feathers, no spare million bucks. Jim could help, and he did.

The following month, March, Stax took another sucker punch from Columbia. Due to the high number of records that Stax had delivered to Columbia, and with no discernable market need for more product, Columbia announced it would begin withholding 40 percent of what it owed Stax to help cover the costs of returned product. Returns? The howl in Memphis could be heard in New York: Get the records to market! There won't be returns, and there will be more money for everybody, if you'll just do the one thing you are supposed to be good at: Get—the—product—on—the—shelves.

Though their relationship was really about one thing—distribution— Stax and Columbia could never get on the same page. "From the beginning of the argument over who would control the branch distributors, record sales started dropping." Jim says. They couldn't agree on the basics of getting records to stores. "So many hours and days were spent trying to straighten these matters out, trying to get the philosophy and the people working together in concert." Jim sighs. "It could never be accomplished. When the principals are involved in something extraneous of producing and marketing and promoting and selling records, which is your business, the inevitable occurs. Records sales start dropping. I'm not talking about a month or two months. This became continuous and it got worse and worse and a dichotomy was struck between the personalities involved—between our people and CBS's people. The problems became monumental—and then the financial problems resulted from that."

The tough times were becoming increasingly evident to Stax's staff. Polydor did not renew its European distribution, and though new deals were made, they were smaller. "There were some speeches that Al gave that were designed to keep the situation together," says Deanie Parker. "None of us was oblivious to what was happening with CBS, and we knew Union Planters was beginning to stink. We could feel it. Several of us had a travel card—could go to an airport and charge a ticket to anywhere we wanted to go. When we got a memo saying to discontinue using them, you knew."

In a late 1973 speech, Al was already acknowledging the company's problems, but attributing their causes to outside sources: "The energy crisis is severely affecting industries which depend upon petroleum and its by-products for its operation . . . Unless the Stax Family can pull together to achieve these [cost-saving] objectives, management will be forced to consider extreme measures, resulting in employee layoffs, possible reductions in salaries, or both . . . Although on occasions in the past the company has given Christmas bonuses during the holiday season, we are unable to do so this year . . ."

The energy crisis *was* raging, and while the resulting higher costs contributed to the problem, including a hike in prices of the raw materials from which records are made, not to mention the cost of shipping them, the Stax crisis also involved a different kind of energy. Al's speech was thirty-one pages long, and it ground over corporate structure and attitude. "Our people didn't have the background or experience in training and management and departmentalization," says Deanie, "but there were some on the staff who'd have held up their copy of that speech and exclaimed, 'Ah, yes! *This* will solve the problem!'" Deanie shakes her head. "Those speeches went on and on and on. It was like a vexation of the spirit."

The cash flow that Stax had so enjoyed began to evaporate while expenses rose. "It just grew too fast," says Earlie Biles, "and we didn't have enough sales to support all the people. We were hiring executives right and left, attorneys, CPAs, marketing and advertising execs." The company's annual payroll rose from $900,000 at the end of 1972 to over $1.4 million in mid-1973.

Stax never stopped producing good music; the releases just became harder for buyers to find. Disco was taking dance music in a new direction, further from the church influence. But Stax's soul music still found an audience. The Staple Singers continued to work with Al Bell, having a solid hit at the start of 1974 with "Touch a Hand, Make a Friend," top-five R&B and nearly top-twenty pop; not as gritty as their previous hits, nor as their next one, "City in the Sky," which went to number-four R&B. They would have four more releases on Stax, staying on the company roster to the end. The Dramatics hit the soul charts, as did William Bell, Eddie Floyd, Veda Brown, the Emotions, and Inez Foxx. Albert King's "Crosscut Saw," a staple of blues bands worldwide, has enjoyed a long life since its October 1974 release. Johnnie Taylor hit number thirteen and broke the Hot 100 with "I've Been Born Again." He almost broke the R&B top twenty that fall with "It's September," and he became Stax's last charting artist with "Try Me Tonight." His final single, "Keep on Loving Me" could have been a pop hit, but it got no real distribution.

The Bar-Kays continued to evolve and grow. Though heavily influenced by Isaac, while he went deeper into the lava lamp, the Bar-Kays moved toward the strobe light. They reworked classic soul sounds with "You're Still My Brother," a tune rife with social message. "It Ain't Easy" is as spare as "Brother" is full, a vocal atop a keyboard riff, and sometimes little more than hand clapping. "Coldblooded," largely instrumental, sounds like they're fishing for a movie soundtrack. The appropriately titled "Holy Ghost" was their last release on Stax and Stax's very last single (November 1975, though it may not have actually reached stores). It's a bridge to the future, proof positive that despite all the business distractions in which the office was mired, good music was still being made.

Quality, however, was giving way to quantity. Between the start of 1973 and the end of 1974's first quarter, Stax placed nine singles in the R&B top ten, and one in the pop top ten. The label released, however, seventy-four singles. The output was multiplying the expenses, and the hits were diminishing. "We had less than a hundred, and all of a sudden we had two hundred on the payroll," says Jim, who was not the kind of boss to return and fire whole departments, even though his wealth was at stake. "Apartments in New York, houses in LA, a quarter-of-a-million-dollar Billy Eckstine contract. Bell needed that conservative bastard saying, 'You can't do these ridiculous deals.' It's high rolling." Jim also believes the music suffered, refusing to blame the lack of sales on Columbia. "We had seventeen promotion men ourselves. We'd been promoting records before and selling them, so why couldn't these same seventeen men go out and make hit records? Simply because we didn't have hit records." Being under federal scrutiny—for taxes, for payola—didn't help either.

Columbia's lack of distribution was not, however, a figment of Stax's imagination. Stax's distributor in Memphis, Hot Line Records, was unable to get Stax product "almost from the day the Columbia deal began," remembers one prominent employee. "We couldn't buy the records to distribute them. It was clear Columbia was trying to put Stax out of business."

"You'd hear the horror stories from the promotions guys about the inability to get Stax product into the marketplace," says Deanie, "and we'd see our records sliding from the charts." Stax addressed the problem by expanding its promotion team, ramping up for a batch of albums geared toward the white market. Joe Mulherin, the trumpet-playing publicist, was on the road with Larry Raspberry and the Highsteppers, a white rock and roll group signed to Enterprise. They had a raucous, traveling-minstrel vibe (à la Joe Cocker's *Mad Dogs & Englishmen*) that included Don Nix (who was also coheadlining the tour), British blues sensation John Mayall, vocalist Claudia Lennear (who'd performed with the Rolling Stones), and drummer Tarp Tarrant (from Jerry Lee Lewis's band, then a free man between felonies). The band had played both *American Bandstand* and *Don Kirshner's Rock Concert*. They were subjects of a forthcoming documentary, *Jive Assp*. Many of their shows were sold-out and simulcast on radio. Larry Raspberry and the Highsteppers were hot. But touring the West Coast in the spring of 1974, they couldn't find their record in stores. "Fans were complaining they couldn't get the recently released *Highstepping and Fancy Dancing*," says Mulherin. "Members of the band canvassed record stores and couldn't find a single copy. People loved that band but couldn't turn their friends on to the album. The shipping had simply stopped." The band did not take the matter lying down. "Our manager addressed this with the Columbia people and was told he was full of shit." Columbia was so powerful that empirical facts could be dismissed.

As the distribution giant unilaterally revamped the deal, Johnny Baylor stepped from his own morass to help. If Columbia's Jim Tyrell was in charge of getting records into the stores—as he indeed was—then surely he'd recognize a demand from Johnny Baylor that Mr. Tyrell do his job. "We had become very close to Al," says Dino. "Johnny was angry that CBS Records was ripping Stax off. They wasn't putting the records out properly. I really felt that they wanted to kill Stax Records, because of the challenge to them. I thought that CBS just did the thing on them."

So Johnny had a brief, charged conversation with Mr. Tyrell. "Johnny Baylor made a threat to Jim Tyrrell," says Logan Westbrooks. "'Follow Al's dictates or else.' And Jim Tyrrell was not intimidated. He came from the streets. He stared it right in the face. So that was the beginning of that little dispute."

That little dispute quickly attained great size. In April, while Stax was down, Columbia hit 'em again: In light of this backlog of stock that Stax refused to acknowledge, Columbia was going to keep the $1.3 million it owed Stax. Stax's *quarterly* payroll in March 1974 was $567,000—well over $2 million per year. Al attacked the problem. He hired his brother Paul away from General Electric (where he was a vice president) to head a new department of new hires at Stax, Retail Relations. "My brother staffed up a division doing nothing but calling retailers so we were able to document for CBS, 'This store number, this person, this is the product they ordered, you didn't ship it.'"

Al assigned Stax's comptroller, Ed Pollack, to sort out the delayed payments with Columbia, and though he made many trips to New York City, he was unable to loosen any cash flow. That same month, behind the scenes in the IRS's Stax investigation, chief bean counter Pollack was given immunity from prosecution, promptly revealing names of disc jockeys and amounts of cash paid. The IRS contacted them all; one admitted that Stax paid his son's college tuition. At the same time, *Washington Post* columnist Jack Anderson was reviving his recording-industry investigations, revealing misdeeds. An ill wind was whipping up to a gale.

During the storm ahead, Stax discovered among subpoenaed Columbia papers a document entitled, "A Study of the Soul Music Environment Prepared for Columbia Records Group." The thirty-page industry assessment, commonly known as the Harvard Report, had been submitted on May 11, 1972, prior to the Stax deal, by Harvard Business School master's degree candidates at the instigation of a Columbia Records executive (and Harvard alumnus). There has been much speculation about Columbia's actual intent with Stax, with some Stax officials citing the report as proof that Columbia was trying to cripple and then overtake Stax. The report, however, does not support the notion of Columbia buying or taking over a soul music label. It encourages Columbia to add soul music to its offerings, recommending the establishment of a black music division, staffing it with black personnel, and also suggesting Columbia make better black music than it had been making (a business school perspective on art). It suggests great profits can be made, but it warns Columbia *against* purchasing or taking over, by name, Stax, Motown, or Atlantic. Clive Davis claims never to have read it, and his dealings with Stax support that, as he ignored the various recommendations as much as followed them. Some parties wanted to make the report into the smoking gun that confirmed Columbia's malicious intentions, but the report's influence seems not as great as the conspiracy theories surrounding it.

There were other dictates that Columbia did follow. "The corporate philosophy of capitalism is, 'If there's a share of the market that you want, either you buy it, steal it, or destroy it,'" says Al with the knowledge of hindsight. "That's the American way. I was talking to Kemmons Wilson [founder of Holiday Inn] and he explained how they took over rug companies to put rugs in all the Holiday Inns. The big fish eats the little fish." The expansion deal that Al thought he was getting into was becoming a suffocation experience; Stax's product was not getting into stores, and money was not flowing in. This was a threat not only to Stax as a corporation, but also to its artists and employees. Isaac's massive payroll, for example, relied on timely payments from Stax.

CBS, to this day, denies any bad intent. "It was never a conspiracy on the part of CBS Records to put Al Bell out of business," says Columbia executive Logan Westbrooks. "CBS was in the business to sell records, to make money. And they did it very, very well. I sat in on every last one of the meetings, and I never got the impression that CBS wanted to bury Stax or take it over. If the retailers are calling for product, then with a very, very short turnaround, we can ship it in there and meet the need." Westbrooks says there was no demand for Stax product.

One of the battles between Columbia and Stax had been a bidding war earlier that year for a hot new United Kingdom act. It wasn't a black London soul singer preaching Black Power to an international audience, it was not a rock band carrying blues to a new crowd. Al's desire to sell more units brought him to outbid CBS for the contract on a prepubescent white Scottish girl named Lena Zavaroni. She was ten years old, the youngest artist ever in the UK album chart's top ten. She sang standards and classics, leaping from a TV talent show into adoring hearts. Her fans included Frank Sinatra and Lucille Ball. "Lena Zavaroni was very good," says Stax publishing executive Tim Whitsett. "She sounded every bit as adult as Rosemary Clooney, and that's the type of music she sang. We were getting away from our core." Though Stax had never had a big hit on a white artist, Al wanted her album, *Ma! He's Making Eyes at Me*, to spearhead his next Stax tidal wave into white America's living rooms. Big money was paid for this coup. And they sold well over one hundred thousand copies, a quantity that once had been a hit at Stax. But in this case, they'd pressed and shipped more than six hundred thousand copies.

Through Zavaroni's manager, Al licensed the soundtrack to a South African stage play. He expanded his foray into that distant market by

Stax won the bidding war for Lena Zavaroni in 1974.

sponsoring a weekly radio program there, an hour in which only Stax records were played. Al had the legal department establish copyright and imprint trademarks there and in numerous foreign markets. "I know they opened an office in Paris," says Don Nix. "I went down there and I just said, 'My God, I wonder how many copies of 'Who's Making Love to Your Old Lady' did they have to sell to pay for this?' It was waste, just rampant waste." Tim Whitsett was equally disquieted about the home front: "It got bloated, especially in some of the projects we took on, some of the artists we tried to put out that just didn't seem to fit, expansive ideas that seemed to stray, like movie production. Our eye was not on the ball anymore. We were looking up in the stands."

◆ ◆ ◆

INATTENTIVENESS TO THE bottom line seemed epidemic in Memphis. The situation at Union Planters got so bad that the president of both the bank and the bank's holding corporation resigned. For its rescue, the bank hired a young man who had shot through the ranks of First National Bank of Atlanta by writing an organizational and marketing manual. Organization was exactly what Union Planters needed, and on May 13, 1974, William "Bill" Matthews was named president of the bank's holding company—at forty-two, the youngest person to ever hold such a position in America. On his first day at work, he learned that the Securities and Exchange Commission was investigating the bank and threatening to sue them. He was also confronted by operational and organizational chaos; when scrutinizing the bank's loan portfolio, he found it so badly managed that it actually cost the bank money to make the loans—the more money it loaned, the more it was losing. Stax was among its largest loan customers.

"The Comptroller of Currency and the bank examiners came in to close the bank," recalls Al. "It was about to go under when they brought in William Matthews. I was called by some of the old officers to come meet this new person. We were high up in their building looking out at the Mississippi River and having this casual social conversation and all of a sudden this gentleman that was sitting over in the corner said, 'Al?' And I looked

William Matthews, chairman of the board, Union Planters National Bank. (University of Memphis Libraries/Special Collections)

and said, 'Yes?' He said, 'Al, I don't want you to think that I'm a redneck from Georgia.' They'd introduced me to him by name but I didn't know who he was. So I said, 'Well, I don't and I won't as long as you don't think I'm a nigger from Arkansas.' And that's the way the relationship started between the chairman of the board of the holding company of the bank and myself. And our interaction from that day to the very last day was like unto that. I knew at that very moment that that was a one-on-one fight."

Matthews had his hands—and fists—full. He held the federal investigation at bay by conducting his own. In July, less than two months after coming on board, he discovered both a kickback scheme and a quarter-million-dollar embezzlement scheme involving loans to fictitious people. One of the participants in the latter was Joe Harwell, a bank employee for nearly fifteen years, and Stax's loan officer.

In 1974, "Stax's total indebtedness to Union Planters amounted to the principal sum of $10,493,220.06 plus interest," trial documents reveal. Pursuing his loans' security, Matthews found no collateral that justified so many dollars and he sent a team of auditors to Stax. "We tried to reconstruct the books," he told a newspaper, "but they didn't really have any books in the normal sense of the term. They appeared to be able to generate $13 to $14 million a year in revenues. The problem was expenses. It was hard to tell what was happening with the expenditures."

On the one hand, Stax's books were no different from any other record company's—or, for that matter, any appliance manufacturer's or any doctor's office's: All would have slush funds that would be hard for an outside accountant to decipher. Some larger, some smaller. Then again, there's Baylor's $2.7 million in nine months; the bank's audit also discovered a $250,000-a-year apartment Stax was paying for in New York—occupied by Johnny Baylor. "Why," Matthews asks, "was Stax paying this man all this money?"

◆◆◆

BY THE SUMMER of 1974, when President Nixon resigned, the music industry was a pop culture pariah. Payola scandals were wide open and CBS-TV broadcast a prime-time documentary, *The Trouble with Rock,* laden with implications of malfeasance throughout the music industry including at Columbia Records, the network's own corporate relation. Stax's relationship with Columbia had, by then, become outright adversarial. The lack of Stax records in stores seemed purposeful: Columbia could prevent sales by withholding shipments, send Stax to its knees, then cherry-pick the talent it wanted. "After Clive Davis left," says Al, "there was really nobody for me to call, because the only person I knew inside of Columbia was Clive Davis."

In July 1974, Stax bought its own pressing plant, a facility in nearby Arkansas. In addition to boosting its brick-and-mortar assets, owning the plant would, after the initial monetary outlay, reduce the cost of pressing, and allow the label to make profits pressing for others. The facility was a converted chicken coop, and its equipment was none too precise, with some records coming out a bit too wide to spin on a turntable.

Jim Stewart, motivated by many factors including the protection of his personal guaranty, stepped up to create additional revenue streams. After a two-year absence from the recording studio, he returned to sign and produce Shirley Brown. She'd been touring with Albert King, who brought her to the label's attention. Her voice had an Aretha Franklin–like quality—she even cut Aretha's standards "Rock Steady" and "Respect" at Stax—but Jim focused more on the intimacy she conveyed, the way she courted the listener's ear. The song "Woman to Woman" had been floating around Stax, rejected by several female vocalists. It has a long spoken introduction—she finds another woman's phone number in her man's pocket, and calls to introduce herself and stake her claim. Shirley's delivery is compelling, like it would be rude to ignore her. Jim proved that his antenna was still tuned, his production skills exquisite.

There was a sense of reunion to the session, with Al Jackson and Duck as the rhythm section (Al also coproduced), Marvell Thomas on piano, Bobby Manuel on guitar, and Isaac's arranger Lester Snell on organ. The resulting song was too good, in fact, to waste on Columbia, who would only warehouse it. Stretching the legal limits of their contract, Stax created the Truth label, a subsidiary outside the Columbia agreement, and put to work its arterial relationships with the distribution outlets where the connections were still strong. Released in August, "Woman to Woman" went to number-one R&B in November and high up on the pop charts; before year's end it became a gold record. "'Woman to Woman,' the last record I did, was, ironically enough, a million seller," Jim says. He pauses, then adds, "Too little, too late."

Stax had been missing payments—to vendors, to employees, to artists. Like weeds, the lawsuits quickly flourished. The initial grievance tore to the company's soul. On September 10, 1974, Isaac Hayes sued Stax for $5.3 million in a federal civil suit. The company's July 26 check for $270,000 had been returned for insufficient funds; Isaac's tax payment to the government bounced with it. (He'd negotiated a $1.89 million contract for the period February 13, 1974, to January 20, 1977, payable in seven equal installments of $270,000; this was the second installment.) Like Stax, Isaac was finding himself in desperate straits. His lawsuit attacked with a vengeance, claiming Stax had cheated his royalty statement since 1968, that the label had not properly promoted his records, and that he'd been billed $100,000 for promotion in violation of his contract. Much of the suit's language expressed dissatisfaction with and anger at Al Bell. Isaac said Al had promised him equity in the company, had declared a "feeling of brotherhood" for Isaac, had told him in 1968, "We are going to be together and share all benefits all down the line." Isaac asked that his relationship with Stax be terminated and he be allowed to negotiate a new contract with ABC Records, the proceeds of which could help satisfy his personal debt to Union Planters National Bank. "Isaac didn't do anything more than the average artist does when he reaches a certain level," says Deanie, "and that is to become a little bit more difficult to work with." The suit was settled a week later, out of court, with a promise for an undisclosed sum and the return to him of all his masters and copyrights, and the release from his contract. Al Bell's organization had been built on Isaac Hayes's back. On what now would it stand?

At that same time, to avoid another court debacle, the master tapes belonging to Richard Pryor were returned, and his contract terminated; he'd sold well, but the income he generated was absorbed before Stax could pay him royalties. Stax had made him a star but couldn't keep him a star; he'd go to Warner Bros., where *That Nigger's Crazy* would be re-released, to enjoy his days in the sun.

Before the month was out, a federal grand jury subpoenaed records of all Stax's financial transactions from 1973. The investigation was part of Project Sound, the ongoing nationwide inquiry into recording-industry kickbacks. Documents covering the two prior years, and all testimony before the jury, were released on October 15 to the IRS "for the purpose," stated US District Judge Robert M. McRae Jr., "of determining whether there are additional tax liabilities due."

On October 9, 1974, in the wake of the success of "Woman to Woman," Columbia sued Stax, accusing it of breaking its distribution agreement. Lawsuits being the day's preferred mode of communication, Stax answered with one against Columbia, suing for $67 million, claiming that Columbia breached the distribution agreement to gain control of the company, citing the Sherman-Patton antitrust laws. Attorneys claimed that during the two-year relationship, Columbia had overordered Stax product, then left the records "unsold in the warehouse of CBS." They stated that Columbia had withheld more than $2.32 million in sales proceeds due to Stax under the agreement and had "willfully, wantonly, and maliciously" attempted to force Stax out of business. Because of the withholding, Stax claimed, it was unable to meet its payroll, causing it to lose Isaac, among other damages.

"I had the international accounting firm of Price-Waterhouse come in and value our masters," says Al. "They put it at sixty-seven million dollars. And we started out fighting with a major law firm—Heiskell, Donelson, Adams, Bearman, Williams & Kirsch—which became Senator Howard Baker's firm. That was one of the most prestigious firms in this state and they wouldn't have taken on an antitrust suit against CBS unless they believed in the validity of that suit." The attorneys claimed Columbia "calculated to destroy Stax as a full service record company and to reduce it to a mere label or production company, completely under the domination and control" of Columbia.

Matthews, the bank chairman, recognized the potential of the antitrust suit, and he wanted to put his team of lawyers on it; helping Stax win it could help his bank. "He called me in," says Al, "and said, 'I want you to give this antitrust lawsuit over to the bank. We can win this, you can't. We'll give you two or three million dollars out of it.' I wasn't going to give him a sixty-seven-million-dollar lawsuit and he'll give me two or three million dollars. If he'd said, We'll split it down the middle, maybe I could have heard him."

During the Stax troubles, Westbrooks remembers Columbia's worry about its reputation in the African-American community. "CBS was concerned about their image on a national basis, especially with black radio stations and black disc jockeys," he says. "Al Bell was a very, very popular figure in the national black community." In fact, Columbia tried to bring Al under its umbrella, offering him a corporate vice president's position overseeing its distribution network. But moving from Stax to Columbia would have, Al felt, been shirking his responsibility and moral obligations. "I said, 'I can't do that. You want me to be a Judas and sell out my people.'"

Al was called to a meeting by Arthur Taylor, the young, starched, and suave president of CBS, Inc., not just the record division, but the man to whom all the media heads—records, television, radio, the whole empire—answered. "I went up to the thirty-something floor in the New York CBS office to see Mr. Arthur Taylor," Al says. "Elevator opened—and it was intimidating. Like going to the Justice Department with all these CBS lawyers running around up there. Here I am arriving with this one little old black lawyer. This huge boardroom runs the length of the floor, could've put forty or fifty people into it. Arthur Taylor was sitting at one end, tapping a pencil on the table, and said, 'Have a seat.' He had a couple of people beside him, and through the door came a guy with a stack of clippings from newspapers that they were getting from all over the country. There was concern building in the streets, and in black media, and in other media, regarding what was going on between CBS and Stax."

That concern was deep. The plug was being pulled on an open microphone from America's African-American heart to the world's ear. Shirley Brown's intimate plea was a whisper that, not too long before, could never have been heard. Isaac's carnal image had been punishable by lynching only a couple decades earlier. Artist after artist, song after song, Stax gave voice to the hearts and minds of a people too long silenced. And with that voice, Stax brought power to its artists and also to its audience. Stax had become the song of a nation. And as Al sat in that huge office high above Manhattan, all of that newfound freedom won with blood and grit was at stake. Columbia cared not a whit about the message. It heard only the cash register. Columbia wanted the sales. Stax was fighting for its voice, its life, and the voices and lives of its people.

Al continues, "Arthur Taylor said, 'Al, I'm not going to argue with you the merits of your antitrust suit. We just have more time than you and more money than you.'" However daunting the scene may have been, Al had the serenity that comes with faith in his position. "I said, 'Arthur, there's no question that you have more money than me but time I question, because I'm not giving up on this.'" If Al was thinking about the hundreds of people who worked for Stax, he must have determined that there was no hope in resolving the issue with Columbia, no hope in re-taining their employment by making peace here, because Al didn't stop; he kept right on going, delivering the goods to the big man on the top floor, saying, "Between me and you, you can call this World War III." With that statement, Mr. Taylor's hand stopped tapping that pencil. The room got quiet, and for a moment it seemed that all sound everywhere had stopped. The two executives were eye to eye, physically locked by an unseen tension. The hand holding that pencil clenched, the knuckles get-ting white, and the silence was torn—*SNAP*—by the angry breaking of that pencil. Arthur Taylor stood and exited the room.

The wrath of CBS, Inc. was discharged upon Stax. "After that," says Al, "I grew to appreciate the power of a corporation like CBS. I didn't realize that they could reach into offices that one would never have thought they could reach into. And they cut off the spigot. They said, 'We don't owe you any money because here's the product that didn't sell that we had in our warehouse.' Several eighteen-wheelers came back to where we housed our goods, returning a substantial portion of all the inventory they had purchased *on the same skids* they were shipped out on. No more cash flow. We couldn't pay many of our artists and other obliga-tions. They were knocking us to our knees, breaking our back."

◆ ◆ ◆

In Memphis, elements of the white population, feeling their majority slipping away, began expressing paranoia and fear. Blacks were taking over the schools, taking over the city council, and, at the end of 1974, whites feared they would lose their voice in Washington, DC.

The congressional election in 1974 was an off year. Nixon had been reelected president two years earlier, and no Senate seats were up. There was the House election, and in contention was the Ninth Congressional District, which represented the heart of Memphis. The seat had been held for four terms by Dan Kuykendall, a staunch conservative. After the 1970 census, districts were redrawn and Kuykendall's, which included Souls-ville, represented a significantly larger black population. (It was also re-numbered from the Eighth.) His opponent in the 1972 race had been African-American, and while the race was close, Kuykendall won 15 percent of the black vote and had the momentum of Richard Nixon's landslide to help him retain office.

In the 1974 election, Kuykendall's opponent was Harold Ford Sr., who'd served two terms in the state legislature. Ford was from a prominent African-American family that ran a funeral home and had a history in politics. He organized a vigorous campaign. He understood the racial fears that ran in Memphis and he sought a wide appeal with statements like "Inflation knows no color." He campaigned on economic development, which would help everyone. With the redistricting in his favor, and the continued momentum from the Voting Rights Act, Ford organized a rudimentary political machine: phone banks, neighborhood caravans, and a proactive voter registration campaign that included rides to the polling places.

Kuykendall, meanwhile, appealed to the city's conservative core, evident in his steadfast support of President Nixon even after transcripts indicting him were made public. And he had a problem new to the 1974 cycle, brought on by the recent implementation of busing: White flight from the city to the county and beyond had changed the district's racial demographic to a larger percentage of African-Americans.

The race grew heated early and as it neared the vote, it was close with an expected Kuykendall win. By nine o'clock P.M. on election night, Kuykendall was ahead by five thousand votes and declared the winner by the major radio and TV stations. But the tally Ford saw on TV didn't match what Ford's poll watchers had been supplying him, and he went to the Shelby County Election Commission offices. "For an hour and a half he sat there," said Election Commission director Jack Perry, "jabbering about 'Something must be wrong,' and 'I know I've got the lead.'" As the tally closed, it turned out that six precincts had delivered their ballots but the ballots weren't among those counted. Soon Ford "and about ten

November 5, 1974. Harold Ford becomes Tennessee's first African-American to serve the United States Congress. (University of Memphis Libraries/Special Collections/ Photograph by Jack Cantrell)

campaign workers found six unopened ballot boxes in the basement of the building." (Ford was quoted as saying, "We found the reports in a garbage can and sent them up to be counted," though he later retracted the statement.) Once those missing votes were tallied, Ford was declared the winner. The Shelby County Election Commission was all white; no African-Americans served on it. Harold Ford became Tennessee's first African-American to serve the United States Congress.

Memphis was a city divided. The population was still a majority white, but just barely. The wounds of Dr. King's assassination had never healed, and the recent busing battles had reopened them. With Ford's election, many Memphis whites were predicting doomsday scenarios, a revolution of the underclass. Black power frightened them, and they sought ways to take back the power.

◆◆◆

STAX'S TROUBLES HAD brought the company much unwanted attention, and Al was feeling the backlash against a black-owned company. "Stax was perceived as a white-owned business until they put it in the newspaper that the blacks were involved in the CBS litigation," says Al, "and that's when the white community in Memphis started reacting." Columbia's stranglehold was keeping any income from Stax, and Union Planters got in the fray by suing both Stax and Columbia. The bank's suit, resulting from Columbia's "virtual ownership" of Stax, asked for $10.5 million in damages from the corporate giant, cancellation of the bank's subordination agreement (so that the bank could then collect its debts before Columbia), and the voiding of a $6 million loan agreement between Columbia and Stax. Union Planters had its own soul to save, and if it had to kill Stax to stay alive, that was basic business; like Columbia, it had millions of dollars invested in the company, though unlike Columbia, the talent of the artists was of no interest to the bank. Union Planters needed the company to thrive, or it needed its assets. Concerned about its reputation in the Memphis community, the bank came to Jim and proposed giving the company to him under some kind of probation. "Jim turned them down right away," says Whitsett. "He said, 'I'm with Al Bell on this, I believe in Al Bell.' And the bank people came back just bewildered. They had to go for the jugular because they did have stockholders, and they had to recoup as much of their loss as they could."

"It did not surprise me, the posture that that bank took," says Logan Westbrooks, the Columbia division head. "It was owned and controlled by white men. I grew up in Memphis, I know the racist attitude of whites in the city of Memphis. The moment they became aware that Al Bell was the owner of Stax Records: 'How dare you, black man, own this company in the city of Memphis!' It was a vendetta from those white bankers against Al Bell and Stax Records." Indeed, though Westbrooks would have reason to deflect blame from his company to the bank, his fundamental point remains true: Many white leaders (and followers) in Memphis were uncomfortable with African-Americans gaining ground in society; further, they'd find the idea of the city being represented by African-American culture embarrassing. Business was first, but reputation was not far behind.

Earlie Biles, Al's secretary, says, "I think the city saw all these black successful people with gold cars, fur coats, gold jewelry, and fancy this and fancy that, flying here and there—they didn't understand what was going on." Deanie Parker, the publicist, concurs: "Union Planters Bank was having very serious difficulties. Being a marketer, I think they were very shrewd. If they could find a scapegoat to position at the center of negative news, and blame their inefficiencies, their ineptness, their shenanigans, on somebody else, then it made a better story for the stockholders and for the customers. And in Memphis, Tennessee, what better target than a record company that's predominantly African-American that's making black

Earlie Biles, left, and Bettye Crutcher. (Stax Museum of American Soul Music)

people wealthy? Where Isaac Hayes is driving around in a custom-made Cadillac that cost more than many white folks' houses did? And what better examples than Carla Thomas or Shirley Brown, or another artist purchasing a fur coat—cash. We were a victim of the times. Now, that said, Stax Records was not perfect. We were like any business, making the best practical decisions that we could, and we were risk takers as well. And the industry itself was changing."

While the label may have felt persecuted, the fact of its indebtedness to the bank remained, along with its lack of collateral, its impenetrable accounting, and the lawsuits against it. These were plenty enough reasons for the bank to pursue it vigorously. "I considered Bill Matthews in all respects an honorable, truthful person," says attorney Wynn Smith. "As far as racism is concerned, my impression was that he didn't recognize but one color, and that was green. I never saw any evidence of his being racist, and I was never aware of any impetus to go after Stax for any racial reason at all."

Each side seems to see what it wants to see, but no matter what the disagreement was about, Al shares an insight that gets to the core of how the disagreement was handled, a reality about the times: "I know that if I had been a white man, Matthews would have dealt with me differently. Assets were sitting here. The language would have been different. The discussion would have been different." Such a discussion with Al, for example, could never have taken place on the golf courses of several prominent Memphis country clubs that were still "exclusive"—forbidding membership to blacks and Jews among others. American society in general, and Memphis society in particular, was undergoing a transformation, trying to make a paradigm shift from a hundred or more years of institutional racism to new equality. It would be harder for those of the older generations. As progress dragged across stasis, the friction was burning Stax.

Tim Whitsett, who had become president of East/Memphis Publishing, remembers an embarrassing proposal made at a meeting between the bank and the publishing company's writers. "Matthews pandered, especially to our black writers," says Whitsett. "I was in the room, Eddie Floyd, Mack Rice, all of our writers." Matthews proposed that, in lieu of payments to the writers, which would be temporal, that the publishing company fund a statue of Dr. King, which would be lasting. "The writers are going, 'Hey, man, we'd rather get paid.' It was so embarrassing. I felt a general uproar bubbling."

In November 1974, Tim Whitsett was in his office when a Matthews henchman named Roger Shellebarger entered. "He announced that the Union Planters Bank was taking control of the publishing company, and the first thing they're gonna do is move us downtown next to Union Planters. It was totally astounding." Stax had defaulted on payments against which the publishing company was the collateral, and the bank was exercising its right to assume control. Jim Stewart had recently met with Whitsett and told him to go along with whatever the bank might say, but Whitsett was not expecting a new boss. Publishing is the music business's constant cash flow, and diverting Stax's stream would wither the company.

Even among the inner circle at Stax, this loss was a surprise. Few saw evidence that the situation was turning so calamitous. "All the news was hitting the trade magazines," says Whitsett, "and I could not fathom the company going under. It was like the Bank of England or the Rock of Gibraltar."

26. A SOUL AND A HARD PLACE
1975

THE INITIAL PAY period in 1975 turned out to be the first gasp of a year-long, agonizing strangulation. Checks usually covered two weeks, and as employees collected their regular pay, they found only half there. "I tried to keep the faith," says Deanie Parker. "I kept thinking, There's got to be a break coming. But I'm afraid that [the missed payroll] was the confirmation that truly the ship had hit sand."

Larry Nix, who mastered the records, had his own rude awakening when he went to cash his paycheck at the grocery store. "At the supermarket where I shopped, in the customer-service window, there was a sign that said, STAX RECORDS CHECKS NO LONGER ACCEPTED." He went to Jim Stewart. "Jim said, 'Don't worry about it, we're pulling our money out of Union Planters and the new bank hasn't caught up yet.' They'd make a check, miss a check. It just snowballed."

As 1974 had ended, banker Joe Harwell was indicted on charges he'd embezzled $284,000 from Union Planters between 1970 and 1973 through fictitious loans and checking accounts; seven other bank officers were indicted on similar charges, though only Harwell also had connections to Stax. Early in 1975, RCA Records sued Stax for failing to pay for nearly $160,000 worth of record blanks used in Stax's recently purchased pressing plant; RCA brandished a $28,000 check that had bounced twice.

"Ouch," Larry Shaw said to the newspaper when told of the lawsuit. "This is a new one. I don't know the details of it. There are so many coming at us."

As the payroll fell further behind, employees began finding other jobs, and artists departed. In February, ABC Records announced it was signing both Isaac Hayes and the Dramatics; Isaac was being given a seven-figure contract, and he initiated a new lawsuit against Stax for continuing to collect his royalties without paying him, and for not fulfilling its promise to return his master tapes. A newspaper article quoted former Stax employees speaking of "salaries that were 'way out of line.'"

Union Planters announced its year-end report in late January 1975; the bank had lost $15 million. On the first of March, Harwell pled guilty to "what was believed to be the largest embezzlement case in Memphis history." He was sentenced to five years, as per the US Attorney's Office recommendation. Other bank officers would soon plead guilty to fraud charges. As for the total bond claims (Stax and otherwise) of $16.5 million, the bank said it "has a reasonable prospect of recovering up to $10 million."

A little good news came in March when Stax and CBS announced an out-of-court settlement. Each company found the other distasteful, but they were bound in a multimillion-dollar obligation. CBS wanted its money and, from its vantage point as exclusive distributor, was willing to take as partial payment both the money it was holding for Stax and the remaining record inventory it was warehousing, valued at—over $4 million. Stax would only owe half of its $6 million, plus interest and back interest if it paid off the debt by August 31, 1976.

The Stax employees who remained were far less concerned about the corporate settlement than they were about their own payments. "People began to say, 'We getting paid this week?'" says promotions man James Douglass. "They changed the pay cycle to monthly, so people worked thirty days before finding out." Al sought relief from a variety of sources. Mayor Richard Daley spoke of moving the company to Chicago. There was talk of relocating to Gary, Indiana. Al signed an heiress to the H.L. Hunt oil fortune as an artist. Looking for piles of money, Al and Stax attorney John Burton turned to the Middle East and made overtures to King Faisal in Saudi Arabia. The king was interested, and talk ensued. They negotiated a multimillion-dollar deal, enough money to pay off all debts and return to the lavish spending that upped the odds for generating a hit. Deanie Parker recalls this as a "hare-brained scheme. But when you're desperate, you have to do something." Engineer Larry Nix stopped in his tracks when he saw three Muslim men in the former church offices, each wearing a flowing robe and *kaffiyeh*. Once the deal points were settled, Burton boarded a plane for the Middle East. Al told Rob Bowman, "I remember talking to him from Beirut while we could hear gunfire on the outside." Bullets were rampant and the king, at his home in Saudi Arabia, was assassinated on March 25, before the papers were signed.

While Al chased the big fish, James Douglass and others searched for kelp. "We went to the mail room guy and got fifteen hundred or eighteen hundred albums up to Randy's Record Store in Nashville, got a quarter on the dollar," says Douglass. "The car, you couldn't even see out the back it was so loaded up. Then Randy wanted them shrink-wrapped, which we could do. Out of the mail room, I was able to generate about ten thousand dollars. I'm spreading money around, people have bills, their kids are sick." Though just a Band-Aid on a bullet wound, he was following Al's old dictate about troubling situations: "Defuse it."

On July 15, in the summer of "The Hustle," Isaac Hayes did the electric slide to the left and released his first album on ABC Records. Disco was his groove, but with a quicker tempo. *Chocolate Chip* was certified gold. The artists still clinging to Stax were reminded, ah, yes, that's how a functioning company works. But Isaac remained plagued by Stax's plights. He'd not been paid his royalties or his settlement money, and was deluged with lawsuits large and small, including seven thousand dollars in unpaid alimony. After his split with Johnny Baylor, Isaac built his own recording studio near where he'd lived as a child in North Memphis, and far from Baylor in South Memphis. Creating a state-of-the-art studio from scratch was an expensive endeavor, and the bills were piling up.

By early September, Stax's phones were disconnected and the workforce had dropped almost 95 percent, to about fifteen people. David Porter paid some salaries out of his pocket, because the loyal few kept coming to work. "It had been so big, a multimillion-dollar company, you didn't think it could possibly go under," says Larry Nix. "Now five or six of us would go into Isaac's old office, sit on that long red leather couch, and David Porter would go along to each of us, say, 'What do you need to get by this week?' By that time, you're hiding your car in your neighbor's garage to keep it from being repo'd."

"Everybody started having problems, divorces and all," says drummer

Willie Hall. "Things got rough. Slowly, they'd come on the lot and start pulling cars, and foreclosing homes, and man, we knew it was on. The IRS came at us with back taxes, audits. Hell, I don't think there was one son of a bitch there that paid his taxes on time, or paid his taxes period. We started watching the demise of everybody." Willie then describes his middle-class life slipping away: "I lost two homes—one that Isaac had helped me acquire for my mother, and then my first wife and I, we lost our home. The IRS—I didn't owe them much, less than ten grand, but I didn't have *any* money. Some guy in the black suit with the black hat and the tie and a gun, he nailed this notice up on my door, told me that from this point on, this property belongs to the Internal Revenue." Guitarist Skip Pitts, vocalist and engineer William Brown, Al's secretary Earlie Biles—the list of people who lost their homes goes on and on, an evisceration of the Memphis Sound.

Big news broke on September 9, 1975, a front-page story in the evening paper announcing a twenty-six-page, fourteen-count federal grand jury indictment against Al Bell, charging that he conspired with Harwell to fraudulently obtain loans, loan extensions, and loan renewals totaling $18,877,983 between December 17, 1969, and May 30, 1974, plus overdrafts totaling nearly $700,000. Harwell was further charged with another $150,000 in fictitious loans, using Bell to guarantee payment. Harwell was said to have received up to $700,000 in kickbacks, and various other bribes including an expense-paid trip to Los Angeles for the 1973 *Wattstax* movie premiere. This indictment was separate from, and independent of, the IRS investigation against Stax and its employees into possible payola. Two weeks later, more than fifty supporters, including Dr. Ralph Abernathy, head of the Southern Christian Leadership Conference (SCLC), and Congressman (and unreleased Stax recording artist) Walter Fauntroy of Washington, DC, packed the Memphis courtroom to hear Al declare his innocence before the judge. Al was represented by James F. Neal, the Nashville attorney who had recently served as a special prosecutor in the Watergate trials of presidential assistants Robert Haldeman, John Ehrlichman, and former US attorney general John Mitchell. Neal—Al continued to go "blue chip" all the way—had received $50,000 up front, and the same had been placed in escrow; it was paid by the Chicago ad agency International Public Relations. (Harwell, accused as Al's coconspirator, was transferred for a few nights from Illinois to the Shelby County Jail; at the hearing, he asked for immediate return to federal prison because the local lockup was "crawling with rats and roaches" and, with no cots available, he was sleeping on a cell floor.)

"Alleging that we had conspired to defraud eighteen million dollars from the bank is laughable," says Al. "To assume, in that period of time, that a black man in Memphis, Tennessee, could conspire with anybody in a bank to defraud it of twenty-five dollars, let alone all these millions of dollars—but they were able to do that. My understanding was that, from a legal standpoint, the bank reflected this $18.9 million on their financial statements to the government's Comptroller of Currency as a contingent receivable, and if they could have gotten the convictions then they would have been able to follow through on what they had represented in their financial statements." In other words, bringing Al down would also prop up the bank and help circumvent its closure.

While Stax was going down, longtime drummer Al Jackson had resumed his friendship with former bandleader Willie Mitchell, who since 1970 had been an executive at Hi Records, around the corner from Stax. Al Jackson began collaborating on songs with Willie and Hi's new artist, Al Green. Beginning with "Let's Stay Together" in 1972, Jackson wrote several huge hits at Hi ("I'm Still in Love with You" and "Call Me" among them), even while he produced and worked at Stax. Al Green's sound was smoother and more lush than Stax's, but with an underlying funk. Green's huge success made Hi Records a major player, and their roster included Ann Peebles, Syl Johnson, Otis Clay, and others who regularly made the charts. Jackson was collecting writer's royalties at Hi and making some session pay (most sessions featured Al's protégé, Howard Grimes, who'd drummed on Carla's "Gee Whiz" and other early Stax hits); Al Jackson Sr. had opened a gas station and Al Jr. had invested in oil wells. He seemed like the one Stax staffer who was surviving the sinking ship.

While driving in his car on September 30, 1975, what would become his last day on earth, Al Jackson Jr. heard the disc jockey discussing that evening's boxing match between Joe Frazier and Muhammad Ali, dubbed "the Thrilla in Manila." Locally, it was being shown on a giant-screen closed-circuit TV at a downtown theater; Jackson was supposed to fly that evening to Detroit to produce a session for Major Lance, a former Volt artist trying to rejuvenate his career. Al rearranged his flight so he could see the fight.

The bout went long, with first Ali and then Frazier ahead. Not until the tenth round did Ali begin to regain the upper hand, then pummeling Frazier's right eye in the eleventh so the onetime world heavyweight champion was increasingly blinded. Ali, who'd been visibly tiring as the fight wore on, took advantage of Frazier's blind spot and attacked from the right. Twelfth round, thirteenth—the intense beatings a torturous endurance test. During the fourteenth round, Frazier staggered like he wore cinderblock shoes. Before the fighters returned for the final meeting, Frazier's trainer signaled the referee to terminate the match. Frazier protested, but to no avail; following the fight, Ali stated, "It was like death. Closest thing to dyin' that I know of."

Afterward, Jackson drove to his house on Central Avenue. He'd been having marital trouble for over a year. Two months earlier, on July 31, a domestic dispute had put him in the hospital and landed his wife at the police station. During that argument, she'd stormed outside and he followed. When she wouldn't say where she was going, Jackson pushed her first onto the hood of his car, then hit her several times, dragged her by the hair, and threw her into the yard. She went inside and pulled a .22 rifle on him; her first shot was a warning, the second one hit him in the chest. She didn't deny the facts, but he decided not to press charges. They filed for divorce.

As that part of his life was falling apart, an MG's reunion was coming together. Steve Cropper remembers the four of them discussing circumstances past, present, and future, and all agreeing they'd clear their various schedules and reconvene in about three months with the intention of devoting three years to the group, recording and touring, to make a new go of it.

It was after midnight when Jackson got home from the fights. Al's wife later explained that she'd come home and been accosted by a robber who tied her up while he ransacked the house. She explained that the robber freed her to answer the door when Al rang the bell, then retied her and made Al lie on the floor. Mrs. Jackson heard the murderous shots ring out.

"I remember getting out of my car at my dad's house in LA and his TV was situated so that you could see it through the screen door as you approached," says Booker T. Jones. "I saw 'Booker T. & the MG's' on the screen, which was eerie, seeing your name on TV as you're walking into your father's household. It was the five o'clock news and that's how I learned that Al had been killed. To this moment, I still can't get over it."

The house had been hardly ransacked, and Al's wallet was not taken. "Al was shot five times in the back," says Duck, "first while standing, then they laid him on a carpet and shot him some more. The bullets went through him, point-blank. It was just, oh, I still have dreams about it."

Al's murder cast a deep pall as the winter of '75 came on. "Oh, it was very grim," says the usually buoyant Eddie Floyd. "We knew by that time that the company was really in trouble, but we still hoped and recorded records. Everybody still believed in the music, and Al Bell was fighting real hard to keep all of that going."

"There was a hope," says Earlie. "A couple of times the administrators went to Europe to talk over new deals for the company. I never saw Mr. Bell not upbeat. I saw him looking weary towards the end, but he was still fighting, and still positive. He kept saying, 'Keep the faith,' and, 'It's gonna be okay.' And he was trying to rally people. He never did give up."

"Every time I looked around, another process server was knocking on the door," says Al. "We must have had about forty or fifty lawsuits going at one time. It paralyzed the company." Al's father had built a successful landscaping company; Al turned to him. "When my capital was zero and I needed money desperately, I was able to call my father—I needed fifty thousand dollars at that time—and tell him I needed it. I was still trying to do what they said couldn't be done and didn't believe that the inevitable was inevitable."

◆◆◆

Stax's new corporate offices had been remodeled, but the church sanctuary had remained untouched. The company held assemblies there, where Al could report to the workforce en masse, where he could inspire the congregated, breathe life into the weary. Before embarking on his music industry career, Al had spent time preparing for the ministry, and in this room, all his interests merged. In this room, he called on all his available resources to uplift his diminishing staff, alternating plain-speech assessments with biblical metaphors of the wicked and the oppressed, of truth seekers and evildoers.

"I hated those meetings," says Deanie Parker. "They went on forever and most of the people sitting there were scratching their heads or their butts." As the size of the company dwindled, the duration of the meetings extended. "It was very weird in there," says Larry Nix. The room hadn't felt full when a hundred people showed up to a meeting. Now it was cavernous. "Big church," Larry continues, "and people thumping cigarettes in the hymn book racks, Al Bell in the pulpit preaching to the employees. I'd look around thinking, C'mon, this is a *record company.*"

On the fifth of December, 1975, the publishing company East/Memphis Music was auctioned on the courthouse steps. There was only one bidder, Union Planters, which got the company in exchange for the balance of their loan. They had assumed control a year earlier, and now they owned it and all the mechanical royalties that the compositions would generate.

Jim's first real lesson in the music business had been about the value of the publishing company. Ellis the barber had explained its importance, and the East Publishing Company is what Jim began with. East reverberated to Stax's inner core, to Jim's very essence. If Jim heard any *snip* now, it was the severing of ties, of the Stax company ship being set adrift without its ballast.

In mid-December, three creditors filed a petition sending Stax into involuntary bankruptcy. The total claim of the three, combined, was $1,910.13—less than two thousand dollars. One creditor supplied toilet paper, one was a photography lab, and one supplied electronic parts. Three creditors is the minimum necessary to commence another company's involuntary bankruptcy, and because each of these was in a different city, it's difficult to imagine they'd have joined together had they not been assisted by a larger creditor. Union Planters National Bank stated that the bank had played "direct role" in coordinating this action.

On December 19, 1975, an enforcer who worked for Matthews barged into Stax. "He jumped up on the receptionist's desk and said, 'You've got fifteen minutes to get out of the building,'" Al, ready to defuse a situation, remembers. "I said to the federal marshal, a black guy, 'What is this all about?' He said, 'It's involuntary bankruptcy.' I said, 'How much?' He said, 'Nineteen hundred dollars.' I said, 'Well, I've got that much money in my pocket.'" But the process had begun. Al was told to lead the way to the master tapes. "My blood went to my head," Al continues, "but I started on through the building. By this time, as I'm going back to the tape vault trying to make a decision as to whether or not I'm going to go off on these people, because it was really nasty, really nasty—I stopped and went into the bathroom near studio A and washed my face in cold water just to cool down. As I came out, the black federal marshal had positioned himself by the door so when I opened it, he said, 'Hey man, be cool. They're trying to off you.' I said, 'Oh, that kind of party.' The guys from the bank wanted to kill me that day.

"I walked them all through the place, very diplomatic, and explained every bit so they would understand that I wouldn't be intimidated. I asked them if I could get some things out of my office and all they would let me take was a little leather attaché case and a little legal pad and my phone book. Nothing else. So we come to the back of the building, toward the guard station. On the outside they had all these black guys with guns—they had recruited them from all the security firms so they'd be all black guys out there. They had an industrial camera crew outside filming the whole darn thing. They were masterful—I have to say they were masterful in what they were doing."

It's telling that even in this moment of Stax's demise, Al can admire the promotional aspect of his expulsion. It harks back to those grim days in Arkansas, cleaning out dog cages, and enduring the disdainful comments about how blacks "can't do nothing but sing and dance." Life had been pelting southern blacks with lemons for hundreds of years, and Al had been making sweet lemonade for most of his life. He'd taken the insult and built a place of real opportunity, a place that rewarded talent and hard work, not white skin and cotton money. It was an oasis, and a fragile one, vulnerable to the economic and social climate surrounding it. Al's eyes were on the heights, the dreams to be made, and the vulnerabilities eluded him, an oversight that would reach into the lives of everyone who worked at Stax, whose family depended on Stax for its milk and bread.

Some would call it hubris, but that is the pat analysis of those looking backward, after the crash. That sort of glibness is like bad music. It is safe, the notes are predictable, and it ignores both the risks and the goals. Al Bell was reaching toward that which was yet to be invented. He was shifting the paradigm, breaking the covenant, pursuing the dream. He was riffing, an economic jam session, a socioeconomic symphony. Determined to reach the next eight bars, and the next and the next, he was lost on the melody and missed the notes.

Standing at the Stax back door, the sunlight jolted him from the reverie, the oversights exploding all around him. Behind him was the achievement of middle-class elevation, of maintenance men becoming recording engineers, of automobile drivers becoming department managers, fan club members inspired to be lawyers. Before him was a frenzied spectacle of police cars, sirens, lights, cameras, weapons, women and men screaming and hollering and crying. This dreaded moment had been barreling toward these stalwart few for months, weeks, and days despite their disbelief, their faith in the forces that averted past disaster.

Al was escorted from the building at gunpoint.

"On one side of me is the federal marshal, on the other side is the guy that's over these security people that are all out here, and on both sides of them there's more security people," Al continues. "We're walking, I see the camera crew filming and the employees across the street and there's this guy that's standing in front of me so if you're on the street you can't see him and he commands me, 'Stop! Open that attaché case and let me see what you have in there.' I thought, God dawg, this is the moment." The man was asking Al to put his hand into the bag, to take his visible hand and put it where its actions would be concealed. "I instinctively dropped the attaché case and grabbed the fence and just held up on the fence. I said to myself, If he kills me, they'll see that I'll be on this fence, because I knew he wanted me to open up that attaché case so he could say I was reaching for a gun."

Al Bell, six and a half feet of black pride and impeccable taste, searched and seized, led on a perp walk, positioned on the wrong end of many guns, clutched the fence for protection. That fence at once offered safety, but also represented a very ugly resolution to his quest for black auton- omy. He'd dealt in the seamy side of business, just as his white peers in New York and Los Angeles had. If his hands weren't clean, they were no dirtier than any other executive's in the record business. But to many people, and certainly in Memphis, a black man with money induced almost as much fear as a black man with a gun. African-Americans, for centuries, had their belongings and achievements wrested from their possession—without recourse of law, with no sense of justice. Black peo- ple could not get too high up without being taken down. Okay, Memphis grudgingly acknowledged, sanitation workers were people. Okay, white society finally conceded, blacks could have new textbooks instead of out- dated white-school hand-me-downs. But our kids sit with your kids in school together? Slow down, slow down. A multimillion-dollar corpora- tion representing Memphis run by an African-American? No way. The bank had Al where it wanted him, in the glare of fear and misplaced guilt that is inevitably part of a confrontation with the law, when even the in- nocent are tainted by the accusatory muzzle of a gun pointed their way—a humiliation to bookend this side of his life.

Al saw a burly employee across the way and called for help. As he came toward his boss, it was a drama within the greater drama, a stillness at the core of the mayhem, a rescue making its way through the crowd and the chaos. Al, clutching the chain-link fence, arms akimbo, needed help, and help was coming. "He came all the way around and came right on through these guards," says Al, "and he got me and carried me back out around." The stillness—not a calm, but a tense, floating quietude— continued as the two moved toward the gate in the fence, all eyes look- ing: "As I walked out of that gate onto College Street," Al says, "I heard myself say, 'Whew.' I felt relief. It was off of me. I still had the other things to deal with, lawsuits and many other things, but all of those pressures associated with keeping Stax open were off of me."

The building was determined to be clear of personnel. The back door was shut. A padlock would be put on the security fence. Stax—the exuberant spirit, the wanton waste, the divine mission, the tumultuous life force, the deep soul, the music, the music!—had ended.

27. "I'LL TAKE YOU THERE"
EPILOGUE

MEMPHIS HAS TORN down more history than most other cities even have, a longtime Beale Street merchant named Abram Schwab used to say. A tour of Memphis is an excursion to empty lots and vacant buildings, an outing to see what used to be. The tour guide's refrain becomes, "Imagine on this weedy site . . ." Memphis despised its African-American culture, was ashamed of exactly what the world loved us for, dismissive of what made us unique. The business leaders and politicians who run this overgrown cotton crossroads so shuddered at being recognized for blues and soul that, somewhat methodically, they tore most of its history down.

The Memphis mentality is to blend with the crowd, to look like the reflection in the 1970s and 1980s mirrored buildings in Atlanta or Houston. Memphis prefers freshly laid plastic to anything historic and distinct. Beale Street was saved, but not before the body that supported Beale, the neighborhood around the street, was mowed down in the name of urban renewal. The rebuilt Beale disdained history, moving signage wantonly, "improving" what it wanted, imitating Bourbon Street's liquor mall. The path where Dr. King marched has been largely erased. The first Piggly Wiggly, the first Holiday Inn—anything old in Memphis, including churches, gets swept away. Hide what we don't like, then pretend it doesn't exist.

The building stood neglected from 1976 until it was torn down in 1989. (Stax Museum of American Soul Music)

This oppressive environment squeezes freethinkers to the margins, creating an unintentional incubator. It provides opportunity for Jim Stewart, for Al Bell, for their unlikely union. Al, born with a vision far-seeing and wide, and a determination to explore its outer reaches; Jim, ever cautious but bighearted and ready for change, with great ears and a strong commercial sensibility. They united, created so much good, so much opportunity—especially for those who'd never had such opportunity. Each man gave careers, wealth, and new life to those around him, but each man also caused many of those gifts to be painfully retracted. Neither intentionally harmed anyone, but like distracted parents, they each, after achieving great benefit, wrought great destruction.

"One day you're making records," says Jim Stewart, then "you leave court and you find out you're not." Less than a month after the forcible eviction, Stax had its day in court. January 12, 1976—gloomy, windy, and gray. Federal bankruptcy judge William Leffler, siding with the creditors, ordered the building padlocked and the company to cease doing business. According to guards posted on-site, Jim sat in his car in the parking lot behind the old Capitol Theater, barred from entering the business he had founded. He looked at the building—fifteen years spent there, rented it for a hundred bucks a month, bought the block, sold it for millions; Jim had had it all. After about thirty minutes, he drove away.

"How can you say it grew too fast when you start at zero in terms of master tape value in 1968 and by 1974 the company is valued at sixty-seven million dollars?" opines Al Bell, indignant nearly four decades after the fact. "Grow that fast for me if you will."

The test of insolvency is whether liabilities exceed assets. There's no doubt that Stax (and its affiliates) owed the bank in excess of $10 million and had many other debts. But much harder to calculate was the value of Stax's assets. Stax was made up of three broad entities: the Stax Record Company/Stax Organization, which owned real estate, recording equipment, subsidiary labels, artist contracts, and master tapes; the publishing companies, primarily East/Memphis Music and Birdees Music, which owned a combined total of over three thousand copyrights, many of which were already classics receiving continued play by their original Stax artists and also covered by other artists; and then various investment offshoots, primarily tax shelters. The value of these shelters, along with Stax's real estate, was easy enough to assess. The valuation problem was in the tapes and the copyrights. "Independent auditors look very, very askance at unusual types of securities," explains the bank's attorney Wynn Smith. "And masters are, to put it mildly, a very unusual type of security. I think the bank's judgment was that the value that had been assigned to those assets was just ridiculous, totally unjustified."

Stax filed a reorganization plan in bankruptcy court in June 1976, over the objections of Union Planters. "I see hope coming my way," declared Al. "There is no doubt about it: Stax can be successful again."

Jim Stewart, in that same period, said, "I am saying to you that the same assets are still within the company now, because it's in the minds of the principals, and the creative people at Stax are still here. It's here [indicating his head]. I'm not asking for credit. I'm just saying, 'Don't underrate Stax.'"

Bill Matthews, the bank's chairman of the board, had other ideas: "I think Stax owes too much money to be viable. There doesn't appear to be enough credibility in the marketplace for it to be the same business it was." Then Matthews took a more solicitous tone. "For the good of the community, [Union Planters would] like to see the music industry prosper and do well in Memphis. But you can't just say it, you have to have a way." Matthews championed the bank's idea of an album comprising vaulted Stax material that would be released in the memory of Dr. Martin Luther King. The album, continued the self-appointed record executive, could generate enough profits to give Stax working capital; he encouraged local African-American entrepreneurs to buy the bank's interest in the firm and use the profits from the album for the record company's further development.

Al Bell was undeterred by the legal lockdown. "Those who forcibly render on us involuntary bankruptcy can only attain liabilities such as empty buildings," he said. "I hasten to caution the hunter to take care that he is not consumed by the prey he seeks to devour."

The bluster on all sides continued until midsummer, when arguments about Stax's viability were made before Judge Leffler in bankruptcy court. The bank argued that Stax's total debt, by some estimates to be over $30 million, made it impossible for the company to recover, especially with their star artist now recording for another label. Stax brought witnesses to substantiate the value of their tapes, including a Motown consultant who estimated their worth at "$21 million not discounted" and also a competing record label owner who suggested a potential "between $4 million and $5 million in revenue for the first year, if Stax were allowed to re-open." The judge ruled that although Stax was a "financial holocaust" with little hope of success, it could reopen if it posted a $500,000 indemnity bond or $500,000 in cash within one week to protect present creditors. Stax proved unable to present the necessary funds, and a week later, Judge Leffler declared Stax out of business, allowing the trustee for Stax's creditors to begin selling off the pieces. The recording equipment netted $50,000 and was scattered among several studios in town. The office furniture was bought by an auction house. Pieces broke off and drifted away.

The publishing companies were sold in February 1977 to Al Bennett—an Arkansas man who'd founded Liberty Records in 1955 and negotiated a variety of music industry deals; he gave the bank a cashier's check for $250,000, with the promise to pay the balance of the $1.8 million sales price over the next five years. *Billboard* described Bennett as "elated." In mid-March 1982, Bennett more than doubled his investment when he sold the Stax publishing catalogs to Rondor Publishing. In 2000, Rondor was sold for $400 million; East/Memphis was one of Rondor's several gems, alongside songs by the Beach Boys, Tom Petty, Michael Jackson, Al Green, and others. The value of the copyrights was proving to be incalculable.

Stax's catalog of master tapes was sold at auction, but not before both Union Planters and CBS tried to claim them. In the court case, according to the appeal ruling, "Union Planters averred that a primary purpose of

CBS in its dealings in this case was to gain control of a substantial portion of the 'soul music market' and specifically to gain control, dominion and beneficial ownership of Stax for said purpose to the detriment of Stax and its creditors." The court ruled that the tapes should be sold, and the trustee should disburse funds to the various suppliers, artists, and other creditors. At auction, Al Bennett, who'd bought the publishing, bid $3.7 million for the tapes, but lost to the $1.3 million bid by the NMC Company, a Los Angeles–based liquidation firm; Bennett proposed installment payments and the judge took cash on the barrelhead. Before 1977 was out, the catalog was sold to an intermediary, Elan Enterprises, who then sold it to Fantasy Records of Berkeley, California. Fantasy was home to Credence Clearwater Revival and was also purchasing catalogs, including jazz labels Prestige and Riverside.

In 1977, Fantasy hired Stax songwriter David Porter to revive Stax, with the intention of not only mining the unreleased material—Albert King's *The Pinch* is a great album from that time, and the Bar-Kays "Holy Ghost" finally got a proper release—but also signing new talent. Despite a solid effort, the label closed after a year and a half. Porter has continued to produce and write songs, and he and Isaac resumed their friendship, like true friends do. The Hayes-Porter collaboration yielded some of the soul era's most enduring hits. A successful businessman, Porter continues to work in music, developing artists and writing songs. Fantasy understood what the Stax catalog offered, and under the direction of Bill Belmont, it kept Stax in the marketplace, introducing the music to successive generations. In early 2005, Concord Records purchased Fantasy for $80 million and reactivated Stax as a recording entity, signing Isaac Hayes, Booker T. Jones, and other artists, in addition to continuing the profitable re-releasing of the classic catalog.

These prices substantiate the latent value of Stax. The music business is built on catalog sales: that is, the artists and songs that sell for decades. The Stax hits have proved timeless, the biggest kind of hits. The performances are honest all these years later; the songs still sing from the heart. That's the sound of the master tapes and the publishing rights accruing value. Hits, however, can't be predicted with any certainty, and so the valuation of the catalog and publishing company at the time of the label's demise is not a scientific determination. Tim Whitsett notes that most of the East/Memphis catalog was recorded by Stax, so if Stax was not releasing records, the publishing company's value would diminish quickly. Conversely, significant value was gained when Congress in 1976 extended the duration of copyright ownership.

There are, nonetheless, authoritative opinions that agree with Al's overall position that the assets decidedly outweighed the liabilities. "If Stax Records had been properly assessed," says CBS's Logan Westbrooks, "they would not have been forced into bankruptcy. But at that time, it was rather difficult to anticipate the value of those master tapes. And even the publishing division, where you think in terms of five, ten, fifteen years ahead—it has proven to be unusually valuable, no question about that—but could you make that analysis at that particular time? It was most difficult."

◆ ◆ ◆

IN THE WAKE of Stax's closing, Al Bell was sued by the Chase Manhattan Bank of New York and the Tri State Bank (an African-American-owned bank in Memphis), by an interior designer, and by a host of others to whom he owed money. The IRS filed a lien against him; Union Planters foreclosed on property he owned.

In July 1976, during the heat of summer, while Stax was in bankruptcy court, Al Bell's biggest trial began: fourteen counts of conspiring to defraud the Union Planters National Bank of $18 million. "They did a marvelous job in putting together the evidence against me, some with forged signatures," says Al. "If I hadn't known me, and if I hadn't known what had taken place, I would have thought I was guilty. Fortunately, James F. Neal, who was my defense counsel, exposed the conspiracy." On the stand, a cohort of Harwell's from the bank (and a former member of the Memphis band Sam the Sham and the Pharaohs—"Wooly Bully" to you) testified that Harwell had shown him how he "could sign Mr. Bell's name as well as Mr. Bell could." Further, Neal brought a witness who'd heard bank officials brag, using a racial slur, about "running those" blacks "and especially the chief" black "out of town."

Al's trial ran for three weeks, and the jury of eight men and four women (seven of whom were African-American) deliberated only seven hours and fifteen minutes. Bell was acquitted on all counts—guilty of nothing—and former banker Joe Harwell was found guilty of making false entries on a bank record and with misapplication of bank funds. Though Harwell's attorney argued that his client was being made a scapegoat to help the bank explain heavy losses, Harwell confessed to signing Bell's signature to loan guarantees, and to having Al sign others without his knowing what they were. Harwell then used the guarantees as collateral for loans not only to Stax but also, according to Harwell's testimony, to fictitious borrowers whose fake accounts he created for his own use.

He was sentenced to two and a half years in jail, in addition to the five years he was already serving.

Al had been through the wars, and was thirty-six years old. His detractors, some thought, had achieved their goal despite the court loss. "Al, in fourteen indictments, freed on all charges," says Jesse Jackson. "But then you've got the bloodstains on your clothes. Don't forget that Dr. King led the Montgomery bus boycott in '55 and was indicted for income evasion in 1957. The case was designed to slow Dr. King down. Dr. King was taken to the penitentiary about traffic tickets in 1960 and put in a cell with killers. That was a form of breaking people, designed to maim and to slow down and injure, and they did just that. Al Bell was and is a man of integrity."

After a respite, Al returned to the record business. He became president of Motown Records in the late 1980s, its last days as an independent label, and assisted Berry Gordy in the label's sale to MCA Records. He founded a new label, Bellmark, that discovered and distributed the song "Whoomp! (There It Is)" by Tag Team; it was certified quadruple platinum for sales over four million. He also worked with Prince, distributing his 1994 hit "The Most Beautiful Girl in the World" and coproducing with him the Mavis Staples album *Time Waits for No One* (which also included contributions from Lester Snell and Homer Banks). Recently, he's returned to Memphis as chairman of the Memphis Music Foundation, and also launched an online venture, AlBellPresents.com. In 2011, he received the Grammy Trustees Award, the music industry's highest honor for a nonperformer.

◆ ◆ ◆

IT WOULD BE another two years after Stax's close before the story ended for Johnny Baylor. In October 1976, Baylor won a judgment against the IRS charging that they had improperly seized his money at the airport; a New York federal court ordered the IRS to return over half a million dollars to him, plus an additional $35,000 in interest. Before Baylor received his returned money, the trustee for the Stax bankruptcy put a claim on it to help satisfy the Stax debts, calling the payments to Baylor "fraudulent conveyances" that were intended to keep the money beyond the reach of any Stax creditors.

Baylor stood trial in October 1978, and Al took the stand, saying, "The management of Stax and Baylor had an understanding. It was a handshake deal." The Union Planters attorney, Wynn Smith, was having none of that, and he set out to prove that Baylor was hiding the money for later retrieval. "You don't earn two and a half million dollars doing nothing," Smith reflects. "There was no documentation whatsoever to justify any such payments. There's no evidence that he ever distributed any product. There wasn't any basis at all for these payments. I argued to the jury that the whole purpose of this scheme with Johnny Baylor was to take two and a half million dollars out of Stax, free and clear of the huge amount of money that Stax owed." Smith told the jury, "Al Bell had a laundry service named Johnny Baylor. Johnny Baylor was a bag man for Mr. Bell, but the bag man got caught with bag in hand."

Baylor, forty-five years old, exhibited no fear on the stand, claiming that the money he received was, in fact, not as much as it should have been. He'd been promised by Bell, he claimed, royalties on all the records he produced, plus a fee for promoting and marketing Stax records. Baylor said he was actually owed about $5 million. "The deal Mr. Bell gave me I would have given him if I had been in his position," Baylor said, "because if we didn't make money I wouldn't make anything." He said Bell gave him one check for $250,000 but he didn't cash it because "it wasn't enough." He later got a check for $500,000. He claimed that when he was first offered a contract in 1968, he didn't sign it because it was "real thin." The next contract was much thicker and thus too complicated to read, so he didn't sign that one either. The only contract that was just right was an oral one. Baylor, claiming responsibility for the scores of Stax records charted by *Billboard* magazine, justified his payments from the stand, saying, "I think I made the major contribution [to Stax's success]. In my opinion I was the difference in Stax being flat and being a major company. I was [as] effective . . . as any record man in this country."

The jury deliberated only about three hours before determining that Baylor was given the money "with the actual intent to hinder, delay or defraud the creditors of Stax." The Stax trustee was entitled to over $2.5 million, and Baylor was forced to turn over what Stax money remained—$300,000 in treasury bills "traceable" to the $1 million payment, and $500,000 associated with IRS money returned to Baylor.

Why would Al Bell turn over so much money to Johnny Baylor on behalf of Stax? Only two people really know. Al Bell says it was money earned. Johnny Baylor died in 1986; the official diagnosis was stomach cancer, but word on the street was that a girlfriend had been, for years, putting ground glass into his food.

"Even though he was a rough, tough dude, people ended up loving him," says Dino. "He cared about people. He suggested to the secretaries that they should speak to Al about the hourly wages. They got a raise. Regardless of the negative things, a lot of good came through him."

"He didn't go around all the time with his gun cocked," says Deanie Parker. "Johnny allowed us to view him from time to time as an everyday guy who liked to have fun, who enjoyed laughing, who had a heart. If he knew someone was in a hardship situation, he would reach in his pocket and pull out money to help. But he could be just the opposite too."

"He helped me a great deal," says Willie Hall. "He gave me a chance to produce when I knew nothing about producing. He gave money to people in need. Now that other side—he did have a talent for whooping people."

No one can deny Baylor's effectiveness at getting records played, though the legality, morality, and civility of his means were dubious. If, as he claims, he was responsible for the success of "Theme from *Shaft*," of "I'll Take You There," of "If Loving You Is Wrong," and the other hits of the period—when those records were selling, Stax was grossing $10-15 million a year. Can one man be worth one quarter of the company's gross, one half, perhaps, of its profit? What Baylor was paid in this nine-month period was more than Stax's staggering annual payroll for two hundred employees.

According to the US Court of Appeals' 1981 ruling against Baylor, "Baylor's flat $1 million promotional fee compares to industry norms of $60,000 to $70,000 per year." Rumors abound—blackmail, extortion, a Swiss bank account. Baylor was ruthless, and however he threatened his cohorts, whatever incriminating information he carried (if any) appears to have as much force a quarter century after his death as it did when the former Ranger walked the earth. No one's talking.

Union Planters National Bank achieved its financial goal, reclaiming slightly more than the $10 million it set out to get on the more than $16 million it was owed by its debtors and swindlers. In the non-Stax Harwell bond claim, the bank was awarded $4.5 million, and the other bond claims were settled at $6.3 million, the bank collecting from its insurance companies. Through novel accounting, that $6.3 million was not taxable. In 1977, Union Planters became one of the largest banks in Tennessee.

Stax's other nemesis, CBS, managed quite well. It signed the Emotions, the Soul Children, and, most notably, Johnnie Taylor, releasing his "Disco Lady." The single's success was so big that the industry had to create a new designation: the platinum record, honoring two million copies sold. (The producer: Don Davis.) CBS was no more accustomed to the workings of the soul circuit than Johnnie was to the corporate record world, and there was a period of adjustment for both parties. Bruce Lundvall, who had become president of CBS Records, was at a company convention, Johnnie's band onstage vamping, but star attraction Johnnie Taylor was nowhere in sight. Rushing backstage, Lundvall was told that Johnnie wasn't performing until he got paid. "I ran upstairs," says Lundvall, "said, 'Johnnie, get onstage willya!' He said, 'I don't go on until I get paid.'" It took some convincing and, reportedly with no money changing hands, Taylor appeared, winning over the audience and helping build the momentum that brought him the biggest success of his career. Stax was always strong at making money for others.

◆◆◆

MEMPHIS OFTEN TREATS its true heroes the way it treats its glorious history. T.O. Jones, the onetime union navy yard worker who tenaciously held to his sense of right and wrong and brought union representation to Memphis's Department of Public Works, did not fare so well. He never regained control of Local 1733, though he did find employment with the national office through most of the 1970s. By 1976, AFSCME had become the largest union in the state, with the Memphis local led by a longtime sanitation crew chief who'd worked with Jones's efforts since 1964. Jones retired in the late 1970s, then suffered a series of heart attacks. This man among men spent his last years living impoverished in public housing, surviving on the support of labor leaders who gave him food and money. He died in 1989. As a younger man, he'd brought dignity and respect—humanity, really—to the city's despised and neglected.

Mayor Loeb did not seek reelection in 1972, and after deciding against a run for the governorship of Tennessee, he retired to Forrest City, Arkansas, where he ran a business selling agricultural equipment. Memphis elected its first African-American mayor, Willie Herenton, in 1991, and he served for eighteen years. Harold Ford served twenty-two years in the House of Representatives and was succeeded by his son, Harold Ford Jr.

Schools in Memphis have never been the same since busing began in 1973. Enrollment in private schools peaked the next year, the number of students and the number of private schools having just about doubled in three years. Private school attendance has held well over the years (census figures showed a dwindling school-age population), but many facilities merged or closed. The Neighborhood Schools of Memphis, run by Citizens Against Busing, had a very short run, failing to reopen in 1974. By 1975, whites in the public schools accounted for less than 30 percent, and their numbers today are about 10 percent. Many whites left the city for the county, and as Memphis has annexed those areas, the nearby towns in Mississippi have grown. At the time of this writing, the public schools are in renewed turmoil, a conflict between rural and urban dwellers, resulting from the redundant, race-based establishment of separate city and county governments.

◆◆◆

POOR ISAAC HAYES. He'd picked cotton before picking up an Academy Award. Money fell on him like rain, and then the money evaporated. He lost more than everything, because ultimately he lost his copyrights—the right to collect future money for the art he'd created.

Hayes's downfall was tied to Stax's inability to fulfill his contract. In January of 1976, after the label had been declared bankrupt, he sued the company and its trustees for $3 million; they were supposed to have given him all his copyrights and master tapes, but they hadn't, nor had they distributed to him his BMI and ASCAP money—funds the company had received for his radio airplay. Meanwhile, Isaac was missing alimony and child-support payments, and his ex-wife was hitting him with lawsuits. The security firm that protected his studio and his house sued him for $15,000. His clothier sued for $11,000. The IRS seized his Hot Buttered Soul studio, and after his lawyers worked out a deal on the $6 million that he owed, he couldn't make the first $100,000 payment in July. On November 11, 1976, he filed for bankruptcy. His largest debt among the more than three hundred creditors was to Union Planters National Bank for more than $1.75 million. Others owed included hotels and motels from New York to California, credit cards and department stores—ten grand to Saks Fifth Avenue in Beverly Hills, another ten to the Saks in Washington, DC. Flower shops, doctors, ex-wives, airlines. His half-million-dollar home was sold on the courthouse steps, scooped up by Union Planters for one hundred grand less than he'd paid for it two years earlier. "Be careful when you take my picture," he warned journalists on his way into court, referring to the glittering initials "IH" on the corner of his sunglasses. "I don't want people to think these are diamonds." Rhinestones. They glitter like real jewelry, but precious they're not.

Never short of ideas, Isaac released three albums in 1977, two in 1978 (one was archival), and one each in 1979, 1980, and 1981. He could keep the money he earned after the bankruptcy—from a recurring appearance on the TV show *The Rockford Files* and his other acting work, from the royalties for his collaboration with Dionne Warwick, 1977's *A Man and a*

Woman, and from his gold-selling album *Don't Let Go,* from 1979. When music sales petered out, he became a respected character actor, then regained a place in popular consciousness when he joined the cast of the animated cartoon *South Park* in 1997 (he'd returned to recording two years earlier . . . with two new albums). His role as Chef on the series proved immensely popular, resulting in an album, *Chef Aid: The South Park Album,* with several tracks sung by Hayes; one, "Chocolate Salty Balls," went to number one in the UK. He quit the show in 2005, unhappy over its mockery of the Church of Scientology, of which he was a prominent member.

In 1992, Hayes was made an honorary king of Ghana, in recognition of his efforts to advance civil rights and to honor the African traditions of African-Americans. As king, he was renamed Nene Katey Ocansey the First. Joining him at his coronation were Chuck D. and Flavor Flav from the hip-hop group Public Enemy; they performed together while in Africa. Isaac helped develop the eastern district of Ada, on the Atlantic. His fourth wife, Adjowa, was from there; she had his twelfth child.

Hayes was inducted into the Rock and Roll Hall of Fame in 2002, and had recently signed to the revived Stax label when he suffered a stroke in 2006. He recovered well enough to resume touring and working up new material. But in August 2008, while exercising at home on a treadmill, he died of a heart attack. His debts were more than his assets, leaving his estate bankrupt; his million-dollar, seven-thousand-square-foot home was sold at foreclosure. One ray of hope: Recent copyright extension acts may allow his estate to soon regain control of his publishing.

◆◆◆

MANY OF STAX'S artists enjoyed continued careers as singers, entertainers, performers, and producers. Few surpassed their Stax success; in addition to Johnnie Taylor, the Staple Singers had a number-one hit after leaving Stax, "Do It Again." Rufus Thomas continued performing, always inviting fans onstage to do "The Funky Chicken" with him. Daughter Carla makes occasional appearances, and her long-unreleased cabaret album, *Live at the Bohemian Caverns,* came out forty years after its 1967 recording, welcome and bittersweet. Marvell Thomas has continued to record and perform, working at various times with Isaac Hayes, William Bell, the Hi Rhythm Section, Peabo Bryson, and the Temptations.

Booker T. & the MG's have occasionally regrouped since Al Jackson's murder, initially with Willie Hall on drums, later with Anton Fig, Steve

Rufus Thomas, the World's Oldest Teenager, had his own parking spot on Beale Street, and a park in Porretta Terme, Italy, is named for him. (University of Memphis Libraries/Special Collections)

Jordan, and then Memphian Steve Potts ("the Smiling Drummer"). Along the way, Booker, Steve, and Duck joined Levon Helm for his RCO All-Stars band, and Cropper and Dunn were part of the Blues Brothers band (which also featured drummer Willie Hall). The Blues Brothers' big hit was "Soul Man," and the album went to number one, introducing a new generation to Stax players and songs. In 1986, Jerry Wexler asked the surviving MG's to be the house band at Atlantic's fortieth anniversary celebration. That led to gigging as the house band at Bob Dylan's Madison Square Garden "Bob-Fest," which in turn led to them backing Neil Young. With their profile high, the band renewed its own touring and recorded a new album, 1994's *That's the Way It Should Be.* In 2007, they were given a Lifetime Achievement Award by the Grammys. Booker and Steve have reignited successful solo careers (Booker has recently taken home two Grammy Awards for Best Pop Instrumental Album; Steve has enjoyed recent nominations).

Duck Dunn, who recorded with Muddy Waters, Eric Clapton, John Prine, and many others after Stax, continued to work with Neil Young after the MG's tour; he called his Florida home "the house that Neil built." "Stax was the greatest thing that ever happened to anybody who worked there," Duck said. "Jim Stewart, I'd love to hug his neck today. He gave me a lot of grief up there in the control room, but he also gave me my life." One night after a gig in May 2012, while touring with Steve

Cropper in Japan, Duck Dunn went to sleep and didn't wake up. He was seventy years young, full of energy, respectful, irreverent, and funny—all of which was reflected in his playing.

Al Jackson's murder remains an open case, and police will not comment on it.

Wayne Jackson and Andrew Love worked hard as the Memphis Horns for many years after leaving the Stax payroll, joining the Doobie Brothers, Steve Winwood, Sting, and U2. Their stamp is all over pop music. "Stax was a cosmic happening," Wayne says. "Little sparks hitting, the fires starting, those records being made. Other people might spout philosophy about being white, being black, but when you saw Wayne and Andrew onstage, you couldn't imagine that anyone had any trouble down South, 'cause we had so much fun. And we sounded so good together. Between us, we raised six children, put them all through school. The more I lived in that environment of magic happening, the more I believed in it." The Memphis Horns were given a Grammy Lifetime Achievement Award in 2012, one of the few backing groups to be so honored. Wayne still keeps his trumpet shined. Andrew Love died in 2012 after a long battle with Alzheimer's.

The Bar-Kays have enjoyed a very successful career. By 1976, within their first year of leaving Stax, they were on the pop and soul charts with "Shake Your Rump to the Funk." From then, well into the 1980s, they were fixtures on the soul charts, occasionally crossing over to pop ("Freak Show on the Dance Floor" comes to mind) and continuing their tradition of wild clothes, energized shows, and party-popping pleasures. James Alexander and vocalist Larry Dodson are the group's mainstays; Ben Cauley sometimes sits in. Their 2012 single "Grown Folks" captures them in fine form, and they played the 2013 inauguration of President Obama. In 2007, on the fortieth anniversary of the plane crash, Ben Cauley returned for the first time to the lake near Madison, Wisconsin, where his friends died in the waters. At a ceremony commemorating the tragedy, he played his trumpet and sang "Try a Little Tenderness" and "The Dock of the Bay" for the several hundred people who'd gathered. In his sleep, Cauley says, he sometimes still hears the final cries of his friends.

◆ ◆ ◆

IN 1981, ON a mid-October day with the weight of winter bearing down, Jim Stewart sipped coffee at his kitchen table while a stream of people he did not know gathered on his fifty-six-acre estate, milling about in preparation for the auction of everything that he owned. The bank was collecting

Jim Stewart's house, and its contents, about to be auctioned. (University of Memphis Libraries/ Special Collections)

on every last bit of Jim's personal guaranty. A reporter approached Jim and asked the reason for the sale. "It's just a real estate sale," he said. "Why does anyone sell his property? I'm just a private citizen and I have no comment." Most of the goods would be gone by day's end. Not long after, the IRS evicted Jim, his wife, and three children during the night.

In hindsight, it's easy to say that Jim bet all his chips on a color not on the roulette wheel. The company's shaky foundation seems obvious, the constant borrowing to finance the next hit—neither the hits nor the borrowing could last. But the stable of artists was still strong, and if Jim gave them the attention they needed, why shouldn't they resume the hits? What had Jim done for years but produce hits from that studio, with many of those same artists? In the moment, the gamble was not as long as it appears in retrospect. He bet on what he'd built. "The only excuse I can give is that I loved the company," he told Peter Guralnick. "I thought it was worth saving."

Epic heroes make epic mistakes. Jim had never done the expected. He'd been told it was unwise to have blacks in the studio, that it was stupid to leave banking. Jim acted from the contradictory heart of humanity: People do things romantic and heroic and regrettable. There may be no sense to it, but the act itself is powerful, emotional, and unforgettable. Jim's bet turned out wrong, but what if he'd been right? What profound belief he'd expressed! In 1974, he was in the catbird seat, and when he leapt out—a beautiful swan dive—he reserved nothing for his family. He lost all that was his. All the savings, all the future income from his sale of the company. He lost the home, the land, the cars, the furnishings. "By early 1974, I was putting money back into the company to protect my investment," says Jim. "And that's what destroyed me. I was wealthy. I had Gulf & Western stock which I had retained from their buyout. I got rid of that and I never cut my losses. I just lost everything." Slowly, with his wife and kids, he reestablished himself, although he avoided the public eye. With some holdings in his wife's name, the family's hard fall had some cushion. A Stax guitarist, Bobby Manuel, would coax Jim into a midtown Memphis recording studio. Manuel, with whom Al and Duck re-formed the MG's, continued to record Stax alumni and newer artists who retained the grit and authenticity that made Stax great. The music was solid, but the distribution less so.

When the world was saying no, Jim and Estelle said yes. They opened their studio the way they opened their hearts, creating opportunity, embracing possibility. A spirit imbues the Stax songs and performances. It is music with soul. "To know that after forty years people still want to hear Otis and still hear Booker T. & the MG's, it's gratifying, very gratifying," Jim says. "I'm just thankful I was blessed to be a part of that. Stax was a family affair, and I don't mean me and my sister. That close relationship of struggling brought us together. None of us had any money. All we had was the desire and the will and the ability to make it happen—which we did. At Stax, there was a lot of soul, the inner soul that's part of all of us. We all gained by sharing that, by respecting our fellow man."

Jim's sister Estelle is the only owner who made any money at Stax. "Lots of people think life ends at thirty," she says. "I started in records at forty. I have to say that my life has been very, very interesting since I was forty." After Packy's death, Estelle forged on with Fretone. "I depended on him," she says. "I almost gave up two or three times. But being around young people, it keeps you thinking." Estelle, after the death of her beloved son, after what she considered a betrayal by her only brother, renewed herself yet again, thinking her young self back into one of the most successful records to ever come from Memphis, "Disco Duck." Created by a popular Memphis disc jockey, Rick Dees (along with producer Bobby Manuel and a convenience-store employee who did the duck voice), the song took off on her label. She was familiar with records getting too hot to handle and she flew to California to cut a deal with RSO Records, a label that had remade the careers of both Eric Clapton and the Bee Gees. Within months of its release, "Disco Duck" went gold, then quickly platinum, selling more than two million copies. As Stax was withering, Estelle was again blossoming. "I got back in the business," she says, "because I had to prove to myself that I knew a little bit more about music than I'd ever been given credit for."

Estelle continued to do it her way. "She spent all her money chasing that hit," says her daughter Doris. Then with a new fortune, she spent it how she wanted. "She blew it," says Doris, describing spending sprees on clothes and home furnishings. "She bought furs." She sold the apartment complex, and Everett died of pancreatic cancer in 1984. When the money was gone, Estelle worked as a cashier in a cafeteria, ringing up Salisbury steaks, Jell-O molds, and corn-kernel bowls, greeting all the customers as if they were stars. She died at age eighty-five in 2004. "You didn't feel any back-off from her, no differentiation that you were black and she was white," Isaac Hayes said at the time of her death. "Being in a town where that attitude was plentiful, she just made you feel secure. She was like a mother to us all." Her grave site features a shaded bench in memory of "Lady A," hospitable and open long after she's left this world.

◆◆◆

MEMPHIS DIDN'T APPRECIATE its musical heritage until Elvis Presley died in 1977. And then it wasn't the heritage or the music it appreciated, just the money that could be made off it. Elvis had brought blues and soul to white society. When he died, Memphis was flooded with tourists from around the world. Phone lines to the city overloaded and service crashed. Florists completely sold out. Locals were shocked by this response, our provincialism laid bare. Memphis experienced a blues awakening like what W.C. Handy describes in his autobiography. At a rural "dance pro-gram" around 1903, Handy's sophisticated band was asked to allow "a local colored band" to play some of the local music. Handy expresses dis-dain for the trio's "disturbing monotony" and was amazed when they finished that "a rain of silver dollars began to fall . . . [There] lay more money than my nine musicians were being paid for the entire engage-ment. Then I saw the beauty of primitive music. They had the stuff the people wanted."

What the people wanted. Elvis died and money rushed Memphis. Stax died two years before Memphis's rain of silver. The Stax building sat empty and shuttered. In 1981, Union Planters sold it to the Church of God in Christ for ten dollars, inserting a clause in the deed that dictated the building's usage as only for "nonprofit, religious, charitable, educa-tional, scientific, cultural and/or civic purposes." If the property were used

June 1991, dedication of historical marker at the Stax site. Ben Cauley remembers what was. (*Commercial Appeal*/Photograph by Dave Darnell)

otherwise, ownership reverted to the bank. The church long claimed it was going to build a community center there—what had Stax been other than the greatest possible community center?—and in 1989, the church began tearing down the building. There was community protest, enough that a stop-work order was issued (there was also report of a gas leak, which may have influenced the order). But, in Jim's words, it was too little too late, and the demolition proceeded, the ending seemingly sealed on this modern-day Greek tragedy. Ben Cauley stood outside the hurricane fence and played a requiem on his trumpet.

"After the close of Stax, and after some time had passed, several years, I would drive back to Memphis, Tennessee, and park across the street from 926 East McLemore, and look at that vacant lot where our hearts once dwelled and see the weeds there, the building gone," says Al Bell. "I'd see beer cans and what have you on that lot, and ultimately, the historic marker that had been placed there. And I would cry. The tears would run profusely, for it was quite painful to know that all that we had worked for and lived for, there was not even a symbol of that in place. It's like someone had tried to wipe all of that off the face of the earth. Never to be remembered and never to be recognized."

The lot stood empty. The movie theater lobby's tile floor showed through the accumulated dirt, and black-and-white photos of the second Bar-Kays would occasionally blow with the breeze. Visitors rummaged through the detritus looking for souvenirs. One local entrepreneur advertised bricks from Stax, shipping them around the world.

As the millennium turned, an idea began taking hold: Stax had assumed its place in the world, now it was Soulsville's opportunity. The sound of Soulsville, and the power of Soulsville, had gripped a post–Jim Crow generation in Memphis. Several burgeoning community leaders saw that around the Stax lot, an infrastructure languished: An African-American college, LeMoyne-Owen, was around the corner, and many of the neighborhood's original, well-built homes still stood. Reaching out to some former Stax leaders, an alliance formed, young and old, white and black, private money and public money. A goal was set: to resurrect not just Stax but all of the neighborhood, Soulsville, with a rebuilt Stax as its beacon. The plan was tri-pronged: A museum to attract outsiders; an academy for neighborhood kids where, after school, they could get homework help and free tutoring; and a neighborhood revitalization plan to remove the blight and strengthen what remained. Stax's longtime publicist Deanie Parker was hired to helm the project.

The Stax Academy opened in July 2000, three years before the Stax Museum of American Soul Music, demonstrating the project's emphasis on community. Rufus and Carla Thomas, the label's seminal hitmakers, were among the first alumni to participate in the academy's summer music camp. Isaac Hayes, Wayne Jackson, Mavis Staples—numerous alumni have returned to inspire the kids.

The Stax Museum of American Soul Music was built on the Stax lot to the specifications of the original building, using the original blueprints. When you stand outside the Stax Museum, you are standing before a replica of the original building. Inside, it's different (take a nap at the original Stax and the layout would be changed before you woke), but Studio A is like the original, and the gift shop is where Estelle's record store was after it moved from the concession stand in the lobby. Inside, the Stax story begins in a transplanted rural church, and as Stax and soul music develop, so does the context of soul music nationally. There are about twenty short films, lots of music and outlandish clothes, plus Isaac's refurbished gold-plated Cadillac (and the razor kit he used to keep his pate gleaming). The Stax Museum even has a dance floor—now *that's* a museum that grooves.

Now, as then, Stax is anchoring a neighborhood. The blight has greatly diminished, there are many newly built homes, and the Stax campus has grown, creating a steady flow of workers and students. Incomes in Soulsville remain low, and there's more crime there than in some other parts of town. It's a work in progress, but the signs of progress are clear, and are everywhere. The Stax Academy proved such a thriving entity that in 2005 the Soulsville Charter School was established. It began with sixty sixth graders, adding a grade each year until it became a middle and senior high school that now pulsates the neighborhood. In its early years, to get into the school, students had to be failing or expelled from their regular program; unfortunately, there were plenty of applicants. The school days are long, and part of the reward for good work is getting to make music; suspension from music rehearsal is a punishment. I saw sixth and seventh graders who'd never known that a cello existed playing symphonic arrangements of Stax hits—"Theme from *Shaft*," "Knock on Wood," and others—and it was one of the most moving musical performances I've ever experienced. The first two classes have now graduated, with 100 percent of each going to college, including one Ivy League recruit.

When the oasis seemed to have become just a mirage, vitality bloomed again from the site. "One day," Al Bell continues, "I turned the corner out on McLemore, looked up and saw that marquee. And it impacted me so much until I stumbled off the curb into the streets. And as I looked at that marquee, I began to cry once again. But this time, they were tears of joy. For not only had the original building been replicated and placed there on that corner, but the most important part of the spirit of Stax Records was embodied there in the Stax Music Academy, for everything about Stax as it relates to creativity, as it relates to administrative experiences and knowledge, was all about teaching.

"It was Booker T. & the MG's that taught these little shoeshine boys called the Bar-Kays how to play music. And it was one artist teaching another. It was one writer teaching another. There were open doors there all the time, where, no matter who you were or what you were, you could walk through those doors and realize an opportunity. Whether you had just been released from jail, or whether someone called you an alcoholic, or whatever the case might be—you could walk in there and somebody cared enough to take you by your hand and teach you and help you. And I saw that there—glorified there—in the Stax Music Academy. And I have not, until this very moment, stopped feeling good about that day and what I experienced in feeling on that day. Because I realized a part of it is still alive. Like Dr. King said, truth crushed to the earth shall rise again."

Lives were made by Stax, and some lives ruined. The tales and fates of these individuals are, like life, diverse and illogical. The Stax story captures our excitement and fears about change, about race and power, about the struggle to find a voice. But the company's results—not just its music, but also its social and spiritual achievements, the camaraderie, the rejection of hatred, the unprecedented successes—are life-affirming. Stax is the story of opportunity, the strides that people will make when given the chance, the growth a community can achieve when closed doors open, when closed hearts open. Had Jim, Estelle, and Al listened to the laws of Memphis and the laws of Tennessee, souls in harmony would never have sung. The beautiful music is something that raises us beyond our confines, that invites the spiritual, that takes us there.

A WRAP-UP OF OTHER KEY PLAYERS

As the work at Stax sputtered and stalled, the music industry in Memphis began circling the drain. "One thing about the banks and the general business community in Memphis, none of those people understood anything about the music business or about the value of a company like Stax to Memphis," says John Fry, owner of Ardent Studios, where Isaac Hayes and the Staple Singers recorded hits, and many Stax artists worked regularly. "The effect of Stax closing was profound and it was widespread. A lot of vendors—studios, photographers, graphic designers, printers, manufacturers, you name it—depended on Stax as a major customer. Many people had to leave town to find work in the industry." Memphis survived as a home for recording studios but not for record labels. There have been start-ups and pop-ups, with forecasts for old school vigor occasionally wafting through. But since Stax's fall, things ain't like what was.

Under Bill Matthews, Union Planters National Bank earned record profits. But by 1984 the bank was again on the skids, and he was relieved of duties that autumn. He joined a cattle-breeding operation, traveling the world selling bull semen and frozen cattle embryos. "He used to say," says guitarist and computer whiz Rick Ireland, " 'The banking business is becoming these bits of ones and zeros flying through the sky, and all we want to do is grab some of them every once in a while and then we'll be rich.'" Matthews joined a credit-card processing facility in Arkansas, but it was underfunded and dissolved under a shady cloud. He moved to California, where he died of a heart attack in 1994, age sixty-one.

Money continued to stick to Johnny Baylor. He spent much of the 1970s in New York rather than in Memphis. Two of his associates, in interviews separated by months and without prompting in either case, each described a drawer full of hundred-dollar bills in Johnny's bedroom.

Dino Woodard received his BA in 1984, when he was well into his 40s, and the year after Baylor's 1987 death, he was licensed to preach the Gospel, soon receiving his Master of Divinity. Presently "Reverend Boom" is a minister at Abyssinian Baptist Church in Harlem, where he's an assistant to the pastor and leads services. Of his late friend he says, "Johnny Baylor, he was a believer. He believed that what he did he had to do to make it in the world. And he made a way for himself." Dino officiated at Baylor's funeral. Luther Ingram died in 2007 from complications related to diabetes.

The Staple Singers maintained an active career through the death of Pops Staples in 2000. In the latter 2000s, Mavis has released compelling albums with Jeff Tweedy and Ry Cooder. The Emotions joined Johnny Taylor at Columbia, and had several big disco hits including the number-one hit "Best of My Love."

Rufus Thomas billed himself as "the World's Oldest Teenager" and "the Funkiest Man Alive." When he'd arrived in Memphis, he couldn't drink out of the same water fountain as white people, and before he died in 2001, the city gave him the only dedicated parking spot on historic Beale Street and named a street for him. In Porretta Terme, Italy, home of the annual Porretta Soul Festival, there's a park named for him. Until he died in 2001, he continued to host a radio show on WDIA.

In 2009, Booker T. Jones returned to solo recording, first making a hard-rock guitar album, *Potato Hole*, in collaboration with the Drive-By Truckers and Neil Young, and then the groove-heavy *Road from Memphis*, collaborating with the Roots. The one-time newspaper delivery kid was sought by the White House as a musical director in 2013. Recently, he's signed to Concord's Stax Records.

Steve Cropper has made two albums with Felix Cavaliere, vocalist and songwriter from the Rascals (*Nudge It Up a Notch* and *Midnight Flyer*). In 2011, he released a tribute to Lowman Pauling and the Five Royales, the group that so influenced his playing. On *Dedicated*, his guitar licks have a foot in the past, a foot in the present, and both feet on the dance floor.

Al Jackson's murder has never been solved. One of the suspects, a man on the FBI's Ten Most Wanted List, was killed in a 1976 police shoot-out in Seattle; another passed a polygraph test and was dropped by police.

Andrew Love played the sax solo on Nicolette Larson's "Lotta Love," and Wayne brought Memphis to Peter Gabriel's soulful "Sledgehammer." ("I hung up the phone," Wayne says, "and asked my daughter, 'You ever heard of Peter Gabriels?'") Wayne still keeps his trumpet handy, recently reprising Otis Redding's "Happy Song" with Frazey Ford. He is an enthusiastic supporter of the Stax Music Academy, where he devotes time to teaching and inspiring young kids. "It had been loose and not that professional, what we had done," says Wayne. "But those records stand up today. The door opened, the wind blew in, and we were smart enough not to fight it."

Saxophonist Floyd Newman, long a first-call Memphis horn player, retired from the Memphis schools' band program and still takes to the stage blowing real soul through twisted brass; lately, he's been featured in the Bo-Keys, a soul band that mixes several younger players with their heroes, including Skip Pitts, Howard Grimes, William Bell, Willie Hall, Ben Cauley, and Archie "Hubby" Turner (from Hi Records).

When the bad winds began to blow, Deanie Parker completed her Master's of Public Administration degree through night courses. "I have to say that the majority of Stax employees, who I think had a great deal to offer Memphis, were blackballed in the work community," she says. When she was hired at the city's first independent television station, it was because, she says, "the manager was not a Memphian. He didn't judge me by the color of my skin. He judged me based on my character and my abilities." After Stax, Larry Shaw established the South's first African-American-owned, full-service advertising agency, the Shaw Group, and later a marketing and communications consulting firm. He passed away in 2003 after a career of positive imaging.

Stax "was one hell of a great company," says Stax's mastering engineer Larry Nix, even though it closed owing him thousands of dollars. "When they say 'Stax family,' it wasn't just words. When my son was born, they bought him a really nice baby bed, they inquired about his health. They were interested in us. I made lifetime friendships. It was so fun, you had to sometimes make yourself go home—afraid you'd miss something." After the Mar-Keys, Larry's brother Don Nix continued to do it the storybook way. He wrote a few hits, including "Going Down," and produced a number of albums. Every big check that came in, he bought another huge item. Beautiful houses, three Rolls-Royces, trips to faraway places. Those opulent items are gone now, but the royalties keep him in bologna and on the edge of trouble, a safe distance between himself and nine-to-five work.

Little Milton continued having hits with Malaco Records in Jackson, Mississippi. Bar-Kays producer Allen Jones helped develop a Stax act named Con Funk Shun, and one of its members, Felton Pilate, was MC Hammer's music director while the star was at the top. When hip-hop stars Jay-Z and Kanye West collaborated, they built their new ideas around samples from Otis Redding's "Try A Little Tenderness," which sounded as fresh in 2011 as it had four decades earlier.

Estelle Axton. (Doris Axton Fredrick Collection)

Eddie Floyd, William Bell, Albert King, and Wilson Pickett all enjoyed successful gigging and recording careers. If their popularity never surpassed what they achieved at Stax, it seemed to almost never wane either. Each continued to work as long as he wanted, drawing crowds with older hits, entertaining them with newer material. "Stax gave me a career," says Eddie. "It's that music, you know? Once you're part of that music, it's till you die." He laughs. "It's just simple as that."

"Somebody asked me what I tell people who come in with a tape," Estelle says, "people who just know they're the greatest songwriter in the world. I never turn anybody off. If I know they don't have any talent, I suspect they know they don't either. I ask them, 'Do you enjoy putting together these tapes? I know it costs you money.' If they say yes, then I say, 'Keep doing it, because the money you spend there, the psychiatrist won't get it.' It's a release, people do it for their own pleasure. They'll never be able to place a song, but for their own well-being they do something they like to do. A lot of things, you're not going to reap any rewards for. If you enjoy doing it, keep on doing it. That's what I tell them."

A NOTE ON STAX RECORDING EQUIPMENT
BY RENÉ WU

The first four Satellite recordings (Burr Road) were done on a one-track Berlant tape recorder model 20-20 owned by Marshall Erwin Ellis.

When Stax moved to McLemore, they had the following equipment:

Ampex model 350 mono recorder
Two four-channel Ampex mic mixers, model 3761
Neumann mic type 67 for the vocals
RCA mic type 44-BX for the horns
Two RCA mics type DX77 for the drums

For monitoring, Stax used the Altec Voice of the Theater loudspeaker, similar to models A5 and A7. The power amp to drive this speaker was a McIntosh model MC30.

By July 1965, Tom Dowd brought in a Scully model 280 stereo recorder in a portable carrying case. Channel one was wired to one 3761 mixer, channel two to the other 3761 mixer.

For a very short period in late 1966 (possibly into 1967), the two Ampex mixers were replaced by a recording "desk" made from two Sigma four-channel mixers. (These were the same as the Ampex mixers but with the Sigma logos; Sigma took over the distribution for the Ampex mixers.) The desk also included echo sends, machine remote control, and a slate/control monitor cluster. This desk was probably made by Phil Iehle.

Welton Jetton, an engineer who would soon found Audiotronics in Memphis, designed a mixing console especially for Stax (no type number). This board was installed in 1966 or early 1967. The control room was upgraded at the same time. A four-track Scully recorder was connected to this new board together with a new mono Ampex recorder model AG350. The Scully two-track that Tom Dowd brought in was replaced by a freestanding Scully two-track. The left console leg was equipped with a Universal Audio compressor/limiter model 175B as well as a Spectra Sonics power supply. For control room monitors, Welton Jetton installed four Altec speakers, model 844A or 9844A.

Jetton next designed a smaller console for mixdown. It was installed in studio B.

In the early 1970s, the Welton Jetton board was replaced by an Audiotronics mixing console model 501, aka "Son of 36 Grand."

ACKNOWLEDGMENTS

The Stax story is complicated, and after years of my own work, I collaborated with Mark Crosby and Morgan Neville on the documentary *Respect Yourself: The Stax Records Story.* Mark and Morgan and I immersed ourselves in Stax, understanding its architecture, parsing its legends, and discovering the story. This book grew from the numerous interviews we did for that documentary, and from many long conversations we had about the label, its characters, its music.

I befriended Deanie Parker through my involvement with the creation of the Stax Museum of American Soul Music. She has been a great sounding board for the documentary and the book, and a great friend. When I told her I was embarking on this book, her look told me that, despite my optimism, she was bracing for another long and involved project; she was right, and she was always resourceful and open with her wealth of material and knowledge, giving me her perspective even after swearing she never wanted to talk about it again.

Peter Guralnick has been this writer's best writing friend. He gives unstintingly of himself, offering opportunities, encouragement, and inspiration. His generosity illuminates everything around him. If you've not read his *Sweet Soul Music*, run now to the nearest bookstore and buy two (you'll love it so much that you'll give one away). It covers a wider musical context—more on Atlantic and Wexler and Ray Charles, more on Rick Hall and the various Muscle Shoals stories, and more on Memphis, including American Studios and Hi Records. Beautifully written, full of personality and personalities, it's a musical story of freedom coming to America (www.peterguralnick.com).

Any contemporary pursuit on Stax is done in the wake of work by Rob Bowman. His exhaustively researched book, *Soulsville U.S.A.: The Story of Stax Records*, is an encyclopedic history and discography of the label. Rob was an early champion of Stax's importance. He was a force behind the three Stax singles box sets, and those include chart information on which I relied.

In his book *Say It One Time for the Broken Hearted*, Barney Hoskyns travels through the South's musical meccas, taking us deeper into the place where this music grows wild. (Shout-out to his Rock's Back Pages—www.rocksbackpages.com—an archive of music writing and a great resource for me.)

My first book, *It Came from Memphis*, will take you deeper into Memphis music and culture without taking you to the obvious places; it's rich reading, and fun.

Living in Memphis, I found myself often at the Stax Museum of American Soul Music, and it proved endlessly informative and exciting. Every visit brought new revelations. The staff there was always supportive and interested in my work. I'm especially grateful to Lisa Allen, archivist Levon Williams, Henry Nelson, Tim Sampson, and Mark Wender.

I'm grateful to my waves of readers, the early ones who slogged through a fat and repetitive manuscript and helped me see the good parts despite the bad, and the latter who took a much cleaner version and made me say what I meant, scolded me for avoiding the hard stuff, and prodded me to rethink what I'd come to accept. All were a big help: Tara McAdams, John Hubbell, Melissa Dunn, Henry Nelson, Joy Tremewan Corcoran, Tamar Cantora, Ross Johnson, Tim Prudhomme, Dan Bullard, Laura Helper-Ferris, and Deanie Parker.

The Memphis-Shelby County Public Library and Information Center is always a great resource, especially its Memphis Room in the History Department, and, within that trove, the goldmine that is the clippings files. Thanks to G. Wayne Dowdy and the History Department staff who lugged many a file to a desk for me. Thanks to Chris Ratliff at the University of Memphis Library's Special Collections desk for his diligent photo research.

Thanks to Trey Harrison and Doug Easley for musical consultation and guidance; to Bob Mehr for leads, collusion, and lunch; to John "J-Dog" Shaw for making me think about Mayor Ingram; to Frank Inman Jr. and William Boyd for their memories of the neighborhood before Stax arrived; Bruce Feldbaum and Mark Cantora for help with legal documents; Robert Smith, Marc Morgenstern, Joel Amsterdam, and Bill Belmont at Concord Records; Anna Esquivel, Tanya Teglo, Drew Paslay, and Lisa Sikkink for additional research; Jonathan Gould, working on an Otis Redding biography, with whom I enjoyed exchanging information and ideas; Will Georgantas copy editor, who had good suggestions; my parents Alvin and Elaine Gordon for their unflagging support and encouragement; and Nancy Morrow, Reba Russell, Richard Pearce, David Leonard, Iddo Patt, Steve Berkowitz, and Jessica Jones.

There are worlds of people essential to Stax and its day-to-day operations, and many great artists who deserve whole books to themselves. I am sorry I was unable to include all the staff and all the bands and all the Stax supporters and friends in this telling. I thank them all for their music, and for their work with and for the label.

Kathy Belden is from the grand old school of the sharpened pencil. Publishing still pulses because of editors like her. Her input, gentle prodding, and give-and-take did what a great editor does: She helped me tell my story. My agent David Dunton knew where to land the deal, and he helped at each step of the way.

My wife, Tara McAdams, read this book over and over in many forms. Every time, she made it better. She, with our kids Lila and Esther, endured the agony, frustration, and depression that most any book entails, reviving me when my energy flagged, slowing me when I rushed to judgment, and helping me see possibilities when I defaulted to the conventional. I'm lucky that Tara's my wife, and anyone who enjoys this book is lucky that she's a reader and a writer. As usual, all my favorite lines in this book shimmer with her touch.

A NOTE ON THE INTERVIEWS

Unless otherwise indicated, all quotes come from interviews by the author. Many of these interviews occurred during the making of the *Respect Yourself* documentary; some interviews come from my prior writing pursuits, and many interviews were done while working on this book.

Peter Guralnick graciously shared his Jim Stewart and Estelle Axton interviews with me. All quotes from Jim or Estelle, unless otherwise stated, come from Guralnick.

Barney Hoskyns readily shared his Estelle Axton interview with me.

The Smithsonian Institution conducted a series of interviews in Memphis in the 1990s. My interviews with Robert Tally, Carla Thomas, Marvell Thomas, Floyd Newman, Lewie Steinberg, and Ben Cauley come from there, as do some of my quotes from Rufus Thomas, Jim Stewart, David Porter, James Alexander, and Steve Cropper. The Smithsonian interviews helped create the Rock 'n' Soul Museum in Memphis (www.memphisrocknsoul.org), which is now also the home of the Memphis Music Hall of Fame (www.memphismusichalloffame.com). Visit them in Memphis, along with the Stax Museum (www.staxmuseum.com), Sun Studios (www.sunstudio.com), and the vast Mississippi Delta (www.visitthedelta.com).

There are several more books to look forward to. Jim Stewart told me more than once that he's working on his own book, and Booker T. Jones, Steve Cropper, David Porter, and Mickey Gregory have indicated they're considering book endeavors. Gents, bring 'em on! This Stax story is complicated and nuanced, and every telling will make it shine a different way.

SELECTED BIBLIOGRAPHY

INTERVIEWS

In addition to author interviews:

Alexander, James. Interview by David Less and John Meehan for the Smithsonian Institution. Memphis, TN, March 2000.

Axton, Estelle. Interview by Rob Bowman. Videotape. Memphis, TN, 1993. Grain De Sable, France.

Axton, Estelle. Interview by Peter Guralnick. Audiotape. Memphis, TN, October 1980. Boston, MA.

Axton, Estelle. Interview by Barney Hoskyns. Audiotape. Memphis, TN, 1986. London, England.

Axton, Estelle. *The Memphis Sound: A Tribute to Our City's Music*. WMC-TV, Memphis, TN, 1994.

Booker T. & the MG's. Interview by unidentified female. CD copy. Unknown location and year. On file at the Stax Museum of American Soul Music.

Cauley, Ben. Interview by Pete Daniel and David Less for the Smithsonian Institution. Memphis, TN, December 4, 1999.

Cropper, Steve. Interview by David Less. Memphis, TN, December 10, 1999.

Dunn, Donald "Duck." Telephone interview by Michael Shelley on WFMU-FM, Jersey City, NJ, July 11, 2009. http://wfmu.org/playlists /shows/32187

Newman, Floyd. Interview by Pete Daniel and David Less for the Smithsonian Institution. Memphis, TN, November 9, 1999.

Porter, David. Interview by Pete Daniel and Charlie McGovern for the Smithsonian Institution. August 7, 1992.

Steinberg, Lewie. Interview by David Less for the Smithsonian Institution. Memphis, TN, December 5, 1999.

Stewart, Jim. Interview by Pete Daniel, Peter Guralnick, David Less, and Charlie McGovern for the Smithsonian Institution. Memphis, TN, May 19, 1992.

Stewart, Jim. Interview by Peter Guralnick. Audiotape. Memphis, TN, October 1980; March 1983; 1983.

Tally, Robert. Interview by Pete Daniel, David Less, and Charles McGovern for the Smithsonian Institution. Memphis, TN, May 22, 1992.

Thomas, Carla. Interview by David Less and Pete Daniel for the Smithsonian Institution. Memphis, TN, November 10, 1999.

Thomas, Marvell. Interview by David Less for the Smithsonian Institution. Memphis, TN, November 11, 1999.

Thomas, Rufus. Interview by Pete Daniel, David Less, and Charles McGovern for the Smithsonian Institution. Memphis, TN, August 5, 1992.

BOOKS

Beifuss, Joan. *At the River I Stand*. Memphis: St. Luke's Press, 1990.

Booth, Stanley. *Rythm Oil*. London: Jonathan Cape, 1991.

Bowman, Rob. *Soulsville, U.S.A.: The Story of Stax Records*. New York: Schirmer Books, 1997.

Brown, Geoff. *Otis Redding: Try a Little Tenderness*. Edinburgh, Scotland: Canongate, 2003.

Cantor, Louis. *Dewey and Elvis: The Life and times of a Rock 'N' Roll Deejay*. Urbana and Chicago: Illinois University Press, 2005.

Cantor, Louis. *Wheelin' on Beale: How WDIA-Memphis Became the Nation's First All-Black Radio Station and Created the Sound That Changed America*. Pharos Books, 1992.

Carmichael, Stokely, and Charles V. Hamilton. *Black Power: The Politics of Liberation in America*. New York: Vintage Books, 1967.

Carmichael, Stokely, with Ekwueme Michael Thelwell. *Ready for Revolution: The Life and Struggles of Stokely Carmichael (Kwame Ture)*. New York: Scribner, 2003.

Danen, Frederic. *Hit Men: Power Brokers and Fast Money Inside the Music Business.* New York: Vintage, 1991.

Davis, Clive, with Anthony DeCurtis. *The Soundtrack of My Life.* New York: Simon & Schuster, 2012.

Davis, Clive, with James Willwerth. *Clive: Inside the Record Business.* New York: William Morris & Company, Inc., 1975.

Djedje, Jacqueline Cogdell and Eddie S. Meadows, *California Soul: Music of African Americans in the West.* Berkeley and Los Angeles: University of California Press, 1998.

Freeman, Scott. *Otis!: The Otis Redding Story.* New York: St. Martin's Press, 2001.

Garland, Phyl. *The Sound of Soul.* Chicago: Henry Regnery Company, 1969.

George, Nelson. *The Death of Rhythm and Blues.* New York: Plume, 1988.

Gillett, Charlie. *Making Tracks: Atlantic Records and the Growth of a Multi-Billion-Dollar Industry.* New York: E.P. Dutton & Co., 1974.

Gordon, Robert. *It Came from Memphis.* Boston: Faber and Faber, 1995.

Graham, Bill and Robert Greenfield. *Bill Graham Presents: My Life Inside Rock and Out.* New York: Doubleday, 1990.

Guralnick, Peter. *Sweet Soul Music: Rhythm and Blues and the Southern Dream of Freedom.* New York: Harper & Row, 1986.

Hilliard, David. *This Side of Glory: The Autobiography of David Hilliard and the Story of the Black Panther Party.* Chicago: Lawrence Hill Books, 2001.

Honey, Michael K. *Black Workers Remember: An Oral History of Segregation, Unionism, and the Freedom Struggle.* Berkeley: University of California Press, 2002.

Honey, Michael K. *Going Down Jericho Road: The Memphis Strike, Martin Luther King's Last Campaign.* New York: W.W. Norton & Company, 2007.

Hoskyns, Barney. *Say It One Time for the Broken-Hearted: The Country Side of Southern Soul.* Waukegan, IL: Fontana Press, 1987.

Jackson, Wayne. *In My Wildest Dreams, Take 1.* Memphis: Jackson and Jackson Publishing, 2005.

Jones, Roben. *Memphis Boys: The Story of American Studios.* Jackson: University Press of Mississippi, 2010.

Nix, Don. *Road Stories and Recipes.* New York: Schirmer, 1997.

Pohlman, Marcus D., and Michael Kirby. *Racial Politics at the Crossroads.* Knoxville: University of Tennessee Press, 1996.

The Rolling Stone Interviews, Vol. 1. compiled by the editors of *Rolling Stone.* New York: Warner, 1971.

Smith, Jerry Lee "Smoochy." *The Real Me: The Story of a Musician and Entertainer of the Fifties.* Bartlett, TN: Blink Publishing Company, 2007.

Wexler, Jerry and David Ritz. *Rhythm and the Blues: A Life in American Music*. New York: St. Martin's Press, 1994.

NEWSPAPERS, MAGAZINES, LINER NOTES, COURT DOCUMENTS, DVDS

"A Study of the Soul Music Environment Prepared for Columbia Records Group." The thirty-page industry assessment, commonly known as the Harvard Report, had been submitted on May 11, 1972.

Abbey, John. "Isaac Hayes: The Most Important Soul Man of Today." *Blues & Soul*, June 1970.

"Adults Join Pickets on Main Street." *Tri-State Defender*, May 21, 1960.

"Al Bell Ordered to Pay $26,232 in Default." *Press Scimitar*, February 18, 1976.

"Al Bell." Stax press release. Released by the Edward Windsor Wright Group.

"Attendance at Schools Increases." *Press Scimitar*, November 17, 1969.

Bayne, William. "AFSCME Seeks Return of Funds." *Commercial Appeal*, January 11, 1970.

Bell, Al. "31 page memo" to all Stax Employees.

Bell, Al. Speech to Columbia employees.

Bell, Al. "These Days Would Come." Memo to all Stax Employees, June 8, 1975.

Black, Kay Pittman. "Al Bell Denies Wrongdoing in Bank Loans." *Press Scimitar*, July 28, 1976.

Black, Kay Pittman. "Al Bell Pleads Innocent to Bank Fraud Charges." *Press Scimitar*, September 24, 1975.

Black, Kay Pittman. "Opponents of Busing Meet with Brock." *Press Scimitar*, May 28, 1971.

Black, Kay Pittman. "Stax Owner Acquitted." *Press Scimitar*, August 3, 1976.

Black, Kay Pittman. "Unrest at Schools Leads 2 to Resign." *Press Scimitar*, November 11, 1969.

Black, Kay Pittman, and Roy B. Hamilton. "Union Ends St. Joseph Strike." *Press Scimitar*, December 26, 1969.

Black, Kay Pittman. "Probe by IRS of Stax Reported by Attorney." *Press Scimitar*, June 19, 1973.

Black, Kay Pittman. "Stax Probe Began After Cash Seized." *Press Scimitar*, June 20, 1973.

Black, Kay Pittman. "New Wage-Hike Plan for City Is Studied." *Press Scimitar*, June 16, 1969.

"Black, White Leaders Press Efforts to Curb Violence Across City." *Commercial Appeal,* October 22, 1971.

"Blacks May Form Antibusing Group." *Press Scimitar,* May 27, 1971.

Beifuss, John. "T.O. Jones." *Commercial Appeal,* April 13, 1989.

Bowman, Rob. Liner notes from *The Complete Stax/Volt Soul Singles: Volume 1, 1959—1968.* Atlantic, Inc., 1991.

Bowman, Rob. Liner notes from *The Complete Stax/Volt Soul Singles: Volume 2, 1968–1971.* Fantasy, Inc., 1993.

Bowman, Rob. Liner notes from *The Complete Stax/Volt Soul Singles: Volume 3, 1972–1975.* Fantasy, Inc., 1994.

"Boycotts: A Mistake." *Commercial Appeal,* April 27, 1972.

Brody, W.W. "Sisson Warns of 'Agitation.' " *Commercial Appeal,* January 9, 1964.

Burch, Peggy. "Federal Jurors Hear 2 Sides in Stax Case." *Press Scimitar,* October 24, 1978.

Burch, Peggy. "Record Producer Takes Credit for Stax' Success." *Press Scimitar,* October 20, 1978.

Burk, Bill E. "Hollywood Company Acquires Stax-Volt." *Press Scimitar,* May 13, 1968.

"Busing to Be O.K.'d by Memphis Board." *Press Scimitar,* June 21, 1971.

"CAB asks Widening of School Boycott." *Press Scimitar,* April 28, 1972.

"CAB Calls for Boycott of Schools for 2 Days." *Commercial Appeal,* April 26, 1972.

CBS Memorandum from Bernard Di Matteo to CRI and CRU Personnel, April 3, 1974.

CBS Memorandum from Bruce Lundvall (CRU) to CRU Organization, November 15, 1971.

"Chancellor Issues Injunction Ordering Municipal Workers Not to Proceed with Strike." *Commercial Appeal,* August 22, 1966.

Chisum, James. "CAB Displays Political Impact Potential." *Commercial Appeal,* June 28, 1971.

Chisum, James. "East Memphis to Feel Misery of Negotiations." *Commercial Appeal,* May 30, 1969.

Chisum, James. "Series of Compromises Gives City and Union 3-Year Work Agreement." *Commercial Appeal,* June 26, 1969.

"City Asked to Employ Negroes in All Depts." *Tri-State Defender,* December 12, 1964.

"City Faces 'Halt' Threat from Epps." *Commercial Appeal,* May 6, 1969.

"Commissioner Sisson Requests Social Security Coverage for All 'Unclassified' City Employees." *Tri-State Defender,* March 7, 1967.

"Confidential T.O. Jones Background Check." September 29, 1969. Henry Loeb Papers, Series III, Box 147, Folder 17. Memphis–Shelby

Country Public Library and Information Center, Special Collections, Memphis, TN.

"Contract Ratified with a Big Cheer." *Press Scimitar,* June 25, 1969.

Cornelius, Lucinda. "Memphis' Stax Records Closes Its Doors, Again." *Press Scimitar.* April 24, 1979.

Cortese, James "Stax Brass Expects Sale to Open Many New Doors." *Commercial Appeal,* May 19, 1968.

Court ruling: A. J. Calhoun, Successor Trustee of Stax Records, Inc., Plaintiff-Appellee, v. Johnny Baylor and Koko Records, Inc., Defendants-Appellants., 646 F.2d 1158 (6th Cir. 1981) Federal Circuits (April 1981).

Covington, Jimmie. "Private Schools Gear for Rise in Fall Enrollment of Students." *Commercial Appeal,* April 29, 1974.

"'Crisis-Weary' Organizations Urge Equitable Settlements." *Commercial Appeal,* November 11, 1969.

Dawson, Diana. "Last Vestiges of Stax Empire Auctioned." *Press Scimitar,* October 15, 1981.

"Don Nix." Stax Records press release. September 12, 1973.

Doughty, Roger. "Isaac Hayes Spreads Memphis Sound in N.Y." *Press Scimitar,* July 24, 1970.

Epps, Jesse. Statement by the Special Assistant to the International President, American "Ex-Banker's Files Subject of Inquiry." *Commercial Appeal,* February 22, 1975.

Federation of State, County, and Municipal Employees. January 13, 1970.

"Evers, Farris Lock Horns on Union/Sanitation Men Want More Pay." *Tri-State Defender,* February 6, 1960.

"Farris Denies That Sanitation Workers Were Dismissed Because of Attempt to Form Union." *Press Scimitar,* July 6, 1963.

"Feelings Run Strong—And So Do the Words." *Commercial Appeal,* October 22, 1971.

Flynn, Brown Alan. "Busing Foes Get Support from Loeb and Chandler." *Press Scimitar,* May 18, 1971.

Flynn, Brown Alan. "Hire Top Lawyer to Fight Busing, Says Kuykendall." *Press Scimitar,* June 8, 1971.

"Foes of Busing March, Then Ride Buses Home." *Commercial Appeal,* March 29, 1972.

"Former Record Producer Defends Role with Stax." *Commercial Appeal,* October 20, 1978.

George, Nelson. "Al Bell, Stax Mover and Shaker, Is Starting Over." *Billboard,* August 2, 1986.

Gordon, Robert. "Soul Man: Booker T. Jones." *Playboy*, June 2009.

Gordon, Robert. Liner notes from *Hi Times: The Hi Records R&B Years*. The Right Stuff/Capitol Records, 1995.

Green, Earl Jr. "Labor in the South: A Case Study of Memphis—The 1968 Sanitation Strike and Its Effect on An Urban Community." PhD dissertation, New York University, 1980.

"Hard, Dramatic Bargainer Acts Tough Role for City" *Commercial Appeal*, February 13, 1968.

Higgins, Chester. "Ex-Con Dancer Finds Savior in 'Black Moses.'" *Ebony*, May 1972.

Higgins, Chester. "Eyewitness Tells of Redding's Violent Death: 'I Guess God Was with Me,' Says Lone Survivor of Plane Crash." *Sepia*, December 28, 1967.

"High Court's Backing of Busing Denounced by Sen. Person." *Press Scimitar,* May 19, 1971.

"Hijack Gang Takes Over Southern Jet, Demands Ransom of 10 Million." *Commercial Appeal*, November 11, 1972.

"Hijacking Increases Airport Security." *Commercial Appeal*, November 12, 1972.

"Hospital Statement Is Firm Against Union Recognition." *Press Scimitar*, November 14, 1969.

"IRS Says Al Bell Owes $527,391." *Press Scimitar*, September 29, 1976.

Jaynes, Gregory. "Epps Rallies 800 with 'War' Talk." *Commercial Appeal,* April 15, 1969.

"Jim Stewart." Stax Records press release. July 1972.

Jimi Plays Monterey/Shake! Otis at Monterey. DVD. The Criterion Collection, 1986.

Johnson, Robert. "Beatles to Record Here," *Press Scimitar*, March 31, 1966.

"Judge Calls for Stax Financial Records." *Press Scimitar*, November 29, 1973.

"Judge Extends Order in Stax-CBS Dispute." *Press Scimitar,* October 30, 1974.

"Judge Orders Stax Evidence." *Commercial Appeal,* August 23, 1973.

Kellet, Robert. "Bishop, Board Still Seem Split on Procedure in Hospital Strike." *Commercial Appeal*, October 30, 1969.

Kellet, Robert. "Top 'Soul' Singer Otis Redding Jr., 5 Memphis Musicians Die in Crash." *Commercial Appeal,* December 11, 1967.

Kingsley, James. "Fate, Luck, Stewart Combined for Memphis Sound." *Commercial Appeal*, July 26, 1970.

Kingsley, James. "Stax Expands with Pop, C&W, Gospel Records." *Commercial Appeal*, January 13, 1974.

Knott, John. "M–G–M Sues Hayes, Stax for Breach of Contract." *Press Scimitar*, February 7, 1973.

Koch, Stephen. "Al Bell Takes Us There: An Interview." *Arkansas Review: A Journal of Delta Studies* 32, no. 1 (April 2001): 49.

Lee, Mary Ann. "Ardent Hitches Its Wagon to Stax." *Press Scimitar*, March 31, 1972.

Lee, Mary Ann. "How Halftime Became Showtime for 'Shaft.'" *Press Scimitar*, December 10, 1971.

Lee, Mary Ann. "Putting the Memphis Sound on Paper." *Press Scimitar*, May 24, 1968.

Lee, Mary Ann. "Singers of 'Soul' Sound Off on Lack of TV Exposure." *Press Scimitar.* May 26, 1969.

Lichtenstein Grace. "Stax Is Accused of Covering Up in Payola Case." *Commercial Appeal,* August 22, 1973.

Lee, Mary Ann. "Stax Is Major Investor in Broadway Production." *Press Scimitar*, February 15, 1972.

Lisle, Andria. "Memphis Sunset: The Mysterious Death of Stax Heartbeat Al Jackson, Jr." *Grand Royal Magazine* no. 6.

Lollar, Michael. "Bell Didn't Participate in Fraud, Witness Says." *Commercial Appeal*, July 19, 1976.

Lollar, Michael. "Bell, Harwell Plead Innocent to Charges." *Commercial Appeal*, September 25, 1975.

Lollar, Michael. "IRS Investigation of Stax Case Results in $1.8 Million Action Against Executive." *Commercial Appeal,* June 20, 1973.

Lollar, Michael. "Stax Records' Owner, Ex-Banker Are Indicted." *Commercial Appeal*, September 10, 1975.

Lollar, Michael. "Stax Tapes Net $1.3 Million; Buyer May 'Resurrect' Firm." *Commercial Appeal*, January 27, 1977.

Lollar, Michael. "Trustee Asks Court to Seize $541,834 to Pay Stax Bills." *Commercial Appeal*, October 21, 1976.

Lollar, Michael. "U.S. Grand Jury plans broadened Stax inquiry." *Commercial Appeal*, November 29, 1973.

"Lunch Boycott Hits 44 Schools." *Press Scimitar*, March 27, 1972.

Maycock, James. "A Black Woodstock: Wattstax." *The Guardian*, July 20, 2002.

McGarvey, Seamus. "The Five Royales, Part 1." *Juke Blues* magazine, issue 31.

McGarvey, Seamus. "The Five Royales, Part 2." *Juke Blues* magazine, issue 32.

McKee, Margaret. "These Nine Memphians Working on Solutions." *Press Scimitar,* November 10, 1969.

"Memorandum of Understanding." Henry Loeb Papers, Series III, Box 267, Folders 6 and 7. Memphis-Shelby Country Public Library and Information Center, Special Collections, Memphis, TN.

"Memphis and Mid-South Population Vol. 1," Memphis Area Chamber of Commerce, February 1972.

"Memphis and Shelby County Population, Housing, and Economic Analysis 1970–1990." Memphis and Shelby County Division of Planning and Development, April 1993.

"Memphis Gets Earful of the Memphis Sound." *Press Scimitar,* March 27, 1968.

"Memphis Market." Memphis Chamber of Commerce, 1963.

"Music Executive Denies Kickbacks." *Press Scimitar,* August 24, 1973.

"NATRA Presents Six Awards to Stax Records." Stax Records press release, September 22, 1970.

"Negroes at Fever Pitch, Vow All-Out Support of Students." *Tri-State Defender,* March 26, 1960.

"'One of Most Segregated in Nation' City Rates Low on Sociologist's Integration Scale." *Press Scimitar,* November 22, 1971.

"O.Z. Evers Gets 1959 Honor Roll." *Tri-State Defender,* January 23, 1960.

Paige Jr., Woodrow. "Stax Says Snags Cleared from Path to Tams Sale." *Commercial Appeal,* March 6, 1973.

Palmer, L.F. Jr. "Story from Inside Jail." *Tri-State Defender,* February 16, 1960.

"Picket Lines Go Up Outside St. Joseph." *Commercial Appeal,* October 6, 1969.

"Piracy on High C's Is Attacked." Stax Records press release. November 20, 1971.

"Population, United States, Tennessee, Memphis MSA and MSA Municipalities, 1980 and 1990." Government document.

Ragogna, Mike. *The Huffington Post,* June 15, 2011: http://www.huffington-post.com/mike-ragogna/van-hunts-free-june-downl_b_877200.html.

"Recording Executive Fails to Convince Federal Jury." *Press Scimitar,* October 26, 1978.

Reid, M.L. "Garbagemen Working in Fear Since More Than 30 Were Fired." *Tri-State Defender,* July 13, 1963.

Respect Yourself: The Stax Records Story. DVD. Concord Music/Universal, 2007.

Riker, Jefferson. "Strike Nobody Wants Looms Close in Confrontation of City, Employees." *Commercial Appeal*, June 4, 1969.

"Role Changes Puts T.O. Jones in Center of Stage." *Commercial Appeal*, July 15, 1970.

"Ronnie Caldwell." *Commercial Appeal,* December 21, 1967.

Sanford, Otis L. "Jury Finds Stax Payments Fraudulent." *Commercial Appeal*, October 26, 1978.

"Sanitation Men Ready to Strike: Accept Union Now Is Demand." *Tri-State Defender,* May 7, 1960.

"Screening of Hijackers Poses Major Questions." *Commercial Appeal.* November 14, 1972.

" '767,050 Live in Metro Area,' Says Census Bureau Report." *Commercial Appeal.* September 24, 1970.

"Soul Sound Opens Heart for Needy." *Commercial Appeal*, March 18, 1968.

"St. Joseph Breaks Off with Union." *Press Scimitar,* October 1, 1969.

Stanfield, J. Edwin. "In Memphis: More Than a Garbage Strike." March 22, 1968. Atlanta, Georgia: Southern Regional Council.

"Stax Announces Plans to Produce 4 Movies." *Commercial Appeal*, February 3, 1974.

"Stax Assistant Talks with IRS." *Press Scimitar,* June 12, 1973.

"Stax Owner, Ex-Banker Named in Indictment," *Press Scimitar*, September 9, 1975.

"Stax Countersues CBS for $67 Million." *Commercial Appeal,* October 29, 1974.

Stax Fax, Issues 1–9.

"Stax Official Believes Firm to Rise Again." *Commercial Appeal*, February 1, 1976.

"Stax Ordered to Open Its Books." *Commercial Appeal*, September 27, 1974.

"Stax Organization Moves into Broadway Play Arena as Major Backers of 'The Selling of the President.' " Stax Records press release, February 2, 1972.

"Stax Oust All Promotion Men." Stax Records press release, February 18, 1971.

"Stax Payments Told in 'Handshake Deal.' " *Commercial Appeal*, October 17, 1978.

"Stax Record Organization Opens Fight Against Record Piracy in Plan Utilizing FBI Methods and Ex-Agents." Stax Records press release. November 22, 1971.

Stax Records 50th Anniversary Issue, *Stop Smiling* magazine, 2007.

"Stax Records Awarded for Creativity." Stax Records press release, April 28, 1971.

"Stax Records Planning Own Office Building." *Press Scimitar*, May 4, 1973.

"Stax Records to Reopen Here Soon." *Tri-State Defender*, December 10, 1977.

"Stax Trustee Asks Seizure of Baylor's $2.54 Million." *Commercial Appeal*, January 29, 1977.

Stewart, Jim. "Copy of Speech Given by Mr. Jim Stewart at Company Meeting." March 14, 1970.

Stewart, Jim. Liner notes for *Otis! The Definitive Otis Redding*. Rhino Records/Atlantic Records, 1993.

Suosalo, Heikki. "Luther Ingram: The Complete Story." *Soul Express* no. 2, 2004.

Suosalo, Heikki. "Tommy Tate." *Soul Express* no. 3, 2001.

"T.O. Jones to Members of the Sanitation Department." July 27, 1968. Henry Loeb Papers, Series III, Box 147, Folder 17. Memphis-Shelby County Public Library and Information Center, Special Collection, Memphis, TN.

Taylor, Calvin Jr. "200 Teachers Rally to Back Fourth Monday of Protest." *Commercial Appeal*, November 11, 1969.

Taylor, Calvin Jr. "Epps, 7 Others Ousted in Move for 'Stability.'" *Commercial Appeal*, May 27, 1970.

"The Stax Organization." Stax Records press release, November 1971.

"3-Flank Attack on Busing Listed." *Commercial Appeal*, May 18, 1971.

"Trash Situation Serious." *Commercial Appeal*, January 12, 1970.

Travis, Dave. Liner notes from *Memphis Rockabillies, Hillbillies & Honky Tonkers Vol. 2: The Erwin Records Story*. Stomper Time Records, 2002.

Trotter, Wayne. "Tear Gas Follows Rocks As Police Stand Firm: March Leaders Arrested." *Commercial Appeal*, November 11, 1969.

"$2.5 Million Is Awarded in Stax Suit." *Press Scimitar*, October 25, 1978.

Union Planters National Bank of Memphis, Plaintiff-Appellant, v. Cbs, Inc., Stax Records, Inc., Alvertis Isbell, A/K/a Al Bell, and James F. Stewart, Defendants-Appellees., 557 F.2d 84 (6th Cir. 1977) Federal Circuits (June 1977).

Unterberger, Richie. "Wattstax." *Mojo*, July 2004.

"UP Bank Sues Stax and CBS." *Commercial Appeal*, November 14, 1974.

"UP Begins Foreclosure On Property of Al Bell. *Press Scimitar*, February 5, 1976.

"UP Buys McLemore Building for 85K." *Press Scimitar*, April 18, 1976.

Vancil, Paul. "Al Bell Remains Optimistic Despite Trial, Bankruptcy Fight." *Press Scimitar*, August 5, 1976.

Vincent, David. "New Coalition of Negro Groups Plan Mass March as First Step." *Commercial Appeal,* October 17, 1969.

Vincent, David. "Threat of Negro Boycotts Looms As NAACP Bolts School Meeting." *Commercial Appeal*, October 16, 1969.

Vincent, David. "Black Coalition Orders End to School boycotts After Board Files Suit." *Commercial Appeal*, November 11, 1969.

Weiler, Joseph. "Many Saw Portents of Stax' End, But Disagree on the Cause." *Commercial Appeal,* February 9, 1976.

Weiler, Joseph. "Stax Backers' Talk Sounds Like Broken Record." *Commercial Appeal,* February 10, 1976.

Weiler, Joseph. "Stax Records: The Dream That Died." *Commercial Appeal,* February 8, 1976.

Wenner, Jann. "Otis." *Rolling Stone*, January 20, 1968.

White, Cliff. "Stax: Fa-Fa-Fa-Fa-Fa-Fa (Sad Song)." *New Musical Express*, August 21, 1976.

Wilson, Robert. "There's Sadness at Soulsville, U.S.A." *Press Scimitar*, January 13, 1976.

Witkin, Richard. "Hijack Rule to Require Armed Airport Guards." *Commercial Appeal* (via the *New York Times*), November 30, 1972.

"Witness Tells About Items in Stax Return." *Press Scimitar*, July 19, 1976.

TURN IT UP, BABY
NOTES ON SOURCES, READING, AND LISTENING

Before specific source notes and recommendations by chapter, here are some broader recommendations. (Note that further reading suggestions are with the acknowledgments.)

Stax has become a label well-reissued. You can get song collections in small, medium, and extra-large doses. The two best ways into the catalog may be the two-CD *Stax 50th Anniversary Celebration*—the big hits are there, and some of the lesser-known artists too. *The Stax Story* four-CD collection is even better, the one you'd want on a desert island. The discs are thematically divided: hits, blues, live, and other good stuff. You can't go wrong with either of these. For a single CD intro, try *Stax Number Ones*. Though these are the big hits that span the label's history, they barely scratch the surface.

The three Stax singles boxes—each box is nine or ten discs—are great, but can be intimidating. This is all of the A-sides released by Stax-Volt, and some of the B-sides. It's archaeological: The chronological sequencing traces the development of the players, the signings, the label's change in direction after the Atlantic years. You can listen to these boxes for years and always discover something new. Each comes with a beautiful booklet full of photos. Grow with Booker T. & the MG's on their three-CD set, *Time Is Tight*. Listen to the band's evolution, along with many live tracks from the 1990s. (If enough people listen to Booker T. and the MG's, wars will end.) The three-CD collection *Take Me to the River* is not exclusively Stax but, as its subtitle suggests, *A Southern Soul Story 1961–1977*. This is a fine introduction to the sounds of the era and the region. *Stax: The Soul of Hip-Hop* collects some of the most popular sampled tracks, combining hits with nuggets.

So where, you might ask, is there room for a new compilation? At the time of publication, I am pursuing interest from several record labels for various new Stax collections—CDs, downloads, and finger-snapping mind implants. No deals are done, but information should be available at my website, www.staxbook.com. Sorry for the tease; more to come, I hope. Getcha one, and turn it up, baby.

At the risk of dismaying many great contemporary soul groups, I must point you to the Bo-Keys, a band that pulls from the ranks of Memphis soul greats, backed by musicians who came up listening to their records. They tour, and they've got CDs, and not only do they keep alive a tradition, they keep soul music originals working (www.thebokeys.com).

To see this book come to life, start with our documentary, *Respect Yourself: The Stax Records Story.* Many of the book's key players are represented there, along with some fantastic archival performances. (Watch the full version, not the one-hour edit.) There are also several DVDs of concerts from the 1967 European tour. *The Stax/Volt Revue Live in Norway 1967* seems the most readily available. You'll see the gang in their prime, and you won't forget it. A few other recommended viewings: *Dreams to Remember: The Legacy of Otis Redding* features commentary from Jim, Steve, Wayne, and Zelma and Karla Redding interspersed through a fine and varied collection of Otis performances. *Sam and Dave: The Original Soul Men* collects many of their best TV and film performances. *Wattstax* is now available in an expanded thirtieth-anniversary edition that includes the originally excised "Theme from *Shaft*" ending, and also features audio commentary, including, interestingly, from Chuck D. And you know that great performance in *Wattstax* of Johnnie Taylor in the velvety-looking club? Now you can see the whole thing: *Johnnie Taylor: Live at the Summit Club.* It makes clear why he was such a heavy hitter.

Tom Dowd finally got his due with a documentary about his amazing life and career: *Tom Dowd & the Language of Music* is a thrill for fans of all pop music since the early 1960s. Last, for a more recent look at some of the Stax artists in concert, as well as some of their Memphis soul peers, you'll love *Soul Comes Home: A Celebration of Stax Records and Memphis*

Soul Music. (More reading, listening, and watching is recommended in the chapter notes below.)

When shopping for these, be sure to support your local independent retailers. If they can't help you, try shopping online at the Stax Museum of American Soul Music. Your purchases will further the great community efforts of the Soulsville Foundation. Their site: http://shop.staxmuseum .com/.

Further information on sources, and more stories, are available at the author's website, www.staxbook.com.

PREFACE: CITY STREETS

Page xii – "the season was always open": This lyric is from J.B. Lenoir's "Down in Mississippi," a song from his 1966 album *Alabama Blues.* My favorite cover version is by Jim Dickinson, one of his greatest recordings from his latter years.

1. CUTTING HEADS AND HAIR

Page 4 – Marshall E. Ellis: Check out the compilation from Ellis's label on the CD *Memphis Rockabillies, Hillbillies & Honky Tonkers Vol. 2—The Erwin Records Story,* Stomper Time Records, Great Britain.

Page 5 – How hard could it be: Memphis seemed preternaturally inclined toward entrepreneurs: Clarence Saunders had founded the self-serve grocery there; the Frederick Smith family, after establishing a river shipping company that led to a bus service that would become Greyhound, would establish overnight air delivery with Federal Express; and Kemmons Wilson's Holiday Inn hotel chain was just exploding as Jim was getting started.

Page 6 – Jim's wife's uncle's garage: This garage was probably on Burr Street, though sometimes it has been remembered as on Orchi, a couple streets away. Both are near Ellis the barber, where Chelsea meets Jackson.

Page 6 – "There were a lot of people": Grain De Sable.

Page 8 – "I really got hooked": Smithsonian.

Page 8 – "They were using a little portable machine": Hoskyns; **"We couldn't talk anybody":** Guralnick.

Page 8 – "My husband, he couldn't": Grain De Sable.

Page 11 – "He asked me if I wanted a job": "LaGrange Native Chips Moman Talks About His Life in Music," Georgia Rhythm (website), November 16, 2008: http://www.georgiarhythm.com/2008/11/lagra nge-native-chips-moman-talks-about.html.

2. A NEW PLANET

Page 15 – Dewey Phillips: Recordings of Dewey Phillips on air are compiled on the CD *Red, Hot, & Blue* (Memphis Archives). There's a chapter on him in *It Came from Memphis*, and a lot of good information in *Dewey and Elvis: The Life and Times of a Rock 'n' Roll Deejay*, by Louis Cantor. You can hear some famed WDIA public service announcements on the CD *WDIA: The History, the Music, the Legend*.

Page 15 – "We used to listen": WFMU Duck Dunn interview.

Page 17 – "He had been taking guitar lessons": For more on guitar teacher Lynn Vernon, see *It Came from Memphis*.

Page 18 – three bucks: http://www.rocksbackpages.com/article.html ?ArticleID=14820.

Page 19 – "Jim liked all kinds of music": Smithsonian.

Page 20 – "I was in love with Hank Ballard": Duck says, "I don't think anybody in the South ever listened to 'Rock Around the Clock.' It was stupid. Bill Haley? Give me a break. 'Shake, Rattle and Roll,' that was Big Joe Turner, and nobody listened to Bill Haley's version. Just compare the two. Jesus. I didn't like the bullshit, you know?"

Page 20 – "the Five Royales": This group was very influential in shaping Steve's guitar sound, and hence the whole Stax sound. See a great two-part history in the British magazine *Juke Blues*, issues 31 and 32.

Page 20 – abandoned ice cream stand: "We went out to the ice cream thing one Sunday afternoon and the tape machine wasn't working," says Memphis guitarist Rick Ireland, who would become a guitar teacher and studio technician. Rick had an early Memphis rock band, the Regents, with Jim Dickinson. Everything was connected properly, and the needle was moving, but no sound stuck to the tape. Rick phoned an electronics expert in town. "The problem was grease," he remembers. "The tape got too greasy running through the machine. I cleaned the capstan and the rubber roller. Burger grease was part of it, I'm sure."

Page 22 – LeMoyne Gardens: "Rich Man, Preacher Man, Soul Man: A History of South Memphis." Prepared by Judith Johnson and Cathy Marcinko.

3. A CAPITOL IDEA

Page 25 – Willie Mitchell's band: How great it would be to find a recording of Willie Mitchell from the Manhattan Club, or one of the West Memphis joints. I've always imagined the late hour that ends a good night in a small club when I hear Booker T. & the MG's "Chinese Checkers." The players are cocky and sure, playing with the loose confidence that says, Let's see how loose we can keep this greasy groove.

Other records that evoke Willie Mitchell's scene and the West Memphis sound include "Calvin's Boogie," on the *It Came from Memphis Vol. 2* CD; the *Hi Times* box set, covering Hi Records, features some early Willie Mitchell; a hard-to-find box set of the Beale Street label Home of the Blues; *The Legacy of Gene "Bowlegs" Miller* features later 1960s material, but sometimes his club roots pop through; and there are choice early Memphis tracks on *The Complete Meteor Blues, R&B and Gospel Recordings*.

Page 25 – Al Jackson Jr.: In *Stax Fax*, March 1969, Al says he learned drums from his father's drummer, Houston Stokes, whom he'd later replace.

Page 27 – "Jim Stewart was standing": Smithsonian Institution.

Page 29 – Robert Tally: See *It Came from Memphis* for more on Tally and his influence on Wayne, Duck, and the others.

Page 31 – "[W]hen the black man": From James Baldwin, *The Cross of Redemption: Uncollected Writings*, edited by Randall Keenan. New York: Pantheon Books, 2010.

Page 32 – SANITATION MEN WANT MORE PAY: *Tri-State Defender*, February 6, 1960.

Page 32 – RECORDS FOR EVERYONE: *Tri-State Defender*, May 21, 1960.

Page 33 – "'What'd I Say' by Ray Charles": If you're new to Ray Charles, there's a world of pleasure ahead. Try the album *Genius + Soul = Jazz*. I've also enjoyed the box *Pure Genius: The Complete Atlantic Recordings*. (But you almost can't go wrong with Ray.) Jim Stewart hit his Ray Charles lick on an early side, Barbara Stephens's "Wait a Minute."

Page 36 – Robert "Buster" Williams: For more on Buster Williams, see *It Came from Memphis*.

Page 37 – an Atlantic Records promotions man: Marty Simon worked for music sales, and he spoke to Norman Rubin at Atlantic.

Page 37 – "mushroomed": *Respect Yourself* documentary.

5. A BANKER AND A GAMBLER

Page 49 – "We were just kids": "put Gilbert and Floyd with Packy": The Mar-Keys are among the great storied bands, and several members are great storytellers: Don Nix, *Road Stories and Recipes*; Wayne Jackson, *In My Wildest Dreams*; and Jerry Lee "Smoochy" Smith, *The Real Me*. See the chapter "Kicks and Spins and All the Flips" in *It Came from Memphis*.

Page 49 – "My dad was going through financial stuff": WFMU interview.

Page 51 – "where the splice is": The dissenting opinion: "Everything that came out of Stax during the first four years," says Jim, "there was not a splice in the tape. It was all live 'cause none of us knew how to splice."

Page 56 – In September 1961, Satellite changed its name: "Satellite Records Switches to Stax," *Billboard*, September 11, 1961, p. 13. The logo was created by Mar-Keys vocalist Ronnie "Angel" Stoots, who would design several early Stax album covers.

Page 56 – "We were surrounded by talent": Barney Hoskyns.

Page 59 – "Chips would rather": WFMU interview.

Page 60 – "I was supposed to get a third": *Nashville Scene* (online), "Chips Moman: The Cream Interview," August 17, 2012. Chips is also quoted in *Memphis Boys*, by Roben Jones: "'I had twenty-five percent—I thought,' Chips said sadly. 'They owed me my share of a million dollars they'd made that year—'61, '62.'"

6. "GREEN ONIONS"

Page 62 – "I'd pick Booker up": Unidentified audio interview in the archives of the Stax Museum.

Page 65 – Jim suggested Steve move his punctuating chords: Leo Fender was a country music fan. His Fender guitars have been essential in defining the sound of popular music from the 1950s on. They were designed to capture the solid wood body's resonance, and to be heard in a loud 1950s dance hall; their sound cuts through. Soon Steve got a Fender Telecaster "probably a '62 or '63. I bought it new." The Telecaster has all the versatility and a bit more *oomph* than the Esquire. Steve went from a Fender Harvard amp to a Fender Super Reverb. Duck played his Fender Precision bass through a 2x15 Standel amp. A young B.B. King got raw, gutbucket sounds out of the Telecaster, and country artists drew cleaner, more refined sounds. George Harrison, of the Beatles, played a Fender.

Page 68 – "We'll move out into the county": *Commercial Appeal*, October 4, 1961.

Page 68 – O.Z. Evers, the men's representative: In February 1960, O.Z. Evers was signing sanitation workers to the Teamsters union. He wanted the city to raise their wage from ninety-six cents an hour to a $1.65 an hour, and he wanted African-Americans in supervisory positions. He was willing to compromise if the city would guarantee a full week's pay. Working with the Teamsters, he drew 200 sanitation workers to a rally in March of 1960, and three months later had 900 signatures on union cards—three quarters of the department. But then Loeb met with the Teamsters officials. The previous year, when Evers had run for a seat on the city commission, he'd been disqualified on a technicality; when Loeb convinced the Teamsters to abandon the African-American workers, Evers quit his effort and applied himself to smaller spheres. The city was too crooked to beat. Evers was a postal worker, and they were one of the first unions to organize under President Kennedy; he also ran the city's Unity League, an activist organization for workers. The *Chicago Defender* named him to the 1959 Honor Roll. (Memphis African-American attorney Russell Sugarmon was also named that year.)

Page 69 – At a truck stop in Alabama: Freeman, *Otis!*, p. 122.

Page 69 – "another company in Detroit": The collection *Soulsville Sings Hitsville* is as good a Stax collection as Motown. It gets under the surface of both—not the obvious Stax players, not the obvious Motown songs.

Page 71 – "It wasn't a preconceived kind of goal": Joseph Weiler, "Stax Records: The Dream That Died," *Commercial Appeal*, February 8, 1976.

7. WALK RIGHT IN

Page 72 – Walk Right In: In 1963, while the Rooftop Singers were having a hit with a jug band song by Gus Cannon, "Walk Right In," someone at Stax realized that Gus was living in Memphis, and he was brought into the studio. The album *Walk Right In* combines his performances (accompanied by Will Shade from the Memphis jug band!) with storytelling and some oral history.

Page 74 – "Everybody was tired": *Respect Yourself* documentary.

Page 75 – The driver's name was Otis Redding: Dive into *Otis! The Definitive Otis Redding*, a four-CD box set, if you can find it. Any Otis compilation will be rewarding. Check out the energy of bandmate Eddie Kirk's "The Hawg, Part 1," and imagine an Otis Redding that took off from full speed. I'm looking forward to Jonathan Gould's forthcoming Otis biography, and whatever new musical releases it will prompt.

Page 75 – water-well driller: Stanley Booth, *Rythm Oil*, pp. 76–77.

Page 77 – broader education: Booker didn't get a music degree, but he took advantage of the musical opportunities, telling me, "I spent hours and hours and hours in their music library listening to composers from five hundred years ago, one hundred years ago, and I learned the emotional lessons that were taught. A piece like 'Finlandia' by Sibelius, how does a man write that? His country has been taken and belongs to another country. When an artist can put an emotion in a piece of music and a listener feels the same emotion, then it's been transferred. That's just a real true thing that you can't touch."

Page 80 – " 'Dowd, you're going to Memphis' ": "When I came down to Memphis," says Tom Dowd, "it was like turning back the hands of time fifteen or twenty years. The people down here were growing up in an era that had already gone by. In New York, we had *googobs* of radio stations, AM and FM. We had stations that were broadcasting Chinese, Greek, Hungarian, Polish. On FM you had classical music and an occasional live performance. Down here, you had preachers saying, 'You send me a dollar fifty, I'll give you a family bible, b-i-b-l-e, and if you send me another fifty cents, I'll give you a fancy packet of chrysanthemum seeds *and* you can have your family b-i-b-l-e.' I was thinking it was a comedy record! They'd be listening to some country station, and they don't even notice how gentle the swing is from the last country record into a couple of blues records. They were being exposed to a different culture. Which is what affected how these people played."

Page 81 – clacking his teeth: Rufus's technique was a way of producing; it was so weird, it freed the player to find Rufus's realm of funk.

Page 82 – " 'I'll worry about the stereo' ": Tom Dowd gave me this advice: "Ultimately, when you're recording, you're storing information. If you record it in mono, it's gonna be mono for the rest of its doggone life. The newest way you can find to store information, you have a chance later of putting it into the state of the art."

Estelle saw advantages to the mono setup, saying, "We survived on that one-track machine until about '63 or '64. But cutting on a one-track wasn't such a disadvantage because the singer felt the musicians and the musicians felt the singer. They did it like they were onstage. That's how you got the feeling."

8. THE GOLDEN GLOW

Page 89 – "Pain in My Heart": Otis and manager Phil Walden affixed their names to "Pain in My Heart," though the song was virtually identical to "Ruler of My Heart," written by New Orleans producer Allen Toussaint and performed by Irma Thomas. It was nothing a judge couldn't settle, and Redding and Walden's names were soon replaced by Toussaint's (or by his pen name, Naomi Neville).

Page 89 – Not giving proper credit: Freeman, *Otis!*, p. 99. The provenance of "Respect" is also a matter of dispute. In *Otis!* (pp. 140–141), the author quotes Percy Welch, a Macon musician, telling a story about Otis's valet Speedo Sims singing "Respect" as a ballad, and written by an unnamed Macon guitarist. "Every time Speedo would get in the studio, his voice would crack up. We'd done recorded 'Respect' five or six times, and each time it'd get worse and worse . . . [Otis told Speedo,] 'You don't need to do that tune, *I* need to do it it. You let me cut it, I'll give you credit.' Speedo should have made him sign a contract."

Page 93 – "Al Jackson was the pulse": "Al always let you know where the one was," says Steve, referring to the time signature in the bars. "Whether it was twelve bars or eight or sixteen or thirty-two bars, he would always give you that downbeat."

The following information on Al Jackson's drum gear comes from drummer Jim Payne's book, *Give the Drummers Some!* (http://www .funkydrummer.com/JPpages/shop.html):

"Al usually used a Rogers drum kit, sometimes with a Ludwig 400 or Ludwig Acrolite snare. The snare mics included Neumann KM84, RCA 77DX, ElectroVoice RE-15, Shure 545. The kick was often mic'ed with an RE-20. The snare was sometimes detuned until the head was floppy and then tightened with the snare's built-in damper. The hi-hat was never mic'ed. Steve told Jim Payne, 'Al Jackson never changed his heads unless he broke one. The same thing with the bass and guitar. If we broke a string we changed it. If we didn't, it never got changed. Al never changed those drums. He had a Ludwig and Rogers mix 'n' match. He had a medium size kick drum, 20-inch, and he had a Rogers floor tom, grey pearl, and then a little 12-inch tom over head.'"

Page 94 – Steve suggested: http://www.vintageguitar.com/3658/ steve-cropper. To write with Otis, Steve bought a second Telecaster, "a good used one, because Otis always tuned to a chord, open tuning. Otis was a one-fingered guitar player, so in his songs, there are almost no minor chords—because he didn't know how to make that form. For things like 'Try a Little Tenderness,' I played in standard tuning; for things like 'Ole Man Trouble,' the intro was all done with a chord on the second Tele."

Page 96 – "I never would have approached it": Freeman, *Otis!*, p. 117.

9. SOUL MEN

Page 97 – The two men: For more on Sam and Dave's long-term and ultimately contentious relationship, see Dave Marsh's *Sam and Dave: An Oral History.* For more on Sam's career, see http://www.sammoore .net.

Page 98 – at the King of Hearts: When Atlantic execs Ahmet Ertegun and Jerry Wexler walked in, Sam and Dave were performing the Ben E. King hit (later a number one for Aretha Franklin) "Don't Play That Song"—which was cowritten by Ertegun. Sam remembers being openly skeptical that they could possibly have been playing a song written by the genteel and tailored Turkish gentleman before him. Ahmet Ertegun—down-home funky within—also produced "Drinking Wine Spo-De-O-De" and wrote "Sweet Sixteen."

Page 99 – white belt, white shoes, pink socks, and bald head: "There was a fad going around among black musicians to straighten your hair," Isaac remembers about the "konk" in the early 1960s. "It was a pain to keep up. So I decided to grow me a fresh crop of natural hair. I went into King's barbershop around from Stax and said, 'Cut it all off.' People were saying, 'Look at that baldheaded guy with a beard.' I liked being different, so I decided to keep it."

Page 103 – the sanitation workers were invisible men: See chapter 15 notes for more on the sanitation department's conflict with the city.

Page 105 – Wilson Pickett was a popular singer: For Wilson Pickett, I've found the *A Man and a Half* two-CD collection to be quite satisfying.

Page 107 – Stax would receive: My specifics on the Stax and Atlantic deal come from Bowman, *Soulsville*, pp. 59–60.

10. A ROCKET IN WING TIPS

Page 110 – the MG's and Isaac supplied the music: The MG's *And Now!* is often overlooked. Good grooves, and also an example of the early stereo recordings with the individual instruments sent heavily to one side or the other, only the mike leakage giving them a bit of stereo balance. The live recording of the 5/4 Ballroom concert is a stone killer: *Funky Broadway: Stax Revue Live at the 5/4 Ballroom*. Outrageous versions of "Boot-Leg" and "Do the Dog."

The Los Angeles recordings by Packy and the MG's have been released on a vinyl album, *Hole in the Wall*, and attributed to the Packers. Packy's other recordings, from various studios around Memphis, have been compiled by Light in the Attic Records on *Late, Late Party 1965–1967.* "Hip Pocket" features Johnny Keyes on kazoo. Johnny and Doris on Packy: http://www.emusic.com/music-news/interview/an-oral-history-of-charles-packy-axtons-late-late-party.

Page 115 – Carla Thomas was at Howard University: With Carla at college, Stax was looking for female vocalists. Wendy Rene came in with the Drapels, and then released "After Laughter Comes Tears," a hit before its time. Later it was sampled by the Wu Tang Clan, among others. The recent *After Laughter Comes Tears* includes her great unreleased tracks. In the zoo of great Rufus Thomas songs, one of my favorites is from 1964, "Can Your Monkey Do the Dog."

Page 118 – **"More important than the record"**: Author's conversation.

11. KINGS AND QUEENS OF SOUL

Page 121 – **one of the greatest soul music albums ever recorded**: There's an expanded *Otis Blue* that includes alternate takes and live versions. Note the flip side of "I Can't Turn You Loose," "Just One More Day." Each instrument gleams in flickering candlelight.

Page 124 – **"Every artist in [San Francisco]"**: Graham and Greenfield, *Bill Graham Presents*, p. 174.

Page 126 – **"There's a gospel tune, 'You Don't Know Like I Know . . .'"**: From the songwriting contract for "You Don't Know Like I Know" between Hayes/Porter and East, dated September 23, 1965: They were paid a nickel per copy sold, and were entitled to 50 percent of any option money.

Page 127 – **"We had one heater"**: The heater was a gas heater, and when I was talking to Deanie Parker about it, she said, "Otis would leave his [dental] partial on the heater and I'd have to pack it up and send it to Macon." That's family!

Page 128 – **"Al Bell saw the potential"**: Mike Ragogna, the Huffington Post, June 15, 2011: http://www.huffingtonpost.com/mike-ragogna /van-hunts-free-june-downl_b_877200.html.

12. UNUSUAL SUCCESS

Page 131 – **Sam and Dave weren't harmonizers**: Experience Sam and Dave through these DVDs: *Sam and Dave: The Original Soul Men* collects a variety of performances, and *The Sam and Dave Show: 1967* is a live show with guests.

Page 137 – **Ardent Studio, an up-and-coming facility in town**: The Ardent studio and label suggests lots of good music. Check out *Thank You Friends: The Ardent Records Story.* Some of the early white Memphis bands—rock and soul groups—are compiled on the two-volume set, *A History of Garage and Frat Bands in Memphis, 1960–1975.*

Page 138 – **Their credulity was further tested**: The Beatles wanted to come to Stax, and you can hear Stax's love affair with the Beatles on *Stax Does the Beatles.*

Page 138 – **"'the Beatles are coming'"**: Don Nix: "I was probably the biggest Beatlemaniac in the world. I always said, 'If I ever meet the Beatles I'm going to ask them how they got that guitar sound on the intro to 'Lucy in the Sky.' And I finally met George Harrison." George had Don assemble the backing vocalists at the Concert for Bangladesh. "Before I could ask, he started asking me questions about Stax. He wanted to know more about Stax than I did about Beatles."

Page 141 – **vacuum cleaners:** Jones, *Memphis Boys*, p. 5.

13. FATBACK CACCIATORE

Page 147 – **England and across Europe:** There are many good visual recordings of the 1967 European tour. The *Stax/Volt Revue Live in Norway 1967* is a whole night from the best seat in the house.

Page 147 – **the lemonade came syrupy:** Brown, *Otis Redding: Try a Little Tenderness.*

Page 152 – **That summer, Al was promoted:** *Billboard*, August 19, 1967, p. 6.

14. WHITE CARNATIONS

Page 155 – **William Bell:** William Bell's first album, *Soul of a Bell*, collects the best of his early career.

Page 155 – **"Hip Hug Her":** Booker says, "That's probably Duck's most aggressive outing and the sound is just incredible. It's almost breaking up but it's not. The bass leads the band. The guitar and bass are playing the same thing, which is a sound I've stuck with in my mind. It beefs up the bottom end, it makes a strong statement for a dance record. I used it later with Rita Coolidge on 'Higher and Higher.'"

Page 155 – **transforming a standard into a truly personal vision:** "If I had to pick the best record that Stax ever made," Jim Stewart says, "it would be 'Try a Little Tenderness.' It has everything that Stax is or was about. It exemplifies what Stax really was, that one record. And when I hear it today, I still get that same feeling that I got when we rolled that tape in the studio." Stanley Booth was at Stax during Otis's last days; see his *Rythm Oil.*

"'Try a Little Tenderness' may be the greatest horn introduction of any record that's ever been made," says Wayne. "That little riff just came off the top of Otis's head, and it went into our hearts and onto that tape." Al suggests just the right optimism in the second verse, tapping the wood side of the drum. Duck says, "That song has got to be Al's. If Al ever created one, it's that one." (Freeman, *Otis!*, 156.)

Page 155 – "Mable John": Mable, who is Little Willie John's big sister, recorded at Motown before joining Stax in 1966. "We would work at the Lorraine Motel," she says. "I was expecting Stax to do me like Motown. You walk in, you're told, 'Sing this.' But Hayes and Porter would sit with me and I would talk to them about my life, my children, my hobbies. And all the time I'm doing that, they're listening to my voice. Isaac would begin to play the piano, because he was getting into my skin. Isaac had a touch that's from heaven. David would start writing, and they would jell like toast and jam." A recent Mable John compilation, *Stay Out of the Kitchen*, manages not to include her biggest hit, "Your Good Thing Is About to End," but does include much unreleased Stax material.

Page 155 – expansion into St. Louis: "Stax Expands with St. Louis, Memphis Move," *Billboard*, March 23, 1968, p. 10.

Page 158 – "After that": Jim Stewart, *Respect Yourself* documentary.

Page 159 – "Soul Man": I like Duck's perspective: " 'Soul Man' is almost Bo Diddley, but in the middle we hold the tonic and Steve does his guitar fills." WFMU interview.

Page 160 – "When 'Soul Man' becomes": Jon Landau, *Rolling Stone*, January 20, 1968, p. 18.

Page 163 – "He was so tired": Freeman, *Otis!*, p. 194.

Page 163 – consider his relationships: When Otis recorded his protégé Arthur Conley, he went to Rick Hall's Fame Studio in Muscle Shoals instead of to Stax. Muscle Shoals was nearer to Atlanta, but Stax was Otis's home. So it's hard not to read meaning into the decision. Several people claim Otis told them he was considering a change in management. Wexler, in his autobiography (p. 202), writes, "Two weeks before his death, he called and asked me to produce his next album. He wanted to move from the Stax sound to the more polished and bigger sonorities of, let's say, Ray Charles. I was flattered out of my mind—but worried to death about the political implication with Jim Stewart. 'No sweat, Jerry,' Otis reassured me. 'I'll take care of that part of it . . . There was no serenity in the posthumous release [of "Dock of the Bay"]. The ocean breeze and the washing of waves on shore did nothing to ease the pain of his passing. There has never been the slightest solace in it. Even now, when I hear 'Dock of the Bay,' I feel a rush of resentment and anger."

Page 163 – "He dissected the *Sgt. Pepper*": Freeman, *Otis!*, p. 187.

Page 165 – Things kept getting better: While at those last sessions, an invitation for Otis came from Vice President Hubert H. Humphrey, a tour of Vietnam in support of the troops; no date was set, but the recognition felt great.

Page 165 – " 'See ya on Monday' ": "Then I Watch 'Em Roll Away Again," the *Wall Street Journal*, January 4, 2013, page D7. Shout-out to band programs in the public schools, and to the Bar-Kays' band teacher, Harry Winfield, at Porter Jr. High School in Memphis. Shout-out to WDIA disc jockey A.C. "Mooha" Williams, who formed the Teen Town Singers, created great radio public service announcements, and who, the Monday morning after the deaths of Otis and the Bar-Kays, read "a touching tribute on his Monday morning radio program." (*Memphis World*, December 16, 1967, p. 1.)

Page 165 – "They did the *Upbeat* TV": The day before their plane crash, Otis and the Bar-Kays were on a Cleveland TV show, *Upbeat!* One complete song, "Respect," is in the *Respect Yourself* documentary, and it may be the most poignant performance you'll ever see.

Page 165 – "told us he couldn't crank it up": Bob Mehr, "Trumpet Player Bears Scars of Deadly Crash," *Commercial Appeal*, December 9, 2007.

Page 166 – "I remember waking up": Higgins, "Eyewitness Tells of Redding's Death."

Page 166 – Otis was seated in the front: Ibid.

Page 168 – "I remember the coroner told the nurse": Ibid.

Page 169 – "never be back": Freeman, *Otis!*, p. 216.

Page 170 – "Trying to work on something like that": Steve brought out the guitar amp he'd used on "Green Onions," a Fender Harvard, to record overdubs on "Dock." Wexler got the mix and thought Otis's vocal was too low. Steve had sent a stereo mix, so he replaced it with the mono mix. That's what was released on January 8; it reached number one on both charts on March 16 and stayed there for four weeks.

Page 170 – "Police skin divers said they were unable": Higgins, *Sepia*.

Page 171 – "We are witnessing": "Thousands Jam Church for Funeral of Three," *Tri-State Defender*, December 23, 1967, p. 1.

Page 171 – The line of cars: *Memphis World*, December 23, 1967.

Page 171 – "Otis was not only an artist": *Dreams to Remember* DVD.

15. "BORN UNDER A BAD SIGN"

Page 175 – "I didn't know it": In an anecdote decades later, Wexler's condescension toward his Memphis friends comes clearer. During a mid-1960s visit, they all left from the studio for dinner. Wanting to impress their visitor, Jim and Estelle chose a fancy place with a revolving floor atop one of the city's tallest buildings—but were turned away at the door because of Al Bell's skin color. Wexler was embarrassed—for himself and for Al—and disdainful of Jim and Estelle. "It shows a certain imprudence," Wexler says. "They didn't have the vision and the wit to know this could be embarrassing."

Page 177 – They'd lost Otis: Stax released two notable tributes to Otis. William Bell's "A Tribute to a King" captures the sadness and heartfelt longing that the studio felt. "Big Bird," a collaboration between Eddie Floyd and Booker, is a an exuberant howl to someone departed. At the crossroads of soul and rock and roll, it's one of Stax's greatest triumphs.

Page 177 – Events leading to Dr. King's assassination: My information on the sanitation department's long struggle with the city comes from the newspaper clippings in the Memphis Room at the Memphis–Shelby County Public Library. However, before immersing myself there, I got renewed enthusiasm from reading *Going Down Jericho Road* by Michael Honey, about Martin Luther King's work in Memphis. (Also check out Honey's *Black Workers Remember: An Oral History of Segregation, Unionism, and the Freedom Struggle*.) The other essential book for the '68 strike is Joan Beifuss's *At the River I Stand*.

The documentary *At the River I Stand* focuses on T.O. Jones and the union's work to settle the strike. A newer documentary, *MLK: The Assassination Tapes*, is an immersion piece, taking you into Memphis during the strike, and into the manhunt. *I Am a Man: From Memphis, a Lesson in Life* is an engaging, ruminative visit with Elmore Nickelberry, a 1968 sanitation worker, forty years later: http://www.iamamanthemovie.com.

Page 177 – "It was horrible": "Witness Tells of Man's Death," *Press Scimitar*, February 2, 1968, p. 10.

Page 181 – Larry Payne: "I was in my living room watching 'As the World Turns,'" Payne's mother says. "A lady ran in and told me Larry had been shot by the police. I ran out. I ran to touch him. The police would not let me touch him. He said, 'Get back, nigger.' He put the barrel of the gun right into my stomach. I could feel it." Officers said Payne had a knife in his hands. His mother's last image was of her son lying on his back with both hands outstretched over his head. "He didn't have anything in his hands." She said there was no knife on the ground. A grand jury declined to indict the officer. He faced no charges. Later, Memphis attorney Irvin Salky filed a civil rights lawsuit against the police department. Police never produced a knife as evidence, claiming the weapon was mistakenly collected with older evidence from the police property room and "it was dumped into the Mississippi River along with other weapons," says Salky. "We had a lot of skepticism over that." (http://www.commercialappeal.com/news/2008/mar/28/mother-grieves-sons-death.)

Page 184 – he leaned forward: See for yourself in the documentary *At the River I Stand*.

16. "SOUL LIMBO"

Page 188 – an assumption of power: In Phyl Garland's 1969 book *The Sound of Soul*, we get a firsthand look as the Gulf & Western–funded takeoff begins. Several record collections cover Stax's second period. *Never to Be Forgotten* is ten vinyl singles (and a download) in a nifty box with photo-heavy, appealing liner notes. "A love letter," they call it, to some of Stax's lesser-known artists. *Nobody Wins* digs deeper into the archives, featuring previously unreleased tracks and the more familiar.

Page 189 – first published statement on Black Power: Carmichael and Thelwell, p. 535. This became the book-length essay *Black Power*, published in 1967. Following Dr. King's assassination, the rhetoric ticked up: "We have to recognize who the major enemy is," Carmichael declaimed a few months after the assassination. Citing the way European whites had treated the "red man," and the way the United States was presently treating the Vietnamese, he continued, "The major enemy is not your brother! The major enemy is the honkie and his institutions of racism!" (Hilliard, *This Side of Glory,* p. 174; the speech is from the Oakland Auditorium, October 21, 1968.) For half a decade there'd been little response to Malcolm X's stated position: "My stand," Malcolm X said, "is really the same as that of twenty-two million so-called Negroes. It is not a stand for integration. The stand is that our people want complete freedom, justice, and equality. That is, respect and recognition as human beings. That is the objective of every black [person] in this country." From *Ready for Revolution*, by Stokely Carmichael with Ekwueme Michael Thelwell.

Page 189 – third-largest industry in Memphis: "Memphis Gets Earful of the Memphis Sound," *Press Scimitar*, March 27, 1968. The article also notes that the local pressing plant, Plastic Products, is shipping an average of 150,000 single records a day, or fifty million a year.

Page 192 – "It was a continuous problem": *Respect Yourself* documentary.

Page 193 – One associate said: Joe Mulherin talked about Baylor's eyes.

Page 196 – **G&W was also negotiating:** James Cortese, "Stax Brass Expects Sale to Open Many New Doors," *Commercial Appeal*, May 19, 1968. The same article notes that the new studio improvements are costing about $50,000.

Page 197 – PARAMOUNT TO BUY: *Billboard*, May 18, 1968, p. 3. The formal announcement was May 13. Also, Bill E. Burk, "Hollywood Company Acquires Stax-Volt," *Press Scimitar,* May 13, 1968.

Page 200 – **NATRA's convention:** Guralnick, *Sweet Soul Music*, p. 382.

Page 200 – **"the nation's problems":** *Billboard*, August 10, 1968, p. 1, by Paul Ackerman

17. A STEP OFF THE CURB

Page 202 – **Detroit disc jockey:** His name was Wash Allan.

Page 203 – **"I knew Johnnie could be in that arena":** Johnnie Taylor's career began long before Stax and ended long after. His *Stax Profiles* collection includes earlier gospel work and later disco hits, with his Stax hits.

Page 204 – **within six weeks of its release:** Showtime, *Press Scimitar*, March 31, 1972, p. 12.

18. THE INSPIRER

Page 212 – **"I had a decision to make":** *Respect Yourself* documentary.

Page 213 – **Redistribution of Earn-Out Agreement:** What a document! So many Stax documents were lost after the bankruptcy, and several are hinted at here. Some specifics:

Estelle gets "$490,000 to be paid at the rate of ninety percent of the first debentures used under said agreement until the total amount is reached, including the debentures to which these parties [Jim and Al] are already entitled for the year 1968–1969."

She waives all right title and interest in any other debentures.

First parties [Jim and Al] waive their right to receive any debentures until total amount in part 1 is paid in full.

This agreement is intended by all parties [as] the final dissolution . . . to the "STAX-VOLT PARTNERSHIP."

The document is painful to study. There are six signatures, in six different pens. It's the dissolution of more than a business partnership. And though the siblings continued to see each other, they'd committed to a legal separation that is a lifelong scar at best, a festering wound at worst. At the same time, there's an unbridled excitement to the moment. This union of six individuals sets Al at the starting gate, ready to roar. This document is on display at the Stax Museum in Memphis.

19. THE SOUL EXPLOSION

Page 215 – "Hit records are the number one thing": *Stax Fax* #1.

Page 215 – "This is a corporate change": "Stax—Many Changes," *Billboard*, May 22, 1971, pp. M12, M14.

Page 216 – Rick Hall and the guys in Muscle Shoals: Stax developed a working relationship with Rick Hall's FAME Studio in Muscle Shoals. Hear their southern story on *The Fame Studios Story 1961–73*, a three-CD retrospective. Also a single-disc compilation, *The Muscle Shoals Sound*. And finally there's a documentary, *Muscle Shoals*, that promises to be a thrill.

Page 216 – Al's visionary soul explosion could be made a reality: A few of my favorite spins from the soul explosion: The first two tracks on Steve Cropper's solo album, "Crop Dustin'" and "Land of 1000 Dances." William Bell's version of "Born Under a Bad Sign," produced by Booker—the two wrote the song for Albert King. "Double Or Nothing" is attributed to the Mar-Keys, but it sounds to me like a great Booker T. and the MG's jam. Otis had suggested the Staple Singers as backup vocals on "Dock of the Bay," but after the crash, there wasn't time; they released their own version on *Soul Folk in Action*.

The new era hits a great note on Margie Joseph's "One More Chance," a song from New Orleans. Don Nix brought Sid Selvidge to Stax, recording his debut on Enterprise, *Portrait*; listen to the track "Amelia Earhart." Recently, the Stax kids were performing at the museum, and I heard the opening piano tinkling of Isaac's "Hypersyllabolic . . ." That's no easy parlor trick, and they performed the song masterfully.

Page 216 – "The lavender carpeting": Steve Leigh from http://www .sl-prokeys.com/stax/stax-mclemore.htm. "Offices and walls could— and they did—just spring up or disappear overnight. That's how things could happen at Stax. On Friday an office—on Monday, a complete editing room."

Page 218 – "the Stax seal of approval": Though Cropper may be accurate on the wider scale of what's to come, the second and third Stax singles boxes are full of good-quality songs. There's a lot of material, and it's not a unified sound like much of the Atlantic era, but Stax continued to release quality music—alongside, granted, some lesser material.

Page 219 – doorbell: From Steve Leigh, http://www.sl-prokeys.com/ stax/stax-mclemore.htm.

Page 219 – "Janis Joplin was there": In 1968, Janis Joplin made her first appearance after leaving Big Brother and the Holding Company. (See *Rythm Oil*, Stanley Booth.) She performed in Memphis at the second annual "Yuletide Thing" event sponsored by Stax-Volt Records. She would kick off her August 1969 Woodstock set with a Stax rouser from Eddie Floyd, "Raise Your Hand."

Page 200 – "Because of my background": Reprint of article from *Record World* in *Stax Fax* #4. In that issue, too, they note Stax celebrating its tenth anniversary; interesting they date it from 1959.

Page 220 – "We're trying to carry a freedom message": *Stax Fax* #4.

Page 223 – Epps could excite: Gregory Jaynes, "Epps Rallies 800 with 'War' Talk," *Commercial Appeal*, April 15, 1969.

Page 223 – "further demands which could not be met": *Press Scimitar*, May 23, 1969.

Page 223 – "spread the misery": *Press Scimitar*, May 23, 1969. "There are citizens out there who think I'm a rascal and disruptive," Epps said. "The people we represent live lives that are totally disrupted because they don't have enough money and their children go to school with no shoes and go hungry during the day because they don't have lunch money. Our trips [to white shopping centers] are not an attempt just to be impudent, brazen or vulgar in our actions, but our way of asking, 'Help us—share the comfort in which you live with us.' "

Page 224 – a settlement was reached: "Contract Ratified with a Big Cheer," *Press Scimitar*, June 25, 1969.

Page 227 – a one-hour TV concert: When making the *Respect Yourself* documentary, we searched for a copy of the "Gettin' It All Together" TV show. None was found. You know where one is? Write me care of this publisher, pally. I'm dying to see it.

Page 229 – "Raymond Jackson brought me over to see Joe Harwell": http://www.sl-prokeys.com/stax/stax-mclemore.htm.

Page 230 – Artists performed: *Commercial Appeal,* May 26, 1969.

Page 230 – the staggering twenty-eight: Along with the MG's, there was Eddie Floyd's *You've Got to Have Eddie*, Johnnie Taylor's *The Johnnie Taylor Philosophy Continues*, William Bell's *Bound to Happen*, Carla Thomas's *Memphis Queen*, and the Mad Lads' *Mad, Mad, Mad, Mad Lads*. Steve Cropper made his solo debut with the great *With a Little Help from My Friends*, and he collaborated with Albert King and Pops Staples to create *Jammed Together*. Pops joined his family on an album while Mavis Staples had her self-titled solo debut. Two gospel-turned-secular groups released their debut albums, the Emotions and also Ollie and the Nightingales. Gospel influences were evident on the Soul Children's debut. Albert King contributed his second Stax full-length album, *Years Gone By*. The Mar-Keys chimed in with *Damifiknow!*

Through Don Davis, they licensed records by Detroit artists J.J. Barnes, Darrell Banks, and Steve Mancha. The newly formed Hip subsidiary label made a couple forays into the rock market with debuts by the Goodees, a Memphis girl group, and by the Southwest F.O.B. (from which later emerged the pop duo England Dan and John Ford Coley). Al presented jazz great Maynard Ferguson on the Enterprise label, where he was also placing Isaac's genre-shifting debut.

Don Nix, who'd been spending time in California, imported some West Coast hip with Delaney and Bonnie (Delaney was from Mississippi). While touring with the Mar-Keys, Don Nix met Leon Russell in Tulsa, Oklahoma. In 1965, they went to California and Don settled there a while (Duck often came to visit). Don brought Delaney and Bonnie to Stax in 1969, his first album production. After that he did more producing for Stax and for Leon's label, Shelter Records. "I had a production contract and a writer's contract with Stax," Don says. "Jim said, 'You go and write, and you go and you produce Jeff Beck, whoever you want to, 'cause that looks good for Stax.' And so he let me produce anybody I wanted to."

Page 232 – **"May I Have Your Ticket, Please"**: The sales meeting's production notebook indicates Stax had big ideas for this album, but perhaps they were too vague to act on: "We are experimenting with this album . . . The album should be a hot underground item; also, if it comes through, it will open the door to establishing Rufus as a comedian . . . Rufus has a very strong following on college campuses across this country and in this album we are attempting to capture him definitely as they know him."

Page 232 – **SAFEE**: *Commercial Appeal*, May 19, 1969.

20. A POT OF NECKBONES

Page 235 – **Isaac was unlike anything else in popular music**: The Isaac Hayes compilation *Can You Dig It?* is a great two-CD overview and includes some video. Don't take anything less than the eighteen-minute "By the Time I Get to Phoenix," the way it was meant to be heard. My favorite part is the extended wind down, with Ben Cauley hitting exuberant high notes with clarity and so much feeling.

Page 236 – **Isaac established the market**: The Beatles had made everyone want to do originals, and Isaac was swinging the trend the other way. "Luther Vandross always said Isaac gave him the courage to take somebody else's song and make it his," says James Alexander. "When Isaac did 'Walk on By,' you forgot about Dionne Warwick's version.

Dionne did 'A House Is Not a Home,' but when Luther Vandross did it, you forgot about hers. Isaac was the innovator who gave a lot of artists the courage to not do an original song."

Page 238 – "physique like a Mandingo Daddy": *Jet*, February 4, 1971, pp. 56–61.

Page 242 – "It's true that we are getting apart": John Abbey, "Isaac Hayes," *Blues & Soul*, 1970.

Page 244 – Stax sold ten million singles: The leading sellers were "Soul Limbo" (700,000), "Hang 'Em High" (800,000), and "Time Is Tight" (800,000), all by the MG's; Eddie Floyd's "I Never Found a Girl" (500,000) and "Bring It on Home" (800,000); Johnnie Taylor's "Who's Making Love" (two million) and "Testify" (500,000); William Bell's "I Forgot to Be Your Lover" (500,000); and the Emotions' "So I Can Love You" (420,000). They'd also sold $750,000 in eight-tracks, and the *Hot Buttered Soul* album had shipped 100,000 copies within a couple months of its release.

Page 245 – "*Soul* magazine was a struggling publication": Bowman, *Soulsville*, p. 200.

Page 247 – "The answers that the board": David Vincent, "Threat of Negro Boycotts Looms as NAACP Bolts School Meeting," *Commercial Appeal*, October 16, 1969.

Page 247 – NEW COALITION OF NEGRO GROUPS: *Commercial Appeal*, October 17, 1969.

Page 248 – "weary of existing": "'Crisis-Weary' Organizations Urge Equitable Settlements," *Commercial Appeal*, November 13, 1969.

Page 248 – "bad wisdom along with bad timing": The quote is from Councilman J.O. Patterson, *Commercial Appeal*, November 19, 1969.

Page 252 – Cropper had to give up: The terms of Cropper's departure come from Bowman, *Soulsville*, p. 213.

Page 256 – paid it off in five months: Michael Lollar, "Bell Didn't Participate in Fraud, Witness Says," *Commercial Appeal*, July 29, 1976.

Page 256 – "The bank, says Joe Harwell": Ibid.

Page 256 – "From that point forward": "Al Bell Denies Wrongdoing in Bank Loans," *Press Scimitar* July 28, 1976.

21. SHAFT

Page 258 – "I try to express myself": John Abbey, "Issac Hayes," *Blues & Soul*, 1970.

Page 259 – "Many theater owners": "Stax—Many Changes," *Billboard*, May 22, 1971, pp. M12, M14.

Page 260 – "When I play rhythm": Michael Ross, "Skip Pitts," *Guitar Player*, June 2011, pp. 52–55.

Page 261 – "When Shaft pops up": From the "making of" documentary that comes with the *Shaft* DVD. It includes a few snippets of Isaac and the Bar-Kays working up the tracks.

Page 263 – "A major film with a black director": "Black Tracks Cue New Sales Mart," *Billboard*, July 24, 1971, pp. 1, 10.

Page 265 – four days of rampaging: "Black, White Leaders Press Efforts to Curb Violence Across City," *Commercial Appeal*, October 22, 1971, p. 1.

Page 265 – "These officers are riding the streets": "Feelings Run Strong—and So Do the Words," *Commercial Appeal*, October 22, 1971.

Page 265 – "A miracle has happened in Memphis": "Racial Protests Ease After an Afternoon and Evening of Vandalism in City," *Press Scimitar*, October 27, 1971. "Adam Oliphant, a Stax Record Co. executive took pencil and paper in hand and for 10 minutes scratched notes on violence locations as dictated by [police Chief] Lux. He then dispatched black officials and rock music stars to the various areas to pass out the free tickets to the benefit show in an attempt to draw blacks off the streets."

Page 265 – all were acquitted: Jim Shearin, *The Commercial Appeal*: http://www.commercialappeal.com/photos/2010/jun/30/175511. They were tried on murder and assault charges.

Page 265 – whipped up dissent: *Press Scimitar*, June 28, 1971.

Page 265 – pass a constitutional amendment: "3-Flank Attack on Busing Listed," *Commercial Appeal*, May 18, 1971.

Page 265 – "reprehensible": Brown Alan Flynn, "Busing Foes Get Support from Loeb and Chandler," *Press Scimitar*, May 18, 1971.

Page 265 – "would guarantee the rights": Kay Pittman Black, "Opponents of Busing Meet with Brock," *Press Scimitar*, May 28, 1971.

Page 266 – Big Star: For more on Big Star, see my *It Came from Memphis*, and also my liner notes to their box set *Keep an Eye on the Sky*. The band released two great albums that coincided with the Columbia distribution debacle's beginning and its end. "We didn't have any problem getting our record on the radio," bandleader Alex Chilton told me. "The problem was getting them into stores." Also look for the documentary *Big Star: Nothing Can Hurt Me*.

Page 268 – "my hands stayed clean": "One big-time guy in New York, when I left out of there," says James Douglass, "he tried to convince me to steal the masters, said he'd press them up and sell them all over New York. 'C'mon,' he said to me, 'think about your kids.'"

Page 268 – **"furnished wholesale lots"**: Jack Anderson, "New Disc Jockey Payola Uncovered," *Washington Post*, March 31, 1972, p. D15.

Page 268 – DISC JOCKEY PLAY-FOR-DRUGS OUTLINED: Jack Anderson, "Disc Jockey Play-for-Drugs Outlined," *Washington Post,* April 21, 1972, p. D19. Anderson reports, "Record representatives . . . deal mainly in marijuana, although insiders have repeatedly told us cocaine is the 'with it' drug this year in show biz." Other Anderson reporting in 1972: "Disc jockeys and program directors across the country are provided with free vacations, prostitutes, cash and cars as payoffs for song plugging. Some big-time disc jockeys have run up thousands of dollars in bills at Las Vegas pleasure houses, all on the expense accounts of record companies . . . The stakes run into the hundreds of millions . . . The more audacious record promoters have simply bribed the record pluggers with cash or with new cars."

22. BALANCE SHEETS AND BALANCING ACTS

Page 273 – **"It got kind of rough around there"**: Willie Hall says, "I became a coproducer with Mr. Baylor, but I had to go through an ass-whooping too. One night we were recording and Johnny came in. You wouldn't see Koko until midnight, the pimp's way. He was kind of full, if you know what I mean. It was James Alexander, Michael Toles, and myself. Johnny said, 'All right, motherfuckers, it's time for a whooping.' There was only one exit and he was standing in it. Michael Toles tried to leave. Johnny punched him. Johnny, beatings were his business. Michael started crying. I'm sitting at the drums, thinking, Oh, God, how am I gonna get out of here? James Alexander was next. James rolled up in a ball behind his guitar and tried to get past Koko, but Koko tapped him too. James played it off but I knew he was hurt. Koko came to me. 'Hall, you ain't going nowhere.' I thought, He is my friend, I know I'm going to get hurt. So I put my dukes up, man, I took a swing at him. He hit me hard. What saved me, I started laughing. He'd hit me, I'd laugh. I can feel those punches today, in my chest, my arm, my back."

Page 273 – **Helen Washington:** Helen Washington was David Porter's niece. After about twenty arrests, she was serving time in the Tennessee State Woman's Prison for five counts of larceny; since childhood, she'd been doing cheap cons with an older counterpart, and was finally sent to the big house for using phony credit cards. Inside, she'd duly reformed, earning "trusty" status and could leave the premises to speak in high schools. Isaac wrote the warden suggesting he could give her gainful employment. The twenty-eight-year-old was granted early release and was assigned to Randy Stewart's team, hawking photographs to fans. "One day she came to me and said, 'I'm tired of concessions, I want to be a dancer onstage,'" says Randy. "She wanted to shave her head like Isaac. I thought, Wow, great idea! We went to the men's bathroom in Stax, I shaved all the hair off her head and took her into Isaac. He said, 'That's a great idea.'"

She was such a compelling figure that *Ebony* magazine quickly put her on the cover. Their profile begins, "She floats on stage as if on invisible wings. Her sylph-like figure, supple, flowing, enchanting, is incongruously topped by a head as hairless as a cueball, a head that glistens brightly in the glare of the spotlight . . . In the kneeling position of a supplicant, she faces the wings, eagerly anticipating *his* coming! The MC, in a circus barker's voice, exhorts: 'And no-o-owww, lay-dees and gennlemene-e-ennn, the one you have been waiting for . . . Eye-sa-ac . . . Ha-ay-ees!' . . .

"Hayes, an incredible figure seemingly straight out of Aladdin's magic lamp, strides on stage, dressed—or, better, adorned—by a maxi-cape with attached hood. He bows, helps Helen to her feet . . . and kisses her full on the lips as he permits his cape to fall into her arms. In burgundy tights, his naked upper torso gleaming like waxed mahogany and also draped with golden chains, he bows again and she kisses the top of his head." (*Ebony*, May 1972, p. 134.)

Randy Stewart: "Then he'd throw that cape off and stand up in those tights—you could see everything! I told him, 'You're going to jail man.' He said, 'The women like that.' He'd kick that cape off, she'd catch it, he'd hit that organ and it was showtime, boy!"

She also told *Ebony*, "My manager is Johnny Baylor. He's been very good to me since I've been out. There are still some cases against me in court, and he's getting them straightened out. He knows a lot about the law, but sometimes he's so tired working day and night, he will sit up in court and go to sleep."

Page 280 – "payola king of New York": *Hit Men*, Dannen.

Page 281 – "800,000 pirated copies": Roger St. Pierre, *Record Collector*, January 1972. Some record labels even pirated themselves, selling albums through nontraditional routes to avoid having to pay royalties to artists and music publishers; the rise of cassette-tape sales also made pirating easier. http://rocksbackpages.com/article.html?ArticleID=14825&Search Text=willie+hall.

Page 282 – "I lost my sales position": "Music Executive Denies Kickbacks," *Press Scimitar*, August 24, 1973.

Page 282 – But Stax's original star was back on top: You can't go wrong with Rufus Thomas. "Walking the Dog" is one of my desert island discs. The early 1970s stuff produced by Tom Nixon has a fuller sound—the funky animal series, and the dances. From his pre-Sun Meteor records to his jam with the Jon Spencer Blues Explosion, Rufus will do you right.

Page 283 – Rance Allen: Bob Mehr, "Gospel with Soul Flavor," *Commercial Appeal*, February 25, 2011, p. 5.

Page 285 – "My fourth oldest brother": Dave Hoekstra, "Staples' Label Boss Takes You There in Retrospect," *Chicago Sun-Times,* January 11, 2009.

Page 286 – "The music in there": Bowman, *Soulsville*, p. 238.

Page 287 – "utilizing ex-FBI operatives": "Stax Record Organization Opens Fight Against Record Piracy in Plan Utilizing FBI Methods and Ex-Agents," press release, November 22, 1971.

Page 288 – Stax had become outsize: Good ideas continued to emerge. A promotion for "Theme from *Shaft*" made the sheet music available to marching bands, resulting in many halftime performances, several broadcast nationally—a perfect reminder of the song's hipness—just in time for the gift-giving season. The response prompted Stax to release arrangements for "Knock on Wood," "Who's Making Love," an MG's song, and two tunes by Rufus Thomas. Mary Ann Lee, "How Halftime Became Showtime for 'Shaft,'" *Press Scimitar*, December 10, 1971; "Shaft as Go, Go, Go," *Billboard*, December 18, 1971, p. 38; "Stax Steps Up Sheet Music Pace Via Its Licensees," *Billboard*, January 15, 1972, p. 66.

23. WATTSTAX

Page 290 – "There was a paranoia": And a counterweight to the paranoia: "Someone gave Isaac a real roulette wheel, ball-bearing precision," says Larry Nix. "So Isaac's valet Benny Mabone started taking bets, and soon everyone's coming in there and gambling. Randy Stewart was producing Inez Foxx, and he couldn't get her in the studio. Benny got a cash box and he was making change. When it got too big it got called off, but it was hot for a while."

Page 290 – A photo from the reception: There's a photo of the newly-weds cutting the cake in the June 29, 1972, issue of *Jet*.

Page 292 – "He wanted most of his life to sing": Heikki Suosalo, *Soul Express* #2, 2004, p. 33.

Page 292 – "Baylor took Luther to Muscle Shoals": There's a great extended Luther Ingram oral history in *Soul Express* by Heikki Suosalo;

also see his piece on Johnny Baylor's artist Tommy Tate. Luther Ingram is in *Soul Express* no. 2, 2004; Tommy Tate in *Soul Express* no. 3, 2001.

Page 293 – "the mastering room": Mastering engineer Larry Nix says, "We got mastering equipment after we put a stereo system in Jim's office. We set up some JBL speakers, turned on the radio, they were playing Motown. Right behind it came a Stax record, and ours just fell down. Everybody said, 'Man, we're getting our butt kicked.' So we bought our own mastering equipment. It cost major money. But with that, you could start with nothing and have a pressed record the next day. Record the tape, we'd master it, Plastic Products would send their truck, press it on their overnight shift."

Page 293 – "One day, Johnny Baylor": Tim Whitsett told *Soul Express* that another Koko artist, Tommy Tate, "was scared to death of Baylor and called the FBI on himself to protect himself."

Page 294 – "into the Broadway play arena": press release, February 7, 1972.

Page 295 – Stax was undeterred: *Press Scimitar*, Feburary 15, 1972.

Page 296 – The scope quickly grew: For more on Wattstax and the Mafundi Institute, see "The State of Art in Watts," by Anthony "Made" Hamilton: http://www.forests.com/caaghist.html.

Page 297 – "We go and find": Jacqueline Cogdell DjeDje and Eddie S. Meadows, *California Soul: Music of African Americans in the West*, p. 184.

Page 298 – The morning kicked off: The night before Wattstax, Isaac performed in Philadelphia. "Isaac would get tied up with people after the show and miss a flight," says Earlie Biles. "And when you had something to be filmed, you couldn't afford to have a person not there. So I was charged with going to Philadelphia and getting him on a Learjet to Los Angeles. After the concert I made sure he stopped talking to people and got on the plane."

Page 298 – "When we played": The Mel Stuart quote comes from PBS's website for the *Wattstax* documentary: http://www.pbs.org/pov/wattstax/interview.php#.URFgzOhrWPc. Also helpful with details was the article "Wattstax" by Richie Unterberger: http://www.rocksbackpages.com/article.html?ArticleID=14218.

Page 298 – "I Am Somebody": When I asked about his composition, Rev. Jackson told me, "Dr. King was killed April fourth, Robert Kennedy killed June the fifth, two heavy blows to our movement and to our sense of possibility. I was in Resurrection City, the March on Washington. I remembered a book by Dr. Howard Thurman, *Jesus and the*

Disinherited. Dr. Thurman said that when we're reduced to our irreducible essence, that we have nothing, no money, no clothes, just nakedness against the world, we're still somebody. We're still God's children. And it just hit me like a bolt of lightning. I said to people, 'Say "I am somebody."' And the Wattstax stage took it to another level, 'cause you had this hundred thousand people in this huge chant, which eventually became a movie. So, where there's life, there's hope. And where there's hope, there's infinite possibility."

Page 300 – "It was almost like a doctor's surgery queue": "Wattstax" by John Abbey, *Blues & Soul*, 1972. Accessed at http://www.rocksback pages.com/article.html?ArticleID=14535.

Page 301 – Their latest album, *Do You See What I See*: James Alexander thinks of the Bar-Kays' *Do You See What I See* as a return to their Otis roots. It opens with the words "America! Do you see what I see?" and ends with a chant, "Young / got to learn / got to live with the old." Stax is giving them a national stage and they're taking it. The CD has bonus tracks of their Wattstax performance!

Page 301 – "His intro is superbly conceived": John Abbey, *Blues & Soul*, September 1972.

Page 301 – David . . . delivered a set both intimate and grand: David Porter released four albums while at Stax. His first, *Gritty, Groovy, and Getting It*, features a beautiful remake of "Can't See You When I Want To" with a gorgeous Dale Warren string arrangement. David, like Isaac, reinterpreted and extended pop hits and he used Isaac's backup vocalists. His fourth album, a "rock/soul opera" titled *Victim of the Joke*, has become a cult classic, including a great take on Sarah Vaughn's "The Masquerade Is Over."

Page 302 – "After the Watts riots": *Billboard*, February 19, 2011.

Page 302 – "An agreement has been reached": Lance Wilson, "Wattstax: Giving Something Back to the Community," *Los Angeles Times*, August 20, 1972.

Page 302 – Little Milton performing his hit: The Hi Rhythm Section told me that when Al Jackson started going back and forth between Hi and Stax in the early 1970s, he got the Hi section gigs at Stax. They're on "Walking the Backstreets and Crying," among other Little Milton tunes.

Page 302 – Johnnie Taylor in a swanky Hollywood club: In *Wattstax*, Johnnie Taylor performs in a red velvety club, and he's owning the place, with the camera tight on him. Now all the audio from the evening is available on *Live at the Summit Club*.

Some versions of the *Wattstax* DVD includes outtakes; the Soul

Children's "Hearsay" is great to see—it's one of my favorite song open-ings. The *Wattstax* concert has been issued in various ways, but go ahead and get the three-CD deluxe edition.

Page 303 – **"interference":** Those sued were Isaac Hayes, Stax Films, Wolper Productions, Columbia Pictures, Stax Records, and East/Memphis Music.

Page 304 – **"It is up to":** "CAB Calls for Boycott of Schools for 2 Days," *Commercial Appeal*, April 26, 1972.

Page 304 – **The response:** "CAB Asks Widening of School Boycott," *Press Scimitar*, April 28, 1972.

Page 305 – **The resistance to:** "Laws, Social Change Cut Shelby Segre-gation Rate," *Press Scimitar*, November 12, 1981.

24. THE SPIRIT OF MEMPHIS

Page 308 – **The Spirit of Memphis:** In 1973, former Mad Lad John Gary Williams released his solo album *The Whole Damn World Is Going Crazy*. What a story! In 1969, he'd come back from risking his life overseas for his country and was angry about the unchanged racial situation at home. He played a role in the local ambushing of a policeman, served several years jail time, and came out to release this beautiful album. His story is being explored by and retold with John Hubbell in a forthcoming mul-timedia project.

Another recently resuscitated obscurity is Lou Bond's self-named al-bum. Bond was a nylon-string guitarist who put out one record on Stax's We Produce label. He had a gentle approach, with probing lyrics and shimmering production. It didn't rock the world in 1974 but has since been sampled by Outkast and Mary J. Blige, and has been recently remas-tered and re-released by Light in the Attic Records. Rest in peace, Lou.

Page 308 – **Lorraine Village:** Working with the US Department of Housing in 1972, Isaac built the Lorraine Village on twenty acres, town-houses dotted with parks and sports facilities. In mid-April 1973, the Memphis Housing Authority asked him to be their spokesperson. Isaac said he could not be bought as a "figurehead . . . in a white-bankrolled entrepreneurial effort to redevelop Beale Street . . . Principles must come before principal. I could not be a 'Judas' to my people—millions of dollars in stocks or 30 pieces of silver, it's all the same . . . Blacks are being pushed into the background, while others are capitalizing on the fruits of our culture and lifestyle. How could we accept the 'crumbs' of participation by one or two Blacks in a $100 million project to redevelop Beale Street which black people had no part in planning, designing, or approving?" See *Commercial Appeal*, September 2, 1972, and *Billboard*, September 9, 1972, p. 3.

Page 309 – "record sales rose": *Time*, "Executives: Clive's Fall," June 11, 1973.

Page 310 – Columbia was loaning: The deal covered distribution of the Stax, Volt, and Enterprise labels. Stax's Gospel Truth and Respect labels were outside the deal, allowing Stax to keep its toes in the indie distribution world. The Columbia deal would last three and a half years from the date Stax paid off the $6 million loan, or ten years (and a few weeks) from signing.

Page 311 – Stax was paid: Rob Bowman, liner notes to *The Complete Stax/Volt Soul Singles Vol. 3*, p. 29. Further, Jack Anderson wrote, "If an album lists for $5.98, the record company sells it to the distributor for about $2.40. He sells it to the 'rack jobber' for $2.90, who sells it to the retailer for $3.05–3.10." (*Washington Post*, April 27, 1974.) In the Stax-Columbia deal, there was no rack jobber; Columbia would sell directly to the distributor through its branches.

Page 312 – a tiff with the engineers: This anecdote comes from Bowman, *Soulsville*, p. 250.

Page 313 – "Now that [hijackers]": Joe M. Dove, "Flights Become Tardy in Wake of Hijacking," *Commercial Appeal*, November 15, 1972, section C, p. 25.

Page 314 – triple the industry standard: See note on Baylor's payment, chapter 25.

Page 315 – a federal tax lien: Kay Pittman Black, "Probe by IRS of Stax Reported by Attorney," *Press Scimitar*, June 19, 1973.

Page 315 – changing the reason: 646 F.2d 1158: A.J. Calhoun, Successor Trustee of Stax Records, Inc., plaintiff-appellee, v. Johnny Baylor and Koko Records, Inc., defendants-appellants.

Page 315 – RECORD YEAR: *Billboard*, January 20, 1973, p. 6.

Page 316 – "Black-oriented films": Nat Freedland, *Billboard*, February 10, 1973, pp. 3, 12.

Page 317 – "Maine lobster for everybody": Larry Nix elaborates: "Al Bell had some land out in the country. They had parking in town and a shuttle bus you could take out there. They had a playground and people to keep your kids. They had a ball diamond, a wooden dance floor with a jukebox, and lights to go on into the night. They flew lobster in from Maine, and had a guy cooking and serving these lobsters. They had two garbage cans full of spaghetti. Food, drinks, softball; it was a company picnic."

Page 317 – "We were major contributors": Jacqueline Cogdell DjeDje and Eddie S. Meadows, *California Soul: Music of African Americans in the West*, p. 182.

Page 318 – annual salary: Bowman, *Soulsville*, p. 287.

Page 319 – finance officer later explained: "Witness Tells About Items in Stax Return," *Press Scimitar*, July 19, 1976.

Page 319 – Clive's personal expenses: Clive states that the billings were the work of Wynshaw. "Wynshaw had forged signatures, falsified invoices, and arranged kickbacks, a few of them involving aspects of my personal business . . . I had never intended to have CBS pay for my apartment renovation or, heaven knows, for my son's bar mitzvah." Clive Davis with Anthony DeCurtis, *The Soundtrack of My Life*, pp. 166–167. The numbers come from "Show Business: Payola Rock," *Time*, January 18, 1973, and "Executives: Clive's Fall," *Time*, June 11, 1973.

Page 320 – "maintains an eighth-floor suite": Kay Pittman Black, "Stax Probe Began After Cash Seized," *Press Scimitar*, June 20, 1973.

Page 320 – "plush Stax apartment": "He had the penthouse overlooking Central Park," says Randy Stewart. "Seventeenth or eighteenth floor. He had two dangerous dogs, big German shepherds. When you'd sit down, they'd come lay and watch you. You could barely move. I used to walk them. I'd come back to the building, take 'em upstairs, as soon as they walked in the house, they'd make a U-turn and start growling at me. 'I just walked your asses!' They were dangerous dogs."

"Johnny had those two stupid ass dogs," says Mickey Gregory. "Their names were Boss and Mean. They were one million percent obedient. If he brought you into the apartment and introduce you to Boss and Mean, you were cool. If he said, 'Have a seat,' and he go into the back, them dogs are going to eat you up. Then he'd drag your ass out on the freight elevator—the doormen were scared of him too. He'd throw you out somewhere."

"At one time Johnny had three apartments in Manhattan," says Daryl Williams. "East Eighty-third and Third Avenue, one at Eighty-sixth and Lex, and Eighty-ninth and Madison was the penthouse." Among his reputed neighbors was an ex-wife of Sugar Ray Robinson, Jeffrey Holder (the 7-Up Un-Cola man), and the president's daughter Tricia Nixon.

Page 322 – "Today he owns": B.J. Mason, "Isaac Hayes: New Wife, New Image, New Career," *Ebony*, October 1973, vol. XXVIII, no. 12, pp. 173–180.

Page 323 – STAX EXPANDS: James Kingsley, *Commercial Appeal*, January 13, 1974.

Page 323 – **ranked number five**: *Press Scimitar*, May 30, 1974, citing *Black Enterprise Magazine*.

Page 323 – STAX ANNOUNCES PLANS: *Commercial Appeal*, February 3, 1974.

Page 323 – **pro sports franchise**: Woodrow Paige Jr., *Commercial Appeal*, March 6, 1974, p. 29.

Page 323 – **bought a church**: "Stax Records Planning Own Office Building," *Press Scimitar*, May 4, 1973. Deanie was moving her department to Union Avenue. "They were going to throw away the steam table, the refrigerator, and all those things in the church kitchen," she remembers. "I said, 'Oh, no.' And we donated them to a church on Parkway."

Page 323 – **Richard Pryor**: Engineer William Brown laughs and says, "In my spare time, I used to edit all Richard Pryor's cuss words together. When I got through, there was a whole roll of just profanity. One day at Stax I got mad. I put that tape over the intercom system, and I locked the editing room door. They wanted to kill me."

25. A VEXATION OF THE SPIRIT

Page 328 – **"The liability ledger"**: *The Turnaround*, p. 101. "There were four or five major bond claims in the five-million-dollar range," says Wynn Smith. "One of them was the Harwell bond claim, which involved Stax Records. There was another big one in the installment lending area, a big one in the investment division, and another big one in the bank itself involving the executive vice president and others."

Page 328 – **"$2 million worth of business"**: *Commercial Appeal*, March 4, 1975, p. 26.

Page 330 – **"I reacted"**: Bowman, *Soulsville*, p. 319.

Page 330 – **"From the beginning"**: *Commercial Appeal*, February 10, 1976, one of a series of three retrospective pieces.

Page 331 – **annual payroll**: Bowman, *Soulsville*, p. 308.

Page 334 – **Harvard Report**: The complete Harvard Report is hard to find, but it's heavily excerpted with good analysis in *R&B, Rhythm and Business: The Political Economy of Black Music*, edited By Norman Kelley—specifically the essays by David Sanjek, "Tell Me Something I Don't Already Know: The Harvard Report on Soul Music Revisited," and by Yvonne Bynoe, "Money, Power, and Respect: A Critique of the Business of Rap Music."

Page 335 – **more than six hundred thousand**: Joseph Weiler, "Many

Saw Portents of Stax' End, But Disagree on the Cause," *Commercial Appeal*, February 9, 1976.

Page 335 – South African stage play: *Billboard*, September 6, 1975.

Page 337 – One of the participants: "Former Bank Branch Manager Pleads Guilty in Embezzling," *Commercial Appeal*, March 1, 1975, p. 1.

Page 337 – trial documents: 557 F.2d 84: Union Planters National Bank of Memphis, Plaintiff-appellant, v. Cbs, Inc., Stax Records, Inc., Alvertis Isbell, A/k/a Al Bell, and James F. Stewart, Defendants-appellees; found at http://law.justia.com/cases/federal/appellate-courts/F2/557/84/272819.

Page 337 – "We tried to reconstruct": Joseph Weiler, "Many Saw Portents of Stax' End, But Disagree on the Cause," *Commercial Appeal*, February 9, 1976. One of Stax's vice presidents says he could never get a budget defined for his division, although he made repeated efforts. He told the newspaper, "How can you run a business when you don't know how much you are making or can spend?"

Page 338 – "Why was Stax paying": Ibid. Testifying in court, Baylor based his windfall of payments on two oral novations, or promises. The lawsuit states: "One novation, made in late 1971 or early 1972, allegedly adjusted the rates for royalty payments to Baylor for sales of Stax records. The second novation, made in March or April 1972, allegedly provided for $1 million in promotional fees, fees to be paid above travel and other business expenses and independent of the number of records actually sold. The novations replaced an agreement typical of agreements in the record industry, putting in its place conditions that were by industry standards extraordinarily generous. Baylor was to receive royalties on seven-inch records (singles) of .22 to .26 per record and on twelve-inch records (LPs) of $1.62 to $1.85 per record, as compared to industry norms of .08 to .13 on singles and .30 to .60 on LPs. Baylor himself testified that a royalty rate of .25 per single would be 'out of reality.' Those rates applied, moreover, to returns and free goods as well as records sold, another feature unusual in the industry. The rates were to be retroactive to the first record Baylor sold for Stax, approximately three years earlier. Baylor's flat $1 million promotional fee compares to industry norms of $60,000 to $70,000 per year. Baylor argues that his unique talents justified those extraordinary terms, but he conceded that nothing he has done before or after his association with Stax would indicate that he possesses unusual money-making talents. He took over full responsibility for Stax distribution in late 1971 and gave it up in late 1972, when CBS took over distribution rights."

Page 339 – Isaac Hayes sued Stax: Deanie Parker on the reaction from Stax's front lines: "We were involved in the Wattstax project and so many other things. Our artists were really very hot and it just went unnoticed until we had finished a couple projects and realized that it looked like we were backing up instead of going forward."

Page 340 – subpoenaed records: *Commercial Appeal*, October 15, 1974.

Page 340 – "willfully, wantonly": "Stax Countersues CBS for $67 Million," *Commercial Appeal*, October 29, 1974; "Judge Extends Order in Stax-CBS Dispute," *Press Scimitar*, October 30, 1974.

Page 340 – "calculated to destroy": "UP Bank Sues Stax and CBS," *Commercial Appeal*, November 14, 1974.

Page 342 – His opponent in the 1972 race: J.O. Patterson.

Page 343 – "For an hour and a half": Joseph Weilder, "Vote Count Proved an Upset," *Commercial Appeal*, November 7, 1974, p. 1.

Page 343 – "and about ten": Lynn Lewis, "Harold Ford Stuns Kuykendall," *Press Scimitar*, November 6, 1974.

Page 343 – "We found the reports": Ibid.

Page 344 – "Stax was perceived": "CBS Sues to Hold Stax to Agreement," *Commercial Appeal*, October 9, 1974, p. 3. The article refers to the CBS attorney acknowledging where the power lay, saying that "Bell gave verbal notice October 2 that Stax would 'no longer abide by' its agreement and that since then the firm has refused to furnish CBS with any records for distribution."

Page 346 – "The discussion would have been different": My friend, the beautiful and late Rick Ireland, who recorded at the Brunswick dairy barn and who worked with the bankers, told me, "Bill Matthews brought in a super brainy guy at bailing out financial institutions, Roger Shellebarger. He bailed out UP. There was a bunch of no good loans in there and he cleaned them out. His job was to collect the assets, to get as much as he could for the bank."

26. A SOUL AND A HARD PLACE

Page 347 – "I tried to keep": Joseph Weiler, "Many Saw Portents of Stax' End, But Disagree on the Cause," *Commercial Appeal*, February 9, 1976.

Page 348 – "Ouch": *Commercial Appeal*, February 19, 1975, p. 30.

Page 348 – " 'way out of line' ": Joseph Weiler, " 'Memphis Sound' Grew from Stax," *Commercial Appeal*, February 9, 1976, p. 1. Article also states: "Reliable sources say that Stewart and Bell had hired several unneeded artists and employees at fantastic salaries and all of this was quickly gobbling up what little money there was." East/Memphis Music "had hired writers and advanced them money on future royalties far beyond anything they could reasonably be expected to produce."

Page 348 – Union Planters announced: *Press Scimitar,* January 31, 1975. Article also states, "During 1974 the bank recognized substantial loan losses which it attributes to the dishonesty and infidelity of former bank officers. Including claims filed relating to the bank's investment division, the bank has now filed claims in excess of $16.5 million under its fidelity bond, claiming that losses in that amount were incurred as the direct consequence of wrongful conduct of former employees, including eight former officers." In addition to embezzlement and thievery, the bank was affected by the depressed state of the real estate market and the state's usury law that limited interest rates. At the year's end, the bank had approximately $63 million in loans on which it was not accruing interest. "Any one of these factors would have harmed our earnings in 1974," Matthews said. "We were unfortunate to have all of them occur simultaneously."

Page 348 – over $4 million: *Commercial Appeal,* March 27, 1975.

Page 349 – phones were disconnected: "Stax Owner, Ex-Banker Named in Indictment," *Press Scimitar,* September 9, 1975.

Page 350 – Big news broke on September 9, 1975: Michael Lollar, "Stax Records' Owner, Ex-Banker Are Indicted," *Commercial Appeal,* September 10, 1975; "Stax Owner, Ex-Banker Named in Indictment," *Press Scimitar,* September 9, 1975.

Page 350 – it was paid by: Kay Pittman Black, "Al Bell Pleads Innocent to Bank Fraud Charges," *Press Scimitar,* September 24, 1975.

Page 351 – "crawling with rats": *Commercial Appeal,* September 25, 1975.

Page 352 – "Al was shot": Andria Lisle, "Memphis Sunset: The Mysterious Death of Stax Heartbeat Al Jackson, Jr.," *Grand Royal* no. 6, pp. 50–53.

Page 353 – "When my capital was zero": Stephen Koch, "Al Bell Takes Us There: An Interview," *Arkansas Review: A Journal of Delta Studies,* April 2001, Vol. 32, no. 1, p. 49.

Page 355 – "industrial camera crew": While making the documentary *Respect Yourself: The Stax Records* Story, we tried to find that film and were unsuccessful. If anyone knows of its whereabouts, please write me care of this publisher.

27. "I'LL TAKE YOU THERE"

Page 360 – in excess of $10 million: Including the bank and all its creditors, Stax's debt may have reached $30 million.

Page 360 – "I see hope": "Stax Official Believes Firm to Rise Again," *Commercial Appeal*, February 1, 1976.

Page 360 – "I am saying": Ibid.

Page 360 – an album comprising vaulted Stax material: This idea morphed over time, and ultimately the Memphis Heritage Foundation paid tribute to Beale Street with an album of vaulted Memphis material. Producer Jim Dickinson put together *Beale Street Saturday Night*, featuring an array of known and unknown players and still available only as a vinyl LP, a thick slice of Memphis, chopped hot please.

Page 361 – "Those who forcibly": *Commercial Appeal*, February 10, 1976. Joseph Weiler, "Stax Backers' Talk Sounds Like Broken Record," *Commercial Appeal*, February 10, 1976.

Page 361 – "$21 million": Cliff White, "Stax: Fa-Fa-Fa-Fa-Fa-Fa (Sad Song)," *New Musical Express*, August 21, 1976. George Schiffer was the Motown consultant who testified as to the tape's value, and Randy Wood is owner of Dot Records.

Page 361 – "elated": "$1.8 Mil Paid by Al Bennett for Stax Publishing." *Billboard*, March 12, 1977.

Page 363 – "could sign Mr. Bell's name": "Al Bell Denies Wrongdoing in Bank Loans," *Press Scimitar*, July 28, 1976.

Page 363 – "running those": Deborah Sontag, "Out of Exile, Back in Soulsville," *New York Times*, August 14, 2009.

Page 363 – false entries: "Harwell would say, 'I can massage this,'" says Tim Whitsett. "Harwell put down as collateral that Stax owned a radio station. The call letters belonged to a shrimp boat that had been damaged in a hurricane and was somewhere in Louisiana."

Page 364 – After a respite: Bell's trouble didn't stop with his acquittal. Six weeks later he was notified by the IRS that he was $527,391 in arrears, taxes and penalties combined. In July 1977, he filed a $20 million federal lawsuit against Union Planters for malicious prosecution; five years later it went to trial, and on August 26, 1982, the bank was cleared.

Page 365 – "Al Bell had a laundry service": "Recording Executive Fails to Convince Federal Jury," *Press Scimitar*, October 26, 1978.

Page 365 – "I think I made": "Record Producer Takes Credit for Stax' Success," *Press Scimitar*, October 20, 1978.

Page 365 – IRS money returned to Baylor: "$2.5 Million Is Awarded in Stax Suit," *Press Scimitar*, October 25, 1978. Also, Otis Sanford, "Jury Finds Stax Payments Fraudulent," *Press Scimitar*, October 26, 1978.

Page 365 – Al Bell says it was money earned: "Johnny was perceived by many as a tough guy because Johnny carried guns," Al told me. "And Johnny didn't have a problem sparring with you like he sparred with Sugar Ray Robinson. And that's Johnny Baylor, my dear friend. I regret that he's not alive to see how things happened after that. But he did achieve that great hit on Luther Ingram, whom he loved so much."

Page 366 – not taxable: "Because Union Planters had carried the bond claims as an asset since 1974, the $6,300,000 received in 1977 was not reflected in current earnings for tax purposes," an analyst explains. "Thus the bank received $6,300,000 in tax-free income in 1977." *The Turnaround*, p. 149.

Page 367 – largest union: "State's Largest Union Local? It's AFSCME," *Press Scimitar*, May 17, 1976. By 1976, AFSCME was representing the park commission, the zoo, and city and county hospitals. It achieved raises of 6 percent in 1975 and 5 percent in 1976.

Page 370 – Blues Brothers band: From the WFMU interview with Duck Dunn: "We were playing with Levon Helm and the horn players from *Saturday Night Live*. Belushi was a big fan of Stax, so the trombone player at *SNL* connected us. Belushi was in New York, I was in California. He called and it was like three in the morning my time, I thought it was Don Nix playing a joke on me. I hung up. But he called back and he wanted me to come to New York. I was scared to death— Paul Shaffer, and Steve Jordan, they intimidated me. But I hadn't had that much fun since the '67 show, and then also playing with Eric Clapton [in the early 1980s]."

Page 372 – "It's just a real estate sale": Diana Dawson, "Last Vestiges of Stax Empire Auctioned," *Press Scimitar*, October 15, 1981.

Page 374 – "You didn't feel any back-off": "Obituary: Estelle Axton, the Founding Force of Stax Records," the *Guardian*, February 27, 2004.

Page 374 – "dance program": Handy's autobiography, *Father of the Blues*, is available online through Google Books.

Page 376 – Stax Museum of American Soul Music: Like their page: https://www.facebook.com/staxmuseum.

When the museum was being built, a fireman stepped forward to say he'd saved Isaac Hayes's Cadillac. He remembered his mother getting him out of school to drive by Stax and see it in the parking lot. Like his Oscar, Isaac's Cadillac was a tangible pride that the neighborhood could share in. He bought it at the bankruptcy auction, put it up on blocks, and decades later sold it to the museum, which had it refurbished (engine removed), and today it spins on display at the Stax Museum of American Soul Music.

Page 377 – just a mirage: Al's noble goal of a wider middle class was achieved in Memphis by Federal Express, the brainchild of Fred Smith. Smith's grandfather had run a ferry line on the Mississippi River. His father had founded one of the bus lines that became Greyhound. Fred put wings onto the idea. A decade after establishing Federal Express in Memphis in 1973, it passed $1 billion in annual sales. Whole swaths of Memphis are populated with nice homes paid for by those earning FedEx paychecks.

Page 377 – "truth crushed": Dr. King was quoting poet William Cullen Bryant.

INDEX

Note: page numbers in italics refer to figures.

"You Don't Miss Your Water (Till Your Well Runs Dry)," 57–58, 122
Bellmark Records, 364
Belmont, Bill, 362
Belushi, John, 438
Bennett, Al, 361, 362
Benton, Brook, 85
Big Star, 266, 424
Biles, Earlie, *228, 345*
  on Al Bell, 244, 250, 282, 306–7, 317
  on backlash against black success, 345
  and collapse of Stax, 350
  on financial troubles at Stax, 331, 353
  as gatekeeper for Al Bell, 268
  hiring of, 228
  on Joe Harwell, 229
  on Johnny Baylor, 228, 314
  on management of Stax, 290
  marriage of, 290
  on staff, growth of, 244
Bill Black Combo, 21, 106
Billboard magazine, 89, 155, 197, 200, 210–11, 230, 231, 245, 255, 257, 263, 294, 315, 361, 364–65
Birdees Music, 210, 255, 360
Black Mondays, 248
Black Moses (Hayes), 286–87, *287,* 288
Black Oak Arkansas, 230
Black Power movement
  Al Bell and, 188–89, 215, 278–79
  goals of, 188–89
  and racial tension, increase in, 200–201
  rise of after King assassination, 418
  and Wattstax, 298–99, *299*
  white fear of, 356
Blackwood Brothers, 23
Bland, Bobby "Blue," 24, 26, 85, 139
blues, as response to racism, xii
Blues Brothers Band, 370, 438
Bluhdorn, Charlie, 255
Bo-Keys, 381
Bond, Julian, *144,* 232–33
Booker T. and the MG's, *66, 91*
  Al Jackson as driving force in, 93
  awards won by, 231, 370
  and Bar-Kays, 377
  "Behave Yourself," 64–65, 66–67
  "Booker Loo," 154
  Booker T. Jones on potential of, 231
  The Booker T. Set, 230–31
  "Boot-Leg," 92, 110, 111
  career after Stax, 369–70
  "Chinese Checkers," 406–7
  contract provisions with Stax, 251–52
  and "Gettin' It All Together" TV concert, 227
  "Green Onions," 63, 65, 66–67, 77, 150, 219
  "Groovin'," 154
  "Hang 'Em High," 423
  "Hip Hug Her," 154, 414
  "Hole in the Wall," 111–12
  and local city sounds, monitoring of, 69
  McLemore Avenue, 252
  on Memphis funk sound, origin of, 67
  and Monterey Pop Festival, 155–58

"Mrs. Robinson," 234
"My Sweet Potato," 154
  naming of, 66
  and Otis Redding, 90–91, 169
  "Outrage," 91–92
  and Paramount Pictures, work for, 198
  production work by, 224, 250–51
  racial mixing and, 92
  reissued CD sets, 403–4
  salaried positions for, creation of, 142
  "Slim Jenkins' Place," 154
  and "soul explosion" at Stax, 224, 230
  "Soul Limbo," 190–91, 423
  as Stax house band, 67, 69, 72–74, 89, 106, 110, 118
  Stax restrictions on outside work by, 251
  and Stax Revue European Tour, 147
  Stax's influence on career of, xv
  success of, 105
  That's the Way It Should Be, 370
  "Time is Tight," 198, 423
  touring by, 69–70
  TV appearances, 110
Booker T. Washington High School, 85
"Boot-Leg" (Booker T. and the MG's), 92, 110, 111
bootlegging, 280
Bowman, Rob, 245, 286, 330, 349
Bracken, Jimmy, 220
Branch, Ben, 25
"The Breakdown" (Thomas), 267, 283
Brewster, W. H., 23
Broadway musicals, Stax funding of, 294–95
Brown, James, 20, 162, 171, 263
Brown, Ruth, 36, 45
Brown, Shirley, 338–39, 341, 345
Brown, Veda, 292, 319, 332
Brown, William C.
  as Booker T Washington High School graduate, 85
  early career of, 28, 39
  and Mad Lads, 124
  and Stax, first contact with, 27–28
  as Stax employee, early jobs, 39, 124, 217, 350, 433
  and Vietnam War, 109, 214
Brown v. Board of Education (1954), 304
Bryson, Peabo, 369
Burk, Arnold D., 197
Burke, Solomon, 41
Burnette, Dorsey, 11
Burnette, Johnny, 11, 26
Burton, John, 348, 349
Bush, Henry "Creeper," 217, 239, *294*
Butler, Jerry, 95, 100, 232
Byler, Fred, 6, 9
The Byrds, 57
"By the Time I Get to Phoenix" (Hayes), 225–26, 235, 236, 422

Cain, Kenny, 101
Caldwell, Ronnie, 143, 166–67, 169, 171
Calloway, Cab, 26
The Canes, 67

A NOTE ON THE AUTHOR

Grammy Award–winning writer Robert Gordon is the author of six books and producer/director of seven feature documentaries. He has focused on the American South—its music, art, and politics—to create an insider's portrait of his home that is both nuanced and ribald. Gordon's first book, *It Came from Memphis*, careens through the 1950s, '60s, and '70s, riding shotgun with the weirdoes, winos, and midget wrestlers who percolated the early forces of rock 'n' roll. Elvis was a marginal figure in that book, but was the focus of *The King on the Road* and *The Elvis Treasures*, both of which were created in cooperation with the estate of Elvis Presley. Gordon also wrote the definitive biography of blues great Muddy Waters, *Can't Be Satisfied*. His films include *Stranded in Canton*, a collaboration with photographer William Eggleston; *Johnny Cash's America*, which examines ideas of justice, penance, and faith— spiritual and national—through the life of Johnny Cash; and *Respect Yourself: The Stax Records Story*, the companion film to this book. Gordon's work has been shown on PBS's *American Masters* and *Great Performances* series, A&E, BBC, Channel Four, and many global networks. His writing has appeared in most major magazines and newspapers. Four of his documentaries have received Grammy Award nominations, and he won a Grammy as a writer for his essay in the 2010 boxed set *Keep An Eye on the Sky*, about the band Big Star. He lives in Memphis, Tennessee, with his wife and two daughters.